Reforming the World

_____

Reforming the World

THE CREATION OF
AMERICA'S MORAL EMPIRE

Ian Tyrrell

PRINCETON UNIVERSITY PRESS
PRINCETON AND OXFORD

Library of Congress Cataloging-in-Publication Data

Tyrrell, Ian R.
Reforming the world : the creation of
America's moral empire / Ian Tyrrell.
p.   . cm.   — (America in the world)
Includes bibliographical references and index.
ISBN 978-0-691-14521-1 (hardcover : alk. paper)
1. United States—Foreign relations. 2. United States—Territorial expansion.
3. United States—Moral conditions. 4. United States—Foreign relations—
Moral and ethical aspects. 5. Imperialism—Moral and ethical aspects—History.
6. Exceptionalism—United States—History. 7. Evangelicalism—Political aspects—
United States—History. 8. Missionaries—United States—History.
9. Transnationalism—History. I. Title.
E183.7.T97   2010
973—dc22   2009050189

British Library Cataloging-in-Publication Data is available

This book has been composed in Sabon

Printed on acid-free paper. ∞

Printed in the United States of America

1   3   5   7   9   10   8   6   4   2

To my fellow historian colleagues in the United States,
who have helped beyond measure
in their generosity and openness

AS WELL AS

Robert James Tyrrell, long lost, but found
and
Doris Priscilla Tyrrell (1910–1994), not forgotten

CONTENTS

ACKNOWLEDGMENTS

IT IS ALWAYS A PLEASURE to thank those who have helped in the long task of writing a book. I have fortunately been funded by a multiyear Australian Research Council Discovery Grant. This has enabled me to employ a series of research assistants, attend conferences and do research in the United States and Great Britain as well as Australia, and acquire copies of a variety of materials from other libraries around the world. Tina Donaghy, Nadine Kavanagh, and Marie McKenzie in turn proved valuable to the research and to the rechecking of material that I have used. Princeton University Press's editorial team has been very helpful in bringing this manuscript to publication. I especially thank Sara Lerner for her work on the photographs and Jenn Backer for her intelligent copyediting.

I received excellent audience feedback from papers delivered at the International Congress on the Social History of Alcohol and Drugs at Guelph, Ontario, in August 2007; the Australian and New Zealand American Studies Association, Biennial Conference, July 2008; the Australian Historical Association Biennial Conference, Brisbane, July 2002; the International American Studies Association Conference in Lisbon, September 2008; the "Making Empire Visible in the Metropole: Comparative Imperial Transformations in America, Australia, England and France" conference, Sydney, June 2008; and the "Competing Kingdoms: Women, Mission, Nation, and American Empire" conference at Oxford University, April 2006. I thank Kittie Sklar and Barbara Reeves-Ellington for the invitation to Oxford; conversations there with Anne Forster, Connie Shemo, R. Bryan Baderman, Jane Hunter, and Jay Sexton were particularly useful. Jay provided a critique of my conference paper, which I much appreciated. A variety of people made helpful comments in the course of presenting several papers during my stay at the École des Hautes Études en Sciences Sociales. François Weil made my time there intellectually rewarding and very pleasant. In August 2008 I spoke at the Sydney Feminist History Group on the Misses Leitch and received further excellent commentary, as I did at the School of History and Philosophy seminars in May 2007 and May 2009. I found especially valuable the penetrating discussion at the University of Mannheim in October 2008, where I outlined the broad themes of the book. I especially thank Prof. Madeleine Herren, University of Heidelberg, and Prof. Johannes Paullmann, Mannheim, for organizing that event and for their marvelous hospitality.

I thank the directors and individual librarians at the Yale University Divinity School Library; Kautz Family YMCA Archives, University of Minnesota; Harvard University Libraries; British Library; Library of Congress; National Archives, College Park, Maryland; National Archives, Washington, D.C.; Bentley Historical Library, University of Michigan; Friends Historical Library, London; Mitchell Library, Sydney; and Australian National Library, Canberra. The University of New South Wales facilitated interlibrary loans. Support from the Faculty of Arts and Social Sciences provided important resources via the Temperance and Prohibition Papers. For earlier research used in this book, I also thank the Fawcett Library, London; Lilly Library, Indiana University; Huntington Library, San Marino, California; Bancroft Library, University of California, Berkeley; and Frances Willard Memorial Library, Evanston, Illinois.

Individuals who have offered advice have been many. I give pride of place to the late Roy Rosenzweig, who, despite an increasingly serious illness, showed considerable interest in probing the theme of the American empire and political lobbying during a broad-ranging conversation with him and Shane White in October 2006 on Pennsylvania Avenue at Capitol Hill. As has become common, I owe inspiration on linking American history to "the wider world" to Tom Bender, as well as Carl Guarneri. James Gilbert was instructive on Dwight Moody, and Duke University's Bill Chafe and Sydney University's Shane White generously commented on my work at the "Making Empire Visible" conference.

Chapters 6 and 7 includes material revised from "The Regulation of Alcohol and Other Drugs in a Colonial Context: United States Policy towards the Philippines, c. 1898–1910," *Contemporary Drug Problems* 35 (Winter 2008), 539–71, used with permission (CO Federal Legal Publications). Chapter 9 includes material adapted from "Prohibition, American Cultural Expansion, and the New Hegemony in the 1920s: An Interpretation," *Histoire Sociale/Social History* 27 (November 1994), 413–45. Place names in the non-western world are rendered in this study as those familiar in the period. Thus Madras (not Chennai), Ceylon (not Sri Lanka), and so on.

Diane, Ellen, and Jessica in Sydney know what it means to live with an historian. As they are all writers of one type or another, it helps, but thanks to all of you and to sister Vicki for your sustenance, love, and advice. And to Bindi, remain cute, but go easier on the barking.

Marrickville, NSW, Australia, July 2009

ABBREVIATIONS

ABCFM	American Board of Commissioners for Foreign Missions
ASL	Anti-Saloon League of America
BHLM	Bentley Historical Library, University of Michigan
BWTA	British Women's Temperance Association
IVA	International Voluntary Association
KFYMCAA	Kautz Family YMCA Archives, University of Minnesota Libraries
LC	Library of Congress
MHC-OHS	Michigan Historical Collections/Ohio Historical Society
NA	National Archives of the United States
NAW	*Notable American Women, 1607–1950: A Biographical Dictionary,* ed. Edward T. James with Janet Wilson James, associate ed., 3 vols. (Cambridge, MA: Belknap Press of Harvard University Press, 1971)
SEAP	*Standard Encyclopedia of the Alcohol Problem*
SVM	Student Volunteer Movement for Foreign Missions
WBMHL	Women's Board of Missions: Supplementary Papers and Correspondence, 1873–1947, ABC 9.5.1, Houghton Library, Harvard University
WCTU	Woman's Christian Temperance Union
WCTUHQ	Woman's Christian Temperance Union Headquarters, Evanston, IL
WLAA	World League Against Alcoholism
WPF	World Prohibition Federation
YDSL	Yale Divinity School Library
YMCA	Young Men's Christian Association
YPSCE	Young People's Society of Christian Endeavor
YWCA	Young Women's Christian Association

Reforming the World

Introduction

GOD, GOLD, AND GLORY. This is the trio of "G's" that many a history student has memorized to understand the motives for European imperialism. The same student would also learn that the 1890s witnessed an upsurge in American overseas "expansion," marking the emergence of the United States as a world power. Not literally for gold did they go overseas, but Americans traded abroad, looking for markets and resources. They also sent missionaries on behalf of the Christian God. In the name of humanitarian intervention, they even acquired colonies across the seas.[1] Rudyard Kipling called on Americans to take up the white man's burden, and for a time they did. Republican Party politicians promised benevolent tutelage and improvement as the destiny for the Philippines, Puerto Rico, and the other islands that fell into the American grasp after the Spanish-American War of 1898. Glory was not absent either. American foreign policy took on a more vigorous tone, and the Caribbean became effectively an American lake in which military intervention was promised—if European powers failed to heed the Monroe Doctrine. Soon Cuba, then Nicaragua, Honduras, Panama, Haiti, Mexico, the Dominican Republic, and other places felt the American military footprint. A pattern of controlling other peoples through military and financial power had been set. All this appeared to be the product of a restless, expansionist economy and culture.

At the time, prominent historians had no trouble conceiving of this activity as empire, nor did many politicians. Those who supported and those who opposed the colonial acquisitions of 1898 tended not to argue over whether the United States was an empire but whether imperialism was a good thing. Yet for decades thereafter, empire came to be a dirty word in the American lexicon. When Admiral George Dewey, the "hero of Manila," returned in 1899 triumphant from the defeat of the Spanish navy in the Philippines in July 1898, the proud citizens of New York raised a victory arch modeled on the precedents of classical Rome. The Beaux-Arts edifice told in its sculptures and inscriptions of an American fleet triumphant, uniting the East and West Indies in one world. But, in 1900, efforts to raise money for a permanent version of the hastily constructed monument faltered, and the original plaster of Paris and cement structure soon had to be removed because the elements had taken their toll.[2] Americans had begun to forget their empire. When the Wilson administration came to power in 1913 it initiated moves for Philippinization of the colonial government. The United States withdrew its occupying force from Cuba in 1902 and Congress affirmed in 1903 the terms of that nation's "independence," though with restrictions that smacked of informal American control, and Hawaii was admitted as a territory in 1898. Distant Samoa, tiny Guam in the Pacific, and Puerto Rico joined the Philippines under American rule, but Americans swept their island empire under the rug with the euphemism of the "insular possessions," and a Bureau of Insular Affairs, not a "colonial office," to run them. Though intermittently raised as an issue or made central to analysis of American history by intrepid scholars in the 1920s and 1930s, the expansionism of the 1890s to 1914 characteristically appeared thereafter in history books as an aberration. Many believed that Americans did not "do" or "seek" empire, as Donald Rumsfeld put it so pithily.[3] A great many books have recently been written about American empire,[4] but scholarly and public debate still struggles over the terms of the discussion, because the American experience did not seem to fit classical European imperialism. This comparative approach tends to treat American expansion overseas and other empires as self-contained entities to be contrasted.[5] The approach falsely creates an ideal type of empire based on formal acquisition of territories, an established imperial ruling class, hostility to decolonization, and the treatment of colonial peoples as dependents.

Whatever the terminological quibbles over the course of empire in American history as a whole, it is clear that the United States did have an empire in the years before World War I. That the formal colonies were limited in scope should not hide that fact; nor should terminology obscure the extensive informal empire that the United States developed through both economic techniques and military intervention. American actions encompassed a "conscious" (if often temporary) "desire to conquer" and a persistent pattern of political and economic domination that arguably conforms to commonsense definitions of informal empire.[6] Nor should the exercise of moral and cultural influence be ignored, where directed toward supporting either formal or informal imperial control. These efforts might simply be ideological, but they may also be material ones in providing support for the colonial state in the contracting out of social and cultural services.

In this book I wish to broaden the context of the drive toward American imperialism—situating it within wider patterns of informal American expansion and the transnational networks implicated in those patterns. While the informal empire of free trade and the Open Door policy is a concept extensively explored by others,[7] nineteenth-century moral reform as another and arguably important part of informal and formal U.S. empire has not been the subject of much analysis beyond a few individual case studies.[8] Americans exported a wide variety of organizations designed for moral uplift, from the well-known and influential

Woman's Christian Temperance Union and Young Men's (and Women's) Christian Association to the less well-known or totally obscure, such as the King's Daughters, the International Anti-Cigarette League, and the World's Good Habits Society.[9] Collectively, I call such groups "moral reformers." In their enterprise to improve both morally and materially the countries to which they went, they were joined by an immense array of missionary forces, including the boards of the denominational churches that administered overseas work, raised money, and kept the faithful at home informed. These groups were not identical in aims, structures, pet causes, or impacts, but they networked and overlapped extensively in their strategies, tactics, and ideologies. They also cooperated and lobbied within the United States to promote moral reform abroad. However, none of this activity was exclusively an American domain. Some of these societies had key foreign organizers and supporters and some were first created in other countries though later adapted or transformed in the United States. Their work exhibited transnational influences upon the United States, even as the tendency over time was for the work to become more American centered and the transnational influence less reciprocal.

All of these groups were part of a larger universe of American cultural expansion that included tourists, popular culture, and sporting groups. Though often of considerable importance, these activities rarely took organizational form or became closely connected with American empire. When they did, as with the export of baseball to the Caribbean, the Pacific, and East Asia, these aspects of the spread of American culture often either occurred through the work of missionaries or mimicked the missionaries. Albert G. Spalding, the promoter who undertook a world tour in 1888–89 to spread the influence of baseball, followed in the tracks of the moral reformers and explicitly called his players "Base Ball missionaries."[10]

American cultural expansion abroad may be analyzed using the terminology of "soft power," but there are better approaches. Coined to describe the cultural and social influences exerted by the United States abroad in recent decades, the term lacks precision, the boundaries between soft and "hard" power are difficult to establish, and little agency can be given to the people subject to this power. More preferable for the study of moral reform is an older term. Cultural hegemony means not "domination" as raw power but the exercise of power under a shared moral and political order in which that power is the subject of multilateral contestation among nations and classes.[11] Power is the product of ruled as well as rulers, of subordinate as well as dominant nations. This power is reciprocal in its practices. Effects do not simply proceed outward but flow inward as events, circumstances, and people abroad influence the United States.

The focus here is not the larger patterns of American economic and cultural integration with the wider world[12] but the organizational and cultural changes in American voluntary reform abroad from the 1880s to the 1920s. Nor does this book concentrate on the reception of American reform ideas outside the United States. That would require not just one study but many, dealing with the complexities and specifics of very diverse societies to which Americans pitched their missionary messages. This is, however, a book about moral reformers exporting their ideas, interacting with one another in the process, and responding to stimuli from abroad in shaping their programs.

Moral reform groups and missionaries often thought of their work as analogous to empire—but a kind of Christian moral empire that rose above "nation," and one nobler in aspiration than the grubby motives of gold and glory.[13] Catholics were not part of this movement. Evangelical missionaries did not regard Rome as an ally abroad, but eyed Roman Catholics and Eastern Orthodox Christians as sources of potential converts to a purer form of faith. And the Catholic Church saw the United States itself as a mission field, not a source of missionary enterprise.[14] The relationship between Protestant reformers' aspiration to create a more Christian and moral world on the one hand and the emergence of American imperialism and colonialism beginning in 1898 on the other is at the heart of what follows. Cultural expansion in the form of missionaries and moral reform enlarged what could be termed the external "footprint" of the United States in the 1880s and 1890s, creating conditions wherein a more vigorous economic and political expansion could be seriously considered. American reformers fashioned their own version of a non-territorial "empire" grounded in networks of moral reform organizations that pursued innovative policies and sought a hegemonic position within the world of voluntary, non-government action across the Euro-American world and its colonies. In the process, American reformers articulated a vision that was global. The emergence of American formal empire in 1898 posed a challenge to this distinctive configuration, and moral reform organizations met formal imperialism's growth by developing a loose coalition of Christian groups that lobbied for changes to the United States' relationships with its colonies and the wider world. This informal coalition settled for a time after 1898 around the work of Wilbur F. Crafts and the American-based International Reform Bureau. The groups associated with his work conceded that American empire did include colonies that provided opportunities for Christian proselytizing, but formal empire was not to be their major focus. The larger project of moral reformers to remake the world in terms of Protestant cultural values was vigorously reasserted by the moral coalition. In the era of World War I and its aftermath, this approach grew stronger and displaced as much as complemented reform of the formal empire. Throughout I argue that the boundaries between Christian evangelical networks operating on a transnational level and formal empire were blurred, with the latter phenomenon essentially embedded within the former.

While talk of networks is now becoming popular in theorizing about transnational political movements in the contemporary world,[15] the deeper pedigree of such movements has rarely been studied and still more rarely theorized. The practical way that networks operated in the history of American empire is imperfectly understood.[16] This book considers the analytical framework of these networks and provides the empirical detail required to trace their operation and impacts. In the process it outlines the fascinating broader context of American moral expansionism from the 1870s to the 1920s. Building up a picture of such networks requires more than theory. Political scientists interested in transnational social movements consider a range of characteristics including denseness of communication, patterns of agenda setting, and lobbying, among other things, but such concepts are essentially empirical and descriptive.[17] Studying networks requires patient documentation of how people across different fields got to know and support one another. These networks depended on the life histories, aspirations, and cultural heritage of moral reformers. This book tells the stories of such people.

Historians are beginning to reassess religion's role in American life, and a key element in this reassessment must be the role of evangelical missionary and moral reform institutions during the era of high European imperialism.[18] "Cultural imperialism" is, as we shall see, too blunt an instrument to fully comprehend these relationships, but connections with the power of colonialism and imperialism there certainly were.[19] The association between religion and Protestant morality on the one hand and American expansion on the other might seem far from new. After all, Manifest Destiny, popularized as a phrase during the annexation of Texas and the subsequent war with Mexico, had an explicit religious justification. The moral movement of the 1880s to the 1920s was not, however, one of rhetorical justification for expansion but intrinsic to that process. It concerned the shaping of expansion and often the criticism of expansion that did not conform to evangelical morals; it was far from simply being a gloss on power. Along a similar vein, it might be argued that the Christian mobilization beginning in the 1880s was merely a continuation of the missions to the Indians of the seventeenth and eighteenth centuries. No doubt the memory of Puritan heroes and heroines of that time spurred missionary zeal into new efforts to carry the Gospel into "heathen lands." Yet the first turn toward overseas missionary work came in the 1810s and 1820s—long before the 1880s, when external stimuli proved more important.[20] Nor is the more general argument valid that

Americans sought an alternative to the "closing" of the frontier of the American West in the 1890s. The sequence of events does not fit. In 1893, the historian Frederick Jackson Turner declared on the basis of Bureau of the Census data that the frontier period ended in 1890, but a good deal of frontier development occurred after this, and the pattern of moral mobilization for expansion revealed in this book began earlier, in the 1880s.[21] Moreover, Christian reformers did not cite the role of the frontier's end as the reason to turn abroad. Their motives almost always raised the external crisis that the global spread of imperialism posed and did not call for acquisition of more land.[22] The connecting thread in what follows is, therefore, not internal imperatives or the logic of evangelistic campaigns but the transnational organizing of American Protestant Christians seeking to change the world.

These campaigns forged in reform what sociologists call transnational spaces. The latter grew on the foundations of the accelerating velocity of international non-governmental organizations in the Euro-American world and the greater cooperation between nations that emerged in the late nineteenth century.[23] Transnational work influenced the United States as much as it did the colonial and quasi-colonial peoples that Americans touched and shaped the architecture of American dealings with the larger world of empires through to the era of Woodrow Wilson. In the process, transnational organizing established strong assumptions and even institutions and practices that survived to become part of the foundations of American global power in the twentieth century.

A word on the use of "transnational" and competitor terms is in order here. The term "international" refers to the formal, political interactions of nation-state institutions. "Internationalism," a concept common at the time, is used here to mean the practice and promotion of interstate cooperation, whereas "the transnational" includes the broader field of non-governmental social, cultural, and economic activities. This more modern term describes the movement of peoples, goods, ideas, and institutions across national boundaries in the era of nation-state building. One common application, used in this study, focuses on the transnational "production" of the nation, in this case the relationship between the United States and the wider world. For the United States, the late nineteenth century to the end of World War I was a crucial period for the growth of the federal state. Through recent historiography, the state's links with overseas empire and war in those years are becoming ever more obvious.[24] Transnational influences helped shape the American nation-state, but transnational history also includes study of the transnational spaces—both mental and material—that individuals and groups created outside of nation. Though culturally influenced by their American roots and newfound national power, Protestant missionaries and moral reformers forged spaces that engaged foreign influences in ways that had their own integrity, yet also fed back to the United States. The complicated dialectic between the national and the transnational is the key theme in this book.[25]

The international and missionary context for the development of American moral reform abroad was the development of communications networks. If the 1840s represented a communications and transport revolution nationally, the 1870s and 1880s saw a global revolution of equally profound proportions. The quickening pace of technological and social change facilitated the expansionist aims of missionaries and moral reformers. These matters are the themes of part 1. Patterns of trade, tourism, transport, and communications highlighted American awareness of the nation's growing international interdependency. As the external connections of Americans grew, the nation became enmeshed in new transnational flows that were global rather than merely transatlantic. In these ways, as chapter 1 shows, the nation's people became increasingly interested in and influenced by circumstances beyond national borders. American missionary work was both transformed by these changes and contributed to them. Two women missionaries, Mary and Margaret Leitch, touched so much of the American project for moral reform that their story helps construct a model for the development of transnational networks and for the impact of experience abroad on the design and practice of cultural expansion undertaken by missionary groups and moral reformers in the era of a global communications revolution (chapter 2). While the material networks that allowed the ideas of missionaries to flourish must be taken seriously, so too must these missionaries' intense enthusiasms rooted in ideology and religious belief.

Within this context of transnational connections and networks, part 2 locates the origins of American empire in the phenomenal growth of Protestant missionary groups and moral reformers in the 1880s and 1890s, starting with the Student Volunteer Movement for Foreign Missions. Rather than dynamic internal development spilling beyond American borders, external stimuli drew Americans abroad, encouraging in the process innovative policies and organizational forms for the missionary endeavor. The experience of missionary outreach (charted in chapter 3) required rethinking the entire organizational basis of the Christian reform enterprises. This process spurred attempts to galvanize the faithful into new practices of systematic giving, lay leadership, non-denominational cooperation, business-church alliances, and departmental specialization.

Reflecting the ferment of missionary enthusiasm, distinctive reform groups arose in the 1880s to extend the American moral reach and provide support for it. They shared tactics, methods, and personnel to produce a matrix of moral reform that pushed an American way of organizing Protestant religion abroad (chapter 4). Christian Endeavor, the Young Men's Christian Association (YMCA), and the World's Woman's Christian Temperance Union (World's WCTU) were representative organizations that campaigned for social, economic, and political assistance for missionaries and their subjects. These groups reveal a relatively equal balance of gender contributions to reform, yet unequal experience and power relations. The efforts of the Young Women's Christian Association (YWCA) paralleled on a smaller scale those of the YMCA and took organizational forms from the latter. Both were products of the evangelicalism stirring manifest in the Student Volunteers, an organization that strongly reasserted the role of men within the mission field. Nevertheless the YWCA, along with the King's Daughters, WCTU, and other organizations revealed the complex gender dynamics at work in the missionary impulse. The tensions inherent in an attempted masculinization of a crusade where women as missionaries were increasingly vital bearers of faith acted as a spur to continual innovation in the structures of organized moral reform.[26]

Chapter 5 develops the theme of "humanitarianism" as a central principle of the reformers' work in the 1890s. From the Russian famine of 1892 to the military intervention in Cuba in 1898, American humanitarianism flourished through relief campaigns undertaken by the *Christian Herald* and its charismatic editor, Louis Klopsch, the WCTU, Clara Barton and the American Red Cross, and missionaries. Historians have mostly ignored these pioneer relief efforts and their connections with the pattern of economic and political expansion.[27] Yet the ideological and practical functions of humanitarian gestures show how reformers developed a culture encouraging intervention in the affairs of other countries that brought the United States to the threshold of the Spanish-American War, and yet how humanitarianism championed the United States as an anti-imperial force.[28]

The acquisition of a formal empire in 1898 cut across the objectives of transnational organizing and further stimulated the moral reform organizations, encouraging them to direct efforts toward a more nation-centered Christian coalition that would reshape the American empire (documented in part 3). These challenges centered on the struggles over the military canteen, the regulation of prostitution, and the licensing of opium in the new American possessions abroad (chapters 6 and 7). American administrators proposed to mimic other empires and adapt morals and manners to the circumstances of colonial peoples. As reformers fought back against what they regarded as errant policies, their work became further interconnected as a moral coalition. Lobbying the national government to achieve transnational objectives became paramount because it was in Washington that the power to effect change lay. These moral lobbyists linked the crusades against "vice" to the creation of a new and more moral kind of empire.

While the main organizations discussed in this book compromised with empire far enough to seek improvement in the institutions of the American colonial enterprise, some individuals challenged the attachment of reformers to the colonial state and the international order of European imperial domination. Intrepid reformers championed the interests of oppressed groups, including the colonial peoples themselves. Some of the challenges that radicals posed were connected to broader Anglo-American imperial networks and drew on patterns of indigenous nationalist reform. The agitation of Ida Wells on lynching, using the anti-racist and anti-imperial platforms provided by Englishwoman Catherine Impey, was one such campaign, discussed in chapter 8. Other dissenters included missionaries whose colonial experience reshaped their later radicalism in the United States. These activists did not shake the foundations of American empire. Nevertheless, their voices registered significant capacity for moral dissent within the reform tradition and exposed mainstream reform's sometimes feeble acquiescence in conventional power structures in the underdeveloped world. Radical agitation also revealed how the reciprocal effects of empire could be felt upon the United States through the experiences of transnational reformers.

Did moral reformers have any influence over the reconstruction of American statecraft brought about by the rise of empire? Part 4 addresses this question. Opportunities there were, but the relationships were complicated. Leading politicians and strategists often expressed moral and Christian convictions comparable to those of missionaries and reformers, yet this is not to say that American imperial adventures were in any sense caused by moral reform entanglements. As chapter 9 shows, presidents and their advisors might be on friendly terms with such people, but the practical politics of government remained paramount. Nevertheless, moral reform organizations subtly contributed to the broader sociopolitical context of American power abroad and aimed at the creation of a Christian state to effect this goal. World War I reinforced this growing allegiance between state and moral reform, and promoted nationalism and American exceptionalism in the process.

The hopes of the Wilsonian new world order affected and expressed the external pattern of evangelical activism after World War I. Though American moral reformers still advocated the movement of ideas, institutions, and personnel across national boundaries, the flow of transnational information became more lopsided. Unmistakably, a flexing of American moral muscle occurred, especially through the World League Against Alcoholism of the 1920s and its ill-fated attempt to apply national prohibition to other countries (chapter 10). In keeping with the American wartime experience, reformers now sought to remake Europe in the image of the United States as a solution to the evils of the world. The strategy struck at the heart of European empire, while ironically contributing to an American alternative. U.S.-style alcohol reform became intertwined with debates over Americanization, anti-Americanism, and the drive for international hegemony in a turbulent world.

History never ends. Change is ceaseless though not unidirectional; continuity is always part of the story, and so too here. The conclusion surveys the broader landscape of the 1920s and analyzes the forces that brought about an apparent decline in missionary enthusiasm. It also explores the dreams and reflects on the achievements of a number of reformers and missionaries from the perspective of the 1920s, starting with the Misses Leitch. Though their overt goals had not been fully realized and, indeed, dreams had failed to materialize, moral reformers had stamped their own imprint upon conceptions of the nation's global role, and attitudes toward a distinctive form of American empire had been substantially reshaped.

PART I

Networks of Empire

Chapter 1

WEBS OF COMMUNICATION

WHEN WILLIAM T. STEAD, the British editor of the *Review of Reviews*, went to a watery grave with the *Titanic* on April 15, 1912, supporters of moral reform wept openly. It was said to be typical of his "generosity, courage, and humanity that Stead was last seen leading women and children to the safety of the stricken liner's lifeboats."[1] Stead was a friend of "America," a country whose efforts on behalf of international cooperation, arbitration, and missionary work abroad he deeply admired. It was this admiration that put him on that ill-fated journey across the high seas. He was traveling to speak on "universal peace" at the Men and Religion Forward Movement Congress in New York City on April 22.[2] Though well-known as the author of *The Americanization of the World*, he did not see Americanization as the message that the United States carried in its cultural and economic expansion abroad. Rather, his admiration of the American republic was part of a much larger story. Just five years before his drowning, he proclaimed that "The Twentieth Century is the Century of Internationalism" in the *Review of Internationalism*, edited at the Office of the Foundation of the Promotion of Internationalism at The Hague.[3] He knew that diplomats, President Theodore Roosevelt, and American peace reformers had played important parts in the events leading up to the Second Hague Peace Conference (1907), and saw Americanization and Anglo-American influence as harbingers of and agents for the spread of internationalism.[4]

Internationalism entailed conceptually and often practically the relations between nations, chiefly as sovereign states operating on a diplomatic level. As critics have pointed out, this internationalism was Eurocentric, hierarchical, and dependent on military strength and economic power. It entailed the spread of European moral and ethical standards of civilization, an observation that should not surprise for an era of imperialism and nationalism. Internationalism was a product not chiefly of the noble aspirations that motivated Stead but of material interests. Groups of nations sought through international action protection from the arbitrary changes that accompanied a more interconnected world.[5] Internationalism depended not only on the fact of nationalism but also on the ability of some powers to exert influence over others to extend higher standards of conduct between humans. In contrast, for Stead internationalism did not operate simply as a set of dealings among nation-states. It extended to a web of transnational influences—influences that embraced groups, ideas, individuals, and institutions across national boundaries. The efforts of transnational reform organizations provided the cultural and intellectual context for the spread of Stead's new internationalism. Europeans, not Americans, took the lead in the growth of International Voluntary Associations (IVAs), but quickly Americans extended and complemented this internationalizing effort with their own distinctive contribution. All this Stead understood. Americanization, reform across national boundaries, and ideologies of internationalism were closely intertwined. In turn, Stead was aware that the United States could be no island, isolated from the world. The great republic was irrevocably drawn not only into closer relations between nations but also into transnational ties through commercial, organizational, and social intercourse.

Vast networks of transnational influences impinged upon the United States in the late nineteenth century. By coincidence, American involvement in this transnational activity surged ahead in 1885, at the exact same time that Stead first burst to prominence as a journalist in Britain agitating against "vice," particularly prostitution, in his famous essay "The Maiden Tribute of Babylon." The transnational activism in which Americans engaged beginning in the 1880s sprang not from thin air but from this wider context of moral reform of which Stead's work was an important part. Material networks' expansion in the 1870s allowed transnational institutions to flourish; an intricate web of connections facilitated and spurred reform across American national boundaries. American awareness of the nation's interdependency with other countries was highlighted by changing patterns of trade, tourism, transport, and communications, by commercial exhibitions and world's fairs, and by media changes, especially in print culture. Though the missionary and moral reform surge of the late nineteenth century in the United States was a product of these influences and roughly comparable to transnational movements in Europe, the American version became distinctively global in its aspirations and highly dependant on new technologies of international communication.

American commerce abroad grew, and not just with its traditional Atlantic trading partner, Britain. Though American exports to Europe remained an important driving force for the American economy, American trade was taking on a global reach. Approximately 72 percent of American exports went to Europe in the late nineteenth century, but imports from outside Europe increased to one half of the total at the turn of the twentieth century. The biggest increase was not from Latin America but Asia, from which imports nearly doubled from 1860 to 1901–5, reaching 15.4 percent of the total. Asia also became an increasingly important export market, from just 2.4 percent in 1860 to 11.3 percent of the total by 1921–25. Much of this increase concerned Japan,[6] but the United States also drew on more diverse international sources for its raw materials and exotic goods. Not only was the United States becoming more commercially interdependent with Asia;[7] closer to home Americans scoured Central America for resources and began to export capital. Railroads, mines, sugar, and fruit plantations in Latin America and the Caribbean became new outlets for American business investment. Cuba and Mexico were especially important targets.

Americans were journeying abroad more often; but they were also living in many foreign countries as businessmen and expatriates, thus raising for the Department of State issues of extraterritoriality. Through their sheer presence, missionaries, traders, businessmen, and even prostitutes widened the American external footprint in the 1870s and 1880s, producing trouble for diplomats and complications for the American legal system on the rights of sojourning citizens.[8] The nation was becoming enmeshed in new transnational flows that were global, not merely transatlantic, and its people were increasingly entangled in circumstances beyond national borders.

As a key element in these changes, the global spread of communications proceeded apace. From the time of the practical demonstration of the Morse code in 1844, enterprising businessmen worked to link nations with the aid of the telegraph. Cables were laid across the English Channel in 1851 and, after earlier failures, a transatlantic cable was successfully completed in 1866. When an experimental and temporary cross-ocean cable was first laid some years earlier, the *New York Times* reported that the infrastructure was "the greatest enterprise of the nineteenth century"; it promoted a "close union of nations in the mutual bonds of interest and amity."[9] At first Europe and North America were brought into closer connection for speedy and reliable information on shipping, trade opportunities, prices, and business conditions. By 1870, rapid European communications had been extended as far as Singapore, and by 1903 trans-Pacific cables linked the United States directly to its new colony, the Philippines, and then on to Hong Kong and Shanghai.[10] Transport timetabling and hotel bookings were thereby made much easier. The expansion of canals, railroads, and steamship lines nicely complemented the growth in telegraph communications. The sprouting of transport networks was most intense across Europe, where rail track mileage trebled between 1870 and 1914, bringing countries closer together and allowing missionaries and tourists to travel more speedily to Asia, especially when coupled with the opening of the Suez Canal in 1869. The Atlantic was shrinking with equal rapidity in travel times and costs, a development that helped integrate Anglo-American moral reform networks. The first steamships, the

Sirius and the *Great Western,* had arrived in New York from London as early as 1838, heralding the future means of ocean travel that would cut travel times and make for more certain passage. Nonetheless, until the Civil War most crossings were by sail, then competition and technology combined to slash the one-way cabin fare by half to less than $100 between the 1850s and 1900.[11] By the early twentieth century about a dozen steamship lines worked the North Atlantic in regular, speedy services and prompted extensive international travel among an elite of Americans. Foreign oceanic travel by Americans reached one hundred thousand passengers per year in 1885. By that time, steamship services across the North Pacific had been working for eighteen years, and the distant South Pacific destinations of Australia and New Zealand were connected to San Francisco by a mail service that became an all-steamer route in the early 1880s.

Not only did middle-class and elite travel across the Atlantic flourish; global trips also became fashionable and newsworthy. Among those who traveled around the world were the inevitable tourists and businessmen, but reformers and missionaries joined in as well. The global excursion was more than an American trend. Thomas Cook, the famous English tour operator, did so in 1872–73, taking 223 days. Gospel revivalists from Britain crossed the Atlantic westward, just as Americans sailed to Europe, and British evangelicals toured the empire, covering vast distances, as did the Glasgow-based Rev. Alexander Somerville. In 1877–79, for example, the Scot "set out for our Australian colonies." In eighteen months of travel from Britain "he journeyed 34,000 miles and spoke to 610 audiences."[12] He also roved across South Africa, Europe, and the Middle East in the 1880s. Nevertheless, the prominence of Americans within the new itinerant style of transnational preaching increased, and reformers and journalists joined in the fetish not just for round-the-world travel but for speedy passages that could gain press coverage and popular acclaim. The obsession with these feats suggested a heightened American interest in the linking of global perspectives and technological achievements in communications. The trend began in 1870 with the exploits of the aptly named American George Francis Train; his speedy circumnavigation allegedly became the basis for Jules Verne's *Around the World in Eighty Days.* An increasing number of intrepid women travelers were among those going abroad and winning—in the case of Elizabeth Cochrane Seaman (writing as Nellie Bly) through her newspaper account of her round-the-world-trip—temporary fame, praise, or influence.[13] Bly's *Around the World in Seventy-Two Days* (1890) was marketed heavily in Joseph Pulitzer's *New York World.*[14] So much of a fetish had this travel bug become that, by the 1890s, going around the world once was not enough. The temperance reformer Jessie Ackermann eventually managed eight trips, but others eclipsed her efforts as the pattern of missionary and moral reform involvement grew. In the new world of speedier and more predictable communications, changing the world for moral reformers became almost a matter of cumulative circulation; reform-minded travel became, in part, a means of demonstrating global awareness and global reach.[15]

The wider experience and awareness of tourism was reflected in the growing interest in travel literature. Returning missionaries gave magic lantern presentations highlighting the exotic places they visited, and missionary magazines became littered with lush images of tropical places— the "palmy plains" and "coral strands" that evoked the memorable phrases of the Reginald Heber hymn familiar throughout the Anglo-American world.[16] More secular clubs developed "travel-by-proxy" programs, provided advice, heard travel talks, watched slide presentations of foreign lands, and promoted "the rise of a tourist mentality." Many of these clubs were founded after 1900 and reflected Progressive Era flexing of women's institutional presence through the Women's Club movement, but some went back a generation or more.[17] Before 1890, missionary outlets were vital in structuring knowledge of foreign places, but secular travel literature was also significant. Of 1,765 travel books published in the United States from 1830 to 1900, 81 percent appeared after 1860.[18] On top of this came the intimidating number of periodical accounts. Thus *National Geographic* became a "dominant force in establishing American impressions of the world, its inhabitants, and the scientific enterprise." With about four-fifths of the magazine's circulation going to such people as businessmen and professionals in the 1880s, it represented the interests of the influential but moved increasingly in the direction of popular middle-class taste. Though geographical information available to Americans from this and other sources did not necessarily dissolve ill-informed representations of exotic cultures, it did multiply the amount of information and whetted the appetite for things foreign. Through newspapers, magazines, and personal tourist contacts, the 1870s to 1890s saw Americans of the middle to upper-middle classes becoming interested in the fashions, food, art, and domestic decorative styles of foreign lands.[19] Exhibits on East Asia at the Philadelphia Centennial International Exhibition of 1876 and World's Columbian Exposition of 1893 excited interest. Japanese decorative art styles penetrated through European fashions, while musicals featuring non-Western themes also flourished. Gilbert and Sullivan's operetta *The Mikado* had an enormously successful New York season in 1885.[20]

From a European perspective, the mid- to late nineteenth century was marked by relative peace in the international arena. Bookended by the Napoleonic and French Revolutionary period before it, and the Great

War of 1914–18 that succeeded it, the era experienced no world wars. This image of a peaceful world was partly an illusion, to be sure. The American Civil War was but one of many bloody conflicts on the periphery of Europe. Numerous "savage wars of peace," as Rudyard Kipling called them, occurred on the boundaries of empires as they expanded and as Europeans sought to suppress the resistance of colonized peoples in Asia and Africa. Nevertheless, conditions existed for more frequent collaboration and negotiation among the political and commercial elites of the European powers in ways that inevitably involved the non-Western world. This process entailed humanitarian, religious, and moral entanglements, and the United States became involved.

Most notably the Congress of Berlin (1884–85) met to organize the commercial development of the Congo Basin and preserve the trading rights of all nations, but American and British missionaries and antislavery societies, such as Britain's Aboriginal Protection Society, pressed successfully for action against the still surviving international slave trade as part of the deliberations. Though it suited the British government's political and economic objectives to use this moral opinion to provide impetus to the Berlin congress, the signatories thereby set precedents in international law on the suppression of slavery. For the first time "in a multinational treaty," nations accepted the principle "that 'native welfare' was a matter of international concern." The Congo would not be owned by an individual European power but would be "internationalized." Ironically, the results of the congress were to cement the power of the privately run Congo Free State, which proved a mechanism for the quasi-enslavement of Africans, not their protection. The shock over the appalling treatment of the Congolese under King Leopold of Belgium's private company rule after 1885 stimulated a further rush of humanitarian sentiment and missionary involvement aimed at curbing the king's power, beginning with moves against the internal African slave trade during the 1889–90 Brussels Conference.[21]

In all of this action, Americans played a role. Missionaries joined American-born Henry Morton Stanley in lobbying for the Berlin congress. In Stanley's case, this action supported the plans of King Leopold, which were not at the time recognized as dangerous to human welfare but promoted it through the imposition of Westernization. Because of trade possibilities and missionary interest, the U.S. government sent a representative to the Berlin meeting and for the first time took part in a diplomatic conference concerning affairs outside the western hemisphere. As Secretary of State Frederick Frelinghuysen put it, the role of the American representative was to argue that "peace and freedom" in the region would come from "the dominion of the white man" and "the development of useful commerce."[22] The action was controversial within partisan American politics, and as a result the United States did not ratify the 1885 General Act of the Berlin congress, but the precedent of greater American international involvement and enhanced humanitarian concern had been set.

The reverberations of the transatlantic anti-slavery tradition could be felt in these humanitarian actions, but post–Civil War moral reform was mediated through the experiences of international organizing in the 1870s and 1880s. The international anti-prostitution movements of that period were explicitly conceived of as "abolitionist" in aim, and the constantly growing women's temperance movement with its themes of women's emancipation also provided a powerful stimulus to missionary activity and models for moral reform. These moral reforms were themselves embedded in a wider network of cross-national interactions in law, commerce, and government.

The impact of industrialization, commercial prosperity, and the growth of rapid communications sharpened intellectual interest in matters international and transnational. Though Randolph Bourne promoted the term "transnational" in 1916, Europeans were, in essence, exploring the concept in the nineteenth century.[23] Lexicographic changes registered increased exchanges of information between national bureaucracies and the beginnings of programs aimed at regulating the new international arena. Simultaneously, Europeans developed international law as a field and, in the United States, parallel champions emerged and ultimately created the *American Journal of International Law* in 1907.[24] Legal scholars such as Simeon Baldwin and Paul Reinsch studied international organizations and treaties,[25] while international peace conferences began to be held, most notably from the American side by the annual Lake Mohonk conferences on International Arbitration in the Catskill Mountains of New York beginning in 1895. On the basis of this burgeoning intellectual interest in internationalism came a series of movements to devise a common international language. Most notable was Esperanto, which was created from the late 1870s to the early 1880s but grew noticeably a decade later to a stage where the first International Congress on Esperanto could be held in 1905.[26]

Intensified communications between nations facilitated a great many international associations. Thus did concrete institutional achievements in exchange and cooperation proliferate across national boundaries. The United States was most definitely not the originator of these trends. American external expansion in the form of transnational organizations cannot be explained by internal movements and dynamics alone, but must be seen as part of European changes toward greater interdependency between nations. It was Europe where international communications were densest and borders crossed more often and more quickly. The growth in the numbers of international organizations began in the 1860s and 1870s in Europe, particularly the second half of the 1870s, fully a decade before Americans became deeply involved.[27] Even more impressive was the up-surge in international non-governmental organizations in Europe from 1885 to 1889, with more than double the number established in that five-year period than in the previous decade. However, this second surge coincided with the creation of highly significant American non-governmental bodies that operated internationally. The American propensity to form voluntary associations in civil society to achieve social and moral goals has been a strong one, yet clearly the trend toward denser associational networks was not linked to national structures alone. An American pattern of voluntarism was not simply projected upon the world stage either. It was part of the larger cross-Atlantic circulation. The American efforts were to a considerable extent stimulated by the example of Europe and by the technical conditions for international action that improvements in global communications created.

The new international organizations were of two basic types. First were those involving relations between nation-states, the second international voluntary associations that were the precursors of modern non-governmental organizations. The first type included international instruments to smooth the path of foreign commerce and communications. The most important of these were the International Telegraphic Union (1865) and the Universal Postal Union (1874).[28] These and others like them were intergovernmental bodies and the products of diplomatic agreements that the United States joined. In some cases, international offices were set up to administer treaties, as was done when the Postal Union located its offices in Berne, Switzerland. That country became the main center for the placement and the growth of this first type of international activity, but it also had a vital role to play in the development of a second type.[29]

Far more numerous were the non-governmental associations or IVAs. Of 462 international organizations created from 1850 to 1914, all but 36 were non-governmental.[30] One category of organization did straddle the boundaries of this simple division, however. These were the international congresses, which were gatherings of experts and government officials to exchange scientific information and to work toward international standards of professional or bureaucratic practice.[31] In some cases these meetings took a more formal intergovernmental role and stimulated the passage of national legislation or worked for permanent bureaus, commissions, or secretariats on particular objects.[32] The most prominent was in health through the International Sanitation Congresses that began in 1851 in Paris when twelve nations met. Prompting this innovation was the spread of epidemics of cholera and other diseases as transport improved in the nineteenth century, making it ever more necessary for governments to establish health quarantine between nations, cooperate with other governments to improve medical intelligence reports on likely carriers of disease, and institute closer surveillance of immigrants.[33] Once again, as in the case of the Postal Union, the United States was drawn into this initially European-dominated work and hosted the International Sanitary Conference in Washington in 1881. Aimed at stopping the spread of cholera, this meeting was the first such gathering outside a European capital.[34]

The idea of holding international conferences had already spread beyond technological and medical questions to social and moral reform. In fact, the boundaries between the medical and the moral were extremely blurred, as physical contagion was often thought to be an expression of moral failure.[35] When an International Congress on the Prevention and Repression of Crime was held in London in 1872, U.S. delegates helped secure the decision to create a permanent secretariat at that meeting.[36] More important for the American reform movements were the biennial International Congresses Against Alcoholism held from 1885 to 1934, meetings that began in Antwerp with 529 delegates assembled from eight nations, including the United States.[37] It was a significant development that these conferences were, at roughly two-year intervals, held more regularly than some other international meetings. They included in their delegates prohibitionists, medical reformers, alcohol treatment experts, and advocates of moderation. Meetings focused on academic and scientific aspects of the question of alcohol use and abuse, but moral questions frequently intruded, as temperance societies sent representatives.[38]

International meetings on moral questions were certainly not new in the 1880s. A World's Anti-Slavery Convention and a World's Temperance Convention had been held as early as 1840 and 1846, respectively, with Americans deeply involved in these deliberations. An Evangelical Alliance joined Protestant denominations in transnational dialogue starting in 1846, but a fiery dispute over the role of anti-slavery in Christian theology and practice hampered American participation until after the Civil War. The first American affiliate was formed in 1867 and the alliance's first international conference in North America, accompanied by sessions on both moral reform and missions, took place in 1873.[39] This was the same decade in which European and then American groups began to look beyond such conferences to form international associations to prosecute their moral aims systematically.

A pioneering example was that of Josephine Butler, an English clergyman's wife from Winchester who, opposing the licensing of prostitution and the medical inspection of prostitutes, worked for abolition of Britain's Contagious Diseases Acts of 1864–69. Butler could not conduct this campaign in splendid isolation because practices and arguments favoring the state regulation of prostitution were becoming entrenched in continental Europe. Such pro-regulation sentiment could easily influence British opinion. Butler therefore decided that taking an attacking position was the best form of defense. She developed networks promoting the alternative approach of abolitionism on the European continent as a way of inoculating British society against a threat from a foreign example and to extend her moral crusade to liberate women from the second-class status of a sex subjected to special medical supervision. Accordingly, Butler fostered a transnational movement. The British, Continental and General Federation for the Abolition of Vice (later renamed the International Abolitionist Federation) was founded in 1875. She tapped into Quaker and anti-slavery networks to spread her message across Europe and through these networks came into contact with like-minded Americans.[40] Her forthright stance and evangelical aura fostered her reputation in the United States, though she did not visit personally. Instead, coworkers Henry J. Wilson and the Rev. J. P. Gledstone toured the northeastern states in April and May 1876 and carried her message. They met with leading abolitionists, such as William Lloyd Garrison and the members of the well-known Blackwell family of Boston-based reformers.[41] Garrison was stirred to tell Henry Wilson of his "feeling the deepest interest in the sublime struggle now going on in your country, and just beginning on the Continent, against the licensing of houses of prostitution, against the so-called 'Contagious Diseases Acts,' and against all other specious but Satanic devices to popularize licentiousness and hold out special inducements for its indulgence."[42] The two English visitors also influenced the Quaker Aaron Powell, who agitated temperance and purity issues from the 1870s to the 1890s. Powell had first met Butler as a delegate to the International Prison Congress in London in 1872, and from this early contact, Powell attended the first international congress held at Geneva, Switzerland, organized by Butler to promote the abolition of state-regulated prostitution in 1877.[43] A New York Society for the Abolition of Vice established as a result of the transatlantic agitation became eventually the American Purity Alliance. Closely affiliated with the International Federation, this society was drawn into European debates over purity legislation, and Powell became a stalwart at the international conferences of the 1880s and 1890s.[44]

Because Powell was a keen friend of the temperance movement, he encouraged opposition to prostitution in that quarter. Elizabeth Wheeler Andrew, Dr. Kate Bushnell, and others who founded and led the Social Purity Department of the National Woman's Christian Temperance Union came under Butler's influence, and ultimately Andrew and Bushnell would take the Englishwoman's side in a rancorous dispute in the 1890s over the direction of WCTU policy toward prostitution. The WCTU, however, campaigned under the more general rubric of "social purity" reform rather than anti-regulation sentiment. This difference, stressing the need for moral standards of purity in sexual matters, conveyed a more "suppressionist" attitude toward "vice" than an abolitionist attitude toward state regulation, a difference from the British movement that reflected the almost total absence of experience with licensed prostitution within the United States.[45]

American reformers were stimulated in a more general way by the growth of foreign interest in their work, coming principally from Europe but also from the colonies of the British Empire. The external stimuli drawing Americans into foreign action was seen especially in the case of temperance. Temperance women in Britain such as the Scot Margaret Parker, who visited the United States and observed the WCTU in its early days of operation in 1875, invited American speakers to their homeland.[46] One of the originators of the Woman's Crusade that picketed saloons throughout the American Midwest in 1873–74, Eliza Stewart, agreed, and campaigned against alcohol across Britain in 1876. She aided in establishing the British Women's Temperance Association in the same year. The American temperance movement was already aware that temperance was a transnational issue from the prior involvement of the American temperance lodge, the Independent Order of Good Templars, first formed in New York in 1852 but prominent across Britain and Scandinavia in the 1860s and 1870s. This mixed-sex organization encouraged non-drinkers to join and drinkers to abstain, but its approach through quasi-fraternal lodges was ritualistic, hierarchical, and inward-looking rather than evangelical. That organization had fractured between the British and (sections of) the American wing of the movement in the 1870s over the admission of African Americans to its order,[47] and efforts to export the principles of American temperance gradually shifted to the more organizationally innovative and proselytizing WCTU. In 1876 the WCTU established an International Woman's Temperance Union at a convention to coincide with the Philadelphia Centennial International Exhibition. Yet the beginning was hesitant and the break with the past not clear; the new body established contacts and passed resolutions but was still not a coherent, unified organization. It aimed at a loose union of national societies in an "international" confederation rather than a globally fused movement. That global approach would have to wait until a decade later. But the meeting of 1876 did indicate the growing network of temperance contacts on which the global vision could later be placed as a more comprehensive layer of work and on which a global organization could rely for support.

The meeting in Philadelphia also drew attention to another influence on international organizing, the phenomenon of the international exhibition "movement" that facilitated many exchanges of information across national boundaries.[48] Though these exhibitions were primarily for trade and to mark important milestones in national history, it was not only technical reformers and governments seeking to spread knowledge of their own countries that took part. The original Crystal Palace Exhibition of 1851 in London had taken "Yankee notions," such as the Colt revolver, to Britain but Americans and Canadians returned with, among many other things, leaflets describing the ten-year-old British movement, the Young Men's Christian Association, and began forming their own YMCAs within a year. For the United States, the centennial of the Declaration of Independence provided a crucial stimulus that the World's Columbian Exposition of 1893 in Chicago consolidated. Purity campaigners such as Aaron Powell and Henry Wilson took part in the International Temperance Conference organized by the National Temperance Society and held in association with the 1876 Centennial Exhibition.[49]

The significance of these European organizations and movements for the subsequent spread of American voluntary reform was considerable. On the one hand, the European achievements gave Americans examples to emulate. On the other hand, they provided a network of public forums for cooperation. The new growth of internationalism made people more aware of what was going on elsewhere in countries that shared certain common features of industrialization and rapid social change. But it did more than that. The new IVAs and the legislation and treaties to which they contributed were creating a "public space" on the international level. In sociologist Jürgen Habermas's terms, "a space of institutions and practices between the private interests of everyday life in civil society and the realm of state power" was developing in the moral reform societies and in the wider pattern of IVAs. Not only was this a public space, it was a transnational space—crossing national boundaries and developing networks and reform cultures within the interstices of global imperialism and capitalism. Historians are familiar with the idea of networks as an element of national communications, but the process of building networks and public spaces operated across nations as well.[50]

Though Euro-American linkages were important in the rise of the IVAs, the American organizations differed from their European counterparts in some key respects. European groups claimed to be "international" and to unite the people of several or many nations. The American equivalents founded mainly from the 1880s onward had a different emphasis. These were self-consciously cast as "World's" organizations, such as the World's Young Women's Christian Association and the World's Woman's Christian Temperance Union. The Young People's Society of Christian Endeavor held "World's" conferences in addition to its "international" conventions, with the latter featuring guest foreign delegates but with formal representation including only Canada and the United States. The Student Volunteer Movement for Foreign Missions similarly planned to evangelize the "world," not just some part of it, and fostered the "World's" (not international) Student Christian Federation after 1895. For all these and many other groups, the aspirations were global and reflected American evangelicalism's mission to take the Protestant gospel to the whole world. Both the American approach and the European approach were Eurocentric, to be sure, but the "World" approach was more revolutionary and more committed to a transnational program because it promised to intervene in individual lives irrespective of nation.

The men and women who were to lead the evangelical crusades of the next two or three decades waxed eloquent about the changes in the international environment that made organizing on a global level promising. They were acutely aware of marked improvements in communications and technology, and sensed the creation of the new public spaces in networks where people could speak across national boundaries irrespective of nationality and without government sanction. As a missionary and university educator in Japan from 1888 to 1913, the Rev. Sidney Gulick found that modern communications "annulled the ancient barriers which so long separated the nations."[51] He predicted the inevitable triumph of a new moral order of international understanding and progress. Many evangelical activists agreed, and sought to enhance this transnational space through their lives and work. One of the key figures in the story to follow, morals reformer and Presbyterian clergyman Dr. Wilbur Crafts, became a champion of internationalism. Crafts was deeply attracted to the potential of the new grid of communications. Speaking on an Atlantic ocean liner in October 1906 he remarked that "international travel and international commerce—and I might add, international reading—are developing an increasing group of international men." He predicted on the basis of these technical advances the emergence of a "uninational" humankind combining the allegiance of all nations and universal values of civilization.[52] Equally eloquent in his approval of the new technologies was YMCA official Sherwood Eddy. He hailed the "students of Christendom awaking, with steam and electricity to carry us to the ends of the earth in a month, with typewriter and telegraph for our epistles, [and] bicycle and railways to speed the gospel."[53]

Crafts also applauded the new intellectual developments, particularly the international peace movement and the growth of Esperanto, but failed to note that the latter was European-biased in its vocabulary choices. He enthusiastically adopted this system himself, and worked with his wife, Sara Timanus Crafts, as an evangelist for a universal language. By 1908 he rejoiced, "Thousands of circles were developed . . . by the introduction

of Esperanto lessons, taught by Mrs. Wilbur F. Crafts," and ideas of internationalism had been widely publicized in the New York *Christian Herald*, which had "about a million readers in many lands."[54] European communications and greater travel opened the eyes of earnest Americans to
the possibilities for moral reform to regenerate the world. The increased
circulation of information also highlighted the specific fields of labor in
which evangelicals could work. As evangelist Arthur Tappan Pierson put
it in 1886, regarding opportunities in "Siam" (Thailand): "The country
feels throughout her extent the thrill of her contact with Western civilization. The telegraphic circuit embraces her and binds her to the Christian
world. The postal system is extending from Bangkok to the bounds of the
kingdom. Mercantile enterprise is developing the exports and introducing imports."[55] According to such accounts as this, the globalizing effects
of British imperialism would lay the groundwork for an Anglo-American
"Christian conquest."[56]

The shared Euro-American spread of technology, communications, and
international organizations aside, a common approach among American
evangelicals venturing abroad reinforced the sense of themselves as different from and superior to Europeans in the ways that they would take
advantage of these great opportunities. The young Wilbur Crafts toured
Britain and continental Europe in 1870 and 1873. He was shocked by
what he found to be great immorality. On his second trip Crafts arrived
in Paris in July 1873, at the same time as Nasser-ed-Din, the shah of
Iran. Crafts reported that the Place de la Concorde and the Champs Ely-
sées were bathed in light for the shah's nighttime edification. Paris was
commonly accorded the title of "The City of Light," but Crafts did not
approve, because Parisian streetlights revealed prostitution and sexual
shame beyond his imagination. "[T]he scenes of wickedness beneath
them," he recorded, conveyed moral darkness amid the spectacular il-
lumination.[57] Not all American travelers agreed, but those who did not
came from a different social class, and lacked Crafts's driving religious
motivation. The young Alvey Adee, who would later be an adversary of
the evangelicals and a high permanent official in the Department of State,
visited Paris a few years earlier. For him, the European experience was
not negative. He could only register the sites of a city "lovely, grand, attractive. The width of the streets, the splendid buildings, the crowds of
pleasure seekers that throng the boulevards, and the splendid shop win-
dows are enough to make up a very beautiful and novel picture."[58] Adee's
was a very different perspective and not the perception of an evangelical. On the other hand, the Methodist Frances Willard was shocked by
government-regulated prostitution in Paris during her stay there on her
1869–70 tour of Europe.[59] When the young Protestant missionaries Mary
and Margaret Leitch and their brother George visited Europe in 1879

on their way to a posting in Ceylon, their response to the morals of the French capital was similarly one of disgust. The mountains of Switzerland pleased them more.[60]

If evangelicals were dismayed by what they saw of European society, their reactions pointed to the forces that motivated them and shaped their perceptions of global trends. Existing networks of international organization provided the means to an end, but not the deepest inspiration for their desire to embrace transnational work and change the world. That came from American Protestant religion. Nor was practical reliance on new technology enough. Sherwood Eddy praised the potential of global communications, but nevertheless stressed the "breath of the Holy Spirit" and the power of prayer. Without those pious instruments, "all the inventions of the century become a pile of rusty iron," the future YMCA leader concluded.[61] Yet technology and morality could work together to form a type of moral electricity. As Frances Willard explained, the sudden mushrooming of temperance versions of internationalism "ran along the electric wires that connect human hearts," making, for example, the conversion of a man in Indiana contingent upon the inspiration received from pioneering women missionaries in China.[62]

These reformers were not only different from many Europeans in the way their evangelical aspirations shaped a global view of American ambitions. Americans were also influenced by intellectual and moral currents coming from other directions than Europe. What transpired on the edge of European expansion stirred them as much as the evidence of European-based moral reform that they saw in the life of Josephine Butler. The colonial world of the European empires and the wider non-Western world greatly shaped American responses and created new moral reform movements in the 1880s. In particular, the nation's most significant spiritual frontiers lay in the Asia-Pacific region. From British India in the 1880s came one powerful set of experiences that encapsulates the missionary transformation of those years. The journey begins in a small town in Vermont and takes us to Ceylon, and back.

Chapter 2

MISSIONARY LIVES, TRANSNATIONAL NETWORKS:

THE MISSES MARGARET AND MARY LEITCH

THE "MISSES LEITCH," as they preferred to be known, had ordinary beginnings but extraordinary lives. Mary and Margaret Leitch were born in Caledonia County, Vermont, in 1849 and 1857, respectively. Of Scottish lineage, these children of a prosperous farmer grew up at Ryegate within sight of the White Mountains of New Hampshire. Evangelical religion was their province from an early age, and they were steeped in the Presbyterian Reformed Church faith and the New School theology that promoted Christian benevolence expressed through good works. After an education at the St. Johnsbury Female Academy, they went from Republican-dominated Vermont (a cousin later served as a congressman for the GOP) to Alexandria in the ex–slave state of Virginia in 1873. The death of their mother in 1872 may have released them from domestic obligations or allowed an escape from sad memories, but, equally likely, the larger events of slavery's abolition and the Civil War shaped their destiny. Their own church congregation had a long tradition of radical abolitionism, and the ethical ideals of anti-slavery were, they recalled, in the blood. "We were children at the time but the questions when discussed burned them selves [sic] into our hearts."[1] It was with this inheritance that they went south, "to do good."[2] In Virginia they taught for "six winters," as they put it, young African American ex-slaves, figuring indirectly in the social movement that became derisively known by southern whites as carpetbaggers. In their spare time they induced hundreds of freedmen to join a temperance society, then, quite abruptly, they turned to foreign fields.[3]

Their progress can be tracked through voluminous letters in the American Board of Commissioners for Foreign Missions (ABCFM) Papers. Let us take this journey with them, viewing it from the perspective of their own experience. Their journey illustrates—from within—the serendipitous yet cumulative nature of transnational network connections. With a brother, George Washington Leitch, the sisters leave Vermont for Boston on the Fourth of July 1879 and enter the service of the American Board in October 1879. Their destination is Ceylon (now Sri Lanka). After a transatlantic crossing, a leisurely progression both charms and enlightens them as they consult with English missionaries and observe the manners, morals, and monuments of Europe and Egypt. On to Colombo they sail, and then to near Jaffna, in the country that would in the late twentieth century be claimed by the Tamil Tigers. For six years the sisters conduct Sunday school and day school Bible classes, and ultimately teach in the Oodooville Girls Boarding School (now Uduvil Girls College), established decades before. The brother is listed in the ABCFM records as "assistant missionary," since the Leitch family is sent with no mission station to administer—that is the province of missionaries of longer standing, led by the Rev. William W. Howland. The sisters have no title. They are simply there, expected to do whatever work they could find. They come with no Tamil, and spend the first year grappling with this enormous deficiency, taking lessons from native Christians in which the role of teacher and pupil is reversed. They learn a great deal about the culture of the Jaffnese in the process.[4] The experience shapes their beliefs and mission strategies. At the end of their missionary lives they argue strongly that no European witness for Christ should be allowed in the field without prior competent instruction in indigenous languages.[5]

At the same time, they avidly consume literature from the home front and are in the vanguard of missionaries introducing innovations such as those of the Young People's Society of Christian Endeavor, a ginger group that proliferates in the years after 1881 in the eastern American states and aims at developing a cadre of hard-core committed Christians working within local churches.[6] The Christian Endeavor movement within the existing Protestant churches pursued an active Christian social life of psalm-singing, flower-arranging, devotional prayer meetings, and missionary studies. Though the sisters could not have known of the movement prior to their departure for Ceylon, they become conduits for it abroad. They also liaise with the Young Men's Christian Association, another vehicle for American moral reform in Ceylon beginning in 1884, as in other missionary fields.

A devoted following they certainly acquire, yet few Tamil are converted. There are just three thousand Protestant Christian communicants in the island's northern province in the 1880s, six decades after the first American missionaries arrived. The Misses Leitch themselves can show for their labor a circle of just fifty-six believers in their own local church in mid-1881.[7] They do battle with the "Shivites" (Shaivites), worshipers of a Hindu god, and other assorted people termed "infidels," enduring the ignominy of a noisy Hindu festival that paraded in front of their church for twelve days each April. They set up tents and bookstores near the shrine to Shiva and sing Christian hymns, employing their native converts during the festival season for the purpose. They ponder the irony that, as the Christian presence has grown, so too have the finances and vigor of

Fig. 1. Margaret W. Leitch with mission children, Jaffna, c. 1882. Reproduced from Mary and Margaret W. Leitch, *Seven Years in Ceylon: Stories of Mission Life* (New York: American Tract Society, 1890), 88.

their opponents worshiping in the Hindu temple. The two faiths market to the masses vigorously in competition in this one physical space—a veritable cacophony of sounds and beliefs.[8] They carry the message of Christ across the northern part of Ceylon, with the aid of a Sciopticon (a form of magic lantern) imported from the United States for moonlight presentations, and introduce Christian singing performances, which Mary accompanied with an American portable organ. A visit to India in 1882 seems to disillusion the brother, who contrasts the rate of conversion in Ceylon with a more miserable one on the subcontinent. The enormity of the tasks facing the missionaries, "with the ever present pressure of the work," is made clear by the inadequate size of the mission force and the entrenched nature of the caste system, especially in Madras Presidency, the only place on the subcontinent they come to know well. Many of these things, especially the caste system that "encouraged and fostered exclusiveness in every circle," clearly offend the democratic ethos of George W. Leitch.[9] In late 1882 he returns to Vermont, to take care of the family farm upon the illness (and later death) of his father. He does not return to the mission field. Later he becomes an itinerant preacher, presenting to churches in the North and Midwest of the United States, including the Seventh-day Adventists in Battle Creek, Michigan, stories of the missions and raising money for philanthropic causes associated with the mission boards. He sings in Tamil to lend authenticity to his performances.[10] The sisters prove more enduring. Except for short visits to India in 1882 and 1885 they do not leave Ceylon until 1886 when they clash with their superiors in Boston over the funding for the school that they run.

Among the ideas they bring with them from their youthful Vermont is gospel temperance and, as in Virginia, they cheerfully organize temperance meetings. Yet their ability to convey the message of temperance is vastly enhanced when they make acquaintance with the World's Woman's Christian Temperance Union in 1886. Margaret becomes vice president for the Ceylon WCTU, and the sisters gather 33,000 signatures for a "monster" Polyglot Petition for the Prohibition of Drugs by the nations of the world.[11] As of 1888, this number stands as a world record for any WCTU auxiliary in the mission field, though the sisters are not in Ceylon when WCTU president Frances Willard's Round the World Missionary, Mary C. Leavitt, visits to organize unions. Nevertheless, Leavitt corresponds with Margaret and writes of her that "I doubt not her usual energetic measures will insure success to the work here." Leavitt concedes that in the northern part of the island "the drink habit is perhaps weaker among the Tamils than among the Singhalese" to the south. Moreover, she finds the English and American missionaries to be total abstainers with "little drinking among the adherents" of their congregations, but "one of the missionaries," probably Mary Leitch, informs her that "there [was] much more drinking at weddings and other festive occasions than was supposed."[12] Despite the apparent moderation in the use of alcohol and Leavitt's candid assessment, Margaret and Mary blame the drug habits of their potential converts for the slow spiritual progress in Jaffna. If it were not for perfidious Albion corrupting the hearts and minds of indigenous people through its revenue policies licensing liquor and opium, the mission would have been more successful. This was a not uncommon reaction for American missionaries, who harbored a kind of moral anti-imperialism designed to advance their own moral stature against the European rulers of colonial people.[13]

In late 1886 the sisters face a turning point in their lives. Told that they must raise their own money to continue the work at Oodooville Girls School, they turn to friends in the United States and quickly get a positive response. Cheered by this success, they plan a return home to carry the story of the Ceylon mission to potential donors. They are convinced that more money must be raised to stem "the tide of infidelity" in British India coming from the expansion of government schools that were entirely secular. Too many students were leaving their local districts to study in these schools or in more academically advanced private Hindu colleges that did not allow Christian teachings. As these schools prepared students for university work, they were more attractive to upwardly mobile Tamils than were the available mission schools. Additional funds were needed to enlarge Jaffna College to teach courses granted credit from a university, so that "Jaffna men could get a full collegiate education in their own province." Affiliation with Calcutta University was achieved in 1893 but, in the meantime, the imperatives of missionary work draw the two back to Europe and the United States.[14] There, from 1887 to 1890 the sisters acquire a taste for the international missionary and moral reform circuits rather than further fieldwork. They increasingly believe the main problem to be revitalizing the mission enterprise at the metropolitan center of operations. They criticize American donors for their parsimony and discover that the Scottish people, with whom they feel strong blood ties of ancestry, are more generous. (In the first three months of 1887 alone they hold more than sixty meetings in Glasgow and its vicinity.)[15] Margaret, the publicly dominant though younger sister, becomes an accomplished platform performer during this period. They raise money for Jaffna College, an institution that aims at producing a native Christian cadre to undertake the missionary work incompletely done by the Americans and Europeans. They personally adopt this strategy to raise money: use the native converts as intermediaries to carry the work to a successful conclusion. In the course of their work they produce in 1890 a handsome book, *Seven Years in Ceylon* that documents their efforts and acts as a brief for their fund-raising.

The sisters remain in the transatlantic orbit, severing their formal appointment to Ceylon with the ABCFM altogether in 1890 to work for five years with the non-denominational Zenana, Medical and Bible Mission of London. Yet as freelancers they continue to work for the people of Jaffna in an ambiguous and increasingly testy informal relationship with the American Board. They appear before the Christian Endeavor international convention in Minneapolis in 1891 and, unmistakably impressed by the Student Volunteer Movement for Foreign Missions and its slogan, "The Evangelization of the World in This Generation," they urge the strategy upon Christian Endeavor groups around the country. Succeeding years are spent raising money for women doctors for the future McLeod Women's Hospital, at Inuvil, near their former home in Jaffna,[16] for Jaffna College, and for other missionary purposes. In the course of this work they return to Ceylon in 1893 to supervise the implementation of their plans for a new women's medical facility.[17] While there, they also investigate the drug question, and in late 1893 they start an anti-opium petition to Ceylon's Legislative Council. Over the next year large public meetings are held and thirty thousand signatures, mostly of indigenous people, are gathered.[18] The sisters' "command of colloquial Tamil enabled them very readily to get full information" and "even to gain admission" to places where opium was sold or produced.[19] Thereby they document the extent of the opium trade and its effects for all to see. Though not successful in swaying the British government to ban opium, this campaign endears them to William S. Caine, a prominent pro-temperance member of the British House of Commons, anti-drug campaigner, and editor of the Anglo-Indian Temperance Association's magazine, *Abkari*. He uses their evidence as part of the English campaign that coincides with the holding of Britain's Royal Commission on Opium in 1893–94.[20]

Once more the sisters return to the United States via England, in time to take part late in 1895 in the next extensive Protestant church campaign.[21] That is the effort to end the suffering of Armenians affected by inter-ethnic violence of staggering proportions within the Ottoman Empire in 1895–96, humanitarian work in which the WCTU and Frances Willard were prominent. Later they are active along with their brother George in the missionary boards' campaign to alleviate terrible famine conditions in India from 1897 to 1900.[22] Margaret also becomes a spokeswoman on—and ostensibly for—Ceylon, appearing at the Ecumenical Conference on Foreign Missions in New York City in 1900.[23] During the famine relief campaign for India, Mary goes to Washington asking politicians to subsidize the shipping of grain from American ports. Eventually some funds for a U.S. naval shipment are appropriated. She applies lessons learned in the Ceylon campaign of 1893–94, where she had made a strong "personal effort with members" of the Legislative Council to pass a bill outlawing hemp and opium.[24] On Capitol Hill, one of the lobbyists filing with her into the offices of powerful Republican Party boss, Illinois congressman Joe Cannon, and other hard-bitten American politicians is the Rev. Wilbur Crafts, the superintendent of the International Reform Bureau in Washington. Formed in 1895, this organization was to become active as an irritating critic of colonial policies when the United States acquired the Philippines in 1898.[25]

Another link to Crafts, a key contact point in the network of transnationally minded reformers, is through the WCTU. Crafts's wife, Sara Timanus Crafts, serves as World's WCTU superintendent for Sunday schools. In 1900, the Misses Leitch team with Sara and Wilbur to write a compendium, *Protection of Native Races against Intoxicants & Opium,* a book reappearing in many editions by 1910 as *Intoxicating Drinks and Drugs in All Lands and Times.* This compendium is widely quoted in reform periodicals and used in political debates over the sins of European empire.[26] The Misses Leitch are immediately in demand at Crafts's side writing petitions to the U.S. government on the sale of alcohol to the soldiers quelling an insurrectionary war in the Philippines, and they condemn the moral corruption of Filipinos at the hands of Americans. With Crafts and his allies they also agitate in 1903 for an American anti-opium policy in the Pacific. They are called in as experts to testify before Congress on drug and alcohol regulation in the colonial world. Their testimony reflects their missionary contacts, because in the course of their work they had met hundreds of missionaries, such as the legendary Scottish missionary to the South Pacific, John G. Paton, who feeds them with statistics on the evils of alcohol among indigenous peoples.[27] Given their ceaseless work and travel, the onset of a series of tropical illnesses is not surprising. These take their toll. After more than two decades in the transnational trenches, they "retire" to a rural section of New Jersey, where they purchase a small property.[28] Yet the sisters never cease to communicate with fellow reformers, and they show a restiveness that irresistibly draws them back to the mission fields. In 1916, the two aging campaigners turn up in Puerto Rico working for a prohibition law.[29] That is the last of their missionary endeavors. Though they disappear from public view in 1917 on the passage of that law, Mary and Margaret leave Puerto Rico in 1922 with brother George and move to California where they remain strong supporters of the mission cause. They die in total obscurity.

It is hard to get a grip on the individual life histories of such itinerant missionary women. It is almost as difficult to get a clear picture of missionary historiography, as little of it has been conducted in the mainstream, and most is relegated to the margins as part of specialized fields such as church history and mission studies.[30] Missionary history has not been a fashionable subject. In the 1960s, those who studied the former colonial regimes focused on the indigenous sources of dissent and the growth of nationalism, and on the deeper continuities of non-Western cultures. The missionaries were part of Europe's past, not the history of the postcolonial world, which must develop its own "autonomous history."[31] Study of Sino-American contacts prospered in the 1970s under the influence of John K. Fairbank and his students, but many within Western historiography disdained the missionaries and neglected the work done in this field.[32] These travelers for Christ suffered this fate because of secularism's triumph in historiography. One exception was the significant work done on women as missionaries by feminist-influenced historians in the 1980s who wrote on transnational American missionary activity. But their chief concern was women's domesticity and women's culture, the projection of that (American) culture overseas, and the way missionary work enlarged or circumscribed that culture.[33]

Gender, to be sure, was one unmistakable driving force for the two women. As feminist historians have observed, mission stations gave women an opening to organize, gain expertise, and assert leadership roles. For the sisters, these opportunities came once brother George had left in 1882. Mary and Margaret fortified each other in the process.[34] Their subsequent struggles with the ABCFM and their criticisms of missionary action and inaction always concerned men, because men were in positions of authority and stood as obstacles in their path to the Christian commonwealth. Unlike some other evangelical women, however, these two missionaries never revealed feminist inclinations. In their letters and publications, they portrayed themselves as sisters in Christ—literally and figuratively. They referred to their female Christian converts as "our sisters," but entered the mission field as a tightly knit family with their brother George. After his return to the United States the sisters maintained strong links with him and another brother, William Buchanan Leitch, who worked in the United States for the mission cause. They dedicated their 1890 book to the two brothers who "cheered and sustained us for all that we attempted to do for the foreign field."[35]

Whether discussing the role of women or not, American missionary historiography has emphasized the outward push of domestic preoccupations. While some have detected the unspoken urge to export the gendered world of Americans, for others a national spirit of progressivism, humanitarianism, and nationalism lay behind the surge of missionary activity.[36] Post-colonial studies explore colony-metropole relations and the missionaries' "orientalizing" of their potential converts.[37] Such work addresses and sometimes contests the theme of cultural imperialism and emphasizes the missionaries as agents of transnational exchanges. Carol Chin notes mission graduates who "transcended the conventional cultural and gender roles," as in the noted cases of Shi Mei-Yiu (Mary Stone) and Kang Aide (Ida Kahn), who were WCTU- and American-trained medical missionaries in China.[38] The ambiguous and reciprocal nature of the missionary project is acknowledged but the focus is still on the push outward, whether that phenomenon is condemned or applauded. Charitably Chin terms women missionaries "beneficent imperialists."[39] Though she aims "to capture the inherent contradiction in the project of American women missionaries," Chin argues that the missionaries came to change, "not to be changed." In mission schools they produced cultural hybrids such as Shi Mei-Yiu, "but their own identities resisted hybridization and remained proudly American and Christian."[40]

Fig. 2. Sisters in Christ. Margaret and Mary Leitch, taken soon after their arrival in Jaffna, 1880. Courtesy Pilgrim Place, Claremont, CA.

In all this study of whether or not the American missionaries were cultural imperialists, little attention is paid to the missionary enterprise's impact on the United States and its people's conception of their place in the world.[41] Still less attention goes to the role of missionaries as connectors in multilateral webs of transnational cultural exchange. It is to this theme that the life histories of the Leitch sisters seem most useful. Missions "were uniquely placed," emphasizes Ryan Dunch, for "intercultural communication by virtue of their institutional structures." They interacted with the host society and with other missionary groups. Through mission boards, they "remained connected to their home countries and churches, and to missionaries of their own denomination or order working all over the world" through "correspondence, periodical literature, and conferences." The influences on them were "highly diverse and international."[42] The Leitch sisters are a classic case in point. Collectively their story contributes in a number of concrete ways to reconceptualize American cultural expansion.

Their lives illustrate how the domestic and foreign missions were closely connected. Work among the ex-slaves influenced the sisters' experiences in the foreign field, and they engaged in racial comparisons, despite their commitment to anti-slavery and the brotherhood of humankind. Early in their stay they reported that "the Hindu native is not excitable like the Negro, but indolent, and slugish [sic] and sanguine." Emphasizing "a parental spirit" of the missionary forces, they saw their task as a hierarchical and supervisory one. Yet they came to respect the land and people of their mission. In reflecting on their role in 1889 they described Indians as "civilized" people alive to the world of science and socioeconomic improvement, and who must be trusted to take part in the administration of the missions and other affairs on equal footing with Europeans. It was the South Asian experience that brought their anti-slavery convictions to the center of their consciousness and practice.[43]

Despite the prevalence in their language of the dichotomies of "heathen" and "saved," the Leitch sisters practiced a degree of cultural interchange. Though not what anthropologists and ethnohistorians call "cultural brokers" or "cultural mediators,"[44] they introduced into the mission schools Christian choral work and conveyed back to European audiences Tamil songs of Christian living and motherly veneration that they and their students composed. At wedding ceremonies they performed melodies sung in Tamil "with the accompaniment of native instruments." They reported with much rejoicing the traditional marriage ceremony combined with a procession of wedding guests in which "an arch of flowers was borne over their heads, a band of music preceded them, and the whole company of people accompanied them on foot in the brilliant glare of torches, blue and red lights, rockets and fireworks."[45] They stressed the role of native "Bible women" who mediated between Tamil and European culture.[46]

The sisters were "in-between" figures organizationally as well as culturally. There is a tendency to see the missions as institutions in which orders came from above, yet the Leitch sisters criticized the home boards' failures, and they usually took the side of the Tamil Christians in their correspondence. They castigated the Congregational Church in the late 1880s and 1890s for attempting to control Jaffna College and for objecting to a larger role for "natives" on the college's board. In an extended correspondence, they successfully fought the efforts of the new foreign secretary of the American Board after 1897, James L. Barton, to retrench its Ceylon mission. To counter these moves, they canvassed Congregational churches and organized the converts of the missionary endeavor in Ceylon to document the usefulness of the work.[47]

In the ways that they associated with Europeans, the sisters further developed their intercultural and transnational perspectives. They did not adopt a pointedly pro-American attitude in the 1880s. Christianity was their focus, not nation: "In the work for Christ and for immortal souls" it was "shame <u>even to mention</u> the question of nationality."[48] They cooperated with English missionaries[49] and scolded the American Board for not contributing to the non-denominational missionary cause of the English Zenana, Medical and Bible Mission and for providing more parsimonious funding for Jaffna College than came from English and Scottish purses. It was to them "a 'daily fresh wonder' that Scottish ministers" allowed them "to speak to their congregations and solicit funds in aid of 'an object wholly disconnected from their own churches and missionary societies.'"[50]

They were also in-between figures in a reverse way. While they argued that people in the mission fields were best able to judge immediate needs, their widening experience in Britain raising money, and their work with non-American missionaries and boards made them critical of conservatism anywhere. They rebuked older missionaries deemed resistant to the newer ideas for organizing missions. The Rev. Samuel Howland (son of William), who had served in Ceylon since 1873 and whose family had an even longer record there, they called a "sponge" incapable of original ideas. He did not have the "larger or hopeful view" that modern missions demanded.[51] They preferred the non-denominational approach to the sectarianism they sometimes found among missionary colleagues.[52] This is why the Leitch sisters were receptive to the innovations of the YMCA and the Student Volunteers, and this experience reinforced a growing sense of Christian ecumenicalism in their thinking. Nevertheless, there were limits to their ecumenical approach. It was specifically a *Protestant* Christianity that formed the backbone of their work. They largely ignored the contribution of Catholics even though these made up the largest proportion of Christians on the island. Within Protestant Christianity, these American women regarded their own church and evangelical churches like it as superior. At the same time, they opposed Protestant denominations that came into the missionary field without either funds or theology and accused the Salvation Army of these and other deficiencies.[53]

Though the sisters were keen to accord the "native" people equality of spiritual treatment, American cultural values inevitably intruded upon their work and introduced hierarchical relations. The sisters depended on American sources of technology and could not use that technology without making silent statements about American prowess and the modernity of American cultural expansion in the mission fields. Their portable pipe organ created "considerable curiosity"; crowds followed them, invitations to play, sing, and even perform Christian hymns that they sang in Tamil in non-Christian schools and hold moonlight meetings for their lantern shows came readily. Testifying to their receptiveness to modern technology was the sisters' "electric pen." Run by batteries, the Thomas Edison designed device would, they hoped, make easy the duplication of letters to send home to supporters.[54]

Accompanied as they were by this impressive paraphernalia in the form of physical baggage, they also carried cultural baggage. Gender as well as technology played a powerful role in the often unwitting messages they conveyed. The very fact that they spoke as women in public became an instantaneous sign of their modernity. They were told they were "very clever speakers," meaning, they thought, "very clever for women." They also became acutely aware of the economic and social pressures on their prospective converts; there was "not a plough in this province," Mary wrote, and no Western medicine unless missionaries brought it. The plea "I will become a Christian if you will tell me where I will get something for my children to eat" impressed them deeply. Modernization was a theme in their work but adherence to the idea was a product of their own colonial encounter, not something forced upon their audience and emanating from a central point as part of a definite plan for mission converts. Rather than emphasize a one-way process of enlightenment at work, they highlighted how the islanders embraced items of American technology and adapted their use to the spiritual purposes of salvation.[55]

The interpretation of motives for—and the mechanics of—American missionary expansion is also affected by the evidence of the Leitch sisters. Traditionally, historians depicted missionaries as "isolated from their home environment" and "slow in adopting a humanitarian emphasis."[56] In this view, homegrown Progressivism generated the new enthusiasm from the ferment of a rapidly changing American society. Yet innovation did not occur purely at the center. Improvements in international communications put paid to isolation in the case of the sisters and many others. It was the experience in Ceylon that led the Misses Leitch to advocate enhanced home participation in the foreign mission work by raising money for Jaffna College; to focus on the idea of a native-led church; and to demand medical and women's missionaries to win the hearts and minds of the locals. They emphasized on-the-spot initiatives over the theories of mission boards. "[We] know every inch of ground ... [and] if we are left alone everything can be carried through to a satisfactory issue....

[T]hose who have been stationed on the field have knowledge that those stationed ten thousand miles distant cannot possess."[57] Recall also that Margaret Leitch's involvement in the WCTU preceded the arrival of the round-the-world missionary Mary Leavitt; it was a product of Leitch's encounter with a temperate and yet theologically resistant people. For this reason she gravitated more toward opium in her search for a serious drug problem among her potential converts.

The story of the Leitch sisters also throws light on the ways that colonial encounters fed back into the metropolitan sources of the missionary impulse. The very birth of the crusade known as the Student Volunteer Movement that stimulated so many young men and women to join the mission field in the 1890s and beyond is commonly treated as a case of spontaneous combustion stemming from revival meetings from 1886 to 1888 at Northfield, Massachusetts. Yet the real sources of this outpouring, shown in the next chapter of this book, lay elsewhere. As the linchpin of the new campaign to evangelize the world in a generation, the student movement produced a dynamic cohort of new leaders, but the conditions behind this development lay in the critique of earlier missionary endeavors from those in the field, and came in part from the demands of indigenous converts that American efforts be redoubled to meet the expanded need realized by preliminary work.[58] The Leitch sisters' return to the United States in 1887 coincided with this feedback from the mission field that the decisive hour of the missions was upon the West. Upon their return they urged an immediate acceleration of the process of sending missionaries.[59]

The Leitch life histories also contribute to our understanding of reform networks and their impact on American cultural expansion and colonialism. They show how, partly by chance, the peripatetic efforts of missionary women could intersect with a large number of causes in the missionary field and bring these together in a cross-weaving of influences.[60] The sisters were skillful in discovering and joining diverse networks that they could use in this process. To be sure, some sociologists find the concept of networks broad and vague. Networks include people who do not know one another, as in the case of newspaper readers, and do not constitute a coherent social movement. For this reason, the idea of "coalitions" of reformers may be preferable.[61] Yet networks may operate in various ways to facilitate the building of interlocking coalitions of social activism. They provide the points of contact upon which transnational social activists can concentrate their work, learn from one another, move from one field to another, develop power structures, and maximize their impact or create impressions of an infallible moral phalanx. Transnational networks among these missionaries generated systems of information gathering and dissemination a century before the invention of the

World Wide Web. Collecting missionary statistics and distributing moral tracts was crucially important and accelerated exponentially in the 1880s and 1890s. But the networks that carried such information should not be seen, as sometimes seems the case in theorizing on the subject, as purely impersonal, self-regulating systems. They are sites wherein the lives of individual activists can be traced. Nor are all within the networks equal, and networks themselves vary in their impact. Empirical studies of these networks enable historians to plot concentrations of power.

Networks developed in serendipitous fashion. Without the World's WCTU and its Polyglot Petition against all drugs, Margaret Leitch might not have acquired the confidence and contacts to become an advocate of opium prohibition on a global level. She might have simply gone back to Ryegate, Vermont, rather than become a transnational organizer. Her cultural background of Republicanism, New England Protestantism, and anti-slavery meant that her work could still be seen in the groove of an older tradition.[62] Yet her interlocking encounters with reform networks enabled her to reshape this antebellum tradition, connecting opium, temperance, and humanitarianism. It enabled her to grow intellectually, to meet Wilbur Crafts and through him to lobby Congress. Together they helped build a Christian coalition in Washington, D.C., that scored blows against U.S. colonial policy and for international cooperation against the supply of alcohol to the indigenous peoples of Africa.[63] For this reason, the sisters' lives show that building up a picture of networks requires careful documentation of how people across fields cross-fertilized their knowledge to produce new transnational missionary objectives. Through interaction with Crafts and the WCTU leadership, the Leitch sisters came to believe that opium and alcohol problems needed solution through concerted transnational reform agitation.[64]

All this does not mean that networking was purely a matter of individual will on the part of the missionaries. Missionary endeavors of the nineteenth century depended on the indirect support of European imperialism and economic expansion. The trajectory of the Misses Leitch shows the importance of improved transport and telegraph communication between the mission periphery and both the United States and Europe.[65] From the technological shrinking of the globe came many things: the importation of the organ that allowed the sisters to develop attractive musical programs; remarkably up-to-date access to innovations in missions and reform techniques, such as those of Christian Endeavor; enhanced availability of reform and mission literature; and the personal visits of reformers, such as Mary Leavitt, to reinforce their work. The Polyglot petitioning that Leavitt undertook on a global level for Frances Willard's WCTU and that the Leitch sisters carried forward in Ceylon was improbable without this infrastructure.

These cases reveal the importance of Anglo-American communications, railroads, cable, shipping, and banking that enabled the long-distance tourism that transnational missionary work often closely resembled. These material networks of power facilitated exchanges of missionary knowledge and practice from different churches and nationalities. They also allowed transnational fund-raising, such as from the English and Scottish evangelical churches that the Leitches tapped for the American Board. The sisters and others like them were drawn from the travail of saving souls in British India toward innovative organizational efforts to sculpt a transnational reform program of missionary revitalization led by Anglo-American philanthropists. From the perspective of Mary and Margaret Leitch, the missions would not be won by specific efforts on the ground alone but by the linkages between them. They did not simply interact within a colony-metropole dialectic but crossed other boundaries and created their own transnational space. In Scotland they learned new techniques for raising money through collecting cards and mite boxes, which, they observed, "are being used with steady and growing success in Gt. Britain and should be introduced . . . more & more here."[66] In the 1890s, they became advocates of systematic, pledged giving from the mass of supporters rather than reliance on a few large donors, and their experience with Wilbur and Sara Crafts's campaigns only reinforced this message of businesslike application of missionary principles. Scottish businessmen such as J. Campbell White (no relation of the American YMCA figure), and several titled English and Scottish men and women, such as the advocate of Muscular Christianity, Lord (Arthur) Kinnaird, lent prestige to their work. They also used their Scottish connections to find patronage among the colonial elite in Colombo, when they returned there in 1893; it was John Ferguson, the Scottish-born editor of the *Ceylon Observer*, who backed their anti-opium campaign in the colony.[67]

Underpinning the causes that the sisters embraced was a growth of missionary "humanitarianism." It has not been fashionable for several decades to focus on humanitarianism as a key element of American foreign relations in the late nineteenth century. More than half a century ago, Richard Hofstadter discussed the spirit of American humanitarian expansionism of the 1890s but related it dubiously to psychological anxieties and an increasingly bellicose temper in the American public.[68] For Hofstadter the sources of this humanitarianism rested within the traditional narrative of American history, not its encounters with the colonial and quasi-colonial world. Yet empirical and methodological weakness in Hofstadter's account aside, the theme of humanitarianism cannot be discounted. The Leitches' missionary zeal was first nurtured in teaching Yankee morals to African American slaves in Alexandria, Virginia. With that crusade cut off by the political termination of Reconstruction in

1877, the Leitches had turned abroad for ways of doing good. They self-consciously connected these two endeavors. When the mission boards began "interfering on the rights of the natives," they recalled the practice of antebellum slave days. Mary hectored her superiors in Boston on the uncanny parallels between white attitudes toward Tamils and views of "the Southerners, Ministers of the Gospel, Members of Congress and Northern Democrats" who "contended that the black man had no rights which a white man was bound to respect."[69] In contrast, the Leitches stood for human rights, which they saw as a direct outgrowth of their missionary work and evangelical faith: "as God was our father and the human race one family."[70] Spurred by the quickening of global communications, the human rights message they conveyed was now a transnational one. The 1880s saw Americans acquire increased knowledge of the wider world, stimulated by pious periodicals that reproduced the stories of the missionaries and their pleas for aid. The missionary causes in which Margaret and Mary took part contributed substantially to the development in the United States of an internationally oriented humanitarian impulse in the 1890s to aid the victims of famine and other disasters in Russia, India, and the Ottoman Empire. Thereby, the provision of information on humanitarian need profoundly affected the course of American empire in the 1890s and beyond.[71]

Though humanitarianism was ostensibly and increasingly secular, the movement was motivated in considerable part by the desire to strengthen the missionary presence in the colonial world. The sisters had come to this conclusion while in Ceylon. The hospital established in Jaffna would be "the *strategic* point in the *evangelistic work* of a medical mission." By coming into contact with the medical staff and seeing "exemplified in their daily lives the spirit and power of the Gospel," patients and their families would more easily convert.[72] Missionaries saw, too, their existing resources drained from the long-term goal of saving souls to the short-term saving of lives unless they could raise humanitarian consciousness in the major metropolitan centers of the Euro-American world.[73] In this work the Leitch sisters acted as witnesses documenting the authenticity of experience among those who "had been a missionary and so could speak from a missionary standpoint."[74] Humanitarianism also served wider ideological functions because the Leitch sisters and others associated with the American Board specifically emphasized the point that material aid came from "far off America," not from colonial governments that oppressed their subjects. Under certain circumstances these arguments could come to justify an American form of imperialism.[75] All this is not to deny the force of economic markets in the arguments over American expansionism. Rather, economic and strategic interest could coincide with webs of humanitarianism, as it did in 1898 in the short American

war with Spain. In these circumstances, humanitarianism served mar-
velously to mobilize public support for the U.S. administration through
the missionary networks. After 1898, the efforts of the Leitch sisters focused more on raising money and on political agitation within the United
States. The American acquisition of a colonial empire transformed the
relationship between these sisters and their government. Now the power
of the state could be used, they reasoned, to achieve moral results.

Yet humanitarianism worked in contradictory ways. When the war
with Spain turned into a vicious four-year struggle against a nationalist insurrection in the Philippines, humanitarians could become critics of
government policy. Wilbur Crafts and his International Reform Bureau
channeled their anxieties over American empire into efforts to reshape
the way the Philippines was run, with Margaret and Mary Leitch joining the chorus. They used their experience with the licensing of opium in
Ceylon and their arsenal of arguments derived from a decade of agitation
in the transatlantic reform circuits to oppose any American policy on
drugs and alcohol that might interfere with missionary work or sanction
the spread of what they regarded as the vices of civilization in the nation's
dependencies. The sisters were among many who worried that drink and
sexual license irrevocably corrupted the American colonial effort. They
could not help but be caught up in the wider anti-imperialist controversy, though they saw the solution as the reform of colonialism, not its
rejection.[76]

Some supporters of the missionary endeavors were more blunt in their
criticism. The Indiana WCTU, especially through its president, Luella
McWhirter, drew the connection between missions, humanitarian relief, and opposition to war and attacked the imperialism not only of the
Americans but also of the British. Under McWhirter's leadership, the Indiana WCTU condemned "such reckless disregard of human life," such
"anger and hatred . . . displeasing to God" as evident in the Philippines
and asked President William McKinley "in the name of Home and Humanity, that you will use your utmost influence and power to bring about
a peaceful termination of the war." For McWhirter, reforming American
imperialism required cutting off its martial underpinning, and she also
audaciously lobbied British prime minister Lord Salisbury over the war
in South Africa, calling for "a speedy termination" of the conflict. "In
the case of England" she drew Salisbury's attention to "the deplorable
thought that the money expended destroying the thousands in Africa
would save the millions who are dying in India."[77] Armenians, Boers, colonial populations in Africa, the people of British India, and Filipinos all
were seen by McWhirter through a humanitarian lens shaped by the role
of missionaries, whom she personally knew and supported through the
Women's Foreign Missionary Society of the Methodist Episcopal Church.

She attended, for instance, the 1897 rally held at the National WCTU convention, called the "grand Armenian Mass Meeting and Memorial Service." Africa showed, according to McWhirter, that "Rum" was not only "the enemy of your homes and mine" but also "the enemy of our sisters' homes in many lands. It hinders our Missionaries in foreign lands."[78]

The Leitch sisters were simply one cog in this vast enterprise of American missionary and moral reform expansion. Their efforts intersected with larger enterprises at many points, and their paths will be crossed in subsequent chapters. They interacted with lobbyists and opinion makers such as Crafts and with grassroots activists in the American homeland such as McWhirter. What metaphor might we use to describe these connections? McWhirter referred to the WCTU as "a great wheel" in which the central union served as a hub from which the spokes of specialized work went out, all "symmetrically enclosed in the rim of the World's W.C.T.U."[79] Though apt for the WCTU, that organization itself was only one wheeling constellation in a larger galaxy, to shift the metaphor. Moreover, McWhirter's analogy was mechanical; to change the metaphor again, the Leitch sisters spun interlocking webs of organic connections. They were makers of constantly shifting and intricate patterns of missionary endeavor. In themselves, the lives of the two sisters from Vermont prove nothing. But they were not alone. The story of these transnational connections and the missionary expansion intersecting with their lives goes back to 1886, just when the Leitch sisters had concluded that they must tour the United States to raise money for the medical care of their beloved Jaffnese. The nation they encountered was far more ready for a missionary struggle than it had been just seven years before when they had left.

PART II

Origins of American Empire

Chapter 3

THE MISSIONARY IMPULSE

THE YEAR 1886 was a turbulent one in the United States, most notably for labor agitation, industrial violence, and riots. Streetcar drivers in New York engaged in a long-running dispute with management from February to September, while in the Southwest, the Knights of Labor's strike against the Union Pacific and Missouri Pacific railroads broke out in the spring, with repercussions far and wide. Across Texas, Missouri, and Illinois, striking railroad workers disrupted the movement of freight and stimulated more radical protests. The summer witnessed the sensational events of the Haymarket Trial where, in Chicago, eight anarchists stood condemned for a bomb-throwing incident that led to the deaths of several policemen. In Cleburne, Texas, angry farmers concerned with high railroad rates drew up in August an important document of what became the agrarian revolt and Populist movement. On the surface, Northfield, Massachusetts, presented a far different proposition. Situated near the border with New Hampshire and Vermont, and straddling the Connecticut River, Northfield's location of surrounding farms, forests, and maple- and elm-lined streets suggested great serenity. It was seemingly removed from the racial and class conflict of industrializing America. Yet Northfield, too, was the subject of upheaval—of a different kind, less observed at the time, but in the long run of great significance nationally and internationally.[1]

The scene was Mt. Hermon, near Northfield; the event the meeting of 251 carefully selected male students drawn from 89 colleges across the United States and Canada; the aim the preparation of these young men for the service of Christ at home and abroad; the forces behind it the college-based groups of the Young Men's Christian Association. These college youths were to be lectured, preached at, and exhorted to action for four weeks by the nation's leading Protestant evangelists. During that month a group of one hundred students joined an historic compact, pledging themselves to be "willing and desirous, God permitting, to become foreign missionaries."[2] Evangelist J. Wilbur Chapman observed how "From eight o'clock in the morning the men considered informally for an hour some phase of College Association [YMCA] work." At ten o'clock formal Bible study was the focus where "[a]ll met and listened to addresses from noted speakers." Afternoons were given over to sports and individual study, while special and public meetings were held in the early evening. Vigorous youths could swim in the Connecticut River, and weekly hikes to the mountains of New Hampshire or Vermont allowed the wonders of God to be contemplated and muscular Christianity practiced. Chapman averred: "All that was best in American culture [was] there epitomised [sic]" and "brought into play through the devotion and singleness of purpose of one man." That man was internationally famous revivalist Dwight L. Moody. Since 1880 Moody had near his home in Northfield invited evangelical ministers and lay Christians to gather for Bible study and to promote spiritual renewal within the churches. Annual meetings were suspended in 1883 and 1884 when Moody was outside the country, but they resumed in 1885.[3]

The momentous meeting of 1886 was the first that specifically targeted the young and future leadership of the Protestant evangelical churches. Additional summer Bible institutes at Northfield in 1887 and 1888 consolidated the approach. Meanwhile, activists toured 167 campuses, persuading more and more young college men to commit to foreign service during the 1886–87 academic year. By 1888, the movement was so strong that its instigators created a formal organization, the Student Volunteer Movement for Foreign Missions. Its task, once clarified, was not to act as an independent mission board (it sent out no missionaries) but to stimulate the recruitment process for the existing boards and to do so across denominational lines. Over 2,200 college students had already responded positively to often high-pressure tactics and committed to serve as missionaries. The movement's slogan was the galvanizing and millenarian "Evangelization of the World in this Generation."[4]

Why did this outpouring of missionary activities in the 1880s centered on the Volunteers occur and what was its nature and significance? Internal American developments stemming from the social and economic upheavals of postbellum America provided the sociological background but did not alone make a new generation of American missionaries. External crises and models for evangelizing stimulated the new missionary movement, encouraging innovative policies and organizational forms. Transatlantic revivalism spurred novel missionary methods and theological approaches, while missionaries "on the ground" in the colonies and spheres of influence of the European imperial powers drew attention to the urgency of missions. Together, these external forces produced new Christian responses to the rise of indigenous religious revitalization and agnosticism in the colonial world. This great outward missionary impulse of the 1880s was not limited to the United States. Part of a broader Euro-American pattern, it was nevertheless one in which American evangelicals sought—and in which they were highly successfully by 1900—to carve their own distinctive contribution and press new patterns upon transnational missionary activity in the wider colonial world.

The student "uprising," or "gusher" as it has also been called,[5] constituted a major late nineteenth-century social movement. As with any social movement, understanding its genesis requires attention to material circumstances and stimuli, the leadership to shape responses to social, intellectual, and moral problems, and the ideologies crystallizing solutions to those problems.[6] The dynamics of this social movement carried its instigators from the galvanic moment of 1886, through establishment of a formal structure in 1888, to the process of normalizing the missionary impulse in permanent bureaucratic forms in the 1890s. As if it were a stone cast upon a lake, the student movement of 1886 made ripples felt decades later in the development of ancillary support services and a business-based reorganization of church work by the eve of World War I. The nature of social movements requires us to move forward in time, but also back, to situate the moment of emergence within longer-term social changes. These processes began well before the students assembled at Mt. Hermon.

From the cohort of young Christians in the colleges of the American Northeast came the leadership. The post–Civil War era saw an expansion of higher education, including for women. Even though only 2.3 percent of Americans went to college by 1900, numbers more than tripled from 1870 to 1890.[7] The elite that did go had Protestant and middle-class to wealthy social backgrounds along with the will and the time that could be devoted to organized religion and missionary activities, if only the right stimulus were to appear. Though business beckoned for many young men, for others the materialism of the era, the rise of corporations, and the ideologies of anarchism and socialism that contested business supremacy in the Gilded Age caused them to seek alternative ways of ordering society. This much is explicable in terms of American conditions. Some historians have emphasized that Christian America was a nation of rising confidence ready to claim spiritual leadership on a global level. Others have pointed to the material context of the changing American society and its discontents as an explanation of the movement's rise. In one estimation, Moody and his disciples made "a half-subconscious effort to divert Protestants from intellectual problems and internal dissensions" to superior "moral and spiritual tasks."[8]

Ideology is a different matter and not so clearly rooted in American circumstances. Young men and (increasingly) women were spurred into action by a cluster of transnational Christian beliefs that shaped perceptions of the problems to be combated and provided tools with which to act. These ideas organized understandings of the past, pointed adherents toward the future, and provided the networks within which the practice of social movements could be advanced. These ideas included strong strains of premillennialism as well as holiness theology. Holiness doctrines were particularly prominent in the Methodist churches, though a more generalized version had become diffused in evangelical circles through the antebellum revivals.[9] The concept of entire sanctification served to revitalize religion, providing the spur to evangelical witness. Individuals would consecrate themselves, that is, renew the formalism of their faith in a deeper spiritualism and piety. Holiness placed little emphasis on formal theology and denomination, and thus reinforced the idea of bearing witness to different church groups, taking initiative in an ecumenical fashion, and forging novel organizational strategies. The doctrine provided one of the sources of a growing non-denominational and emotional emphasis within the Protestant churches more generally. It drew energy and reputation from the revivals of the 1870s in the transatlantic world that stressed personal commitment, action among and by the young, and the urgency of the spiritual outlook. Though not always explicitly champions of the holiness movement, the Northfield delegates expressed these doctrines as "a recognizable part of the general atmosphere of spiritual enthusiasm and personal reconsecration that Moody sought to kindle."[10]

Premillennialism was another potent influence in some evangelical denominations. Many clergy and laypeople unimpressed by the growth of materialism and secularism in Western societies felt that a revitalization movement was needed in the churches, and ideas of premillennialism were important in formulating how this change might be effected and interpreted. This doctrine emphasized the sinful world of the present and the need to repent; it reflected concern over the perceived moral and spiritual deadness of denominations that had routinized church work and missionary endeavor begun in the first two decades of the nineteenth century. Premillennialists conveyed the sense that Christians could not rely on modernity as implementing God's will but needed to embrace an otherworldly emphasis on spiritual renewal. In contrast to the previously dominant postmillennialism, for premillennialists the coming of Christ would precede the thousand years of earthly Christian rule. The role of the Christian preacher was not to build gradually the kingdom of God on earth through the material extension of the churches but to prepare for a divinely controlled Second Coming. Premillennialists took literally the biblical command to preach the Gospel not as a fulfillment of the millennium but as an urgent preparation of a millennium that might begin at any time. This doctrine favored the moral and theological imperative of bearing witness to all peoples as a precursor of Christ's return. Though postmillennial beliefs of witnessing God's work in the world clearly intermingled in the Student Volunteer Movement, premillennialism gave great urgency to the tasks of revivalism, including missionary work abroad. It was from this confluence of ideas that the concept of the evangelization of the world in one generation came.[11]

As much as new ways of perceiving material problems, new social movements require novel tactics and strategies. Though it is often assumed that innovations were American centered, in fact they were commonly derived from, or forged in partnership with, the larger transnational Christian community. Key architects of the Student Volunteer Movement were well aware that campus-based student Christian missionary movements began to emerge in Norway, Sweden, Denmark, Great Britain, Canada, and the United States at almost precisely the same time, during the academic year of 1883–84, and that a quickening of Scandinavian missionary activity had already occurred with the founding of the Svenska Missionsförbundet in 1878.[12] The Princeton Foreign Missionary Society was formed in October 1883 with Robert Wilder as its leading light, but the Student Volunteer Movement founder knew that he was not alone. He reported: "the source of the modern missionary uprising among students must have been in heaven, appearing as it did on earth at the same time in lands so remote."[13]

Providential or not, the events were stimulated by a widespread exchange of information and institutions across the Christian European world made possible by the improvements in transatlantic communications. Whatever the hand of God in the matter, the answers to the upheaval of the times linked American events with opportunities and inspiration abroad, even though the events of 1886 have been typically interpreted as the product of internal American conditions. Fast steamship lines and almost instant cable communication made transatlantic revivalism an important precondition for the American awakening.[14] The quickening pace of emigration from Europe to the ports of North America after 1870 strengthened transatlantic influences too. Nineteenth-century Scandinavian and German evangelicals joined the movement west, sometimes mingling with British evangelists they met in Liverpool and other intermediary English ports on the way west across the Atlantic. There they mixed with and influenced views of pietism, premillennialism, and non-denominational evangelism. An important early figure was George Müller, who had come from Prussia to Britain as a young man and upon the death of his wife developed after 1875 a seventeen-year worldwide evangelizing ministry, including stints in Australia, in India, and on the West Coast of the United States, where he influenced American clergy later involved in the Student Volunteers to accept premillennialism.[15]

Though American revivalists had interacted with English and Scottish colleagues for several generations, cooperation intensified after 1865. Moody first visited Britain in 1867 and conducted extensive revivals there in 1873–75 that touched millions, and again several times in the mid-1880s, at the very time that the Volunteer movement began. Revivalism is typically associated with American culture, but its characteristic features in Britain were similar, if not quite as successful, and its innovations sometimes preceded the American ones. Moody's style was uncannily anticipated by the immensely popular Baptist preacher Charles Haddon Spurgeon, born just three years before the American. Both emphasized lay leadership, both lacked a university education, both appealed to a non-doctrinal Christianity, and both adopted elements of holiness and premillenarian doctrines. Spurgeon had an American as well as an English presence; his sermons were telegraphed each week to the United States, and among his admirers was President James Garfield.[16] Moody had a reciprocal appeal in Britain. He met and influenced important British missionaries such as Sir Wilfred Grenfell, when the latter was a student in the mid-1880s.[17] Also under Moody's sway was the English Baptist minister Frederick B. Meyer, who in the 1890s would tour widely in North America and around the world, preaching an essentially "transdenominational" theology among student Christian groups and the YMCA.[18] But Moody not only spurred revivals and evangelical innovation while in Britain. He also took inspiration and concrete precedents home. The Northfield conferences established in 1880 built upon British innovations, notably the small Mildmay conferences of holiness-oriented evangelicals held from 1870 in Islington, and the larger Keswick assemblies from the mid-1870s onward.[19] The latter was a mainly middle-class and Anglican phenomenon convened in the Lakes District every year that itself was inspired by Moody's revivalist feats in Britain in 1873. Up to six thousand people attended these Keswick meetings annually.[20]

The student meetings of 1886 were not Moody's idea, but they, too, reflected the transatlantic ferment. Young American college men influenced him. The Inter-Collegiate YMCA had been founded in 1877, with Indiana-born and Princeton-educated Luther Wishard as its secretary. Wishard did not originally have an overseas missionary aspiration; his job was to tour North American colleges, but he and his close collaborator, Charles K. Ober, were influenced by events across the ocean. The catalyst came from the university town of Cambridge, England, where Moody had preached in November 1882. Moody inspired the English test cricketer and Cambridge Blue Charles T. Studd to commit to Christ. Other Cambridge students joined Charles in November 1884 to form the group of missionaries to China known as the Cambridge Seven, whose story spread throughout the Anglo-Saxon world. It seemed a clarion call to Christian effort abroad because young men of vigor and intelligence from the English social elite had forsaken secular glory for a mission from God. As the Student Volunteers saw it, the Cambridge students embarking for China were "noted for their scholarship, their prominence

Fig. 3. The Mt. Hermon gatherings of prospective Student Volunteers and college YMCA delegates were frequently addressed by speakers from abroad. Here, English preacher Frederick B. Meyer, center, left, addresses a meeting. Reproduced from J. Wilbur Chapman, *The Life and Work of Dwight L. Moody* (Philadelphia: Bradley-Garretson Company Limited, 1900), 330.

in athletics, and, above all, their consecration and spirituality."[21] Studd's message could not be avoided in America. The Northfield meetings of 1885 heard Studd's equally evangelical brother J. E. Kynaston Studd bear direct witness to the Cambridge movement, and another brother addressed the 1888 meetings.[22] After witnessing his 1885 appearance at Northfield, Wishard booked Kynaston Studd for a lecture tour to rouse enthusiasm and commitment among the American college students, then urged Moody to use the Northfield meeting of 1886 as a college revival. When graduates of the meeting vowed to canvass American colleges in order to gain recruits for the mission fields, they mimicked the Cambridge example. During a hike across the mountains of Vermont, it was suggested that a deputation to colleges, "something like the 'Cambridge Band,' be sent." The student leaders picked four to campaign but only Wilder was able to go, and others were substituted.[23]

Focusing only on the transatlantic evangelical exchange is, however, Eurocentric. The missionary impulse cannot be explained as an Atlantic-based movement alone. Calls to enter the mission field came insistently from those on the edges of European expansion. The meetings at Northfield from 1886 to 1888 were peppered with the speeches of young students or returning missionaries from the field in Asia. Improved transportation since the 1860s had made furloughs more possible, more often.

The opening of the Suez Canal in 1869 was particularly important in allowing swifter and more comfortable passage. The Leitch family was only one of many in the 1870s that used the rail routes across Europe to Brindisi, before boarding a Colombo-bound steamer for India or beyond, and who returned by the same route.[24] Later, improved transportation across the Pacific also facilitated quicker passage. In 1886, the Rev. Dr. William Ashmore of Ohio, who had served the American Baptist Missionary Union since the 1850s, returned from China because of his wife's illness and issued to the assembled at Mt. Hermon a "summons to Christian duty" on behalf of East Asia.[25] The 1888 meeting would be addressed by no less than the great English missionary James Hudson Taylor, the founder of the China Inland Mission. He, too, emphasized the enormous opportunities for soul-winning in the Chinese empire. Present at the original 1886 meeting were young men such as the Japanese Kotaro Shimomura, a student at Worcester Polytechnic, but most important were the sons of missionaries who had returned to study in the United States, yet felt strong allegiance toward the lands of their youth. The program for July 22 saw opening prayers by foreign students speaking in their native tongues. All were "fitting for missionary work in their native lands," and twenty-five others had already declared for foreign mission work.

Some of the Americans present had parents in the mission fields and had been born there.[26] Robert Wilder was the most notable of these. Born in Maharashtra in 1863, he was the son of Royal Wilder, a Presbyterian missionary in India for three decades beginning in 1846. The young Wilder grew up almost entirely in the absence of contact with other European children; he spoke Marathi as much as English and frequently visited the palace of the local maharaja, whose wife supported the Wilders' efforts to educate women. In broken health, Robert's father had returned with his family in 1875 to live in Princeton at the end of his missionary career and, in 1877, founded the *Missionary Review* (later the *Missionary Review of the World*), which he edited until his death in 1887. Royal Wilder had several times clashed with missionary superiors for their failure to heed fieldworkers, and he brought back with him a message parallel to that of the Leitch sisters: he stressed in the *Missionary Review* the urgent need to reorient missionary tactics to something more responsive to the needs of indigenous converts.[27] Though Robert Wilder enrolled as an undergraduate at Princeton in the early 1880s, he considered himself a product of India. Studying Sanskrit as well as theology, he longed to return to the field to carry on his father's work.[28]

During the 1886 meeting at Northfield, it was Wilder who convinced Moody of a plan to make foreign missions the showpiece of the program by using the testimonies of young students from abroad and the sons of missionaries studying in the United States. Thus sprang the idea of the "The Meeting of the Ten Nations" within the 1886 convocation. Students representing Japan, Persia (Iran), "Native America," Siam (Thailand), Germany, "Armenia," Denmark, Norway, China, and India spoke for three minutes each on the pressing needs of their countries and the transformative effects of missions. Wilder's testimony followed his father's arguments, focusing on the huge potential of South Asia for soul-saving and the absence of an adequate missionary force. Boon Itt, Siam's representative, described his nation as newly opened to the "gray dawn of Christianity" for "you, young men, to come and reap her harvest of souls for Christ."[29] Similar tactics were used at the follow-up meetings in 1888. There, Junzo Kawamoto, a graduate of Oberlin, claimed to represent thirty-five thousand in Japanese Christian churches and stood up for the international allegiance of the missionaries, criticizing the imperial powers and urging a transnational and non-denominational program of missionary involvement by students. His call for "a union of denominations" was "greeted with a round of applause."[30]

Quite apart from the direct stimulus coming from the missionary field, the mission boards at home were acutely aware of European imperialism's expansion in Asia and Africa. The political division of Africa facilitated by the Berlin congress of 1884–85 heightened the stakes for American missionaries. The Rev. Judson Smith, a secretary of the American Board of Commissioners for Foreign Missions (ABCFM), found "no movement in our day more interesting or significant than that which draws the eyes of all the nations toward the great Continent of Africa. Annexation and colonization and conquest are rapidly giving new and permanent political relations to all parts of the land and to all its peoples." At home, Henry Morton Stanley's "great work" on the Congo Free State published simultaneously in America and England was "everywhere meeting with enormous sales."[31] In the view of many American churchmen, European territorial expansion and the thirst for knowledge of the "dark continent" created opportunities for Christian missions. For Judson Smith, the "thread of fate for this new world" proceeded from the "hand of God." That unseen force moved the "great powers" to plan for "empire."[32] From the days of the earlier interest in the American quasi-colony of Liberia, Africa was an American mission field of the Congregational, Methodist, and other churches. Indeed, "American churches played a central role in evangelizing the continent" yet, a modern authority avers, African mission work was more "pronounced in black churches."[33]

The European carve-up of Africa stimulated a general interest in revitalizing missions, but Africa was not to be the key target of expansion in the 1880s and 1890s. When Wishard toured the world from 1888 to 1892 seeking allies in the evangelization of college youth, his single

African stop was Egypt, which he pronounced a "difficult" field because North Africa had only a few Protestant missions and Western colleges to build upon. A later trip to Cape Town in 1896 proved more promising, but the promise lay only, he believed, in the leadership of white society and underlined the fundamental problem. Africa lacked the educational changes introduced or unleashed by the European impact that in Asia produced a potential cadre of student converts to become the movement's indigenous vanguard.[34] Moreover, the call for Africa came from the mission boards, while that from Asia and the Pacific came from the missionaries on the ground and students who addressed the Northfield meetings. The student movement's energy and direction would come not from above but from below. The student movement would focus in its response more commonly on Asia.

Enhanced opportunities for soul-saving created great anxiety because they arose in the context of declining domestic participation in missions among some churches and mission boards. There was, stated the American Board, "a faltering zeal" among Christian peoples easily distracted by the "din and strife," the "bustle and stir of daily toil."[35] In 1882 the Rev. Dr. Nathaniel G. Clark, a secretary of the ABCFM, had called for an increase in missionary personnel but reported in 1886 that "Four years have past [sic] and practically no addition to the working force of ordained missionaries has been made, while the necessities of the work have become more and more urgent."[36] Dr. Josiah Strong, general secretary of the American Evangelical Alliance, an interdenominational body, claimed in 1885 that "the world would have been evangelized long ago if Christians had perceived the relations of money to the Kingdom, and accepted their stewardship."[37] To this alarm was joined the historicist theme of a critical anniversary in the American mission enterprise. For the Congregational, Presbyterian, and Reformed churches providing the backbone to the SVM, the mid-1880s meant an end to seventy-five years of pioneering labor from the American Board. Missionary officials were convinced of the unity of past, present, and future under God's direction. For them, 1885–86 was an auspicious time. Missionary supporters could, noted Judson Smith, "look forward to the work which is still to be accomplished, and in the light of past experience to plan for its prosecution."[38]

The Northfield gathering of 1886 therefore became a cathartic event designed to renew a missionary effort perceived to be flagging. According to supporters of missions, one cause of the decline was a secularism that relativized faiths and proclaimed them spiritually equal. Western unbelief and its effects on potential converts in the mission fields disturbed Presbyterian advocate of global evangelism Arthur Tappan Pierson, whose oratory stirred the 1886 Northfield meeting with the "intense earnestness" of his speech, "God's Providence in Modern Missions."[39] One of the leading intellectual architects of the renewed missionary enthusiasm, Pierson argued that it was "time disciples were done with spiritual Darwinism." Pierson's *Crisis of Missions* was a best-selling book in 1886, wherein he proclaimed: "the religion of Christ is no evolution from other faiths." He condemned as a misconception the leaving of the "heathen" alone in "the peaceable enjoyment of their religion," as some moderns allowed. His position placed the onus on the American people to respond to the secular challenge at home and competitor faiths abroad, and re-dedicate to missionary giving and service.[40]

Pierson's anxieties had great impact because competitor faiths in the mission fields had been gathering strength for several years. The alarm came from India rather than China at this time. Concurrent with the Northfield meetings of 1886–88, British and American missionaries warned of the dangers from European theosophists operating in Madras, who acted, evangelicals charged, as a stimulus to Buddhism and Hinduism among potential Christian converts.[41] Samuel H. Kellogg had for several years been a missionary of the Presbyterian Church in the U.S.A.'s Board of Foreign Mission's station in Allahabad. After he returned to a teaching post in the United States in 1876, Kellogg wrote *The Light of Asia and the Light of the World* (1885) to measure the role of Buddhism as a competitor faith "about which of late in the Western world we have been hearing so much."[42] Only Christianity he found to be the true light of Asia, not Buddhism. Hindu revivalism had also strengthened as a reaction to the attempted Christian conversion of India. Between 1877 and 1888, Hindu mobs in Madras Presidency picketed missionary meetings, stoned houses, and tried to drown missionaries out with noisy counterdemonstrations, as happened to the Leitches in Ceylon. There, the Wesleyan-educated Arumuga Navalar incorporated Western teachings into his scholarship critiquing Christianity, established his own Hindu schools in competition with Christian ones, and became a prominent Shivite (Shaivite) revivalist before his death in 1879. His was the sect that George W. Leitch and his sisters reported to their ABCFM superiors in Boston as a militant threat after 1880.[43] When Pierson and others called for renewed missionary efforts against the rising tide of unbelief, this resurgence of competitor faiths was the vital context. The missionary impulse was a reciprocal one with roots in the colonial world's experience itself, not simply a unidirectional thrust from the United States.

Transnational perspectives also help recover the lost sensibilities of the movement by drawing attention to the Christian rather than a specifically American ethos. The mental map of these visionaries punctures ideas of an American exceptionalism. The Volunteers cooperated with the Canadian Intercollegiate Missionary Alliance and saw themselves as involved in a joint activity with other groups such as the later Student Volunteer

Missionary Union of Great Britain. "For the first time the students of the Anglo-Saxon world are united in a mighty enterprise," the SVM executive rejoiced.[44] The revival of missions had global aspirations and included a highly important European role. While Asians were key targets, continental Europe was also a candidate for evangelism, and alliances with European evangelicals were as vital as those with people in Europe's colonies because an evangelized Europe would renew the Christian values of European empires and rebound to the benefit of all colonies. Pierson's *Crisis of Missions* highlighted the news of the opening of Europe as well as Asia. When even the Vatican relented and allowed Protestant missionaries to work within sight of St. Peters, Pierson took the concession as a sign of supernatural intervention and an invitation to a global offensive for a Bible-based revival. As part of the preparation for the Second Coming, Christians must prepare, he argued, by bearing witness to all countries.[45] The SVM followed this injunction. Simultaneous with its recruitment of missionaries for service to Asia and Africa, SVM leaders almost immediately took the message of Northfield to their fellow Christians in Europe. Wishard went there in 1888 and, before beginning service in India in 1893, Wilder went to Britain for a year, where he founded the British Student Volunteer Missionary Union.[46] After returning permanently from India in 1902 after nine years of service, he did further work in Scandinavia and Britain, while making his home in Norway, where his wife had been born. From the SVM, too, came the impetus for the World Student Christian Federation, founded in Sweden in 1895 through the work of John Mott, who evangelized there and the countries of central and eastern Europe. In the view of the Volunteers, "Christian" regions needed, as much as anywhere else, the rebirth that the SVM offered.[47] The field was not international but global evangelism.

The larger global rather than American context of missionary work is perhaps the single most neglected feature of the SVM's history. Yet there are other myths and misconceptions about the movement's genesis that need dispelling. The cosmopolitanism of the early meetings has often been exaggerated. Of the 1886 "meeting of the ten nations" only two representatives were actually indigenous to Asia. Another was a Native American. Persia (Iran), China, India, and Japan were represented by American students, all children of missionaries or would-be missionaries themselves. The missionary impulse drew on ideas fermenting in the mission stations of the Euro-American periphery, but the bearers of these ideas were mostly Euro-Americans, not truly "native." It is significant if arrogant that they regarded themselves as spokesmen for these foreign peoples. The student leaders conceded no inconsistency in that stance, for they assumed that a native-born Christian vanguard would rise up to take charge from the stimulus that their novel missionary tactics elicited.

Myths are useful ways of organizing social movements, fashioning inspirational history and crystallizing perceived truths. The SVM's founding myth is that the movement sprang suddenly, gushing forth with an enthusiasm that was the hand of God, inherent in the concept of an "uprising."[48] In reality, the meetings were the result of continual pressure, agitation, and careful organization, work that came not from Moody but from the young sons of the missionaries and their allies in the YMCA. The apparent suddenness of the "uprising" also hid the deeper wellsprings of missionary work in the 1870 and 1880s. Not all churches had experienced a crisis of missions, and some were able to maintain a steadier pace of work. The Methodists were more content with the existing supply of missionaries, the Congregationalists much less so.[49] The call for evangelization of the world in a generation was not new either; the theme had a long pedigree, but interest in the idea surged after 1881 in response to an article in the pages of the *Missionary Review of the World*, edited by Wilder's father. It was written by Pierson, the author of *The Crisis of Missions*. The Philadelphia Presbyterian's "Can the World Be Evangelized in Twenty Years?" was widely reviewed and reprinted. It occasioned much debate, both supportive as well as critical.[50] Pierson wrote: "These are days of giant enterprises in the interests of commerce, science, art and literature. Why not carry the spirit of sanctified enterprise into our religious life and work! I wish by voice and by the aid of the press to set forth a practicable business proposition, namely that before the year 1900, the gospel shall be preached to every living soul!"[51] Pierson exuded premillennialist influence taken from the Anglo-German preacher George Müller, who converted him from a postmillennial position just a few years before.[52] Though the concept of an "uprising" was exaggerated, it served its ideological purpose in spurring action. Whether consciously modeled on the labor protests of the 1880s or not, the idea of a popularly inspired insurgency connoted a new beginning. This was precisely the stance that a new social movement needed because it emphasized a decisive break with existing practice.

The passionate commitments made at Mt. Hermon did not necessarily translate directly into overseas missionary service. This was another of the misimpressions one might gain from hagiographic missionary literature. Those pledging their lives in 1886 contained a number of whom nothing was heard again, and only Wilder and Benjamin Labaree of the speakers at the "meeting of the ten nations" became overseas missionaries, the latter suffering martyrdom at the hands of Kurds in Persia in 1904.[53] James Garvie (Tatanka Kinina), the half-Sioux who represented Native American peoples at the meeting, taught at the American Missionary Association's Santee Normal Training School in Nebraska in the 1890s.[54] Kotaro Shimomura returned to Japan to become a prominent industrial chemist though he served from 1904 to 1907 as president of the (Christian) Doshisha University in Tokyo. George E. Talmage was more typical in his missionary pedigree but one whose career underwent unexpected twists and turns. As the son of the Rev. John Van Nest Talmage, D.D., a Reformed Church missionary to China since 1846, his connection with the missionary movement was a strong one. Talmage was an undergraduate at Rutgers when he signed the pledge, but after graduation in 1889 he did not head for the mission fields. Rather, he held a variety of Reformed Church pastorates, switching denominations to become an Episcopalian in 1908. Though his sister Katherine spent sixty-four years as a missionary at Amoy until 1937, Talmage's career was chiefly distinguished by a long stint as Theodore Roosevelt's pastor at Christ Episcopal Church, Oyster Bay, where he officiated at the ex-president's burial service in 1919. In the 1920s Talmage was an opponent of fundamentalism and had outgrown his evangelical roots.[55]

The army of Volunteers pledged to serve was enormous, the number actually going overseas much less so, and the reasons for attrition complicated. By 1892, about 6,200 had signaled their missionary intentions, a figure that rose to 13,789 by 1904. By 1920, a total of 8,742 Volunteers had sailed. Because of the time lag between pledging and sailing, measuring attrition exactly is difficult, but around one-quarter of all Volunteers eventually served as foreign missionaries.[56] The enthusiasm worked up under the pressure of mass meetings could not always be maintained. For many "the novelty wore off," as the Volunteers' own magazine candidly admitted.[57] This was especially the case when combined with many concrete impediments. To start, students had to complete their college studies, a process that could take several years, years in which they might change their mind or fail to finish. Then they had to find a suitable board willing to take them. Though at least 630 volunteers had left by 1894 for foreign fields, mission societies did not have sufficient funds to send many others who wanted to go. Parental opposition stopped some (candidates occasionally asked Volunteer leaders to pray for their misguided parents who refused to give consent or provide financial help).[58] Moreover, the churches at home were not united over the issue. Some in the Presbyterian Church felt that the home front would be neglected, as did many Episcopalians.[59] "So many Christian people" were "so little in sympathy with any widespread and intelligent effort to evangelize the world speedily" that they urged spurious objections.[60]

There was a marked conflict between the desire for external expansion on the one hand, and protection of the spiritual needs of Christian civilization in the United States on the other. The Rev. Arthur Mitchell, a representative of the Presbyterian Board of Foreign Missions, told Wilder in October 1886 that his board could use a thousand missionaries but that the Volunteers "ought to take no more than the church at home can wisely spare." The reluctance in part reflected conflict within the churches over the practicalities of the premillennial claims made by Pierson and the SVM. Mitchell asked what was meant by evangelization of world. If it literally meant global conquest in the generation of the 1880s, many thousands of missionaries would be required immediately; "more practicable" and more in line with "necessities" was the training of "native" workers, but that would be a longer-term project.[61] Parallel to this criticism were rumblings over the pledge from those who said it privileged mission service over other church work. Moody himself had reservations because he believed that "the Kingdom of God" was "everywhere," not just in the mission fields.[62] To some critics, the pledge threatened to give the movement a cult-like status above the churches. For this reason, the statement was watered down in 1892 to read "It is my purpose, if God permits, to become a foreign missionary" and became a non-binding "declaration."[63]

Because sections of the evangelical churches remained skeptical and outsiders scoffed at the idea of a two-decade evangelization of the world as an increasingly remote proposition, the movement had to become routinized. It needed to rationalize its operations, introduce bureaucratic procedures to raise money and personnel, and build alliances with the American business community. Its links with the YMCA and with the American Inter-Seminary Missionary Alliance founded in 1880 (an earlier college group among those in theological training in the Protestant seminaries) had to be worked out. The latter group merged with the SVM in 1898, while Volunteer leaders achieved a demarcation of interests and a formal alliance as a solution to the conflict of interests with the YMCA and YWCA. Therein the Volunteers became the YMCA's and YWCA's arm for missionary liaison and organization. A supervisory executive committee that began work in January 1889 drew one representative from each of four groups: the college branch of the YMCA, the YWCA, the Inter-Seminary Missionary Alliance, and the Canadian Intercollegiate Missionary Alliance.[64] A traveling secretary, a recording secretary, and a corresponding secretary were appointed to coordinate local and state SVM organizations and to raise funds. Beginning in 1891, the SVM held international conventions every three years.[65] Even the missionary enthusiasm was routinized, with the introduction for college students of a systematic plan of mission studies in 1894 through an Education Department. Specialized administrative functionaries, departments of work, and links with business benefactors allowed the specifically American contribution to come to the fore. By 1895 the movement was thoroughly institutionalized. Though the evangelization of the world in a generation remained the goal, increasingly the commitment became qualified, the

emphasis shifted to human services such as education, and the lines between pre- and postmillennial thinking became blurred.[66]

As this consolidation occurred, a new breed of leader emerged. The
Princeton-educated Presbyterian Robert Speer was one of the early recruits Wilder made in his tours of the colleges, and Speer became in turn
a recruiter himself and an important intellectual influence on the evolving movement. But he never served as a missionary. After working as a
secretary of the SVM between 1889 and 1891, he found his calling at the
Presbyterian Board of Foreign Missions, commuting from suburban New
Jersey to the board's New York offices where he was "a great board secretary," according to the YMCA's Sherwood Eddy.[67] With Wilder working in India as secretary of the College Department of the YMCA from
1893 to 1897 and Wishard undertaking roving missionary tasks, overall
leadership at the center gravitated toward John Mott, the Iowa farm boy
and Cornell University undergraduate. Though Mott was among the one
hundred original Volunteers at the Northfield meeting of 1886, he did not
designate a specific missionary field and served as neither a conventional
missionary nor a YMCA secretary abroad. Instead in September 1888 he
became national secretary of the Inter-Collegiate YMCA and chairman of
the executive committee of the SVM. Above all, Mott's role would be as
an organizer and manipulator of committees, a speaker, and a fund-raiser,
particularly through friendship with such wealthy American donors as
International Harvester magnate Cyrus McCormick and the family of
John D. Rockefeller.[68]

The SVM's leadership, growth, and business links made the issue of
masculinity critical. It was men, particularly young men such as Mott,
who seized the initiative and worked with businessmen to promote the
organization financially. The well-known "feminization of American religion"[69] was on the minds of American Board officials in the 1880s when
they exhorted the churches to new efforts abroad. When missionaries
noted the rising participation of women such as the Misses Leitch,[70] they
knew that men were becoming proportionately scarcer in the mission
fields; they worried at the possible loss of male authority and the absence
of ordained ministers, since in almost all churches only men could be
ordained. A missionary support society claimed that men must "look out
for their laurels."[71] Newly fashionable ideas of muscular Christianity put
a premium on such strengthening of masculine roles. Principal backer
John D. Rockefeller Jr. was particularly keen to advance the cause of
what he called "Christian manhood."[72] In unconscious company with
this push to reassert masculine identity and power, the visitation groups
sent to campuses mostly went to men's colleges until 1895. Published accounts and private correspondents of the SVM's leading organizers rarely
mentioned women, even when, as in the case of Wilder and Mott, their

Fig. 4. The young John Mott at the time of the Northfield meetings, 1886–88. Courtesy Special Collections, Yale Divinity School Library.

spouses accompanied them abroad on mission service. This undervaluation entailed a great irony because women's prayer and missionary support groups predated and exerted indirect influence on the Northfield proceedings of 1886. Wilder's sister, Grace, with whom he had grown up in Maharashtra, was a leading member of the students' Missionary Association at Mount Holyoke College and, prior to the formation of the SVM, urged upon her brother a movement to stimulate action in the mission fields. Women's ideas provided an indispensable context of the movement's gestation and growth, but that contribution was rarely acknowledged openly.[73]

This masculine ethos served the SVM not only in its founding myth but also in its attempts to reproduce its networks across the globe. Though American religion and missionary activity featured a considerable role for women in the churches of the late nineteenth century, this was not so true of other countries, particularly in Europe. There the opportunities for women in higher education were far fewer. Masculine leadership gave the SVM's emissaries easier entrance to male society in eastern Europe, and more so in non-Western countries, where they could cultivate young, educated, Westernizing colonials without having to challenge the profound sexual divisions of those societies. The key SVM aim of converting Asian students into the avant-garde of Christian expansion in Asia could necessarily be achieved in the first instance only through male missionaries, since formal education was largely restricted to men.

Yet there were obvious disadvantages in this approach; only women could reach women in the secluded spaces of the zenanas of India and the Muslim world, and in many other colonial settings similar circumstances applied. Targeting women had a great, long-term strategic advantage, because missionaries could thereby mold "the habits of thought of the coming generation."[74] At home in the United States—and in the mission fields where women's work was increasingly important—assertions of masculinity were also problematic for different reasons. A yawning gap existed between the SVM's overwhelmingly male leadership and a rank and file that was increasingly female. From 1892 to 1900, women made up 41 percent of Volunteers while women constituted 60 percent of the total American missionary force by 1900. As a consequence of the supply of willing female labor, the numbers of women among the Volunteers grew despite the demands for a masculine leadership. By 1920 women comprised 55 percent of the Volunteers compared to less than a quarter in the late 1880s.[75] Ultimately this female-driven growth underpinned the SVM's achievements; without the interest of women the organization could not have sustained its idealism and reputation as an efficacious means of missionary recruitment for long. But the rising importance of women missionaries meant changes in the organization that after the 1890s tempered the muscular Christianity of the movement's early years. Neither the Northfield summer meetings before 1893 nor the college organizing that raised the first two thousand volunteers had a formal role for women, but change was already under way on the early committees by virtue of YWCA affiliation from 1889. In 1898 there were two YWCA members on the executive committee.[76] Nevertheless, the SVM remained an organization in which the assertion of masculine leadership and identity was a central ideological claim. This tension between the reality of female missionary contributions and anxieties over its implications was in fact productive because it imparted considerable moral energy to the crusade and shaped the male leaders' responses to the crisis of missions.

Though many Volunteers did not fulfill their pledges by becoming missionaries and the churches divided over the efficacy of the pledge itself, the SVM had an immediate impact.[77] Presbyterian SVM convert Speer noted in 1892 certain "hopeful features" in the quickening interest in missions. The spin-offs occurred in both financial and personnel matters. In forty colleges and thirty-two seminaries that he surveyed, a great increase in foreign mission giving had occurred since 1886; colleges that gave $500 before the SVM emerged gave $40,000 afterward.[78] Speer also cited a great increase in the percentage of men in seminaries training to go into foreign service. In the Presbyterian Church, only 5.5 percent of those training for ordination became foreign missionaries up to 1875, whereas 11 percent of the contemporary theological seminary students had volunteered by 1892, and Bible study in those places had been stimulated. Speer also boasted about a new ease in Americans' sense of the religious vocation—beyond the United States because "the field was" now "the world."[79] Though many lapsed from their pledges, the Volunteers assisted in recruiting over ten thousand of the more than fourteen thousand Protestant missionaries who went to foreign fields before the end of the 1920s.[80] Even obscure Volunteers who did not enter work overseas took their experience of the SVM back into the domestic stream of American society. The Sioux Indian, James Garvie, became not only a teacher among his own people but also an ordained Congregational minister to them.

One result of the Volunteer movement was to tip the balance in favor of American moral hegemony within the world's Protestant foreign mission force. This was not a field dominated by Americans in the nineteenth century, despite celebration of the stories of pioneers and the role of the American Board from its founding in 1810. Britain remained the leading missionary country through to the early twentieth century, and the United States had only nine hundred missionaries abroad at the end of the 1880s. Yet American numbers grew faster from 1886 onward, trebling in the first ten years beginning in 1889 when Volunteers began to enter service. Early comparative statistics are notoriously unreliable, especially in regard to women, partly because Americans counted the wives of male appointees as bona fide missionaries but Europeans did not. However, figures from 1900 onward are sounder. In 1900 the United States produced 27.5 percent of the world's Protestant foreign missionaries, compared to 38.35 percent by 1910 and nearly half by 1925. The foundations were laid in the 1880s and 1890s for the later American Protestant ascendancy within the missionary world.[81]

The impact on the international missionary community was considerable. Adapting the growth of secular non-governmental and governmental networks to their purposes, missionaries began to organize internationally. Germans and British contributed to this drive in the 1880s, but the missionary collaboration occurred increasingly on an American model thereafter. After European as well as American work spurred the holding of a centenary missionary conference in London in 1888, the next meeting held in New York in 1900 subtly marked the growing

American presence in the international missionary community.[82] By the time the World Missionary Conference convened in Edinburgh in 1910, the American contribution to the global organization of the Protestant missions had substantially expanded. The American delegation included Bishop Charles Brent and John Mott, who was elected to the critically important position of chairman.[83] From there, Mott was instrumental in arguing for establishment under his leadership of a Continuation Committee of the Conference. Though interrupted by the war in Europe in 1914, the Continuation Committee became a de facto secretariat for the international mission movement.[84] Mott had cultivated many colleagues in the Euro-American world in the course of his travels for the Student Volunteers and the Student Christian Federation, and none was more helpful than the Indian-born Scot Joseph H. Oldham. Together Mott and Oldham steered the missionary movement toward greater cooperation, culminating in the founding of the International Missionary Council in 1921.

This marked a great step in the development of Christian ecumenicalism, but the meaning of the change was not so straightforwardly positive. The size of the delegations at Edinburgh had been determined "by the size of missionary-giving budgets" where the Americans' dominance was already becoming obvious. The imbalance caused no end of discomfort for their British partners. Because Americans were "undertaking the entire expense of the preparation of the Statistics and Missionary Atlas," British officials were "anxious to avoid the appearance of dictating to them."[85] The focus on formal reporting, specialized studies by tasked committees, and compilation of data adopted by the 1910 conference flowed from the methods already pioneered by the Student Volunteers and their American allies in the mission societies and partly implemented internationally at the 1900 conference. In these respects the meetings from the turn of the century represented a decisive break in approach. The Continuation Committee conformed to this practice, stressing "business efficiency" and standardized formats for the subsidiary conferences that Mott convened in a dozen cities across Asia after 1910 as he promoted Christian ecumenicalism.[86]

Not only did the Student Volunteers spur the growing prominence of the United States as a missionary nation. The movement also changed the nature of religious institutions around them within the American sphere of operation. Though the YMCA predated the SVM and influenced it, the Volunteers effectively transformed itself into a missionary ginger group within the YMCA promoting international action and a newly militant evangelicalism. In addition, some key figures made their commitment as missionaries not to a regular board but to the YMCA. Thus the "evangelization of the world" theme propelled the YMCA (and the YWCA) toward greater international prominence. Wilder served in India as National YMCA secretary, while John Mott took on, among other duties, the associate foreign secretaryship of the YMCA of North America. He, more than anyone else, drove the appointment of YMCA secretaries to posts in India, Japan, China, Mexico, and many other countries from the 1890s to the 1910s. YMCA secretaries such as Sherwood Eddy sometimes served as roving evangelists, moving from country to country as the need arose. Missionary work thus took innovative forms outside the missionary boards. This change flowed from the non-denominationalism of the SVM, an idea that the missionaries in the field and indigenous Christians had urged in the formative period of 1886–88.[87]

Beyond the missionary impact of Americans going abroad was the work that other foreign nationals did in response to American organizing. In 1898, the Third International Convention of the SVM heard how the movement had spread to Britain, Scandinavia, Germany, Australia, New Zealand, South Africa, China, India, Ceylon, and France, with student missionaries drawn from these diverse places. All reportedly expressed "gratitude" to the American movement for help "in the formative period of their work." The SVM declared boastfully that students of "Protestant Christendom" had united to make Jesus "King" "among all races of mankind."[88] The reach of these networks of young volunteers was revealed when, in 1903, Mott visited Australia seven years after his first trip to find the organization had grown from 70 to 1,370 members. Australia was, he stated, no longer ignorant of the world missionary scene and the number of Australian theological graduates going into foreign missionary work had more than doubled.[89] The networks of the World's Student Christian Federation in which European, American, and colonial students were partners provided a receptive audience for Mott's books and their organizational messages. When Mott's *Evangelization of the World in This Generation* was published in 1900, it was reprinted in England and sold out in Norway, Germany, and Sweden.[90] These networks flowed in many directions with reciprocal influences felt in the United States. The Volunteers claimed that they could bring "Some of the best missionary works of Great Britain" into wide circulation in the United States through their international contacts.[91]

The Volunteers also spurred greater interest in lay development within the foreign work of the American churches. Among the most prominent of the early leaders of the SVM—Mott, Wilder, Speer, Charles K. Ober, and Wishard—none became ordained ministers. Their emphasis on lay involvement created greater flexibility and was essential for fund-raising by giving a greater role to businessmen, who could maintain their commercial careers while aiding the SVM. By 1901, one immense financial contribution stood out. Though Rockefeller family charity cards showed

gifts to the YMCA as far back as 1884, the International Committee of
the YMCA of North America's work was heavily supported beginning
in the late 1890s by John D. Rockefeller Jr., who contributed $100,000
toward both Mott's salary and foreign buildings for the YMCA work.
Rockefeller bankrolled Mott's second world tour in 1901–2 and at that
time began systematically supporting the foreign work with an annual
grant of $10,000. "I believe in this work and in your special fitness to
carry it on," he told Mott. Already, the YMCA of North America had
received $288,390 in funding for its international work, a huge sum in
the values of those times in comparison with puny gifts to the WCTU and
other reform organizations.[92] Donors such as department store magnate
John Wanamaker also gave heartily, but the link to business produced
an unexpected bonus beyond money—the expertise of businessmen
prepared to organize campaigns to improve the efficiency of the missionary effort.

The Laymen's Missionary Movement of 1906 was the key beneficiary.
Inspired by an SVM convention in 1905, businessman John B. Sleman
joined in 1906 with evangelical leaders Mott and J. Campbell White to
form this new group. Behind the movement was the idea of "the infu-
sion of an increased spirit of practicability and businesslike administration into missions."[93] Systematic canvassing for the mission field became
the single most important input of the Laymen's Missionary Movement
through "an ever-widening circle of pledged contributors" as the church
membership increased.[94] As befitted the practicality and informality toward doctrine that went with lay leadership, the Laymen's Missionary
Movement was non-denominational, just like the SVM and YMCA. Its
program included visits by businessmen to the mission fields to report on
efficiencies, while General Secretary White was drawn from the YMCA
and was the brother-in-law of John Mott. The Laymen's job was to galvanize the churches, not to provide a permanent organization. It engaged
in fund-raising, including "crusade" dinners at which up to two thousand businessmen attended.[95] As further evidence of cross-organizational
transfer, the new group's tripartite slogan of "Investigation, agitation and
organization" closely resembled that of the Woman's Christian Temperance Union. Unlike the WCTU, however, the Laymen's Movement was
self-evidently for men. Its masculine orientation reflected the experience
and ideology of the Volunteers and the YMCA, whose missionary leaders
inspired it. The Laymen's Movement spurred a succession of efforts to
strengthen the connections between businessmen and religion in the years
before World War I, thus powerfully affecting in the process the domestic
American practices of the churches. The way in which the Men and Religion Forward Movement of 1911–12 enhanced the role of men within
the Protestant churches of the United States was but one prominent out-

come.[96] In addition to the parent Laymen's Missionary Movement, the Canadian Council of the Laymen's Missionary Movement, the Laymen's Missionary Movement in Scotland, and the Laymen's Missionary Movement in England were soon organized. By 1909, the movement had also spread to Germany and Australia.

The SVM and groups derived from it did not initiate but added to the growing missionary impact on American society. The stimulus to organize systematic laymen's support came from missionaries themselves. The revitalization of the churches in the various "forward movements" before World War I did not emanate only from within the world of American business. Despite the masculinism of the "laymen" ethic, the reorganization of giving within the home churches represented the more complex reality of the missions, where women's labor was vitally important. The ABCFM used such techniques as systematic community canvassing in the 1890s and took the cue for their funding drives from Ceylon's Leitch sisters, who in 1896 "inaugurated" the first explicit "forward movement" for that board when its funds appeared to be diminishing sharply. Their move was based on the collection of money from special organizations formed within these churches such as the "young people's societies" of the Congregational churches, the Christian Endeavor movement. The sisters also distributed personalized collecting cards for shared sponsoring of missionaries, a method they encountered in the late 1880s during the Scottish and English campaigns in support of the Ceylon mission.[97] These systematic methods were infectious, especially when put in the hands of men with business experience.

When he returned in 1902 from extended service as a YMCA secretary in India, David McConaughy met an old friend, John Converse, president of the Baldwin Locomotive Works in Philadelphia, and enlisted him in a systematic plan involving the canvassing of businessmen. It was from this convergence of strategies that the idea for the Laymen's Movement came. As Converse argued, the aim was "not so much to increase the comparatively small number of comparatively large gifts, but rather to enlist a far larger number of comparatively small gifts on a weekly basis."[98] The Laymen's Movement was also institutionally and directly connected to the mission experience. J. Campbell White spent ten years as a YMCA secretary in Calcutta and claimed that the real problem in the global spread of Christianity was not the ineptitude of missionaries but the inadequate financial support in the home force.[99]

Such missionary impacts in the metropolitan United States became increasingly important as improved international communications underscored the need for missions and provided examples of how missionary endeavors could be more effectively organized. The rising numbers of missionaries on furloughs not only fostered recruitment drives[100] but also brought back news of both crises and opportunities when they canvassed churches for money. Returning workers published in missionary magazines, and the reports of their comings and goings were also carried in the popular press. The great missionary meetings, such as the Ecumenical Conference on Foreign Missions held in New York in 1900, featured in the major metropolitan dailies and gave welcome platforms for returning missionary heroes or heroines. After 1900, the churches used improved marketing techniques drawn from the international exhibition movement to enhance these occasions as celebratory festivals of missionary achievement.[101] "The World in Boston" Missionary Exposition of 1911 included pageants and other representations of the diverse ethnic and religious groups to whom American missionaries carried the Gospel. Later pageants moved to cities such as Chicago, Baltimore, Cincinnati, and Providence, Rhode Island.[102] The Women's Missionary Jubilee held two-day meetings in forty-eight major cities and many smaller towns across the country in 1910.[103] Every missionary society duplicated these activities in far more mundane but regular meetings. Methodists from all over the United States did so when seven thousand gathered in annual summer camp meetings at Ocean Grove, New Jersey, to hear, as in August 1906, the testimony of missionaries from India, China, and the Philippines that Methodism had "made rapid strides in the Far East."[104]

Information presented to the home audience often contrasted a "heathen" society with the progress of Western civilization and called for the former to be saved by the latter. "The World in Boston" included "The Pageant of Darkness and Light," a musical drama representing great events in the history of missions. These views of the non-European world, with their "Vivid Reproductions of How Natives Live in Foreign Lands," reinforced existing stereotypes of development and underdevelopment, but they did make audiences aware that the United States was part of a wider world of attempts to transform non-white peoples.[105] Digging a little deeper, it becomes clear that the mission movement conveyed greater complexity while never losing sight of the central message of Christian salvation. After 1902, the Young People's Missionary Movement led by the youth secretaries of twelve of the nation's leading Protestant mission boards held summer conferences that attracted thousands and combined to establish courses of study for church groups. They published a series of primers accompanied by maps and sets of statistics that contemporary observers judged to be "of great value."[106] Works such as *Daybreak in the Dark Continent* conveyed the messages of cultural superiority and spiritual transformation of an Africa considered deeply entrenched in backwardness.[107] Others in the series, such as *The Christian Conquest of India* by Bishop James Mills Thoburn of Calcutta, provided more learned evidence on the "races and religions," history, politics, village life, and climate of its chosen missionary target. A series of detailed maps acquainted readers with the geography and culture of the subcontinent, and a glossary of cultural terms promised a more informed church constituency. The book aimed at creating "an intelligent interest in India and its teeming millions."[108] In such works missionaries could convey some awareness of the social context and complexity of their work to American audiences.

Significantly, the representation of the mission fields within the United States was a transnational phenomenon. The organizer of "The World in Boston," the Rev. A. M. Gardner, designed the "Orient in London" as well as earlier but similar pageant expositions in the capital city of the British Empire.[109] The fact that both the SVM and the missionaries in the field shared a common Eurocentric framework for conceptualizing their task reinforced doctrinal assumptions. Evangelical reformers did not envisage an American empire but a Christian one. This Christian "empire" included a number of significant transnational organizations with which regular American Protestant missionaries interacted and upon which they depended for ancillary support. From the interaction of these organizations came considerable innovation in the way that Americans fashioned moral reform abroad. In ensemble, these movements began in the 1890s to shape their own version of a networked constellation of reformers. Therein, quasi-imperial features of power relations began to emerge, but in different ways from those of European empires. Nevertheless, the practice of sending out missionaries enmeshed the Volunteers within the imperialism of the Euro-American world.

Chapter 4

THE MATRIX OF MORAL REFORM

The United States was "a nation of joiners," remarked historian Arthur Schlesinger Sr. in 1944. That epigram echoed the famous observations of French traveler Alexis de Tocqueville on the role of voluntary societies in a republic.[1] Tocqueville would not have found the 1880s disappointing in this respect. Nowhere was the phenomenon of joining more obvious than for the evangelical reform infrastructure developing in that decade. A host of new societies expressed concern for revitalizing the churches and missions, but the impact was not simply national. The new surge of voluntarism did more than "mirror the structure" of the nation with the development of the national economy and polity after the Civil War.[2] It reflected engagement with the larger world that paralleled the growth of international organizations in Europe. The Student Volunteer Movement for Foreign Missions was just one of several innovative groups demonstrating new techniques of non-denominational religious and moral reform. All involved conceptual innovations that made organizations bearing the new ideas controversial abroad and disruptive of the existing social order. The same characteristics made them popular among foreign nationals seeking to sharpen the appeal of their particular reform enthusiasms. These American-inspired organizations were mutually supportive of each other through the sharing of tactics, methods, and personnel. Some, like the YMCA and the WCTU, predated the missionary revival of the 1880s but were transformed by it. Others, such as Christian Endeavor and the King's Daughters, arose at much the same time as those missionary enthusiasms. Both types helped change the climate for home support of the missionaries and established a considerable presence abroad. These groups' experience of missionary outreach in turn spurred further rethinking of the whole organizational and funding basis of Protestant cultural expansion. In each case Americans served in coalition with non-American groups and used these groups to export American ideas and organizational forms; they networked within the British Empire and extended ideas of informal influence within that empire. American evangelical reformers began to engage in transatlantic exchanges of ideas before the Civil War, but the flow was carried to greater lengths and on a broader geographical scope beginning in the late 1870s. Moral reform organizations promoted global aspirations and fostered departmental specialization, statistical analysis, administrative reporting, geographical and demographic strategies of cadre placement, and encouragement of "native" workers. These ideas were not developed by any one group but by societies in constant interaction with one another and with the mission fields. The strategies advanced had to be adapted to the circumstances of those fields.

One of the earliest models came from the temperance movements that, by the 1880s, ceased to be largely transatlantic and became global in achievement. Despite its first, tentative international action at the Women's International Temperance Convention held in Philadelphia in 1876, the WCTU had to wait until external circumstances and internal changes made the moment for effective organizing across national boundaries propitious. Not until the president of the WCTU from 1879, Frances Willard, embraced a global vision in the early 1880s did a change come with the founding of the World's WCTU in 1884, a move foreshadowed by Willard the previous year. This move expressed the changes in American attitudes toward missions reflected in the ideas of Dwight Moody's transatlantic revivalism. As a Methodist-centered organization in its early days, the WCTU was close to Moody's style of evangelism, and ideas of consecration (holiness) theology were influential in its rhetoric and practice. Though predominantly led by Methodists, the WCTU was also non-denominational, a factor that gained it strong Presbyterian, Quaker, and Congregational support. Temperance non-denominationalism paralleled that of the Student Volunteers and reflected the conviction that Christianity must rise to the challenges of social change at home and abroad by moving from doctrinal divisions to practical application of evangelism.

The other influence came from outside the Atlantic world. The emerging global—as opposed to "international"—vision of the World's WCTU operated in a transnational intellectual space derived from beyond Europe or the United States. Willard acknowledged the impact of "missionaries to the Orient" who urged her to send temperance organizers to China, Japan, and Hawaii. She was spurred by "the magic transformation in the civilization of Japan" brought about by Protestant missionaries and the newly open nation's willingness to adopt Western customs such as temperance. Yet there was a negative side to closer international connections to match these positive hopes. A visit to the opium dens of San Francisco's Chinatown in November 1883 brought home to Willard the indissolubly transnational nature of the fight against drugs. To defeat opium in the United States, it would be necessary to send temperance reformers advocating prohibition of drugs and alcohol to East Asia and Europe, places that were sending immigrants to the United States.

Armed with this global vision, the World's WCTU grew into a more cohesive force than older international organizations. It would have a bureaucratic structure at a "World" level and a transnational missionary force allied to or responsible for no one country. On the basis of its innovative global approach, the WCTU grew in more than forty countries and dues-paying membership climbed past three-quarters of a million by the 1920s. Its work promoted across the world such secular causes as woman's suffrage and higher wages, as well as moral and religious campaigns from temperance to anti-prostitution.[3] The WCTU cooperated closely with missionaries, forming a Temperance and Missions Department, while sending its own round-the-world missionaries beginning in 1884. From San Francisco on to Hawaii, Japan, Australia, New Zealand, India, Africa, and beyond, Mary C. Leavitt was the first to go. She toured the globe intrepidly until 1891, preaching temperance and organizing affiliates. Protestant evangelical church missionaries in China, India, Japan, and Africa as well as the Pacific islands became receptive to her message.

The WCTU's contribution to global temperance and prohibition campaigns is well-known. Less known is its contribution to the organizational revolution of American moral reform. The World's WCTU created concrete work that could instill a global identity among women. Recognizing in 1885 that women could not vote but could attest their moral commitment, temperance women undertook a ten-year petitioning campaign to raise women's consciousness of collective identity and injury. This was the same work that the Leitch sisters carried on in Ceylon. The work for the Polyglot Petition gathered support against the use of drugs and alcohol, and gave women a sense of definite activity in countries where they lacked elementary rights of citizenship. A deputation first presented the petition, weighing 1,400 pounds, to President Grover Cleveland in February 1895, with 1.1 million signatures physically mounted and many more waiting to be added.[4] Seven million signatures and proxy signatures by attestations of societies were claimed worldwide.

The petition was the brainchild of Willard. Beginning in 1880, her "Do-Everything" policy allowed the WCTU to grow rapidly by appealing to women whose interests extended beyond temperance. The WCTU became an umbrella network attracting people interested in a wide range of moral reform causes linked in some way by temperance commitment. It borrowed the idea of "departments" of work from the structures of American business and encouraged specialization with "superintendents" appointed to coordinate work in each area, from flower missions to kindergartens to Sabbath observation to anti-narcotic work. The WCTU pursued its own "moral bureaucratization" that operated hierarchically with each local and state level reporting upward to the national union.[5] Reporting requirements encouraged the collection of statistics to show progress, and the statistics could be used to define where organizers and round-the-world missionaries should be sent. Reporting also emphasized

Fig. 5. The Polyglot Petition of the World's WCTU, 1886–95, collected by scores of workers around the world. Reproduced from Anna A. Gordon, *The Beautiful Life of Frances E. Willard: A Memorial Volume* (Chicago: Woman's Temperance Publishing Association, 1898), 144.

a clear program of work and agitation for that program to be uniformly adopted across affiliates. The WCTU mirrored the growth of American federalism with Willard announcing that the local, state, and national unions were "natural" developments, but the new society did more that that.[6] Its leaders wished to foster the nascent internationalist sentiment that they found in the work of transatlantic purity reformers. The WCTU wished to take advantage of the proliferating networks of international organizations and moral reform societies in the process of formation in Europe after 1875, but the WCTU would extend its own networks globally because of the pull coming from its missionary contacts in Asia. By using transnational organizers in addition to sending missionaries to be stationed in particular countries, the World's WCTU pioneered an approach subsequently elaborated by the YMCA and YWCA. The WCTU also profoundly influenced one of the key reform movements to spur the home churches into moral reform and missionary activity abroad, the Young People's Society of Christian Endeavor.[7]

Founded in 1881 by the Canadian-born Congregational clergyman Francis E. Clark in Portland, Maine, the Young People's Society of Christian Endeavor (YPSCE) targeted young people of both sexes and sought

to create an environment for Christian living within the evangelical Protestant churches. The group mushroomed in the mid-1880s at precisely
the time that the SVM inspired college youth. Unlike the Volunteers, the
Christian Endeavor movement was not limited to college students but
embraced all young people, and it crossed the gender barrier more effectively than did the WCTU, which enrolled men only as a small minority
called associate members. Like the SVM, growth was rapid. In 1883,
the second annual Endeavor conference boasted 56 societies with 2,870
members but a spurt of growth in the mid-1880s saw numbers reach
almost 15,000 by 1885, double that for the previous year, and 50,000
in 1886.[8] By 1890, over 660,000 members had joined.[9] Formed as an
umbrella institution, the United Society of Christian Endeavor presided
over the state and local affiliates and provided speakers and templates
for organized action. Signaling its national ambitions, in 1886 Endeavorers met in "national" convention for the first time outside New England.
Soon, the growth of membership required bureaucratic administration
to promote systematic organization. Anticipating the drive for efficient
business methods in financing within the Protestant churches themselves,
this restructure introduced a full-time paid secretary to run the organization.[10] The society's growth was helped by the establishment of a print
publication, the *Golden Rule* (1886), though this paper was run by sympathetic businessmen and not under direct Endeavor control until 1897
when it changed its name to the *Christian Endeavor World*.[11]

The Endeavor societies introduced distinctive methods that greatly
aided their advance. These included dedicated young people's prayer
meetings, pledged daily prayer and Bible study, and specialized committee work including flower arrangement, hospital visitation, and social
and church music committees. The systematic organization enabled a rationalizing of work within churches that many pastors and congregations
welcomed. Music committees took control of young people's choirs, while
church temperance societies were folded into the Endeavor movement's
temperance committee work. State and national conventions featured in-
spiring speakers, booths for the distribution of literature, and colorful
spectacles through pageants and the display of state banners and national
and state flags. Through the conventions, rank-and-file delegates became
part of a much larger movement, and the reward of attendance provided
incentive for further work within local affiliates. Holiness doctrines were
emphasized to commit attendees to service, with preachers leading by example when they consecrated themselves to Christ in highly orchestrated
moves. Group identity was promoted through adoption of a badge that
displayed public profession of the faith. These meetings became steadily
larger with more elaborate activities that mimicked church attendance on
a vast scale. The 1905 Baltimore convention featured 8,000 official del-

egates, a "Chorus of 2,800" leading the worship, and a crowd estimated at 20,000 people bowing in prayer.[12]

Much of the Endeavor work aimed at securing young Christian youth against temptation by providing "the element of sociability" to match the attractions of "the world." The society asserted that 75 percent of young men never saw the inside of any church, while only 15 percent were regular churchgoers and 5 percent were communicants. Christian Endeavor gained ground when it was able to bring "a halt to these drifting masses," boasting by 1886 that "the society has greatly increased the ratio of conversions in the churches where it has been introduced."[13] This success was achieved by systematic methods. The anxiety over and desire to protect youth gave the Endeavor movement an inward-looking aspect that belied its aggressive expansionism. It was concerned with recruiting church people at home, ensuring that those born in the church stayed in the church. This purpose was not, on the surface, easily compatible with Endeavor's other notable feature: a rapid duplication of its organization across the globe. Yet the latter process was also striking, and the impetus came from outside.

The Endeavor movement embraced the SVM's millenarian message of the "crisis of missions" at the urging of returning missionaries and Volunteer officials such as Robert Wilder, who addressed its conferences.[14] General Secretary George M. Ward could claim in 1886 to be part of the global evangelist movement started by the SVM. "God showed his approval of the cause," Ward claimed, and "placed the Society of Christian Endeavor in a prominent position among the ranks of the organizations which have for an aim the evangelization of the world."[15] Missions were from the start "a core element" in YPSCE work with mission study groups formed, but this work received increased practical and financial emphasis by the 1890s through active missionary committees in the local affiliates. Many societies adopted the "Fulton Plan," named for the Presbyterian missionary Rev. A. A. Fulton. On furlough from Canton (Guangdong), China, he electrified the 1891 Minneapolis convention with his scheme. Therein, "each member pledged two cents per week for missionary work and sent the collected funds to denominational mission boards."[16] Fed by the contacts with missionaries and the money raised by the home societies for mission work, the movement's expansion into missionary fields bounded ahead.

Almost from the beginning, the society's methods and achievements won international notice, and efforts were made to export the institution. These efforts came not from the leaders of Christian Endeavor but, as with the SVM movement, from the periphery. As early as 1884 missionaries wrote unsolicited letters to Clark asking for information. In other cases missionaries on furlough discovered the attractions firsthand. The

Rev. J. E. Walker, a missionary with the ABCFM in Foochow (Fuzhou), China, spoke to Clark's congregation in Portland, Maine, and noted "the enthusiasm and commitment of the young people in Christian Endeavor." He thought that the society would help school Chinese converts "in the practices of a Christian way of life."[17] With a fellow missionary who had worked with Christian Endeavor in the United States, Walker founded an affiliate in China, whose Chinese characters translated as "The Drum-Around and Rouse-Up Society." The Endeavor movement soon became "a key vehicle for exporting Protestantism" with missionaries using Endeavor methods to "organize and train young people on the mission field."[18] With the recognition that role models were otherwise absent for the young converts, missionaries valued the training that the YPSCE gave in public expression of faith and Christian acts of service. By 1886 Syria, Japan, China, Africa, Micronesia, Spain, Scotland, and England boasted societies.[19] This pattern of dissemination underscored the importance of missionaries on the frontiers of European cultural penetration soliciting information and support from within the American Christian Endeavor.

The "missionary" expansion of the movement, like that of the World's WCTU, was not limited to the obvious targets in the colonial world. Francis Clark's own Canadian background and the growing intellectual concern in the larger society for a strengthened Anglo-Saxonism encouraged him to see the movement as an Anglo-American phalanx in which the people of the "white settler societies" such as Canada, Australia, and New Zealand played strategically critical roles. Clark talked up the mission cause, noting "a foothold in Great Britain, and in many mission lands."[20] His comments referred to the conviction that the society must expand globally and exploit networks of communication and cultural ties that linked the United States to Britain and its colonies. While Christian Endeavor did not do well early on in Britain and some English church leaders believed the movement was "an American fad,"[21] the internationalization process was underpinned by personal Anglo-American connections made by Endeavor leaders, who traveled frequently to overseas conventions. The swelling of the YPSCE into a society of millions across more than forty countries was vastly stimulated by the regular circumnavigating trips of Clark, who embarked on his first world tour in 1892. Yet the trips undertaken also reflected prior success in far-flung places. Australia was one of Clark's favorite destinations, partly because of the attraction of the Protestant churches to his methods.[22] Secretary John W. Baer reported in 1892 that the growth of the movement in Australia was "phenomenal" and rivaled in per capita terms that of the United States.[23] Spurred by attention to international organizing, the society became one of the largest voluntary associations in the world by 1900. Fifty thousand people attended the 1900 World's Convention in London, and by 1909 there were seventy-one thousand societies with nearly four million members worldwide.[24]

Leaders credited a flexible structure with facilitating this rapid spread. As the Connecticut affiliate stated, "Experience has taught us the adaptability of this society ... to heathen and to Christian lands. The constitution is substantially the same everywhere.... . The perfect adaptability of methods, combined with uniformity of principles, is one reason for the rapid progress of this movement."[25] Yet the YPSCE also prospered as part of a wider network of mutually supporting organizations. It worked in interlocking ways with the YMCA, whose officials frequently addressed its meetings. Thus Christian Endeavor's fourteenth annual conference in Boston in 1895 saw the YMCA's John Mott deliver an address prior to his own first world trip. Mott also conferred with Clark to gain a sense of how to approach missionary work in other countries.[26] Networking occurred through personal sharing of experience but also through imitation of tactics and organizational forms. Christian Endeavor drew on the surrounding infrastructure, and little about it was truly original. In his book *Christian Endeavor in All Lands*, Clark admitted that the departmental methods of work reflected the WCTU's "Do-Everything" policy.[27] The pledge was applied from temperance societies and the Endeavor badge copied that of the WCTU in form if not exact appearance. So thoroughly was the WCTU duplicated organizationally that temperance women called Christian Endeavor "Our Unlisted Allies." Indeed, Christian Endeavor was strongly supportive of alcohol prohibition. Yet there was a difference. Because the movement ignored or airbrushed many controversial subjects with which the WCTU grappled, and because it actively recruited both sexes, it was able to achieve much higher membership numbers than those of its temperance sisters.[28]

This close networking was grounded in Clark's activity as a roving organizer and publisher, just as John Mott served this function in the SVM. Clark toured the world four more times in the decade to 1903; in all he visited Europe twenty times. Clark's trips were copiously documented for his followers in his printed travelogues; these were celebrations of Christian Endeavor's global reach and numerical strength but also conveyed information on the exotic customs and religions of foreign peoples. His books sold well and helped finance further forays into international ministry. In 1897 he published, with his wife, Harriet, *Our Journey around the World*. In part an extended traveler's tale, the book's underlying message was twofold: the diversity of colorful world cultures, yet the homogeneity of humanity in need only of the Christian gospel, and the example of Christian living that the Endeavor movement embodied.[29]

The movement had its critics within the United States. Its pledge implied, said many Baptists and Methodists, the substitution of external manifestations of worship for a "spiritual religion." Some Christians also objected to its apparent takeover of church youth work or its unwillingness to affiliate with denominational groups. The Methodists organized the Epworth League as a defensive and highly successful counter, while Baptists established their own competing society with an optional pledge, and Christian Endeavor had to modify its own.[30] But these societies in many other ways were stimulated by and responded to the Endeavor movement; they actually documented the extent of its influence and the way it changed church organization. Abroad, the movement did not always face such denominational opposition. This fact became one secret of its rapid growth there and explained the appeal of foreign affiliates in the propaganda war over the organization's controversial features. Clark pointed out that in Australasia both the Church of England and the Methodists participated without qualms in the Endeavor societies and in many places formed the backbone of its support.[31]

Clark exploited the numerical strength of his organization together with his widespread international experience as a platform speaker to influence American foreign relations. In 1901 he led the interorganizational deputation petitioning Secretary of State John Hay for laws against the supply of opium and alcohol to the "native races,"[32] and three years later he met with King Oscar of Sweden to get endorsement of a "proposed world treaty" on the supply of alcohol to those same peoples.[33] In keeping with this effort, Christian Endeavor emphasized Anglo-Saxon leadership of the world as promotive of international stability and progress. The organization displayed the British flag at its St Louis convention of 1890, united with the American to represent "the international fellowship fostered by Christian Endeavor."[34] Clark wished to promote internationalism, but it was an internationalism based on a cultural hegemony of progressive, English-speaking peoples. "If the peoples of England, America, and Australia knew more of each other, they would love each other far more," he opined. Through the young people's fellowship in Christian Endeavor, "English arrogance and American spread-eagleism and Australian provincialism would each receive a deadly blow."[35]

This Anglo-Saxon hegemony would supposedly transcend racial division. Photographs of happy Asian and African affiliate conventions and individual members abounded in the movement's publications. The movement's leaders promoted Christian Endeavor as an "interracial fellowship" or "kinship."[36] A transnational reach and ideology committed the society to a progressive attitude on advancing racial equality at the national level, since to do otherwise would be inconsistent with its international stance. Non-white delegates were accepted from abroad, so equal status had to be accorded the descendents of American slaves. Though claiming to cut across racial divisions and enroll people of color in many

Fig. 6. Christian Endeavor leaders stressed its cross-racial and cross-national reach. Here the All-India Christian Endeavor Convention in Allahabad is depicted in Francis Clark, *Christian Endeavor in All Lands: A Record of Twenty-Five Years of Progress* (United Society of Christian Endeavor, [1906]), 169.

places around the world, the movement nevertheless operated within the racial parameters of the social groups wherein it flourished. Attendees at the 1898 convention in Nashville were housed in racially segregated accommodations, though the convention controversially seated African American delegates in its midst. Black activists attacked the organization in Seattle in 1907 for failing to integrate the hotels in which delegates to the national and international conventions stayed. This unsettling incident was almost entirely erased in the public record and played no part in the self-image of the Endeavor movement.[37]

Racial divisions repressed internally were matched by more obvious international hierarchies, but the latter were shaped by prejudices toward culture and underdevelopment rather than overt racism. Christian Endeavor's duty and that of its allied networks was to uplift the "backward" colonial world. For William Shaw, who attended the 1909 World's Convention in Agra, India, as the general secretary of the United Society of Christian Endeavor, that country was "mysterious" and "marvellous." It was a land without a sense of progress where ambition found "no place in the life of the Hindoo," but it was not racial inferiority that created this static society. Rather it was the mystery of a place when God "is ruled out ... and the worship of the creature is substituted for the worship of the creator." In comparison with the West, India's neglect of progress resided in this fact, since numerous taboos and caste restrictions prevented social change. "Cattle are deified, and children are neglected," exclaimed an exasperated Shaw.[38] Similarly China was, in Francis Clark's eyes, a country where "Ancient conservatism" thwarted "modern progress." His gloomy assessment of "The Empire of the Dead" came in the wake of the repression of the Chinese Reform movement of 1898 and the Boxer Rebellion of 1900 with all its "heartrending accompaniments." A formal partition by the imperial powers was "most desirable" in Clark's view but did "not seem to be a solution" to the "real problem of the regeneration of China," which was the need for a "transformed character." Chinese people had to be modernized by the Anglo-Saxon cooperative reform coalition. Clark praised the missionaries for their contribution to the task and urged solidarity from his own coworkers. There was "no such force at work to-day for the regeneration of China as the army of missionaries sent out from America and Great Britain."[39]

The Endeavor movement and the WCTU were by no means the only organized Protestant reform groups that mobilized young people for Christian service from the 1880s to World War I. Others performed almost invisible but valuable ancillary roles. At the urging of the Lend-A-Hand Club club founder, charity worker Edward Everett Hale of Boston, Margaret Bottome formed in New York a parallel movement within the churches, the King's Daughters, in 1886. Its method was to form "circles" of young women of ten per circle, who chose some particular aspect of Christian service. Prominent among Methodists, Episcopalians, and Presbyterians, the King's Daughters crossed denominational lines just as Christian Endeavor did and promoted a sisterhood of Christian service among young women. Though boys could join beginning in 1887 and a separate King's Sons group was soon created, the organization could not compete effectively with the YMCA. It remained female dominated for decades and was still known commonly as the King's Daughters. By the 1890s, it had established circles in more than half the American states and published a magazine, the *Silver Cross*. Unlike the Endeavor movement, which supported prohibition, the King's Daughters fashioned an apolitical agenda. They did nursing work and supported visitations to the poor and prisoners. Their organization did not specifically address the agenda of missions; indeed it became swept up in urban reform and organized a tenement house settlement in New York, which it renamed in 1900 after slum reformer and journalist Jacob Riis, who supported the organization's work.[40] For this reason the King's Daughters' social conscience took largely domestic American courses. Nevertheless, it spread as part of the export of American cultural institutions to—and duplicated "circles" in—more than a dozen foreign countries, including Japan, China, Syria, and India by 1900. It became part of the network of home-based support for international humanitarianism and was tapped by the Leitch sisters to assist with famine relief for South Asia.[41] By 1916, a commentator could note its "large membership" on "every continent except Africa."[42]

A more potent vehicle for projecting American values abroad was the YMCA, though ironically this organization was of British origin. Founded by George Williams in London in 1844 in the wake of revivalist meetings that were American inspired, the YMCA was soon exported to the United States, where it thrived among middle-class Protestants.[43] In 1866, Americans introduced a complementary Young Women's Christian Association whose genealogy could be traced to mid-century female prayer societies in Britain. By the 1880s, the new burst of religious revivalism created the incentive and energy to expand the American YMCA (and later the YWCA) overseas. Initially, individuals established their own YMCAs in the mission fields, the first being an association in 1884 at Jaffna College in Ceylon led by Dr. Frank K. Sanders, a son of Jaffna missionaries and associate of Margaret Leitch.[44]

At first the American YMCA was reluctant as an institution to seek targets abroad, as it was bound by an informal understanding not to trespass upon the colonial possessions of European powers where these already had YMCAs at work. The Scottish missionary Dr. Alexander Somerville had established affiliates in Bombay and other places in India in the 1870s though, in the judgment of American YMCA officials, these had not prospered.[45] The American YMCA had something better to offer, its supporters believed. That was its specialized college associations. The American YMCA had already developed a structure in which college students were targeted through their own YMCA chapters as part of the Inter-Collegiate YMCA formed in 1877. With the SVM institutionalized in 1888, Luther Wishard departed from his work as Inter-Collegiate YMCA secretary to undertake a three-year world tour beginning in 1889 and founded college YMCAs in Japan, South Africa, China, and India. In all he visited over two hundred mission stations. This was essentially an expedition to assess the "advisability" of extending the American work among college youth around the world.[46]

Yet the stimulus for systematic American intervention had already come from abroad, several years before. Discontented with the ineffectual effort of British moral reform societies in Asia and inspired by the beginnings of the Student Volunteers, missionaries in the field solicited American help. An American medical missionary, the Rev. Jacob Chamberlain, who was working at the Reformed Church mission at Arcot in Madras Presidency, campaigned hard on this issue. He believed the American YMCA would systematically organize the educated youth of India, introduce effective non-denominational methods, and heighten the evangelical temper of youth work. Chamberlain raised alarm at lost opportunities because "India's educated young men" were "deprived of their ancient faith running off into infidelity, Rationalism & Agnosticism and poisoning the minds of their uneducated friends," while the missionaries were "failing to reach them and apprehend them for Christ."[47] The American YMCA was attractive to South Asian missionaries because its collegiate institutions catered specifically to this group that missionaries regarded as the future leadership of British India. Two decades later, the same arguments were used to solicit YMCA support in the Americans' own colony in the Philippines. Episcopal Bishop of Manila Charles Henry Brent desired YMCA help in view of problems posed by Westernization. Brent noted that "the breaking down of old traditions through the sudden influx of Western thought" had created "a tendency to agnosticism and scepticism among the youth of the land"[48] but believed the YMCA could help combat this secular virus.

The appeal of the American YMCA was not restricted to American missionaries, however. In Madras, Chamberlain reported that an interdenominational meeting of all of the missionary workforce supported an American YMCA introduction as early as 1887: "Many of us missionaries in India think the time has fully come" for an American intervention and "missionaries of different denominations, and the secretaries of several of our leading Boards of Missions have expressed their full approval of the proposals."[49] Despite the sometimes prejudicial judgments of visiting YMCA officials toward regular British missionaries and their social and cultural institutions, American innovations were welcomed by British coworkers where they promised new methods to combat the rise of secularism and indigenous religious revitalization.[50]

The YMCA's work in Asia and other locations was thoroughly transnational. It employed recruits from Britain and Canada as well as "native" workers, but the leadership was largely American and the program informed by American experience of how the YMCA should be run. Though party to an international agreement dating back to 1855 that laid down the terms for YMCA membership and international cooperation, the American-dominated International Committee of the YMCA of North America (the peak body) decided in 1889 to act unilaterally on Chamberlain's advice. Citing missionary demand and "Providence," it sent its own missionaries to the non-Western world, thereby creating competition with nations holding colonial possessions.[51] Upon adoption of the memorandum of international work in September 1889, a committee appointed John Trumbull Swift as YMCA secretary for Japan and David McConaughy Jr., the secretary of the Philadelphia YMCA, as secretary for India. The YMCA argued that the American body should not have its "international" work "restricted to United States and Canada" because "Young men of other lands need help as much, and they are rapidly coming into places of power and leadership." This need would open opportunities for foreign lands to "profit" from the "accumulated experience" of the Americans, so that the newly enrolled national affiliates would "not make the same mistakes." The mission of the American YMCA in the colonial world would from the first be "Not to control but to bring out native leadership and initiative."[52] The aim was not to send regular missionaries to compete with general evangelizing but "corresponding" secretaries—both "national" and provincial—to focus on the recruitment of indigenous youth and to work particularly in the growing ranks of college and high school students in India and Japan.

Women had long been involved in missionary support groups in the American colleges, and soon women emulated the YMCA's feats abroad on a somewhat smaller and less well-financed scale. When the SVM became institutionalized in 1888, Nellie Dunn of the Inter-Collegiate YWCA became part of the executive. After Anglo-American women jointly established the World's YWCA in 1894, the YMCA and YWCA continued to tread closely connected paths. The YWCA followed the men's approach of appointing "national" secretaries to India (Agnes Hall, 1894) and China (Grace Paddock, 1906). Among those who went to India and China were women stirred by the Northfield meetings and the college crusades that male recruiters undertook but who found it difficult to get a satisfying missionary posting with the regular boards due to bureaucratic or gender bias.[53] Nevertheless, the YMCA led the overseas work because it commanded the better finances and had a head start.

While the Christian Endeavor movement followed in a serendipitous fashion wherever the missionaries solicited aid, the YMCA soon began to target strategic areas for development.[54] The areas chosen differed in some respects from the regular missions, which had longstanding and major involvement in the Ottoman Empire. Despite British and American missionary involvement in Africa, little of the YMCA's efforts went there because Africa lacked the development of a student cadre that could be targeted.[55] The early focus on Japan and India reflected the two areas in the 1880s that the influential American churchman and evangelist at the Northfield Volunteers' meetings, Arthur T. Pierson, regarded as most open to Western influence among the major non-Christian communities of the world.[56] Only after 1900 did China loom large in the YMCA's strategy as the Chinese empire began to crack at the time of the Boxer Rebellion and evidence of Westernizing reform began to multiply. D. Willard Lyon, the first official secretary to China, was appointed in 1895, six years after the appointments in Japan and India began. By 1904, eight YMCA foreign secretaries had been appointed to China, but the body's global aspirations were reflected in the wide range of appointments elsewhere—to Argentina, Brazil, Ceylon, Cuba, Hong Kong, India (ten), Japan (six), Korea, and Mexico (two).[57] By 1916, the organization had 157 secretaries in 55 countries, but it was still heavily concentrated in Asia.[58] The organization also conformed to the American global aspiration symbolized by the round-the-world trips of YMCA leaders John Mott and Luther Wishard.

The strategic approach of the International Committee of the YMCA of North America differed from the British organizations in emphasizing the need for special infrastructure as a beacon of modernization and businesslike achievement. Backed by funding from rich businessmen such as John D. Rockefeller and department store magnate John Wanamaker, the Ys from the United States were able to push impressively into Asia and began an ambitious program to erect headquarters in each association outpost. Bricks and mortar gave YMCA affiliates funding targets to focus organizing at home, and the beneficent results abroad connoted for the recipients images of American modernity and practicality. Frequently these buildings included residential hostel accommodation and sports facilities. Athletic fields, gyms, and equipment symbolized in the Philippines and elsewhere the efforts of the YMCA to build a new colonial man, modeled on Euro-American ideas of a muscular Christianity. The ability to command large amounts of money gave the YMCA a prestige that even the highly respected WCTU could not hope to match among modernizing students in China, Japan, and the colonies of the British Empire. Though a women's version of muscular Christianity emerged in the YWCA, donors exhibited no equivalent largesse toward the latter, which had to scrounge for smaller sources of funds.[59]

These new organizations spearheaded the post-1880s phase of American missionary expansion abroad. Though the regular mission boards were the beneficiaries, the missionaries in the field sometimes did not anticipate the vigorous change that the Americans would bring. Despite the initial appeal registered in the international and interdenominational support within Madras Presidency, one set of antagonisms grew in India, where the YMCA raised hackles by pushing for more aggressive methods in line with the new ethos of YMCA masculinity. YMCA leaders spoke in sometimes polarizing language of "American" and "British" missionaries, where the latter symbolized conservative resistance to change. In 1890, Robert Wilder derided the Bombay YMCA because it was run by Englishmen whose work, he said, "is of the old fogy kind. Every one of their meetings was attended by women."[60] In Japan, the organization needed to skirt the regular missionaries because of the divisions between them. The secretary of the Osaka YMCA, George Gleason, proclaimed of the regular missionaries: "There are so many diverse elements to deal with, many of them out of harmony with each other, that I often tremble for fear I may make a mistake and lose the confidence of some." Gleason took a more direct evangelistic approach than the missionaries who, he argued, tended to "lecture around the Gospel instead of giving the direct message which leads men to decision."[61]

On occasion, antagonism sprang from the fact that the YMCAs challenged the authority of the missionaries and their ability to change the "heathen." The YMCA wanted to stir up the mission fields, especially where these were not dominated by Americans. This is not to say that international cooperation was lacking, but Americans wanted to select "men" from Britain or Canada who conformed to their own ambitions, not accept the British YMCA hierarchy's own claims. The Student Volunteers arranged a tour for the noted evangelist Frederick B. Meyer of London, "believing that Christian India would have to be awakened before non-Christian India was ever evangelised."[62] To Philadelphian David McConaughy, who established the YMCA in Madras, there was a pressing need for "a missionary to the missionaries." In effect, he criticized those who had acquiesced in his own appointment, the British missionaries, arguing that "There must be a revival among them, before we can look for spiritual quickening among the heathen."[63] The regular missionaries from Britain had failed and must give way to the tactics of the American YMCA all across India.

The latter deployed aggressively evangelical methods. They objected to organizations that attempted to water down doctrinal content. They favored the American plan of work over the European approach, which tended toward an introspective pietism. Steely evangelical doctrine rather than the broader and more moderate "Paris plan" that had been accepted by the YMCA as its international basis of cooperation in 1855 was the aim of YMCA officials sponsored by the International Committee of North America. They also threatened to disrupt the existing social order in the colonial world by challenging hierarchies of politics and race. The "race problem" was one that "crops up on every hand," wrote Canadian Archibald Grace, the committee's secretary in Allahabad.[64] McConaughy, too, showed signs of a distinctive approach. In Bombay, he argued, it would "be most difficult" to get the English "to change their base of operations." He took "radical exception" to the English YMCA's policy of "practical exclusion of natives" and the custom of "their meetings being for everyone, instead of for Young Men." In McConaughy's view the English policy catered only to the social hierarchies of the imperial government, which were exclusive and racist ones that showed little interest in aggressively promoting the Christian gospel along the lines of the "American" (evangelical) plan. The English objective was to preach to the converted rather than to non-Christians.[65]

Concern over the methods of both the American YMCA and the Student Volunteers ruptured the fragile unity of the Protestant Christian world and reached the highest levels of the missionary community. As early as 1888, at the Centenary Conference on the Protestant Missions of the World in London, German and other continental delegates expressed alarm at the American obsession with numbers, publicity, and "quick results."[66] Delegates to the Continental Mission Conference in Germany in 1889 voiced similar fears, which festered over the next two decades. A key source was the Christian pietist theology of Gustav Warneck, who, in 1897, attacked the millenarian extremism of Pierson that had inspired the SVM. Three years later, Warneck refused, along with some other European delegates, to attend the Ecumenical Conference on Foreign Missions in New York, and he singled out the tendency to "export western language and culture along with Christianity." The Gospels, the German theologian argued, called on Christians to "go into all the world," not to "fly" there.[67] Warneck opposed Pierson's *Crisis of Missions* as an attempt to "push forward the hands of the clock in advance of the true time."[68] Those who attacked the excesses of the American missions and their devotion to the millenarian evangelization of the world in one generation targeted the rhetoric of the religious reformers in America, but the same objection was made to the actual methods that evangelists from the United States adopted. The 1910 World Missionary Conference in Edinburgh impressed Europeans with what historian William R. Hutchinson called "a growing and heedless, Anglo-American and even American domination" of the mission field.[69] The forays of the Volunteers and the YMCA into Scandinavian countries raised hackles, too. Swedish Lutherans split over resistance to Americanization. Because some conservatives equated true religion with the state-supported church, they looked upon the United States as the "godless land" of "sects."[70]

Resistance to American theological and organizing methods was also registered in the World's Student Christian Federation. As a result of his world travels for the YMCA in the early 1890s, Luther Wishard hoped that the "colleges of foreign mission lands" could be converted into "strongholds and distributing centers of Christianity." These could be agents of the "Church Militant" in the colonial world, once the young American professors coming from the American collegiate YMCAs had, as in the case of Frank Sanders in Jaffna, introduced methods for student conversion among them.[71] Yet the tight, American-led plan that Wishard envisioned for the Student Christian Movement did not eventuate. Key European groups had leaders resistant to "Anglo-Saxon superficiality." Even the British universities had been reluctant to join in a uniform scheme until 1894.[72] John Mott diplomatically concluded that it would be maladroit to fashion student affiliates according to "any one plan"; diversity must be recognized. In individual countries, the movement should be "adapted in name, organization and activity to their own particular genius and character" and linked in a federation.[73] The compromise gave Europeans more say within the organization than they would otherwise have had but allowed Mott greater access to work within the Orthodox churches of eastern Europe, especially Russia, which he visited several times.

The YMCA met another formidable foe in the form of the social changes going on in the communities of the colonial world. YMCA official Sherwood Eddy lectured to Indian students in 1902 and reported home that "The national consciousness is awakening. They defend all that is theirs, they resist all that does not praise or tolerate the national religion."[74] Some YMCA agents emphasized that a nationalist reaction reflected their own missionary influence. By 1902–3, Englishman J. N. Farquhar noted "Neo-Hinduism" as a "great encouragement" because it showed the influence of the "missionary attack." National revitalization movements were, in Farquhar's opinion, "imitations of Christian methods": the Dawn Society established in Calcutta in 1902 by Satish Chandra Mukherjee copied the YMCA's modernizing tactics within a purely Hindu belief system.[75]

The dialectical battle over faiths was not a simple one between colony and metropole, in which the Christian challenge from the West met the indigenous response. It was a far more complicated and multilateral struggle in which the colonized developed alliances with Europeans, and in which Europeans fought among themselves. Nationalist sentiment came from a wider transnational discourse of which the YMCA's own intervention was a part. The nationalist reaction itself was stimulated by the complicated nature of Western cultural penetration. In the revival of Krishna in India, Eddy saw the hand of European influence. "The heroes of this new movement," he wrote in 1902, were Swami Vivekananda, Mrs. Annie Besant, "the famous London convert from materialism to theosophy," and "Col. Alcot, of America" (Henry S. Olcott). Olcott and the Russian "Madame" Helena Blavatsky had established the headquarters of the syncretic theosophy movement in Madras in 1882, where they proceeded to play "an active role" in both the Buddhist and the "Hindu renaissance" of the 1880s.[76] It was this outpost of theosophy marketing a non-Christian religion to Indians that had in 1886–87 disturbed the missionaries of Madras to call upon a vigorous American YMCA effort to match the challenge of new faiths.[77]

The visits of Hindu proselytizers to the United States brought the battle of the faiths home to American mission supporters. At precisely the time that the American religious offensive was set off in the mid-1880s, travelers from India were bringing knowledge about Hinduism directly to the American public. The first significant incursion came from Gopalrao Joshee, a Hindu man who toured from 1884 to 1886 and attracted wide attention in the press when he proclaimed the superiority of Indian culture.[78] American liberal churchmen were not impervious to this influence. In 1893 the World's Parliament of Religions held in conjunction with the Chicago Columbian Exposition gave a platform to Islam, Buddhism, Judaism, Catholicism, and other competing faiths. Presbyterian minister John Henry Barrows promoted the event "to liberalize Christianity, [and] encourage interreligious activities" but simultaneously wished to demonstrate "the splendors of Jesus and the Christian faith."[79] The possible impact of resurgent "Eastern" beliefs contesting Christianity was brought home with great force by this event, and it polarized the evangelical churches in ways that foreshadowed the coming of the fundamentalist-modernist split. Hindu revivalist Swami Vivekananda attended the meetings in Chicago and received a polite hearing from liberal church leaders seeking to be diplomatic and ecumenical.[80] Both alarmed and unimpressed, the *Missionary Herald* attacked Vivekananda for launching "an aggressive movement" to promote "heathen propaganda."[81] David McConaughy and others from the American and British YMCAs encouraged indigenous Christians to combat this new syncretism and Hindu revivalism head-on. In 1895, S.C.K. Rutnam, an Indian Christian from the Belgaum district of Bombay Presidency and secretary of the local YMCA, was delegated by his colleagues to go to England. There he attacked the Parliament of Religions as a "baleful" influence. According to Rutnam, many people in India mistook the Parliament of Religion's intent. He told the *Christian Herald* that Americans "did not realize how far you allowed truth to give way to courtesy" and unwittingly encouraged Indians to believe that Westerners conceded all religions to be equal. To Rutnam and fellow Indian allies of the missionaries, the "horrible side of Hinduism with which we are so familiar in India was not presented in Chicago" and was "unknown" to the unsuspecting people of the United States.[82] Sherwood Eddy understood these battle lines. He verbally confronted Vivekananda onboard ship on the way to India in 1897 about the illogicality of the Vedas, later claiming what he believed to be an ideological and moral victory.[83]

Though the YMCA and its allies set out as defenders of the faith, they were forced to adapt to the changing circumstances of religious belief within their own target audience. As far as the missionary practice of the YMCA was concerned, neither conventional evangelical theology nor the aggressive interdenominational proselytizing could prevail. Because of concern with the rise of anti-Christian faiths and Hindu revivalism, an effort had to be made to find common intellectual ground. The Englishman Farquhar had been in India since 1891 and was a professor in the London Missionary Society's Bhowanipore College. Tapped by Mott in 1902 to be educational secretary for India, based in Calcutta,[84] Farquhar claimed "the power of Christ to lay hold of men" because "it reaches the innermost center of their being."[85] But Farquhar also sought to adjust the Gospel message. His book, *The Crown of Hinduism* (1913), would, historian C. Howard Hopkins has written, "be a major contribution to the dialogue with Hindus and a force in the changing attitude of Christians toward other religions."[86] Rather than dwell on the unique doctrinal claims of Christianity, Farquhar began to stress the social Christianity of "conscience," "heart," and "intellect."[87] In addition to its efforts at acknowledging cultural complexity, the major strategies of the YMCA in India incorporated as soon as possible "native" Christian secretaries. Farquhar considered the Indianizing of YMCA positions "a very wise move" because the YMCA had become "in certain respects the leading Christian organization in the country, and we have exercised a very large influence." Yet by the early 1920s, Farquhar thought that the process had gone too far. "Our leading Secretaries, being Indians, and really living Indians, necessarily experienced to the full the tremendous impact and transforming force of the National Movement." While this assiduous attention to local needs could be salutary, nationalism tended to "swallow up" everything else, including "culture, ethics, [and] religion," becoming in the process its "servants." To the true nationalist all religions were equals. Christianity was left behind and "the average Indian Secretary gave up our urgent Evangelism and fell back on Social Service, which had the double advantage of being [a YMCA] activity and also a support to Nationalism." Farquhar urged conservation of the "British and American Secretaries" at the expense of further indigenization, but the American YMCA itself had turned at home to the same sorts of social service that had been pioneered in India and, as it turned out, in China.[88]

In East Asia, adaptation was also extensive. The YMCA in China tended to "soft-pedal its outward religious manifestations," according to historian Shirley Garrett. In Shanghai, YMCA secretary Robert Lewis aimed to be a "powerful force for righteousness throughout the Empire,"[89] but he had to compromise with Chinese culture. He left the character chi-tu (for Jesus) off the association headquarters' door, and the word "disciple" was not used. In Chinese, the YMCA generally became known as the "youth association."[90] Instead of Christianizing, the YMCA found its niche in modernizing. Its leaders argued that YMCA values were "the Western counterpart of that ancient and honoured tradition, the Confucian ethic," through "linked concepts of morality as the core of a great society."[91] By this means the small and little-known Chinese YMCA achieved "during the years from 1900 to 1911 a scope and reputation disproportionate to its size." By 1907 eight cities on the mainland had branches of some sort, and its growth "was explained by the fact that the Association stood for gradualist Western change."[92]

Fig. 7. Sherwood Eddy with a Chinese Christian leader, Professor Chen Wei Ping of Peking, studying a YMCA campaign poster, illustrating the missionary target, 1918. The text above the circle translates as "The five essentials for strengthening a country: humaneness, righteousness, politeness, knowledge, trustworthiness" (the five basic Confucianist virtues). At the center of the target is the concept of "spirit," which for Eddy and the YMCA approximated the soul. Reproduced with permission of Sidney D. Gamble Photographs, Archive of Documentary Arts, Duke University; Item 178–999. Translation courtesy of Dr. Barbara Hendrischke, University of New South Wales.

Japan was the other great world civilization that the YMCA tackled in the 1880s and 1890s, but the association's earliest appointee, John Trumbull Swift, was not successful. He faced numerous problems, from ill health to anti-foreign feeling among the Japanese and sectarian rivalry between different missionary groups.[93] The Protestant community in Japan remained very small compared to the five hundred thousand in India. In this case the YMCA did not bend as far as it needed to do. Galen Fisher, another YMCA secretary in Japan, noted the antagonism of "liberal" theological leaders in Osaka and Kobe toward "the pillars of Association work," which remained staunchly evangelical as late as 1903.[94] Not until the Russo-Japanese War of 1904–5 gave the YMCA a role in the utilitarian purposes of the Japanese state did it gain a foothold by providing comfort stations for the soldiers in Manchuria. Japanese supported this work and donated to the local YMCA affiliates as a patriotic duty. As historian Jon Davidann shows, "the nationalism of Japanese Christianity modified goals within the American YMCA," but these goals paralleled the shift toward social service elsewhere in the Asian outposts of the American organization.[95]

Adaptation occurred not only because of insistent indigenous pressure but also because of the conflicting demands of European interests. Religious doctrine was a key point of contention. David McConaughy discovered that rigid insistence upon the evangelical plan would simply alienate Anglican Christians among the established elite in Madras, a vital group because of its wealth and prestige. He had to modify the Madras YMCA constitution to appease missionaries from the Society for the Propagation of the Gospel, as they would not accept a clear reference to Protestant evangelicalism as the basis of the movement.[96] In the American-occupied Philippines, the problem of denominational resistance came from Catholic rather than Episcopalian sources. YMCA executive secretary Alfred T. Morrill reported "The ever-present problem is the opposition of the Catholic Church," as well as "the extreme political unrest in the Islands." Because of the state of the Catholic Church, which American evangelicals did not accept to be fully Christian in the moral standards of its clergy in the Philippines, YMCA officials felt that they could not foster religious convictions among Catholics. They wondered whether the YMCA could "conscientiously bring a man to the point of belief where a program for his expression of that belief should be laid out for him and tell him to go to his own church."[97] That would be to send YMCA converts back to unsound moral doctrine and undermine the evangelical mission. From Colombo, YMCA secretary Louis Hieb also reported Catholic-Protestant rivalries, though of a slightly different kind. Roman Catholics joining the YMCAs in Ceylon were threatened with excommunication from the church, and Hieb was the subject of personal intimidation.[98]

When adaptation to foreign circumstances involved, as it often did, greater attention to social service, the process generated social, intellectual, and political currents similar to those manifest in the mainland United States. American industrial conditions encouraged diffuse ideas of a Social Gospel and the golden rule as ways of dealing with social conflict in the 1890s by linking personal salvation with an imperative of helping others materially as well as spiritually.[99] Missionaries were not immune to these broad intellectual developments.[100] The American Missionary Association, a home missionary body working among southern ex-slaves, had as vice president between 1894 and 1901 the prominent Social Gospel minister Washington Gladden. Far from being immune to Social Gospel influence, Christian Endeavor gradually espoused ideas of labor arbitration to settle interclass disputes, and the YMCA became noted for its social service programs. Yet the Federal Council of Churches, which would become a stronghold of socially conscious Christianity, adopted only a weak form of the Social Gospel at its formation in 1908, and in neither the Endeavor movement nor the YMCA did discernable change toward a social Christianity come before the first decade of the twentieth century.[101] By the time the Federal Council of Churches acted, both the YMCA and Christian Endeavor had already expanded dramatically across Asia and had made inroads into southern Africa, Latin America, and the Caribbean. The timing does not support the notion of an outwardly expanding Social Gospel influence from within the United States.

More plausible is the argument that a socially conscious Protestant Christianity developed among evangelicals in a parallel fashion abroad. European versions of Social Gospel ideas can be found, and the Anglo-American context of social Christianity cannot be ignored. The settlement house schemes that some socially conscious Christians, including the King's Daughters, adopted in the 1890s were first tested in Britain by Christian social reformers.[102] Yet for the American missionaries and moral reform organizations, experience of the non-Western world was a separate source of such ideas. In both China and India, the YMCA grappled with the practical context of its work. Whereas the 1897 Indian Student Congress of the YMCA discussed a purely evangelical agenda of Bible study, prayer as a method of work, techniques for soul-winning, Christian work in the colleges, "the holy spirit and the deeper Christian life," and strategies for India's evangelization, after 1900 the YMCA began to show greater attentiveness to social unrest, religious heterogeneity, and racial and ethnic conflict.[103] YMCA secretaries in China and India began to emphasize technical improvements, such as educational courses on English and the use of sports as a means of building national character. The right of entry for Chinese emigrants wishing to come to the United States was taken up by YMCA officials with the American consular authorities in Shanghai.[104] In American possessions and occupied territories such as the Philippines, Puerto Rico, and Cuba, public health and the physical development of youth became important issues.[105] In many of these places, but particularly in India and China, the YMCA confronted nationalism as a fact, and the idea of a "New Era" in Asia took root in YMCA thinking as a consequence.[106] The origins of a greater social consciousness went deeper, however. They could be traced to the 1890s, when ethnic violence, war, economic dislocation, and climatic disasters tested the willingness of American evangelicals to help their foreign brethren. The issue was most clear-cut in the case of Indian famines, but the same themes resonated through natural and social calamities in Russia, the Ottoman Empire, and Cuba. Here the social conscience of the missionaries and moral reformers would face one of its sternest ordeals—and greatest opportunities.

Chapter 5

BLOOD, SOULS, AND POWER:

AMERICAN HUMANITARIANISM ABROAD

IN THE 1890s

FLOOD, FIRE, FAMINE, DISEASE, and the blood of collective violence stalk much of human history. Generation after generation buried its dead and could afford precious little time or money for the sick, injured, and displaced. At some juncture in the nineteenth century, the practical indifference of those observing disaster from a distance began to decline in the Euro-American world. When the catastrophes of failed harvests, religious persecution, ethnic cleansing, and the upheaval of war provoked headline after headline in the international press of the 1890s, nothing was new. And yet the response in the United States was. The theme of "humanitarianism" became a central principle of evangelical reformers' work through famine and refugee relief undertaken by the WCTU and missionaries. These groups became linked to other emerging sources of humanitarian activity, notably the Red Cross. Together, they stimulated a sense of international engagement and tapped new philanthropic networks.

American reformers' philanthropic endeavors abroad served transformative ideological and practical functions, promoting a collective culture of humanitarianism through the historical experience of organized giving. That culture had its dangers. It encouraged well-meaning intervention in the affairs of other countries and yet championed the United States as an ideologically superior and anti-imperial force. This production of moral power occurred despite the fact that Americans were not the only givers, nor the greatest in the 1890s. Britons gave more, and many other countries contributed to relief work. Professing "internationalism," American humanitarians revealed a variable mixture of Christian, patriotic, economic, and political power motives. Enthusiasm was not constant either. It waxed and waned with the economic swings of prosperity and depression in that tumultuous decade. Giving was genuine, but never simple. Internationalism was ambiguous though equally genuine. Together, the humanitarian drives of those years softened up the United States to the processes of empire and contributed to circumstances bringing the nation to the verge of war in 1898.

Long before the 1890s the people of the United States had shown interest in the plight of the less fortunate abroad, but earlier humanitarian urges were more episodic and less religiously based. Americans were moved by the stories of people seeking political liberty, such as the Greeks against the Ottoman Empire, and Poles suffering oppression at the hands of tsarist Russia in 1830. Material aid flowed from individual Americans, who rushed to help the Greeks in their struggle and, in the mid-1840s, to feed the victims of the Irish famine. More specific roots of 1890s philanthropy abroad lay in the growing tendency of moral reformers to participate in non-denominational reform work in the 1880s.

The formation of Ramabai Circles to build and support a school in Poona, India, for high-caste Hindu child brides became a prototype for later activities. The movement's founder, Pandita Ramabai Sarasvati, studied and traveled in the United States from 1886 to 1888 and covered thirty thousand miles observing American society and campaigning for pro-woman causes.[1] Ramabai's tales of young girls of Hindu faith ruined for life by child marriage to old men whose death left the child widows with no means of support touched the hearts of middle-class women. Prominent Americans such as WCTU president Frances Willard and Dr. Rachel Bodley, dean of the Woman's Medical College of Pennsylvania, took Ramabai under their wing, and the first Ramabai Circle group was formed in Boston in 1887. By 1889 there were fifty-seven circles across the North and West, mostly in cities and on university campuses, with over four thousand members and funds of $36,000. One individual moved by the Indian woman and her cause was Student Volunteer leader John Mott, who persuaded the University of Michigan to organize a circle.[2]

Like the international humanitarianism that was to follow, these groups took on a transnational issue, displayed an ideological commitment to relieve suffering, pioneered systematic fund-raising, and were non-denominational and non-sectarian. The Ramabai Circles of middle-class evangelical women identifying with the oppressed of other nations anticipated important themes exhibited later. Support came from a variety of "church, humanitarian and philanthropic activities" in a process of networking that drew on the missionary experience and bequeathed these patterns to larger enterprises that followed.[3]

It was the catastrophic Russian famine of 1891–92 that saw widespread, organized international philanthropy come to the fore as a theme in American life. In the Johnstown floods of 1889 and other earlier domestic disasters, the American Red Cross was instrumental in providing relief, but from the time of the famine, it and its coworkers turned to international affairs.[4] Failure of the harvests across huge swathes of the

Russian wheat belt threatened twenty million people and brought about three to four hundred thousand deaths.[5] Americans gave "out of a sense of justice rather than compassion," concluded historian Merle Curti. A combination of "unprecedented prosperity, a traditional friendship with Russia, and a belief in . . . personal dignity and worth" propelled the effort forward.[6] Five relief ships heavy with cargoes of flour took to the oceans when relief efforts started. Yet the Russian campaign was part of a larger pattern of response to disasters in the 1890s. American giving went beyond Russian food relief to include attempts to avert disease and deal with refugee problems in a variety of settings around the world. From 1897 to 1900, India, not Russia, was the focus of relief efforts, upon news of the terrible famine on the subcontinent, while the Armenian victims of Ottoman persecution held the nation's moral spotlight in 1895–96. By 1897–98, humanitarianism also encompassed the sufferings of the Cuban people in their struggle against Spain. The consequences of intervention in the latter case were to be momentous for missionary efforts for a generation to come and brought into question the meaning and impact of American humanitarian concern abroad. Could humanitarianism survive empire? Was the former a condition for the development of the latter?

The upsurge of interest in famine relief stemmed from several sources, not simply "humanitarianism."[7] Because the United States was still partly a farm-based export economy, some of the interest in famine relief was, in reality, self-interest. As the *St. Louis Globe Democrat* bald-facedly stated in regard to the Indian crisis of 1897: "The famine in India is deplorable but it has a bright side in the way of promoting the use of American corn as a food product, and thus teaching the world that it ought to buy and consume more of that cheap and nutritious article."[8] The desire to sell abundant agricultural products was of growing importance in American foreign policy and economic expansion. Production of wheat (and corn) boomed greatly with bumper harvests in 1891–93 more than double those of 1890.[9] Agricultural preoccupations with distant markets made Americans sensitive to the vicissitudes of both commerce and nature— and their impacts upon peoples. In the western agricultural regions, interest in the progress of foreign farming was high. American farmers could not help but be aware of the changes in weather in the lands of their competitors, and the effects of loss (or gain) of harvest, because farmers benefited from the removal of competition that they had felt in international markets for two decades, particularly from Russia. The Russian steppes often supplied from one-quarter to one-third of world wheat exports in that period and had made substantial inroads on traditional British consumers.[10] Farmers were also aware of the possible indirect effects on other agricultural products such as cotton, where the need for Russians to substitute food for cotton crops might influence trade.[11] Awareness of the foreign plight induced feelings of guilt amid the prosperity of American agricultural production in the early 1890s and influenced decisions about how much to give, and precisely when.[12]

Advancement of opportunities for American industries and, more important, American power abroad, cannot be discounted as a motive.[13] The Russian famine relief was begun late in 1891 by William C. Edgar, the editor of the *Northwestern Miller* in Minneapolis and a great booster of the North American wheat region's role as the coming breadbasket of the world.[14] Demonstrating the superiority of American-style agricultural production and distribution served the nation's milling interests. Edgar later became more explicit on this point when, in *The Story of a Grain of Wheat* (1903), he reflected on the Russian and other experiences of humanitarianism and portrayed food as the key to world dominance by the Anglo-Saxon race in general, and by the United States in particular.[15] Foreign trade also intervened in another way. Early reports of the Russian crop failures had come from foreign agents of the McCormick Harvester Company, which could no longer sell their reapers due to the competition of cheap labor from peasants driven off their own holdings into itinerant work.[16] It served the interest of harvester manufacturers to be able to restore economic stability to Russian agriculture. Yet Edgar's interest went beyond the self-interest of either farmers or exporters of machinery. He met with English humanitarian campaigner W. T. Stead in London to coordinate Anglo-American relief efforts and expressed considerable concern that the grain should reach those who needed it most. At the same time, he believed that humanitarian actions had to be seen to be done, as well as done, and so Edgar accompanied the first shipment.[17]

Food politics and the quest for hegemony in a global economic struggle were not the only themes in the rise of American international humanitarianism. Another was the sense of what scholars call "histoire croisée." A greater "entanglement" in the affairs of the world had grown in the 1880s, registered in the rise of a wide variety of international conferences and organizations, as discussed in chapter 1.[18] None was more important than the Red Cross. The formation of the American Red Cross in 1881 under the leadership of Clara Barton and the ratification by the United States of the Geneva Convention in 1882 were interconnected events as Barton sought to respond to the international movement to implement the Geneva Convention of 1864. This confluence of circumstances strengthened the hand of those working to extend humanitarian relief by providing a structure and mandate for Americans to link with international efforts. Upon its founding, the American Red Cross immediately affiliated with the International Red Cross. In 1891–92, it made perfect sense to put the Russian project under the auspices of the Red Cross and Clara Barton's charismatic leadership. By February 1892, much of the Russian famine relief was being channeled through her organization.[19]

At first blush, this humanitarian campaign seemed to have little or nothing to do with the revivalism of the 1880s. Tsarist Russia was not a missionary field at the time, but the causes of this condition gave evangelical reformers an ideological interest in the relief program.[20] They complained that the autocratic government there persistently sought to "stamp out all [other] religions," including evangelical Christianity, as forces subversive to the established religious order.[21] Moral reformers supported opposition groups, especially dissident individuals opposed to authoritarian controls over individual conscience, such as the celebrated novelist Leo Tolstoy. When Tolstoy publicized the ordeal of the Russian peasants in 1891, American evangelicals responded. They hoped for the opening of Russia to Western influences but, because of the absence of missionary contacts, they did not have the observers on the spot to stimulate American concern, nor the networks to distribute aid as the millers and their commercial allies did. Nevertheless, moral reformers used their limited contacts to good effect.

The WCTU's leadership was the first into the campaign of giving, channeling $200 raised in impromptu fashion from delegates at the November 1891 World's WCTU convention. Interestingly this meeting was held before Edgar made his own appeal. The WCTU was the first organization to provide funds for the Russian campaign, completed a day before Edgar telegraphed a proposal to the Russian minister in Washington.[22] When the Russians accepted his offer on December 4, Edgar began soliciting aid.[23] Meanwhile, further WCTU financial contributions went through the different channels of Tolstoy's family; Tolstoy's work was well-known to the sorority of the WCTU because of his temperance convictions and his contribution to peace reform, a topic that loomed large in the WCTU's "Do-Everything" galaxy of causes. Frances Willard had communicated with him since 1890 and had taken an interest in his work even before that.[24] Tolstoy's daughter Tatyana praised the WCTU's contribution as a product of that group's peace work and as part of a growing thicket of international cooperation; it was "a new token of the universal brotherhood which is not violated by the difference of government and nationality."[25]

Yet another circumstance prompted the humanitarianism first manifested in the response to the Russian famine; this was an awareness of what went on abroad that came not only from missionaries and travelers but also from the widening scope and innovative forms of modern journalism. Historians associate the rise of the yellow press with William Randolph Hearst's *New York Journal* from the precocious tycoon's arrival in New York in 1895. The term was first used to connote the sensationalizing of news, a "generous and imaginative use of illustrations," and a "penchant for self-promotion."[26] While it is perhaps significant that Hearst's influence became manifest precisely in the middle of the humanitarian upsurge, some of his tactics were already used by the religious press through the work of Louis Klopsch, an up-and-coming newspaper editor. German American in background, Klopsch had become an evangelical Christian in the 1880s and married the daughter of a prominent Methodist minister in 1886. By this time, Klopsch had taken charge of the New York–based *Christian Herald*, which became the best-selling religious paper in the United States and one that exercised a growing influence on humanitarian activities. Over the next two decades, Klopsch would raise $3.3 million for international charities. Klopsch had a marked capacity for using media-driven relief campaigns to sustain interest in and subscriptions to his newspaper. He accepted the need to use "sensationalism," including pictorial journalism, to develop his cause.[27] Courtesy of Klopsch, the *Christian Herald*'s impact was enhanced by the outlandish comments of his ally in the business of the paper, the Rev. Thomas De Witt Talmage. A controversial preacher "eccentric in his habits and manner of speaking,"[28] Talmage was given to addressing at his Brooklyn Tabernacle each Sunday "an immense assemblage of *seven thousand* souls," whom he held spellbound by investing with "thrilling interest" every topic that he touched.[29] Klopsch had initiated the journalistic partnership by syndicating the Presbyterian Talmage's sensational sermons in the *Christian Herald* after 1885, and Talmage became a partner in 1890.[30]

The Russian famine saw the two begin to work for foreign causes. Talmage preached the gospel of help for Russia across America, then in July 1892 accompanied along with Klopsch a shipment of food aboard the steamer *Leo* and reported in the *Christian Herald* on the appalling conditions of the Russian peasantry.[31] In this work Klopsch and Talmage followed the prescripts of the later yellow journalism with their graphic accounts. There had "probably" been no more "remarkable spectacle of disinterested Christian charity than this," proclaimed the self-promoting Klopsch. "No more beautiful and complete obedience to the command of the Master" he could imagine.[32] This was to be the beginning of an important linkage between evangelical Christianity and a cluster of humanitarian initiatives. An important theme was the self-congratulation in the reform and religious press over the generosity of the American people. "No other country has as yet sent help save ours," boasted the WCTU's national organ, the *Union Signal*.[33]

Just two years later a far different emergency arose in which Klopsch and Talmage took an important part. Massacres in the Ottoman Empire of Christian Armenians began at Sassoun in September 1894 after the sultan, Abdul Hamid II, fearful of his waning central power, encouraged sectarian fighting led by Kurds against the Armenian population. After repeated Armenian protests for freedom and protection, the struggle turned in the following year to repression by the Ottoman authorities in Constantinople and across the Armenian districts of the empire in Eastern Turkey and Syria. What then happened the American supporters of Armenians called "a wholesale carnival of lust and blood."[34] Episodes of near genocidal scope stirred the hearts of many in the United States; it was not just the ransacking of churches, the burning of mission compounds, and the loss of life that disturbed but the stories of massacred parents leaving countless orphaned children. The WCTU reported three hundred thousand to half a million destitute young people.[35] In addition to the growing number of refugees came shortages of food, with disease spreading on the back of malnutrition, as it had done in the Russian case.[36] But that was the least of it. Missionaries in Turkey and Armenian survivors reported the "boring out of eyes," the "gouging" out of stomachs that were then filled with gunpowder to explode or with oil to burn the bodies, and the torturing of victims with red hot pokers, not to mention "atrocities so dreadful that the worst must be held from public print."[37] One eyewitness claimed that babies were tossed from soldier to soldier at the end of bayonets.[38] Even though the British organized their own relief appeals as befitted the nation with a greater foreign policy interest in the eastern Mediterranean, Americans felt that relief could not simply be left to a rival power.

The competitive spur of the British example aside, one plain fact could not be ignored. Despite the growth of American missionary interest in India and China since the 1850s, the Ottoman Empire was still a leading American missionary field, and it was the Americans among Western nations who had the strongest Christian mission presence there in churches and colleges. The missionaries of the American Board of Commissioners for Foreign Missions had a position of "extraordinary importance" in the region.[39] The Union Signal argued that demands for freedom issuing from Armenians had led to the repression and that this action entailed an American obligation. From the churches founded by missionaries in Armenian territory came the "American spirit and example" that had "stimulated the Armenian spirit of independence." In this crisis it was the "duty" of all American Christians to provide aid.[40]

The American conscience was directly stirred by the transnational campaigning of the Armenian diaspora. Converted to evangelical Protestantism or influenced by American missionary educators in Turkey, young Armenians migrated to the United States in the 1880s and 1890s, some before and many after the troubles began. One of the former was Moses Gulesian, an up-and-coming real estate developer in Newton, Massachusetts, who had voyaged west in the mid-1880s and became, reputedly, a millionaire in New England.[41] He harangued the National WCTU's annual meeting in 1895 at Baltimore, pleaded with Secretary of State Richard Olney for action, and lobbied Clara Barton to go to Turkey.[42] Another to supply the reformers with the information they needed was Herant Kiretchjian of Minneapolis. An Armenian educated at the American-founded Robert College in Istanbul who came to the United States in 1888, Kiretchjian participated in the debates at the World's Parliament of Religions in Chicago in 1893 and served as secretary of the Persian Committee there. He "wore a fez, and counted himself a loyal Turkish subject"[43] until the first of the massacres, then founded the Armenian Relief Association (the Phil-Armenic Association) in late 1894.[44] Like Gulesian, Kiretchjian lobbied politicians and reformers in Washington.[45] Rebecca Krikorian, on the other hand, was a refugee, the daughter of an imprisoned Armenian pastor, and a teacher educated by American missionaries. She toured the United States with the Leitch sisters to chaperone her and school her in the ways of Western oratory.[46] Krikorian could tell of her own family's travail and did not mince words over gory details. Her broken English made her testimony seem even more eloquent, and at one meeting "the vast audience was moved to tears."[47]

The national response to these claims for aid from the periphery of the American evangelical empire was coordinated through an ABCFM-inspired body, the National Armenian Relief Committee, based in New York. The secretary, Frederick Davis Greene, was a Turkish-born American missionary who had served in the Armenian region of eastern Turkey as an employee of the ABCFM. He had many friends and converts caught up in the slaughter. He used his local knowledge to give credibility to his accounts of "the terrible atrocities and wholesale murders committed in Armenia by Mohammedan fanatics."[48] His *Armenian Crisis in Turkey* reportedly contained the best documentation of the struggle.[49] Brown Brothers of Wall Street, a financial house whose principals were Presbyterians who had contributed heavily to the Union Theological Seminary in New York, served as banker for the relief funds and the committee's members included well-known Congregational clergyman Leonard Bacon. Local committees complemented the national work, with the ABCFM very prominent in the New York and Boston affiliates. In Philadelphia, wealthy businessman such as the Presbyterian John Converse served on the Citizen's Permanent Relief Committee alongside Rudolph Blankenburg (later a Progressive Republican mayor of the city).[50] Also important in the City of Brotherly Love was the work of Quaker peace, animal rights, and women's temperance advocate Mary S. Lovell and her prominent coreligionist and pamphleteer Josiah W. Leeds.[51] In Chicago, the Armenian Relief Association had at its head Dr. Sarah Hackett

Stevenson, who was president of the Chicago Woman's Club, a prominent physician, and president of the National Temperance Hospital.[52]

Evangelical women were especially important in providing aid to Armenians. "God distinctly called us to that work," the Leitch sisters argued. It would have been a "great sin" not to act.[53] Not only did they,
along with the Christian Endeavor women, the King's Daughters, and
the WCTU, raise money for food and clothing; they lobbied for refugee
entry to the United States and found homes for orphans. Boston feminist
and social reformer Alice Stone Blackwell was moved by this Christian
people's plight. She translated, edited, and published *Armenian Poems*
in 1896, a book that British luminary James Bryce described as "A most
interesting product of Armenian poetical genius." To Bryce, Blackwell's
labor made "Americans and Englishmen realize that the nation for which
we plead is a cultivated one, with not only a history, but a still living and
productive literary power."[54] This comment spoke to the common theme
of a struggle between Christian civilization and Muslim savagery. To be
sure, men as well as women shared the horror over civilizations collid-
ing. The Armenians were proxy Westerners in Asia. Dr. James L. Barton,
the secretary of the American Board in 1897 and former president of
Euphrates College in Turkey, remarked, "I know the Armenians to be,
by inheritance, religious, industrious and faithful. They are the Anglo-
Saxons of Eastern Turkey."[55]

For many supporters this struggle had an aspect of quasi-racial solidarity, but what touched the droves of women stirred to action was the way
the experience of the Armenians seemed to highlight the clash of their
own civilization's progress on the issues of woman's emancipation and
the allegedly circumscribed position of women in the non-Western world.
The WCTU, especially, made the Armenians a cause célèbre. Members
saw the plight of the victims as representative of the struggle of men
and women to achieve Christian domesticity amid the polygamy of the
Ottoman Muslims. Frances Willard took to her heart the testimony of
Rebecca Krikorian and others as the true stories of exemplary sister
Christians. Armenians were idealized for "their loyalty to a pure home"
and as standard-bearers for companionate marriage in a struggle for "the
home against the harem."[56] Especially important to the women of the
churches was the herding of Armenian Christian girls into harems as "the
unwilling slaves of their brutal captors."[57] This rhetoric mixed issues of
women's rights with sexual fears, and evoked the idea that Islam exercised total power over women.[58]

Reflecting her society's concern with domesticity and family values,
Willard solicited aid for the orphans and appealed for funds to help her
close companion, English aristocrat Lady Henry Somerset, in a scheme to
colonize Armenians in Bulgaria.[59] As supervisor of the work, the World's

Fig. 8. Armenian refugees in Marseilles helped by Frances Willard and Lady Henry Somerset. Reproduced from Anna A. Gordon, *The Beautiful Life of Frances E. Willard: A Memorial Volume* (Chicago: Woman's Temperance Publishing Association, 1898), 241.

WCTU sent to Bulgaria as its agent Laura Ormiston Chant, who was a British feminist, social reformer, and frequent visitor to North America.[60] Meanwhile, Somerset and Willard met refugees in Marseilles and directed their passage to Maine and Massachusetts. The WCTU did battle with stony-faced American immigration authorities to allow these immigrants to get beyond Ellis Island and join the Europeans whom poet Emma Lazarus argued were yearning to breathe free. Along with the Salvation Army and Christian Endeavor, with whom the WCTU worked, Willard helped find places in United States for five thousand Armenian refugees.[61]

This pro-Armenian group was not a single force; the missionaries and evangelical reformers could not function alone. They needed bankers, consular support, farm products, and the funds of the wider community, hence the importance of the Red Cross. Because of the hostility of the sultan to the missionaries, whom he and other Ottoman government officials regarded as fomenting rebellion among their Christian subjects, it was necessary to seek aid through a neutral source that was truly international rather than a product of American cultural expansion. The Ottoman Empire had sanctioned its own Red Crescent movement allied with the International Red Cross and it was expected that Ottoman officials would allow the American affiliate's emissaries free passage. The campaign therefore utilized the expanding experience of Clara Barton's society forged in the Russian campaign. The missionaries approached the ABCFM's Judson Smith, who in turn called on Barton to intervene. The missionaries were decisive in impelling her to action but were joined in their lobbying by Armenian community spokesman Herant Kiretchjian. With fifteen assistants, Barton left in January 1896 for Constantinople.[62] Endorsing American commitments to internationalism wholeheartedly, the *Union Signal* claimed that Barton stood for the "great international principle" of the Geneva Convention to which the United States had given its assent.[63] The missionaries accepted the Red Cross as an arm of their own movement, and one with which they claimed ideological affinity. An announcement by the National Armenian Relief Committee stated: "Clara Barton and her Red Cross associates and the missionaries are at their posts. Great efforts are being made to force them to leave. America should stand behind them and support them. Humanity and duty demand it."[64] Missionaries linked the role of the Red Cross to the broader cause of Western civilization. The Rev. Edwin Bliss portrayed Barton's work as an example of American righteousness and ignored the role of the Red Crescent. The missionaries were, Bliss claimed, "joined by Clara Barton, representing altogether that highest reach of American help for the needy. A grand company, an object lesson to the world of American Christianity."[65] Though the cultural if not theological link between the Red Cross and Christianity was obvious enough from the symbolism, this boasting of Christian influence was precisely what upset Ottoman officials and the Turkish public.

For this reason alone, tensions were bound to develop between the evangelicals and Clara Barton, who understood that outrage in the United States over Ottoman actions threatened to wreck her efforts. She observed the strict neutrality that the Geneva Convention and the Red Cross required, praised the sultan for providing security after she entered the country, and at the end of her mission proclaimed it a success, by recalling for reporters the images of cheering crowds as she left.[66] For the missionaries, the position was more pressing. They had educated Armenians, and developed strong personal and institutional ties with them. When the slaughter began, Armenians sought refuge in mission compounds, and Turkish reprisals threatened church property. In a symbolically important case, rioters tore down the American flag at the mission in Hasse Kui, looted the compound, and killed the Armenian caretaker.[67] Thus the crisis threatened the survival of the missions themselves. Because of these deep emotional ties and material interests, the missionary Henry O. Dwight and others tried to exert political influence for the protection of church property. Dwight asserted the value of the missions for

American commercial penetration in order to justify diplomatic support but did not ask for military intervention.[68] In September 1896, the Rev. Cyrus Hamlin, founder of Robert College, publicly chastised U.S. senator John Sherman in the *North American Review*. The Department of State, charged Hamlin, had failed to provide any show of strength that might relieve the precarious position of the missionaries.[69] Similarly, evangelical reformers in the United States passed resolutions calling for action on the part of the American and other governments. Aware that a comprehensive program of emigration was potentially so vast that it could only be successfully undertaken by cooperation between peoples, the WCTU internationalized the American campaign by sending appeals to Queen Victoria, other monarchs, and European governments. The effort strengthened the sense of unity among evangelical women, who claimed that nations were "moved" by a "public opinion" increasingly marshaled across national boundaries.[70]

The attempted meddling of the evangelicals upset Ottoman officials who, angered by Anglo-American press reports of the massacres, initially reneged on promises to give Barton access. She had to use the offices of the U.S. minister in Constantinople, Alexander Terrell, and her own diplomatic skills to retrieve the situation by continually emphasizing the neutrality of the Red Cross as an international body. This stance conflicted with the implicit patriotism of some of the humanitarians and the pro-American stance of their Armenian allies. The latter asserted an ideological position in which humanitarianism embodied American values, not international ones. Articulating these bellicose and patriotic concerns, Rebecca Krikorian spoke at a mass rally in Washington organized by the WCTU on January 13, 1896. She argued that American missionaries were the ones hated the most by the Turks because of the ideological freight of liberty that they carried with them. According to Krikorian, Turks feared that "we, the people, will get ideas of liberty" from Americans.[71] Noting that Europe would not act, she urged the United States to send a fleet of "war vessels." The dire circumstances were "too urgent for diplomatic interference" alone, she spluttered out amid tears. Her compatriots begged American intervention "to stop the horrors at once and forever." Certainly there was an ideological dimension to this humanitarianism, as in the case of the Russian famine. The WCTU petitioned Congress to act not in terms of national interest but for "our home-loving republic . . . and its moral and material influence."[72]

Barton professed to be pleased with the Armenian campaign. Her presence and the publicity given by the missionaries and their American allies had raised transnational consciousness over the massacres and contributed to curbing hostilities. The eyes of the world were on the Ottoman Empire, as they would not be in 1915, when the carnage of World War

I preoccupied minds during a far more dramatic example of attempted genocide against the Armenians. The missionaries and their allies had also succeeded in raising the issue of humanitarian relief as a legitimate and important international enterprise, in which Americans participated in a wider diplomatic campaign alongside the British.

Yet the missionaries' more ambitious political pressure was not completely successful. To be sure, the impact was apparent when, the day after Krikorian's electrifying speech of January 13, Representative Elijah Morse, a Republican and prohibitionist from Massachusetts, moved in Congress for the United States to join other nations in a campaign to "wipe the Turkish nation off the face of the earth."[73] However, Congress in its wisdom passed a more moderate resolution from Senator Shelby Cullom asking President Grover Cleveland to apply "appropriate pressure on the Ottoman government" and assuring him of support "in any move he might make to induce the powers to respect their treaty obligations to the Armenian people."[74] Even this did not move the administration. Cleveland did not provide a show of force in the Mediterranean, as he feared any remonstrance against the Ottoman Empire might completely close off Red Cross access. He resisted the entreaties of a deputation of businessmen that included financier William E. Dodge, who was an important conduit for the evangelical forces.[75] A growing division of opinion within the humanitarian coalition reinforced government caution. After she had been given entry, Barton repeatedly cabled that her work went unmolested by the authorities. Moreover, some humanitarian reformers such as the Quakers exercised a strong voice against any belligerent action. Josiah Leeds wrote *The Help of Armenia*, a tract warning against armed intervention by the great powers as likely to provoke more massacres.[76]

Missionary lobbyists nevertheless claimed to be happy with the results of their benevolence. They noted that the American missionary enterprise had been salvaged by the combination of financial aid and political pressure. As the Leitch sisters stated, "the hold of the missionaries upon the whole Armenian community [had] been strengthened."[77] Moreover, with protracted diplomatic pressure from the new president, William McKinley, in 1901 the sultan finally paid an indemnity for the destruction of mission property. But the emphasis of the Armenian people after 1896 was on emigration to the United States and elsewhere. Undoubtedly the events of the previous few years had checked the expansionist aims of the missionaries in the region while simultaneously solidifying the allegiance of the Christian community of Armenians to American missionary endeavors.[78]

If the political outcome was not entirely satisfactory from the missionaries' point of view, neither was the financial work. The evangelical public gave generously but inadequately. Of the money raised during the financial year 1895–96, the ABCFM furnished $130,000, or about one-seventh of the board's worldwide operations for the same period, while the Armenian diaspora alone provided an additional $80,000.[79] The estimated total raised for 1894–97 was $300,000. This compared well with the cash for the Russian relief ($250,000)[80] but fell short of Britain's $480,000 (£100,000 sterling) Armenian contribution.[81] In any case, American giving was not enough to sustain Barton. Despite simmering discontents and sporadic outbreaks of violence in the Armenian areas, she returned home in August 1896 after exhausting available funds.[82]

One limiting condition in the performance of giving was unspoken: women's philanthropy mobilized large numbers of small givers but rarely did quite as well as when rich businessmen contributed. Women had taken a larger proportionate role in this case, and they lacked the resources to provide the really big gifts. John D. Rockefeller gave $1,000; he could have spared more. Yet there were many circumstances that made the $300,000 a highly respectable figure. American donations were worth nearly $1 million during the Russian famine, but the case was not comparable, because so much of the "money" had originally been given in grain at a time of bumper harvests. In the Armenian case, the gathering of funds was more limited than had been hoped because economic conditions had changed.[83] Unemployment, harvest woes, and competing claims for funds made it harder to get commitments in the Midwest during 1895–96. More important, the Armenian appeals competed with yet other calls upon the largesse of Western nations. The most pressing came from the Indian famine of 1897. Reports that up to three million South Asians had died made the Russian famine pale into insignificance and even challenged the importance of the Armenian crisis.[84] Though little known today, the effort to save starving Indians was to be the most extensive campaign of the 1890s in terms of its organizational complexity and funds raised. Forty million people were in peril and, one farm-state paper concluded after receiving testimony from missionaries, the famine's "grim shape casts a shadow clear around the world."[85]

When Mary and Margaret Leitch returned from Ceylon in mid-1895, they were among the women stirred to action by the Armenian tragedy; in 1897 they turned to the new cause of India when the ABCFM's James Barton gave the alarm.[86] There was a definite humanitarianism in this campaign. The Leitch sisters wrote: "Contrasting the awful destitution there with the abundance to be seen here on every hand, we felt that, as God was our father and the human race one family, the people in this country had a duty to perform to their suffering brothers and sisters."[87] After failing to interest a number of prominent politicians, Mary and Margaret remembered the role of the *Christian Herald* in the Armenian case and sought an interview with Klopsch. At first he was reluctant to cooperate, concerned that his recent campaign over the massacres had exhausted the public's interest and its purse. But the sisters showed him letters and pictures from missionaries; Mary Leitch told him that he would "endear himself to the best people" and "far from losing subscribers undoubtedly his subscription list would largely increase." Quickly persuaded, week after week Klopsch published the firsthand evidence that they gave him. The Leitches also induced him to reprint 25,000 copies of the *Christian Herald* issue of March 17, 1898, because it "contained such a touching presentation of the need and appeal."[88] Klopsch raised money for the *City of Everett* to be sent to Calcutta with grain and arranged for a representative of the *Christian Herald* to go with it. In the campaign that followed, the paper alone gathered $641,000, more than double the total American commitment to the Armenian massacre relief.[89] This was "the greatest of all the foreign charities in which Dr. Klopsch engaged."[90] The *Christian Herald* collected in all $732,000 and another $557,000 over a longer period from 1896 to 1910 for the Indian orphan fund that was an offshoot of the immediate relief work.[91] In comparison, Klopsch garnered $63,867 over the shorter period of two years for Armenian refugees. Klopsch was, however, the central figure through which funds were channeled for the Indian relief, and this was not true in the Armenian case.

Those raising funds for India benefited by building on the networks developed in earlier campaigns. The Leitch sisters wrote the ABCFM: "Our experience in the Armenian Relief work has brought us a host of new friends, and will be helpful to us in many ways." Such friends included Klopsch, but the sisters also called on the Ramabai Circles, King's Daughters, and the Christian Endeavor groups that they had cultivated during the Armenian campaign.[92] The Ramabai Circles responded to the call after receiving the Pandita's "thrilling word-pictures of the sufferings of the famine children." The circles named in her honor were not only spurred into action; they reorganized and incorporated as the American Ramabai Association. With an improved organization and enhanced publicity, their "prayers" for gifts were then "richly answered."[93]

Boosting the prospects for Indian famine relief was the surge of American wheat and corn production from its mid-1890s slump. By 1897, grain supplies reached levels far in advance of 1892's harvest.[94] Giving away grain was back in fashion. Guilt was also present in the new spurt of giving, when allied to the sudden turn of fortunes in the agricultural sector. Granaries were so "full to bursting" that a "great sin would rest" with those who did not give, warned the Leitches.[95] More than disinterested benevolence was involved, however, even for the evangelicals. In the first place, missionaries wished to fortify their religious work, fearing

Fig. 9. Images such as these of Indian children taken during the great famine of 1897 were used by missionaries and their supporters to elicit sympathy from donors in the Anglo-American world. Reproduced from Ramabai Sarasvati, *The High-Caste Hindu Woman*, new ed. (New York: Fleming H. Revell, 1901), 52.

that money would be drained away from longer-term endeavors in order to feed the starving.[96] Second, they hoped that Indians would feel grateful for aid and that the power of Christianity would be better advertised, giving a "great impetus to mission work in India."[97] Third, the provision of food involved complicated questions of morals as much as survival.[98] Pandita Ramabai and the WCTU joined the YMCA in raising alarm about "the moral side of the famine in India" when destitute parents sold children into prostitution to gain money for food. Nevertheless, the missionaries admitted that bad conditions led to sin and felt that material aid would alleviate moral temptation.[99]

To further these aims and especially to stamp the name "Christian America" upon the enterprise, the philanthropists again insisted on accompanying shipments of grain. Klopsch complied by sending Illinois Methodist Rev. Richard G. Hobbs in July 1897 with the *City of Everett*, and Klopsch himself accompanied another shipment in 1900, after famine resumed its hold. The Leitch sisters did not return to India but wrote officials and missionaries there to make sure that the message of Christian giving sank in.[100] In its ideological impact the campaign succeeded admirably in promoting the selflessness of American Christians. "Indian appreciation of American generosity" was evident, reported the YMCA. "[T]he people are beginning to see that the underlying motive is the sympathy which the religion of Christ arouses in the hearts of His followers," YMCA secretary in India David McConaughy noted. McConaughy was one of a number of missionaries who depicted famine relief as an ideological and religious battleground. Klopsch and the Leitch sisters criticized the British administration, and the YMCA took note that the episode cemented the roles of Americans as givers and as bearers of a possibly superior civilization. The *Subodha Patrika*, a Brahmo paper, gave American Christians cause to celebrate: "The critics who drew so largely on the War in Transvaal for illustrations of inconsistency in the practice and preaching of the professors of Christianity will do well to reflect on the munificent gift which America has sent to India." The five thousand tons of donated maize the paper found remarkable, because it came from a people with whom Indians shared only "the common bond of humanity." These "acts of kindness" were "the basis both of a man's and a nation's true greatness."[101]

Specific political circumstances aided the cause of giving in this case. The stories of the famine told by missionaries, newspapermen, and the bearers of grain shipments reinforced anti-British feeling within sections of the American population. Some observers noted the "indifference of England to the sufferings of the famine-stricken."[102] The captain of the *City of Everett* reported meeting "ungrateful Britons" upon arrival in Calcutta. English officials told him they would rather he brought "a cargo of rapid firing guns with which to kill off the native Indian population instead of food."[103] Irish Home Rule sentiment also contributed to the fund-raising because, by giving, Irish Americans could conceivably embarrass the British government. The *Irish World and American Industrial Liberator* proclaimed of the Indian crisis that "Plague, Famine, and Increasing Impoverishment of the People" was the inevitable result of "English rule."[104] Other observers condemned the "Cold-Blooded Method of Evading Responsibility for Famine" evident when colonial officials told a visiting American that Indians must always starve if their population went above a certain level.[105] When the famine reoccurred in 1900, YMCA secretary for India Sherwood Eddy similarly blamed the British. Deeply moved by the situation, he condemned an England preoccupied and "overtaxed by the war in South Africa."[106] Time after time, the American public heard and read how American humanitarianism and British imperialism were different. The foundations for an anti-imperial form of empire were being laid.

Unmistakable was the impact of missionaries in making Americans aware of the circumstances in India and in providing networks for the distribution of funds. The *City of Everett*'s cargo was dispensed entirely through mission sources under the committee headed by James Mills Thoburn, Methodist Bishop of Calcutta. Even where not overt, the missionary connection was never far from the surface. The Reverend Talmage, with whom the Leitch sisters appeared at many meetings across the United States to promote giving aid to the famine victims, was a brother of prominent American missionary John Nest Talmage, who spent forty years in China.[107] Though the role of the press was important through Klopsch's *Christian Herald* in all of these campaigns, the information on the Indian famine was fed to Klopsch by missionaries and partly orchestrated by the Leitch sisters. The *Christian Herald* published wrenching testimony of starvation and disease derived from on-the-spot mission sources.[108]

Women missionaries and their supporters at home were important agents in this work. The executive committee of the Woman's Foreign Missionary Society of the Methodist Episcopal Church met in Denver, Colorado, in November 1897 to hear from missionary committees in Minneapolis, Des Moines, Pasadena, Topeka, and other cities. The editor of the *Woman's Missionary Friend* spoke alongside missionaries from China and Bengal, as well as Sarah S. Platt, president of the Woman's Club of Denver. Men participated, too, providing witness to the essential role that women played. The Rev. Homer Stuntz, who had returned from protracted missionary duties in India, spoke "in admiration of the work being done by the [Woman's Foreign Missionary] society in India and told of the good it was accomplishing."[109] The organizational structure of the local and national mission boards linked the American heartland with these far-off places in chains of information gathering and personal testimony.[110]

Historian Merle Curti invoked the "spirit" of humanitarianism to explain the upsurge in giving in the 1890s; he did not place the missionary and reform networks at the center of his analysis. Yet the presence of these networks was a common thread running through disparate causes. The proliferating webs of missionary and moral reform groups gathering "facts" concerning bad conditions abroad, and collecting resources to aid suffering, were first constructed in the late 1880s when the missionary expansion had begun. This timing may explain why earlier famines in Russia and India had not received the publicity and support that the later ones did. The missionary connection became stronger over the course of the 1890s, from a peripheral role in the Russian famine case to a central role in that of the Indian famine. But even in the early 1890s, moral reformers provided infrastructure for the gathering and dissemination of relief. Regarding the shipments to Russia, Klopsch's coworker Talmage had hinted at the Christian networks brought into play: "A committee of the King's Daughters had decorated the ship with streamers and bunting, American and Russian flags intertwining."[111] Along with the Christian Endeavor societies in thousands of churches and the WCTU auxiliaries that had earlier sent money to Tolstoy, it was the same local cells of King's Daughters that the Leitch sisters tapped for the famine relief in India just five years later.[112]

This alliance of philanthropy and evangelical reform in the mission fields faced a new challenge in 1897. This came from the growing concern with Spanish repression of the Cubans rebelling against colonial rule. The atrocities committed by the Spanish general Valeriano Weyler competed with those of Muslims against Armenians in raising the level of moral outrage. As in the campaign on the Indian famine where the *Christian Herald* dramatized the events, the yellow press fomented outrage, even though the press did not cause the war that followed.[113] The immediate experiences of the Ottoman Empire and India contributed to the way evangelical reformers framed the issue and sensitized them to take the Cuban crisis as a grave challenge. Frustration at the inability of the missionaries to stop Turkish attacks brought evangelicals to see Cuba as a place where Americans could seriously consider intervening militarily. Here there was no problem of interference in European affairs, no entangling alliances to avoid. Though emphasizing in 1896 that the dispute with Spain had not yet come to war, the *Union Signal* editorialized that "we must not consent to have another Armenia at our very doors."[114] When Clara Barton saw the casualties in Cuba, she proclaimed that the Armenian massacres paled in comparison.[115]

The humanitarian aid to Cuba won support from the full range of evangelical reform organizations. The King's Daughters established a committee to secure cotton goods and other clothes for Cuban women and children.[116] In the interests of his newspaper but also to express his own personal dismay, Louis Klopsch became involved in the Cuban relief. Along with other papers, the *Christian Herald* publicized the terrible conditions, stressing that the Spanish army's deliberate crop destruction was a "sterilization of the country" that caused famine and wholesale population movement. The appeal echoed the concern of earlier campaigns for the ill fed.[117] In response to discussions with Clara Barton, during Christmas 1897 President McKinley called for American citizens to give, and Klopsch telegraphed Secretary of State John Sherman his cooperation and that of his newspaper. He immediately donated $1,000 of his own money. When the State Department created the Central Cuban Relief Committee, it appointed Klopsch, Charles A. Schieren of the New York Chamber of Commerce, and Clara Barton's nephew Stephen Barton to be the members. The committee met in Bible House where the National Armenian Relief Committee had convened, and evangelist Dwight L. Moody "sent a stirring message" in support of the work.[118] In Moody's 1898 New York evangelistic meetings (the last there before his death in December 1899), "Cuba figured conspicuously." He prayed for those "who are dying in Cuba" and devoted part of the collections to their relief. During the short Spanish-American War that followed, Moody chaired the evangelistic department of the Army and Navy Christian Commission of the YMCA, though he earlier feared war and hoped it would be averted.[119]

Klopsch similarly wished for war to be avoided, and he went to Cuba "to see for himself the situation." Arriving in March, after the sinking of the *U.S.S. Maine* on 15 February 1898 but before the United States declared war, he became both a dispenser of aid and a government intermediary. He cabled home comments on the conditions he and his wife noticed, scenes that "touched them as human hearts are rarely touched."[120] He gave money to the American consuls for relief work. Mirroring his Armenian and Indian famine work, Klopsch was especially concerned about the orphans.[121] But the strong-minded Clara Barton had concluded from her Armenian experience that the Red Cross must control the entire relief effort itself in the interests of international coherence; she clashed with Klopsch, whose work she tried with some success to marginalize.[122] In early April Klopsch was back in the United States,[123] where he briefed Assistant Secretary of State William Day.[124] Klopsch's information was considered impressive enough for him to counsel McKinley and the entire cabinet.[125] Though "war was inevitable" in the estimate of many, Klopsch cautioned against such action, as Moody did with his parishioners.[126] Klopsch told McKinley that independence for Cuba would be "a curse" and claimed that "autonomy" under Spanish supervision would be preferable.[127] Momentarily McKinley seemed to favor peace, swayed in part by Klopsch's account, but quickly swung back when the philanthropist was criticized for having become too close to the Spaniards.[128] Instead, the prevailing views were those of Senator Redfield Proctor, who painted a much blacker picture of Spain's intentions. Throughout the country, sentiment congealed in favor of dispensing "justice" rather than philanthropy.[129]

Moral reform's ambivalent relations to military action and imperialism were on full display in this contest. Neither Klopsch nor the WCTU favored a martial course but, when war came, humanitarians faced new dilemmas. Patriotism rose sharply, with the Student Volunteers' John Mott vowing that "the American flag floating over us" was "an inspiration."[130] Opportunities for the advancement of missionary interests surged too, and humanitarians took hope that the defeat of Spain would be followed by the annihilation of moral evils.[131] Cuba and Puerto Rico were not missionary fields, and yet could be so once Spain was vanquished. The Pennsylvania Synod of the Presbyterian Church extended congratulations in

October 1898 for the way the president was "enabled to speedily conduct the war for humanity's sake with the Kingdom of Spain and to bring it to a successful and happy conclusion." They also congratulated him "that the flag of the Union, the emblem of civil and religious liberty and token of sovereignty, [had] been raised upon the fair isle of Puerto Rico." Presbyterians suggested that this might not be the end of American ambition: Liberia might now be taken as a protectorate, and they proclaimed an expansive version of America's moral mission because "the barriers to the spiritual life are the same at home and abroad."[132] The geopolitical horizons of the evangelicals were beginning to merge with their moral aspirations.

The flowering of international humanitarianism organized in the United States in the 1890s did not end with formal imperialism's onset. New demands soon came for relief as a result of volcanic eruptions and storms in the Caribbean, not to mention other disasters further afield. The Red Cross and Klopsch's *Christian Herald* both continued to provide substantial aid to the unfortunate. Klopsch immediately threw himself into further famine work for India, traveling there in 1900 to proclaim famine "the century's greatest tragedy."[133] However, personnel changes and the circumstances of formal empire tipped the balance of forces and altered relationships between humanitarianism and imperialism. Klopsch's partner Talmage died in 1902, his reputation sullied by financial wrangling at his church, while Barton's role in the Cuba crisis came under increasing attack, largely because she had insisted on going to Havana to direct affairs herself and had neglected her leadership role in Washington. She was also thought by many to be too old. The American Red Cross reorganized in 1904 under new leadership, and its ties to the American government became stronger.[134] By the time of Klopsch's death in 1910, his reputation had diminished too, and his passing revealed the murky state of his finances; it transpired that his personal funds and those of his charities had been sloppily mixed to the extent that obtaining probate on his will became difficult. When his debts were repaid, a sizable part of his fortune had been hived off, though Klopsch still died a well-to-do man revered by evangelicals.[135] Yet the era of personality-driven appeals for humanitarian donations seemed at an end for entirely different reasons.

Philanthropy was turning from donations centered on human interest and personal idiosyncrasy to the more systematic work of foundations. Such work began with Andrew Carnegie's generously funded institutions formed after 1901, later augmented extensively by the Rockefeller Foundation in 1913. Moreover, increasingly the voluntary organizations' humanitarian aid abroad would become allied to the state. Aid to India in 1897–98, when Congress had belatedly supplied naval transport in response to the missionary lobbying, presaged this move. The plan to move grain with government help anticipated the beginning of U.S. foreign aid. Yet the sights of government were now firmly set on the administration of the Philippines and other island conquests. Here would be a new outlet for American humanitarianism, but one that raised fresh challenges. The Leitch sisters would make this transition and come to the center of efforts to make the new American empire moral.

PART III

The Challenge of American Colonialism

Chapter 6

REFORMING COLONIALISM

WHEN WAR BROKE OUT between the United States and Spain in April 1898 over the sinking of the *U.S.S. Maine* in Havana Harbor, the leading missionary and moral reform organizations immediately responded with patriotic enthusiasm. While they saw "new dangers in the tropics" in the American course of action and had ambivalent feelings about war, evangelical reformers sensed fresh opportunities for influence. Just a month before the peace treaty was signed in Paris in December, a group representing the leading reform organizations issued on November 5, 1898, an invitation to a National Christian Citizenship Convention, to be held December 13–15 in the nation's capital.[1] The meeting called for the extension of certain American laws to the new territories, including those "forbidding prize fights and bullfights, restricting divorce, and forbidding bigamy and related evils." The "social evil" of prostitution must be eliminated from American-controlled territory, the meeting proclaimed, the "policy of prohibition . . . in Alaska and the Indian Territory" extended, and the military canteen system abolished. The group aligned its enthusiasm for moral reform potential with the extension of American power. According to the *Washington Post*, "Expansion received the unqualified and unanimous endorsement of both speakers and audience."[2]

The mastermind behind the conference was the Rev. Dr. Wilbur Crafts, the irrepressibly energetic Presbyterian minister we have already encountered waxing eloquent upon the rise of modern international communications. His chief work was, however, as superintendent of the International Reform Bureau in Washington.[3] Formed in 1895, this organization aimed to be a central lobbying office in the nation's capital for the various Protestant evangelical causes, particularly those centered on alcohol and drugs. By 1904 the bureau had, in addition to Crafts, an assistant secretary, a field secretary, "and ten other secretaries and clerks." Crafts and his fellow workers published a journal, the *Twentieth Century Quarterly*, distributed specially designed leaflets and books on an industrial scale, placed articles strategically in missionary and evangelical journals, and addressed local churches and reform groups in person. The *Los Angeles Times* noted in a feature article his "novel but effective methods." Crafts's officers organized formidable campaigns with standardized petition forms, provided petitioners with lists of congressmen and government officials to target, and personally lobbied politicians. The bureau developed systematic canvassing using a nationwide set of telephone books and city directories to contact constituents and prepared indexed profiles of influential religious people—and their interests. When a pertinent issue arose these people would be sent form petitions to use.[4] Crafts believed fervently in the persuasive powers of information and the role of cheap printed material. He equated rational thought with moral enlightenment and saw better technology as the way to achieve moral goals. He utilized the great communications revolutions of the nineteenth century—steam presses, railroads, the telegraph, and the telephone—to concentrate the power of the nation's large numbers of evangelical Christians upon Washington. Crafts's work had limits in itself, but it presented a funnel for the opinions of many millions.[5]

The meeting that Crafts organized in 1898 set an ambitious moral agenda. Of the themes that delegates discussed, two became the principal moral reform issues between 1899 and 1903: the anti-canteen campaign designed to ban the sale of alcohol in the military, and the social purity crusade after the U.S. Army in the Philippines began medical inspection of prostitutes to protect the health of its soldiers. The latter practice had given de facto government recognition to prostitution. Reformers and missionaries allied against the government-sponsored evils of drink and sexual license sought thereby a more moral kind of empire. As Crafts later pointed out, the convention of 1898 "was not 'anti-expansion' but against the extension to our new people of American evils, such as the saloon and the spoils system"; instead the convention favored extension of "good" American institutions such as the little red schoolhouse and the American form of the Sabbath.[6]

In the Washington meetings, an informal coalition of interests converged at that decisive moment in U.S. history. Speakers included the Rev. Josiah Strong, the author of a leading text that reformers appropriated to justify expansion, *Our Country*.[7] Other luminaries present were WCTU officials Mary H. Hunt and Katharine Lent Stevenson,[8] education reformer and Sabbatarian ex-senator Henry Blair of New Hampshire, Howard H. Russell of the Anti-Saloon League, and retired general Oliver O. Howard, the "Christian general" and former head of the Freedman's Bureau during Reconstruction (1865–74).[9] The coalition now faced the task not simply of exporting American values but of conducting campaigns to create a moral nation-state and a moral empire. Though relying still on the spadework of missionaries in the field, the target was Washington. Christian Endeavor, the WCTU, and the missionary societies took leading roles, but the campaign was coordinated by Crafts, who acted as chief lobbyist, collector of information, and conductor of the moral orchestra. This coalition has been studied in regard to domestic American

Fig. 10. Wilbur Crafts at his desk in the International Reform Bureau, Washington, D.C., just months before his death in 1922. (Author's personal collection.)

legislation, but foreign policy forays and transnational activities were at least as fundamental to its aspirations.[10] More important, the campaigns outside the United States and those inside were inextricably linked. Crafts wished to use the martial spirit of wartime to advance the cause of evangelical social reform not only abroad but at home as well. The Philippines and Puerto Rico would be models for a domestic moral housecleaning.[11]

In the years that followed, the same forces stressed the importance of these measures to the making of an American style of empire. The image of the United States in the world was central to the coalition's thinking. While the 1890s was an era of Anglo-American rapprochement, moral reformers were concerned with the international community's response to the American assumption of world power status. As the WCTU's *Union Signal* stated in 1901, "European jealousy of the United States" was considerable. "The good natured friendliness with which Europe had heretofore regarded us" had "changed in a moment to suspicion and dislike." The war with Spain and American trade inroads in Europe rankled abroad. Only Britain had remained friendly. "With the exception of our British cousins," the editors believed, the United States must "teach the world a lesson in national chivalry by furnishing an example of a powerful nation which uses its power not to prey upon the weak but to succor them" and seek the "cooperation of the nations."[12] Reformers would thereby counter anti-American reactions to the sudden growth of American power.

Of the moral causes that the National Christian Citizenship Convention recommended, none was more potent than the military canteen. After many years in which the sale of alcohol to the army had been carried on by private traders under government licensing, earlier temperance movement criticism had led in 1889 to regulations forbidding the sale of spirits and establishing the post exchange system for military camps. There, the army itself ran the sale and consumption of alcohol on what amounted to licensed premises. Gradually private traders were driven out and their contracts terminated. Though Congress made post exchanges theoretically dry in prohibitionist states in 1890, the majority continued to sell light beers and wines under army dispensation. The government sale of liquor within the army in any state or territory conflicted with the prohibitionist stance that there should be no compromise with evil. To prohibitionists, the government should not give a bad example by sanctioning the alcohol trade in the eyes of the American people.[13]

The issue had enormous political importance because so many young American men had joined the military during the war and the subsequent Philippine resistance that began in 1899. Approximately 126,000 troops served in the Philippines alone during the resistance to American rule. Half of all the American army regiments were stationed in colonial outposts at any one time as late as 1907, and 89 percent of troops served in the new tropical possessions in 1900.[14] Crafts and the WCTU leadership understood these facts and their significance in the struggle for prohibition nationally. The campaign against the military canteen in the Philippines became a covert way to experiment legislatively with particular incremental forms of prohibition and demonstrate the clout of prohibitionists. In "all great battles," explained the WCTU's legislative tactician, Margaret Dye Ellis, there existed a "central point of attack."[15] In the looming war for national prohibition, the provision of alcohol to the troops was the weak link in their opponents' chain. On that basis, the prohibitionists pushed forward from 1902 to demand wider alcohol exclusion zones in areas surrounding dry canteens. This tactic was part of the strategy of incremental implementation of state and, ultimately, national prohibition.[16]

Beginning in December 1898, an enormous petitioning campaign coincided with the national organizing effort and circulated through the

Protestant evangelical churches, starting with Crafts's own Presbyterian brethren. At first the reaction to the war had been largely positive, but the euphoria did not last. The Presbyterian Synod of Pennsylvania made no mention of imperialism in its minutes of the October 1898 meeting. Instead the church gave "sincere appreciation of the patriotic and valorous conduct of our soldiers and the brilliant achievements of our navy" and extended sympathy to the bereaved. This resolution was passed before the United States had publicly committed to retention of the Philippines, but when this position became widely known, the church petitioned President McKinley against the canteen system as a stain on the nation's international reputation.[17]

The avalanche of petitions that followed focused on such issues as the need to abstain in tropical countries because of perceived threats to health. Episcopal Bishop of Manila Charles Brent called drink "the curse of the tropics." It weakened the entire physical system and made young men more susceptible to infectious disease. Yet the main concern initially was moral protection of "our boys," with Brent noting how quickly they "go down."[18] This concern for the moral welfare of young men in the army expected to stray from the straight and narrow path was especially clear in the case of petitions from women, which comprised about one-third of the total, where the protectiveness of mothers toward their sons was strongly represented.[19] Though the petitions were partly orchestrated by and often represented on templates designed by Crafts's own bureau, the arguments made were not uniform. The WCTU had an important role, with national legislative lobbyist Margaret Ellis in Washington coordinating the women's campaign, but it was often small unions that were making protests as much as the National WCTU executive. Clearly this was grassroots petitioning and it represented widespread community concern, even though rich men of national standing such as former Republican postmaster general John Wanamaker also took part in this mobilization of opinion.[20]

The petitions and personal lobbying had their effect. The canteen for the navy was easily abolished in 1899, under an order from Secretary of the Navy John D. Long, a strong temperance supporter and friend of WCTU president Frances Willard.[21] While the opportunities to use canteens in the navy were strictly limited and port access to saloons that could relieve sailors' thirst while on leave extensive, the army's many encampments presented a more intractable problem. Not the navy but the army bore the brunt of the fighting and the colonial occupation. Christian reformers were effective in intimidating legislators against the military canteen, but the army and the McKinley administration itself resisted. Secretary of War Elihu Root was a trenchant opponent, both out of principle and in line with the opinion of most of his commanders.

Crafts drafted a bill abolishing the canteen on February 28, 1899, pushed through by his congressional allies, but Attorney General John W. Griggs judged the law poorly written and the administration declared on his advice that prohibition was not enforceable. Liquor sales could continue, provided they were dispensed not by military officers but civilian employees. This position outraged the WCTU.[22] In the opinion of temperance groups, the army provided a poor example for Filipinos.

Another outpouring of petitions followed, calling on the government first to uphold the law and then to pass a revised one.[23] Capitulating to immense political pressure, Congress passed a more explicit law on February 2, 1901.[24] Not until then did the opposition mobilize comparable though smaller grassroots support because only then did the dry canteen system take practical effect. Opposition came from a variety of sources but was centered on the military itself. Outsiders petitioning against the law and asking for it to be vetoed included the wives of military officers or doctors unimpressed by prohibition and favorably disposed toward regulation of drug and alcohol problems. Arguments against the law were not based on the right to drink but the most effective course of promoting temperance in the military.[25] An estimated 87 percent of soldiers agreed, and many petitioned against the law, but too late.

The law applied everywhere, including the continental United States, and was not simply a response to the situation in the Philippines. It had effects in heightening tensions over white American drinking in Puerto Rico, Samoa, Hawaii, and in the protectorate of Cuba, as well as in the Philippines. Emboldened by the success with the canteen, the churches and missionaries both in the colonies and through the International Reform Bureau lobbied for an extension of controls over the drinking of "natives" and for the suppression of saloons.[26] Missionaries and American residents in Puerto Rico railed against intemperance among the American occupying forces. "The scenes of debauchery and drunkenness were disgusting in the extreme," wrote one such observer in 1900. American rule was thus thrown into disrepute: "The Spaniards look at these things with contempt."[27] Though the government reduced liquor licenses in response, it was not until the extraordinary circumstances of 1917, when the U.S. Congress debated wartime prohibition for the mainland, that a law for Puerto Rico allowing the dependency to vote on prohibition was enacted.[28] In Samoa, the position was different. The naval authorities controlling the islands reversed an initially lax policy and curbed the liquor trade to the indigenous people and the operation of saloons in March 1901 in response to reformers' pressure.[29] However, it was in the Philippines that the impact on the new colonial possessions was most controversial, as the major American colony, the one with the most troops, and the one most resistant to foreign rule.

Because the American occupation's impact was so considerable in the Philippines, reformers began a campaign to go beyond the anti-canteen law to cut saloons—invariably given the generic title "American saloons"—and curb the drinking of soldiers and civilians in the wider community. The Ecumenical Conference on Foreign Missions in New York in May 1900 decided to support this drive against the "American" saloons in the nation's island possessions after hearing missionaries and churchmen such as the Rev. Theodore Cuyler denounce the role of drink. Delegates wished to eliminate the embarrassment for American colonial rule and to avoid the possibility that the bad habits of Europeans and Americans might catch on with the Filipino people.[30] By early 1900 petitions organized by the International Reform Bureau and its grassroots allies had already begun to include this issue. Journalist William E. Johnson traveled in the summer of 1900 to investigate alcohol use in the Philippines. Johnson was one of the most colorful and newsworthy characters in the prohibition movement. Later labeled "Pussyfoot" for his nighttime snooping on illegal liquor selling, he undertook a tour of Manila and upon his return wrote a widely reprinted report in the prohibitionist paper, the *New Voice*. There, in August 1900, he documented the enormous increase in the quantity of beer available under the American occupation and the absence of saloon regulation. In 1893 there had been only one-eighteenth the quantity of malt liquor imports that were consumed in the first ten months of U.S. occupation.[31] In *Protection of Native Races* (1900), Crafts and his coauthors drew on Johnson's evidence and that of novelist and journalist H. Irving Hancock in *Leslie's Weekly*, claiming that, in Manila, "slowly but surely the natives are veering around to the temptations to be found in the saloon."[32] In response, the International Reform Bureau circulated a new wave of petitions.[33]

When arguing against the "American" saloons in the Philippines and Puerto Rico, reformers stressed their pernicious effects on both the American population in the islands and the reputation of U.S. colonialism. Harold Martin, the Associated Press representative in Manila, claimed that Filipinos "believe the whole American people to be on a par with the drunken element of our present army of occupation. They don't like us, and decline to give us the benefit of the doubt. A temperate people themselves, they have a deep contempt for drunkenness."[34] In the estimation of many observers, prohibition would prevent the Filipino people from harboring resentment against American occupation and contempt for American authority. It would also prevent Filipinos from being corrupted by American practices.

Concern with "native" intemperance in the Philippines existed in this way but took second place to concern for American soldiers. In response to the canteen law, enterprising American civilians and others had set up saloons around the perimeters of the army camps, outside the control of the canteen system. Soldiers had only to go beyond the boundaries of the camp to get liquor. In addition, Filipinos ran their own wine bars and liquor shops that soldiers could frequent, and where drinking could be joined to illicit sexual contact with racially diverse Filipino populations. Opponents of the canteen law claimed native liquors made from palm oil and sold at such shops were more potent and dangerous to the health of soldiers who abused them than to Filipinos, who did not. That circumstance made it desirable to lobby the Bureau of Insular Affairs, the Department of War, and the Philippine Commission government for laws to extend zones of prohibition around the camps.[35]

Petitioners against the "American" saloons used Kiplingesque language to justify an anti-saloon campaign, to be sure. They argued that the "responsibility of promoting the happiness, welfare and prosperity of the less favored and enlightened inhabitants of the Islands of Cuba, Puerto Rico and of the Philippine archipelago [had] fallen . . . upon the government and people of the United States."[36] These responses reflected the currents of humanitarianism that flourished in the 1890s food relief campaigns. Some petitioners went so far as to recognize explicitly a common humanity demanding equal treatment. A mass meeting in Warrensburg, Missouri, on November 25, 1900, protested the presence of Western-style liquor "especially" in the Philippines, "where it was, until recently, unknown." Even though "Pagan and Semi-civilized," the Filipinos were "moral and sober" and deserved protection from the "ruinous, desolating and soul-blighting consequences of this, one of the greatest of human curses." Those petitioners concerned with the impact of drinking on the indigenous peoples of the Philippines averred that "all Mankind, wherever found, came from a common parentage, possess like appetites and propensities, and are tending to a common destiny."[37] In this respect they presented images contrary to that of the Philippines administration, which based its policies on racial division as a means of implementing American rule.[38] While these attitudes still represented a hierarchical view of colonized people, the tensions were resolved in reformers' minds by resorting to ideas of social and religious evolution. The deleterious European impact in moral matters held colonial subjects back from a natural developmental path. It was the role of the United States to retrieve the situation and return these people to a "common evolution towards a higher civilization."[39]

Prohibitionists had some success with these arguments. Under pressure from the missionaries and the government in Washington, the Philippine Commission cut the number of saloons by more than half between 1900 and 1903, raised taxes, banned Sunday trading, implemented prohibition on gambling and musical instruments in saloons to discourage the

Filipino attraction to them, and removed saloons from prominent commercial thoroughfares and other areas where the public could not avoid them and where families would congregate.[40] In 1903, colonial authorities enacted a two-mile prohibition zone around all army camps. "Native" wine shops were also literally decimated over the same period to four hundred. Secretary of War Elihu Root claimed: "the powers of the [Philippine] Commission are ample" to deal with the alcohol problem. "This traffic is more rigidly and effectively regulated . . . in the city of Manila than in any city of similar or greater size in the United States."[41]

Agitation over the canteen and the American-style saloons also heightened concern about a much broader question, one that went far beyond the conduct of the army in the formal colonies acquired in 1898. American interest in the protection of the "native races" against alcohol in the wider colonial world suddenly increased, and reform of American liquor policy became part of Anglo-American humanitarian lobbying on a global scale. European colonists had penetrated Africa, disrupted kinship networks, pressed workers into quasi-slavery, and, particularly in the Pacific, demoralized indigenous tribes by taking their land and plying the trade in alcoholic beverages among them. Missionary groups distinguished between good and bad European commerce, and blamed unscrupulous traders for introducing non-European peoples to new "vices."

Interest in the issue in the United States was initially limited mainly to Africa, stimulated by the unexpectedly negative results of the Congress of Berlin (1884–85) and the festering sore that was the Congo Free State. Denunciations of the rule of King Leopold of Belgium as inhuman were made by the African American George Washington Williams, the American delegate to the 1889–90 Brussels Conference on the suppression of the African slave trade. But the persistence of coerced labor was not the only issue raised by critics of European rule.[42] The supply of alcohol became a touchstone for wider anxieties over colonialism's oppressions. Well-known Brooklyn naturalist William T. Hornaday's *Free Rum on the Congo and What It Is Doing There* had already led the charge in 1887 in attacking a "too free trade" in rum in Africa. His book drew on missionary expertise for evidence but also provided a spur to action. He cooperated with the WCTU in the publication of this work, which included a foreword by Anglo-American Quaker Hannah Whitall Smith urging the WCTU to petition for an international response. As the close friend of Frances Willard and frequent returnee to the United States from her adopted home in Britain, Smith was in a strong position to exploit transatlantic networks to get action on the topic.[43] This call was taken up by the WCTU's round-the-world missionary Mary Leavitt, who traveled across West Africa in 1889 as far east as the Congo basin[44] and presented the evidence gathered on her travels to audiences in Europe and the United States in 1890–91. She took the issue to the highest ech-elons of the anti-alcohol movement when she read a paper titled "Liquor Traffic and Native Races" at the Third International Congress against the Abuse of Spirituous Drinks held in Norway in 1890.[45]

Action from the U.S. government was slow, however, and followed on the heels of concerted British and European negotiations. In line with its traditional political isolationism, the United States remained suspicious of anything that might encourage further intervention by colonial powers in Africa and the Pacific alike. In 1892, the United States belatedly ratified the General Act of the Brussels Conference, which included a provision to restrict the entry of alcohol to central Africa, the area on which Hor-naday and Smith's agitation had focused. Yet U.S. ratification was neither held up nor accelerated by this particular provision. Rather, it was on is-sues of trade and the partition of Africa that the Senate dragged its heels for a year.[46] Not even this minimal concrete achievement occurred in regard to the Pacific Islands, the other focus of the evangelical campaigns. This inactivity contrasted with Britain. As early as 1879, a series of gov-ernment regulations and laws began to exclude Britain's alcohol exports to the New Hebrides and surrounding region, in response to lobbying in Australia and Britain by the tireless Scottish missionary John G. Paton.[47] Paton pleaded with the U.S. administration for a parallel American law in 1892 in the wake of the Brussels agreement, but without success. Not until the nation was drawn to the concept of the white man's burden in 1898 did the issue gain wider political currency.

The assumption of American colonial power challenged this inaction. As Margaret Leitch emphasized, "The reason for silence no longer exists. God has entrusted to us millions of human beings in our new posses-sions."[48] In 1900 Paton traveled to New York to attend the Ecumeni-cal Conference on Foreign Missions, where he lobbied for a similar law to Britain's and for the United States to join British diplomatic efforts to form an international humanitarian coalition to achieve anti-alcohol objectives.[49] His visit was organized by Crafts, who also arranged for Leitch to speak at one of the supporting church meetings and had the "native races" question inserted into the program.[50] There the former medical missionary from the Church Missionary Society Mission in Ni-geria, Charles F. Harford-Battersby, called on Americans to join the strug-gle in "An International Native Races Committee."[51] As a result of the 1900 meetings Crafts convened an American Native Races Deputation with a heavy representation of prominent missionaries, with Mary and Margaret Leitch as honorary secretaries. This body became part of the International Native Races Committee to cover "all" Christian nations, though in fact it consisted of British and American committees working in cooperation.[52]

Under the impact of the 1900 missionary meetings and representations by Crafts, the administration and politicians in Congress began to move. On December 3, 1900, President McKinley recommended action by the Congress to suppress the liquor trade among Pacific Island peoples. Two days later, the Senate Foreign Relations Committee belatedly urged ratification of the new Brussels International Convention on the Liquor Traffic in Africa (1899) that extended the provisions of the 1890 agreement, and Congress ratified the convention on December 14, 1900. One powerful argument for Americans to join this agreement was international reputation. Britain had already acted and the United States must do the same to maintain its high moral credentials. As Paton put it, America must "keep step with England in protection of island peoples" while Crafts urged Americans to "do what Christian Britain has done in the interests of humanity."[53] The campaign was a novel one because it was an episode of transnational cooperation alongside British reform workers involved in an exchange of information, coordination of tactics, and promotion of a British model for stimulating American interest in drug problems. The American Native Races Deputation that Crafts formed was a self-confessed copy of a British organization. This, the Native Races and the Liquor Traffic United Committee that Harford-Battersby represented in 1900, had been established in London more than thirteen years before in response to revelations on the liquor traffic in Africa by the British and Colonial Congress of the National Temperance League. When temperance reformers called for "protection" of "helpless" Filipinos and other colonials against American alcohol in 1898, they joined this transnational campaign and utilized the Anglo-American language of benevolent humanitarianism and paternalistic reform.[54]

The native races campaign was indeed highly paternalistic—rooted in ideas of weak tribes at the predatory whim of liquor sellers and drug peddlers. Indigenous peoples were not considered capable of initiating involvement in the liquor business of their own free will, and reformers played down what modern anthropologists have found to be the pre-colonial use of intoxicating liquors, especially within African cultural traditions.[55] Crafts stated in 1900, "The cultivated native is still only a cultivated child. There is not an island to which this refers where the cultivated native is not a child, although he is cultivated, like the colored men of the South."[56] This racially influenced attitude fit the campaign of the National Citizenship Convention of 1898 to extend existing U.S. policy on prohibition of alcohol in the Indian territories, where paternalism had increasingly applied since the 1880s. As wards of the federal government and heavy users of alcohol, Indians presented for temperance reformers a cautionary model on Westernization's impact on colonial peoples. Crafts quoted H. Irving Hancock that the American Indian was being "wiped off the earth by permitting disreputable white traders to supply him with ardent liquors." Crafts did not wish to see indigenous peoples elsewhere suffer the same fate.[57] When the reform coalition petitioned for a halt to U.S. liquor exports to the South Pacific islands at their meeting with Secretary of State John Hay on December 6, 1901, they stressed American responsibility and the helplessness of the indigenous to resist. Crafts emphasized the need to "protect the child races," and Francis Clark of Christian Endeavor dwelt on the "effects of strong drink" that he had observed "especially among those in the dark corners of the earth."[58] At the meeting Margaret Ellis appeared for the WCTU alongside Charles Lyman, president of the International Reform Bureau.[59] Dr. Howard Russell of the Anti-Saloon League (ASL) spoke, though only "briefly." The political message of this emerging Christian coalition was manifest at this meeting; its spokesmen and women claimed to represent more than twenty-five million people, with eight million voters through missionaries and the combined membership of twenty-one "great societies."[60] This lobbying, which Hay received favorably, cemented administrative support for passage of a law in 1902, the Gillett-Lodge Act, banning American trade in alcohol with the New Hebrides and surrounding islands, as Paton had implored, and in cooperation with the British legislation.[61]

Though heavily critical of American inaction before 1900, by 1902 the Christian reformers regarded the Republican administration in Washington as highly receptive to their cause. They applauded what they saw as advances in the matter of alcohol policies. Those adopted in the Philippines were far from an achievement of prohibition and yet prohibitionists seemed reasonably satisfied with the Philippine Commission's response. Noting that off-base drinking facilities had been a "scandal" since passage of the anti-canteen law, Methodist missionary to the Philippines Homer Stuntz hailed the passage of the two-mile anti-saloon provision. This was "a great victory for righteousness" that made "drunkenness hard and temperance easy," he claimed. When Stuntz spoke, government officials knew that he had behind him the authority of the Manila Evangelical Union that brought the Methodists, Baptists, and other Protestant churches (including the Protestant Episcopal Church after 1903) together as a local lobby group.[62] Wilbur Crafts went further than this implicit endorsement of government policy and praised the administration. In correspondence with Philippines governor-general William Howard Taft, he "publicly expressed appreciation of what he and his associates have done ... to lessen the evils due to drink."[63] Arthur Judson Brown, secretary of the Board of Foreign Missions of the Presbyterian Church of the U.S.A., avoided discussion of prohibition completely and similarly lauded regulation as "the earnest desire of the Commission to place such restrictions upon the liquor traffic as can be enforced." Secretary of War Root explicitly called the adopted policy "high-license," which was in the United States anathema to prohibitionists, yet Brown openly approved of such a policy for the Philippines and Stuntz and Crafts implicitly accepted it.[64]

In part this apparent satisfaction entailed bowing to the inevitable. Prohibitionists demonstrated considerable political pragmatism and willingness to adapt to circumstances. Congress delegated the licensing power to the Philippine Commission authorities, a body far more impervious to direct missionary lobbying than was Congress. Beginning in 1901 there was no focal point in Washington to which the petitioning could be applied in order to change the law to one of prohibition. (The moral lobbyists had tried to tack an anti-saloon measure onto the army bill in 1901 but were defeated.)[65] The commission's administration was composed of civil servants, albeit political appointments at the higher echelons, like Taft, who had presidential aspirations back home. Administrators were also typically infused with a conservative view of empire in which British and other European imperial precedents on the regulation of drugs were taken seriously and where pragmatic dealing with local political elites was practiced.[66] Commissioners and their staffs knew that their action impinged directly upon the Filipino people at a time when insurrection was present and did not share the conviction that drink was a great danger to their colonial charges. One key Philippine Commission official, William Cameron Forbes, served as governor-general (1909–13) after four years as secretary of commerce and police, where regulation of saloons was his responsibility. Forbes believed "blue laws" to be draconian; his diaries contain numerous references to his own personal love of good times, including polo, drinking, and dining. He clashed repeatedly with Mercer Johnston, an aide to the Episcopal bishop and a prominent member of the Evangelical Union, over alcohol licenses for carnivals.[67] Yet even if the Philippine Commission had taken a view more favorable to the prohibitionists than it did, administrators in Washington would still have been obstructionist. Root and Roosevelt were not teetotalers; both were supporters of conservative regulation, not radical measures such as prohibition, and Root had openly opposed the anti-canteen law until overridden by Congress.[68]

Even among the temperance groups, the rhetoric on the dangers of alcohol to the Filipino people wore thin on their own supporters and within the leadership of the reform coalition. For the Presbyterian Rev. Arthur Brown, the "native" wine shops had been "numerous" before 1898 but sold little alcohol. The Filipino "always dilutes" his "vino," Brown claimed, whereas American soldiers were commonly caught "gulping down whole glasses of the raw liquor."[69] Prohibition was no longer a high priority in 1903 when Brown wrote, and it continued to be downplayed thereafter. The Evangelical Union agreed to withdraw its opposition to the licensing of intoxicants at the Manila carnival, preferring instead to concentrate on what they regarded as the greater evil of cockfighting.[70] Not only did reformers and missionaries concede the limited nature of the alcohol problem, but also the balance of petitioning had swung sharply away from alcohol after 1902 because Crafts and his allies had other campaigns on their minds. The first was the lobbying to prevent the army in the Philippines from licensing prostitution, an issue that elicited a vast array of complaints.[71]

The anti-prostitution crusade followed a similar pattern to that of the treatment of drinking. In both cases the objection was to state regulation's encouragement of sinful practices. In both cases colonial officials tolerated local customs. In both cases, too, the reformers campaigned to get (largely) symbolic concessions that divorced the American state from the "vices" that they identified. The coalition of missionaries and their representatives in Washington mobilized against each perceived "evil" through mass petitioning and claimed to represent millions. Their electoral intimidation moved government policy to varying degrees and for motives that differed between administrators and reform lobbyists. But both reformers and the government could by their action portray the American approach to the regulation of morals as superior to that of other empires. That is, the United States could, if cleansed of state-sanctioned "vice," proclaim itself as a moral empire.

The broad outline of the facts of prostitution and American soldiers at war quickly became known. Journalists covering the Spanish-American conflict produced reports from the field that camp followers accompanied the armies in Cuba, Puerto Rico, and the Philippines.[72] In the Philippines the prevalence of widespread prostitution was a particular cause of concern because of the large numbers of occupying troops, the drawn-out nature of the military conflict, and the highly controversial attempts to deal with the problem through regulation. The racial mixing of white soldiers with Filipino women heightened issues of physical and moral contagion. It was assumed that these women would carry disease and infect soldiers and sailors alike.[73] Manila came to be known to critics as a "Hell upon Earth," a Sodom and Gomorrah that was "a blot on our fair country" that "for the good of both branches of the Service" should be "eradicated."[74] Venereal infection rates rose as a result of the overseas military postings from 1898 and quickly raised alarm among doctors.[75] To this fear of sexual contagion was added the inflow of Asian women, especially Japanese, who represented the twin themes of immoral camp follower and racial contagion through "oriental standards of morality."[76] Yet the objection was not simply racial, since European and American women had also flocked to the colony in search of trade from the troops.

The army's answer was not eradication of the world's oldest profession, but closer regulation to improve military health. Army commanders introduced inspection of prostitutes for venereal infection soon after the arrival of the occupation forces. Suspected prostitutes were to be examined weekly and issued certificates of clean health. Details would be kept in inspection books. If infected, women were consigned to quarantine in a specially designated hospital.[77] Japanese and other foreigners found to be prostitutes could be deported.[78] For the administration a brothel was nothing other than a prudent innovation to protect American troops from the locals, but it also represented an accommodation with the preexisting social situation. Even as regulation was considered a novel operation for the American army, it was not novel for the Philippines. In fact regulation was to a considerable degree an extension of the system operating before the Americans arrived. The army had tried to reinstitute a type of regulatory regime already adopted by the Spanish colonial authorities. It drew on the Spanish regime's system of funding by compulsory fees and "penalties paid by the prostitutes themselves."[79] Though the need for efficiency to prosecute the war was a high priority, the army also stressed that Progressive-style health regulation of the island's sexual economy would simultaneously benefit the American public. Without strict regulation, contamination would spread to the American mainland. "[V]enereal disease carried to innocent women and children in the United States, as it certainly would be," represented additional "evil consequences which would follow unregulated prostitution here," stated Major Charles Lynch.[80] The theme of contagion was spurred also by the difficulty of defining what a prostitute was. The lines were blurred between professional whores and women who joined as casuals to get cash on the side and "help out" friends or relatives when too many soldiers visited; thus policing boundaries became difficult. All the more reason to institute a red-light district with a clearly demarcated line to separate the clean from the unclean, and to do so with the power of government.[81]

These were not the arguments of the reformers. The latter opposed the establishment and maintenance of any system of regulation and linked their condemnation to a moral indictment of all kinds of vice, including drinking, gambling, and cockfighting. It was not specific to prostitution. Unlike the army's approach and that of the colonial state more generally, it did not emphasize racial contamination of white society, except insofar as the presence of European prostitutes put a blot upon Christian civilization.[82] When moral reformers made reference to the large numbers of Japanese, Chinese, and Filipina sex workers, they sometimes objected to the categorization of prostitution as white slavery. For Wilbur Crafts, the evil was as much "brown" slavery as white, because all women were oppressed by the system.[83] It was the symbolic aspects of regulation that most concerned reformers, the association of the American regime with a tainted system that raised shrill alarm. The campaign was a part of the larger attempt to make American expansion abroad more moral.

How did the practice of regulation become known in the mainland? When politically well-connected soldiers such as former Kansas lawyer Major William Bishop returned home, they told stories of life in the islands and reported to congressmen and newspaper editors.[84] Enlisted soldiers and officers from a strong Christian background who were shocked at the regulation system also informed their ministers of religion, who in turn raised concerns with administration officials. As a result of the evidence filtering through to the mainland, the Christian coalition quickly gleaned useful documentation. But word of mouth from the soldiers was not the only source of evidence. The troop ships that carried soldiers also carried newspapers, touring clergyman, and investigative reporters to and fro.[85] With the occupation there came, too, the beginnings of an American civilian community in the Philippines. These included missionaries, especially the Methodists led by Homer Stuntz, but also the clergy of the New York Protestant Episcopal Church, which organized a missionary diocese in 1901.[86] Then there were the family members that sometimes followed the army. The WCTU sent Carrie Faxon of Bay City, Michigan, whose sister Cornelia Moots was already in the Philippines, to work with the Woman's Foreign Missionary Society of the Methodist Church. Moots had gone to be closer to where her adopted soldier son had died of disease, and Faxon had strong sisterly reasons to join her,[87] but she took on the task of investigating the allegations against the Philippine Commission's policies and was given the brief of promoting "social purity" among the troops.[88] These and other people sent back information. Although designed as a missionary cooperative organization, the Manila Evangelical Union also campaigned to raise the moral tone of the American community. American businessmen were sometimes associated with the proliferation of saloons, but others such as the editor of the *Manila American* sided with the missionaries.[89] With information from such sources, the righteous anger of mainland reformers was sure to be aroused.

The most important stimulus for the anti-prostitution case came from the visit of the colorful Pussyfoot Johnson when he investigated the alcohol issue in 1900. As Johnson's sponsorship indicated, prostitution could not be divorced from the reformers' concern about alcohol and from the organizational mechanisms of the temperance movement; reformers could reason that alcohol fueled sexual desire and provided places (saloons) where prostitutes met clients. Yet the original mission was overshadowed by the evidence of sexual license that Johnson uncovered. His visit to Manila not only documented the reality of prostitution but also highlighted the inspection of prostitutes paying four pesos a week for the privilege of working. "With the advent of the American troops there came abandoned women from every corner of the earth," Johnson reported. He found about two hundred licensed houses in the city, with examinations of sex workers conducted under the military government's Department of Municipal Inspection. Six hundred prostitutes, including "the swarms of loose women who have rooms and who prowl about the streets," were directly under military control, representing what Johnson derisively called "American civilization." If unwell, women were forcibly confined to the San Lazaro Hospital and, when released, could be arrested again if they did not take prescribed treatments. Johnson found most houses of prostitution "decorated with American flags inside and out" to serve notice of their licensed status and to attract American troops. His article in the *New Voice* carried pictures of houses of ill repute and a facsimile of regulation book entries signed by a government physician. The impact on the army was a subject that Johnson also closely noted, since one in six illnesses among the troops treated in the Manila military hospital was said to stem from venereal disease. Nevertheless, Johnson did not forget the lessons of the simultaneous campaign going on to quash the canteens and "American" saloons. To open a brothel, a proprietor had to get a wine and beer license; drink and sex appeared to go together. Johnson also echoed the campaign to protect the native races: "The natives, who had never before seen a house of ill-fame, are much interested in the concern, but watch their own girls with unusual vigilance. They are afraid that they may become 'civilized' by the Americans."[90]

Johnson's exposé stirred responses from anti-imperialists, suffragists, and social purity workers, but these groups were not distinct; they shared information, membership, and arguments. They all provided foot soldiers to conduct a campaign ultimately channeled by Wilbur Crafts and the International Reform Bureau. Anti-imperialist sentiment was present in these arguments across a wide spectrum of church people and reform groups. All agreed that licensed prostitution was another indictment of the U.S. occupation, but some singled out prostitution as the ultimate confirmation of the evils of empire. Boston-based woman's suffrage supporter Henry Blackwell noted: "To this department of moral degradation has the curse of militarism already degraded our government. A system outgrown in England and rejected in America is to-day in force in the Philippines."[91] *The Crowning Infamy of Imperialism* published by the anti-imperialist American League of Philadelphia proclaimed "a record of national dishonor" and sarcastically scorned "the civilization we have introduced." Here was a shameful story of national disgrace evidenced in the very "sentinels posted on guard to keep inmates prisoners."[92] This moral anti-imperialism tinged other critiques, including those of suffragists and the social purity reformers of the Christian coalition such as the redoubtable Mary A. Livermore, the Massachusetts WCTU official, suffragist, and peace campaigner. In her "Remarks at the Annual Meeting of the New England Anti-Imperialist League," Livermore charged that the nation had "gone astray in the principles of the Republic." By the acquisition of colonies the United States was no longer an exception in the world. She denounced "the delusion we have all been living"—of America as the "Messiah of the race."[93]

Social purity activists had a keenly developed sense of the dangers of empire from their contacts within Anglo-American reform networks. The American agitation against licensed brothels in St. Louis and attempted licensing elsewhere in the 1870s had spurred and then been stimulated by the visit of Englishmen Henry J. Wilson and W. P. Gledstone in 1876. American "abolitionists" (favoring the abolition of the state regulation of vice) were well schooled in the "evils" of regulation. They were aware of licensed prostitution in the British army in India and determined to keep it out of the U.S. Army. Taking their cue from the British battles of Josephine Butler, these abolitionists regarded medical inspection as discriminatory against women.[94] This line of thought was attractive to activists such as Blackwell, the renowned editor of the Boston-based *Woman's Journal*, who sent clippings of Johnson's work to Secretary of the Navy Long, charging the War Department with "fostering social vice." Blackwell's views could not be easily dismissed as he was, Long told Elihu Root, "a very reputable man" and "a life long Republican."[95] Blackwell urged women to make the agitation part of the 1900 elections. With a more "elaborate system of regulated vice" postponed until after the November poll for fear of losing votes, the time to act was "while the Presidential election impends." Blackwell called on women "of all religious, reformatory, and social organizations" to "utter an effective protest" and petition McKinley.[96] Yet since women could only vote in a handful of states, a parallel conclusion was to use the "depth of moral degradation" as a "striking object lesson" of the need for universal female suffrage.[97] Blackwell, his daughter Alice Stone Blackwell, and Mary Livermore were not the only suffragists to take up these arguments. The North American Woman Suffrage Association issued a parallel complaint on behalf of all American women at its 1900 convention in Rochester, New York.[98]

Despite opposition from apparently disparate groups with different agendas, the major source of political protest came from the WCTU and the evangelical churches. The form of their petitions and the issues were remarkably similar to those for the canteen. Arguments centered on how alcohol and sex acted as reinforcing evils and on the imperative of separating the state from vice, but there was one difference. More than in the case of the canteen, petitioners were likely to be women because this was a feminist issue, registered not only among suffrage organizations per se but also in the WCTU. Though the aggregate numbers of petitions was less than for the canteen, the social purity campaign came strategically after the anti-canteen victories and built on that issue's momentum and the electoral fear it created. The Roosevelt administration soon sensed the pattern of lobbying. As Bureau of Insular Affairs chief Clarence Edwards later put it, Crafts "had so much to do with drawing out all legislation against the canteen" that his machinations could be detected behind other moral agitations. Roosevelt was quick to forestall any further uproar by making concessions.[99]

The anti-prostitution campaign paid scant attention to the fact that Filipina prostitution preceded the American invasion. To recognize this point would have been to downplay the theme, derived from the "native races" discourse, that Filipinos were being ruthlessly transformed by the evils of Western civilization. Instead, the reformers drew on their experience of prostitution reform in Britain and the British Empire. Yet reformers were hardly the sole source of this comparison. In 1901 the military governor, General Arthur McArthur, stated that critics had "very imperfect information of general conditions in the Orient." He justified regulation with reference to how "in Asia unusually strong measures have been taken to protect the English speaking soldier from the results of temptations which confront him." It was not simply abolitionists who raised a false parallel suggesting the system had been copied from India. It was the army itself that stressed the connection. Critics, opined McArthur, did not understand the "Orient" and its problems, problems the British had already faced. Reformers in the mainland United States had "less direct responsibility" than "that felt by the Army officers." McArthur suggested that critics visit other Asiatic ports where they would realize by comparative study just how much the American army in the Philippines was "a civilizing agent."[100] Nevertheless, the government took conciliatory action to appease the moral lobby. In response to rebukes from Johnson, Blackwell, and others, the Philippine Commission instituted military order No. 101 of May 21, 1901, introducing regular inspections of the soldiers to remove the element of sexual inequality involved.[101] But the attempt was ham-fisted because soldiers were not issued with certificates of compliance, and the admission that regulation was routine and justifiable merely stirred reformers and missionaries to further indignation.

References to British Empire experience touched off a deep surge of concern because the WCTU had already confronted this issue just a few years earlier.[102] The World's WCTU had become embroiled controversially in the case of the British army in India, when the WCTU's combative round-the-world missionaries Kate Bushnell and Elizabeth Wheeler Andrew had in 1897 castigated World's WCTU president, Lady Isabel

Somerset. The target of their ire had endorsed the system sanctioning licensed prostitution in brothels established for the benefit of the British army in the Indian military cantonments. Frances Willard initially supported her friend Somerset, thus causing huge dissension within the American WCTU and abroad, where Josephine Butler threw her considerable moral weight behind efforts to unseat Somerset and denounce Willard. Somerset was eventually forced at the 1897 World's WCTU convention to repudiate her own stance, an action interpreted by the abolitionist forces as a triumph over state regulation. As this embarrassing episode had concluded just prior to the acquisition of the Philippines, the WCTU was especially concerned that the American version of empire should not be morally stained, as was the British Raj. The WCTU stressed the need to remove the sanction of vice from the American flag—to make it, as the WCTU missionary Katharine Stevenson later observed, "stand in the Far East as the symbol of righteousness."[103]

As in the canteen issue, another huge flow of petitions poured forth. The WCTU's Margaret Ellis led the campaign, joined by Wilbur Crafts. Ellis and Crafts lobbied even Theodore Roosevelt himself, and Ellis was particularly effective.[104] Reflecting women's emancipation and the social purity heritage in about equal degrees, she argued against "segregation" of the women and examination on "suspicion." Though prepared to call prostitutes "vicious women," she held it "a violation of justice to apply" to them "compulsory medical measures which are not applied to vicious men."[105] Early in 1902 she obtained an official army book of medical inspection documenting the existence of a child prostitute and her examination by army doctors. Ellis circulated this information among the missionary communities at home and abroad, and used it to great effect in embarrassing the military. She then threatened electoral reprisals by getting her supporters to lobby their fathers, husbands, and brothers to vote against the Republican Party. Secretary of War Root, other officials, and ten departmental clerks were inundated with hostile letters and personal callers. President Roosevelt also felt the brunt of the constant stream of protests and intervened to reverse policy, ordering Root to ban formal inspections. After February 1902, no fees could be charged for medical examinations to determine the existence of a sexually transmitted disease.[106] Roosevelt combined this edict with issuance of an order that borrowed from British regulations. He called on officers to encourage personal morality and to provide information on clean living for the troops. This action was especially targeted at neutralizing temperance opposition. Under Circular No. 10, Root directed the army to "control the diseases due to immorality" and noted that "Excessive indulgence in strong drink is absolutely certain to ruin any man, physically and morally." Regimental commanders were instructed to point out these dangers and to lead by example. This was music to the ears of the WCTU, because it put the state on the side of the promotion of morality, not "vice."[107]

As in the issue of the canteen, the impact of the lobby on medical practice was only partially effective. Resistance to any change from Washington came from army doctors who dragged their heels in implementing the new policy. Lt. Col. Louis M. Maus, chief surgeon for the 2nd Division, Eighth Corps, did not discontinue issuing certificates of inspection to prostitutes for more than six months after the order to rescind was given, but the reformers' continued vigilance gradually forced higher levels of formal compliance.[108] In addition, neither reformers nor the government was able to stop the selling of sex by Filipinos and others. "Resistance" to U.S. colonialism consisted not only in well-recognized armed conflict but also in Filipinos' maintenance of social practices that predated the American occupation. By his later complaints, Crafts himself conceded the continued existence of "sex slavery" in the Philippines in the years before World War I. On a trip to Iloilo in 1907, he observed Japanese prostitutes onboard ship and was told that women were once again being imported routinely. The law prohibiting immigration of women of immoral character was not faithfully enforced by customs officers in the way it was allegedly being done by the Immigration Bureau in the United States.[109]

On a more technical but equally important level, the new procedures did not stop de facto inspection, as Ellis well understood. The keeping of records of inspection ceased, but informal medical surveillance continued, and lists of known prostitutes were kept. In 1908, a former Bureau of Health official reported that, if diseased, a woman must still be subjected to medical care, but the place for treatment "is not stated." She had to be pronounced cured by the medical officer of the district even if treated privately. The government's facility where lockups of prostitutes occurred had been turned over in 1906 to the private Mercy Hospital, but under Catholic control it continued to receive the government's clients and was "devoted" to such cases. Even though the WCTU had opposed geographic segregation of prostitutes between 1901 and 1902, a red-light district had effectively been established at Sampaloc. Police made sure that houses of prostitution were not allowed outside a prescribed area; they reported on the numbers of inmates and on the attempted evasion of treatment. Meanwhile the Sisters of Paul de Chartres at Mercy Hospital worked to divert the patients into "better channels," in what amounted to conventional Victorian "rescue" work for "fallen" women.[110]

Yet to focus on moral reform's limited impact in the Philippines would be to miss a key point. Along with its allies, the WCTU was victorious in preventing the stain of legalized prostitution upon the American flag; the *Union Signal* boasted that "no other philanthropic society in the world" had an organization able to make such an impact; and members could begin to trumpet the superiority of the American type of empire amid the growing competition among Europeans for supremacy in East Asia, where regulation of prostitution was still common.[111] A policy of official promotion of temperance reform and discouragement of immorality had been adopted by the president and the Department of War through Circular No. 10. Moreover, reformers' anti-prostitution campaigns undermined any possibility that Philippine-style sexual regulation would become a model for the American mainland.[112]

After 1902, it was difficult to keep the political controversy at white heat. With the insurrectionary war declared over and increasingly out of newspaper headlines, social purity "activism" seemed to "decline."[113] Yet the decline occurred mostly because reformers had gained concessions that put them in alliance with the state and made it harder, though not impossible, for them to criticize the subterfuges adopted. The WCTU under Ellis's lobbying was the architect of this compromise that gave important symbolic concessions to the moral coalition and made social purity the stated government policy for the army. Ellis was a Republican and anxious to take advantage of an alliance with Root. It was she who suggested that outlawing inspections should be matched by adopting the alternative model of Lord Wolseley's order as commander of the British army, in his directions to his own officers in April 1898. It was she who offered in return that the WCTU would broadcast the administration's moral credentials. Margaret's husband and coworker for reform, John T. Ellis, called on Root, who summed up Ellis's advice: "many of your better informed members now realized and appreciated that much information from prejudiced and inspired sources had gone abroad" and you are "today only anxious to gain the facts." Like her husband, Margaret Ellis had professed to be "glad to make public the 'favorable showing'" Root had given "regarding the whole 'Philippines business.'"[114] She printed and distributed hundreds of the circulars illustrating the new moral policy of discouraging sexual activity and promoting positive, wholesome recreation for soldiers. Moreover, she was "desirous that the people [all] over the country shall be informed as to the nature of this circular."[115] This was a similar denouement to the tacit compromise in the alcohol case, where the government refused to adopt full prohibition and both Homer Stuntz and Crafts had supported the reform/government cooperative position in return for concessions. This denouement came close at times to Crafts's objective. He had in his 1895 Princeton Theological Seminary lectures envisioned a Christian state in which godly citizenship and "Patriotic studies" cleansed the government of evil. Such a state was to be based on a non-doctrinal but evangelical Protestant religion. It was to be a relationship in which reformers acted in coalition with the government through the work of a "Christian lobbyist."[116] The outcome of each agitation—liquor and prostitution—was mutually reinforcing on this point.

Although the reformers had been appeased, this was not the major reason for the shift away from agitation on the purity question. After all, Crafts was still prepared to complain in subsequent years against brothels and any violation of the tacit agreement with the government. Rather, in 1903 a new danger to the evangelical view of a moral empire emerged. The Philippine Commission's plans for the sale of opium paralleled the social purity question because licensing was the commission's answer to the opium "problem." Licensing would deal better with the reality of "Oriental" practices through progressive but gradualist policies. These would be informed not by utopian moral reform but by practical experience. Here reformers and missionaries discovered what they believed to be a unsurpassed threat to the Philippines' moral progress and the reputation of the colonial state. Uniformly, missionaries and their supporters in the United States argued that the moral obtuseness of the Philippine Commission made opium the cause célèbre. Protestant Christian agitation not only shifted to this new issue; it moved to a new dimension wherein reformers could gain greater influence in the United States and across the region.

Chapter 7

OPIUM AND THE FASHIONING OF

THE AMERICAN MORAL EMPIRE

IN JUNE 1903, William Dix of Philadelphia wrote Secretary of War Elihu Root an indignant letter. An item on American policy in the Philippines published in the *Philadelphia Ledger* enraged him: "If I were a pesky anti-imperialist I would say—thus do the superior swiftly fall to the level of the inferior." Dix hoped that a righteous people such as the Americans would be spared "the obloquy of being no better than the perfidious British." He urged Root to "Spare us that disgrace under our glorious flag."[1] The source of his anger was not inspection of prostitutes nor the supply of drink to soldiers but U.S. policy on opium in the Philippines. Dix was not alone. Most moral reformers and missionaries now believed opium to be a more serious problem for the Filipinos than either alcohol or the "social evil."

From the outset, American drug policy in the Philippines was caught in a series of contradictions that exposed it to the wrath of evangelicals. Most Americans frowned on opium smoking, but opium importation to the U.S. mainland was not illegal under federal law. The American administration in the Philippines, first the army, then the Philippine Commission beginning in 1901, wished to maintain revenues and knew that opium was an excellent and reliable source, if taxed. The commission and the army also knew that outlawing opium would once again mean interfering with local customs at a time when the administration was concentrating on the very real rebellion that threatened the American hold on the territory and that produced immense controversy at home. Moral scruples over opium might fuel further unrest. Yet U.S. administrations did not want to spread the opium habit. At the takeover in 1898, a high tariff was introduced to restrict opium imports in a system that dovetailed with customs operations on the mainland. Imports to the islands nevertheless increased and smuggling prospered. The experience with enforcement and detection provoked attempts within the Philippine Commission to frame a new policy. Early in 1903 the change came in the commission's move to license the opium trade on a contract system similar to that existing before 1898. It was to this policy that Dix and a legion of other Christian reformers objected in April to June 1903. Ostensibly the new measure was to be one of regulation and restriction in which a contractor paid fees to the colonial government for the privilege of dispensing the drug. It went further than the old Spanish system by allocating only one monopoly importer in a bid to maintain easier surveillance and control, but followed the Spanish in restricting the categories of legal use to the single case of ethnic Chinese. In a major departure, the commission attempted to confront the otherwise unthinkable by proposing that the revenue raised would defray the expenses of "young Filipinos to be educated in American schools."[2] Drug money would pay higher salaries to Filipino teachers, schools would be built, and other useful policies implemented. Bureau of Insular Affairs chief Clarence Edwards simply could not understand the objections that this scheme faced. To this attempted sop, moral reformers responded with furious opposition. Evangelicals attacked any use of opium revenues, even if it were for good purposes. Good and evil could not mix, especially not in American government policy.

Missionaries and their supporters in the United States mobilized through the already battle-hardened ranks of the evangelical coalition of reformers. By deploying the coalition's transnational networks against American policy, reformers achieved a substantial victory, one with far-reaching consequences. Yet in the treatment of the opium issue, it was not simply a moral coalition triumphing over a passive government. The American government adapted to the new moral lobby and used drug reform as an instrument in regional and ultimately global policy. Collusion between reformers and government began to shape American diplomacy in distinctive ways. The impacts ended neither in the Philippines nor in East Asia; rather, the prohibition of opium use would require dramatic changes in federal law regarding the import to and use of opium in the United States. The colonial empire fed into domestic politics.

The arguments drew on objections to an immoral government similar to those that pervaded the anti-prostitution and anti-canteen campaigns. When reformers initially opposed any idea of high license or government monopoly as a way of regulating the drug trade, they followed lines familiar to the anti-drink cause. The difference was that reformers split over just how serious the evils of alcohol were if used in moderation, while for opium they regarded any use as inherently addictive. Greater similarities could be found in the campaign on prostitution. Oriental customs could not be overcome, officials had argued in both cases; instead, both prostitution and opium must be tolerated but controlled. Just as prostitution control rested for the government on military and administrative necessities, so too opium policy. One could not have, for example, decent Chinese labor to provide logistical support for the troops outside Manila without supplying an opium ration to the workers. This was one of the first lessons learned by Clarence Edwards, a strong supporter of the opium policy. Edwards related his own experience as chief of staff to General Henry Ware Lawton, when the army marched north from Manila in 1899. The regiment took three hundred Chinese laborers with them, who promptly developed withdrawal symptoms without their drug of choice. On Lawton's orders, a representative of the group was given a pass to go back and buy more smoking opium from Manila. This was the first time Lawton had heard of opium used as an army ration. Edwards drew the conclusion for Bureau of Insular Affairs policy that opium use in the islands was "a condition and not a theory, and it must be worked out practically with one end in view" for "the good of the people of the Philippine Islands."[3] Impractical moral schemes hatched far away should not be allowed to interfere.

The government claimed with some justification that opium was tolerated in other colonial regimes, but this was precisely what worried people such as Dix. Licensing opium challenged the whole basis of what missionaries and reformers saw as the purpose of American colonialism, that is, moral uplift and an example to other imperial powers. The great seriousness with which the issue was regarded across the evangelical networks cannot be understood without grasping the transnational nature of the missionary project. Missionaries and their allies at home did not simply seek to civilize and evangelize Filipinos. Their mission went far beyond the borders of the U.S. formal empire. Opium smoking sanctioned in the most prominent colony, the Philippines, would undermine the efforts of American evangelicals in their informal moral empire being established in India, China, Southeast Asia, and the Pacific Islands.

The American response to the opium problem was a transnational one. Opposition to U.S. policy did not start in the Philippines itself; American missionaries had already joined their British coworkers in an agitation against opium in China. Dr. Hampden Coit DuBose, a South Carolina native and long-term Presbyterian missionary in Suzhou, China, had organized the Anti-Opium League in 1896.[4] Though less important than reformers would have liked in the eventual renunciation of use by the Imperial Chinese government,[5] the league's agitation was an important factor in raising consciousness of the issue within the United States, in fostering cooperation between American and British missionaries, and in lobbying with missionaries and American residents in Manila. The league published *Opinions of over 100 Physicians on the Use of Opium in China* (1899), a widely distributed work with fifty-eight American missionary contributors. Dr. William H. Park, an American medical missionary, surgeon at Suzhou Hospital, and consultant to the Imperial Maritime Customs, collated the testimony. It emphasized the drug's addictive properties that went far beyond those attributed to alcohol and made it a greater scourge. The general consensus among reformers that opium was even more dangerous in the "Orient" than alcohol allowed very broad support for an anti-opium campaign to develop. It could easily encompass people like Bishop Charles Brent, who believed that alcohol was not inherently evil provided it was used in moderation but that no moderate use could be made of opium.[6]

Underpinning this assessment was the American identification of opium as a serious problem in the culturally distinct Chinese immigrant communities. Opium was used medicinally by American women and present in many patent medicines, but this was not the original source of American anxieties. Americans' images of opium users were of Chinese "celestials," with a foul-smelling subculture of opium smoking. In Chinese society opium was used recreationally during sexual intercourse, and white Americans found this practice repellent. Newspaper reporters and police described opium dens in the United States inhabited by "semi-naked" men and women lying about in variously compromised states of semi-consciousness. By the turn of the twentieth century, the opium-smoking habit appeared to be both growing and spreading across racial and class lines, with young, white, middle-class men and women starting to fall victim to recreational opium use. In the late nineteenth century the use of opium measured in imports to the mainland rose sharply. High tariffs on the drug had not worked, and considerable smuggling occurred whenever the tariff was raised. To ensure the protection of Americans, opium smoking needed to be interdicted abroad, with the source of supply cut off, much as with cocaine from Colombia one hundred years later. Thus there were domestic American reasons for supporting opium prohibition.[7]

Yet foreign policy issues and concerns relating to the new American colonialism also intruded. Across the entire region of the Far East, missionaries made the issue partly a symbolic one that defined their moral outlook and separated them from the sinful, especially from Europeans who supplied opium under coercive colonial or quasi-colonial regimes. From the experience of China, missionaries gauged the limitations that opium placed on Christian conversion when Chinese associated Christianity with such a debilitating practice.[8] Esther Jerman Baldwin, who had first gone to China with her Methodist missionary husband in 1862, declared, "We missionaries find this opium traffic a more deadly obstacle to the uplifting of the people than all their idolatry and superstition." Chinese, she argued, equated foreigners with Christianity "just as they represent heathenism to us."[9] In turn, American missionaries argued, China could not be modernized and made a place receptive to Western commerce without dealing with the scourge. The Open Door policy needed opium reform as its necessary condition. Nor could opium smoking in the Philippines be prevented without dealing with the problem in China. The trading links with Hong Kong were too close; Chinese business families smuggling or legally importing opium had connections with those in the Philippines. It was DuBose who wrote in 1899 the letter that started the American agitation by pointing out that this highly addictive drug already had a hold upon the Chinese population of the Philippines. A "great responsibility" was "placed upon the Government" in the "sale of this poison to a semi-civilized people," DuBose concluded. Here the white man's burden and the concept of "protection of native races" appeared as prominent themes.[10]

In response to the government's policy, Protestant missionaries associated with the Manila Evangelical Union rose in righteous anger. Led by Homer Stuntz, they petitioned the president and the secretary of war in May 1903, but they did not do so alone. As in the other moral issues of the canteen and prostitution, soldiers themselves sent home information on opium's use and sometimes wrote congressmen when they returned.[11] In coordinating the flood of protests, it was not the missionaries but the lobbyists in Washington and their legions of followers who were decisive. A petitioning campaign that rivaled the anti-canteen drive required central organization. Wilbur Crafts sent out his trademark circulars and petition forms across the nation and channeled the thousands of responses to the president. Most of the petitions were domestic and came from businessmen, church groups, women's club groups, Christian Endeavor chapters, the WCTU, and like-minded individuals, not the Manila Evangelical Union.[12]

That did not mean that missionaries were unimportant, but their deployment was as exhibits for the arguments. In the knowledge that their firsthand experience gave them greater persuasive power with politicians, Crafts organized missionaries to call on President Roosevelt and Secretary Root. An important witness was James Mills Thoburn of Ohio, the Methodist who had served in India for forty years and who had become Bishop of India and the Straits Settlements in 1888. Crafts arranged for him to meet Root on July 9, 1903, where, along with Crafts, he briefed the secretary of war on the "practical workings of opium revenue laws all over Asia and the great superiority of Japan's wise and effective prohibition of all sales except in medical prescriptions." Thoburn brought testimony of the system's weakness in India and of the similarities between those arrangements, the British Straits Settlements system (for Singapore, Penang, and Malacca), and that being proposed in the Philippines. Thoburn denied that the problem could be quarantined to the Chinese alone and reported the many Indians addicted in Calcutta as evidence that opium respected no racial boundaries.[13]

In response to the flood of petitions and personal visits, the government put the proposed contract system on hold. After reading two letters from Crafts, Roosevelt demanded of Root: "What is this proposition, to grant a monopoly for opium selling in the Philippines," and called for a full report.[14] Yet Root himself had already moved to take evasive action against the onslaught of petitioners. Prior to meeting Thoburn, the secretary of war telegrammed Governor-General Taft to take "no course which either in substance or appearance will promote such traffic. Feeling in this country has always been strong against England's course in China and will condemn any regulation which seems to sanction the traffic rather than to plainly reduce it."[15] Yet the impact of Thoburn and the lobbying by Crafts in the following month was clear. On July 10, 1903, the day after receiving the submission from Thoburn and Crafts, Root wrote Taft that "the more I study the opium question the more reluctant I become to have your government sell opium concessions." These concessionaries would inevitably try to increase sales "as it has been [shown] in India; the large profit which the government expects to make would insensibly but inevitably throw it into the attitude of fostering the business." This would be "contrary to the declared and established" American practice. Root inclined toward supporting prohibition, in which there "would be some smuggling, but that would not spread the habit like an active authorized opium trade under whatever limitations."[16] In all these arguments, Root echoed Crafts and his fellow lobbyists.

The petitioners mobilized by the International Reform Bureau did not dwell on the evils of opium, which were left to the missionaries' firsthand testimony, but on the impact of the policy on the United States and its new colonial regime. They revealed a very broad frame of reference about American global aspirations and followed the precedents of the native races campaign, as well as deeper assumptions of the Christian humanitarianism of the 1890s. J. W. Magruder, writing on behalf of the Methodist Episcopal Church of Portland, Maine, referred to the Senate resolution of June 4, 1901, on the native races question and highlighted its extension to opium "of the principle, that native races should be protected against the destructive traffic in intoxicants." The humanitarian principle was evident in the words of the prominent Presbyterian John Converse, who argued for a policy consistent with the "Christian and humane character of this nation." The WCTU was more conciliatory toward the government but made thinly veiled threats of electoral reprisals should the opium policy remain unchanged. Though anti-imperialist arguments surfaced, petitioners professed a desire to improve the position of the American state by reconciling Filipinos to American control. To do this, it was argued, the discontents that opium created in terms of economics and ethnic division must be removed. According to Elisha Kane, a businessman from Mt. Jewett, Pennsylvania, American military policy did nothing more than provoke the "rebelliousness of the Filipino" and his "disgust and hatred of the vicious and brutal among our Americans." But, Kane reasoned, opium would further inflame community tensions. Opium smoking could not be limited to Chinese. It was "impracticable to legalize vicious indulgence and then attempt to keep it within bounds." Inevitably "race hatreds" would be "aroused and stimulated by the acts of the vicious and degenerate" among the Chinese and Filipinos. These race hatreds would rebound against the regime and make the Philippines ungovernable.[17]

The reformers did not use the United States as an example of how to control opium but rather engaged in comparative colonialism. They argued that American policy was below the standards of other colonial powers in some cases and imitative of the worst ones. These comparisons exploited the missionaries' sense of a rising "new" Asia, with its syncretic experimentation, its nationalism, and its restiveness against Western ways, to argue that the United States must seek not to impose on but learn from the "Oriental" world. Crafts and Thoburn stated that American politicians must legislate for Filipinos as "Asiatics." The only place "Asiatics" had had their say was Japan and there the evidence was clear. To Crafts and Thoburn, the Japanese were exhibit A for the correct path of Asians to modernity, since the "superiority of Japan in energy and progress has been attributed in part to Japan's successful prohibition of opium."[18] Crafts depicted Japan as a nation that had adopted the best of both worlds. Later he elaborated on this point: "So should every student traverse all centuries and all countries to gather for himself and his people the best of past and present, of East and West."[19] Though their arguments were framed under the rubric of "native races," reformers moved subtly from the idea of helpless natives to concede a vigorous new nationalism to which the United States must respond if its own status as a great power in East Asia were to be developed.[20]

Even as the native races campaigns were highly paternalistic, the anti-opium campaign subverted simple dichotomies. To be sure, within the United States the anti-opium drive had a racist tone in which the Chinese contagion must be prevented from infecting American bodies, but missionaries were highly supportive of indigenous Chinese efforts to combat opium and followed this through with support for Chinese emigration to the United States and against the expanded Chinese Exclusion Act of 1902. Moreover, by holding Japan up as an example, they argued that race should not determine the pattern of hegemony in East Asia but moral stature. Crafts was far from alone on this point. John Mott expressed similar sentiments and lobbied the government, as did the Federal Council of Churches.[21] Prominent pro-Japanese opinions came from Congregational missionary Sidney Gulick, born in the Marshall Islands of an American missionary family. At the age of twenty-eight in 1888, he became a Protestant missionary educator in Japan after graduating from Yale University, and after 1900 served with Crafts on the International Reform Bureau's board.[22] After twenty-five years in Japan, he returned to the United States in 1913 where he opposed racism and advocated better treatment and understanding of Japanese and Chinese people in California.[23]

Awareness of the International Reform Bureau's tactics in parallel moral reform crusades profoundly shaped the administration's response.[24] Because he knew the history of the recent canteen and anti-prostitution agitations, Roosevelt was in no mood to defend an opium policy unpopular in the United States. In the lead-up to the 1904 presidential election, he would not associate his administration with the sanctioning of opium production and thereby alienate the reform/missionary coalition that now claimed thirty million supporters in the United States.[25] Roosevelt and Root ordered the Philippine Commission to change its stance: it must appoint a committee to follow the advice of the missionaries and travel to China, Japan, Formosa, Saigon, and Singapore to study the various regulatory systems.[26]

While the government accepted the political realities, it was suspicious of the sources from which opposition came. Root and Bureau of Insular Affairs chief Edwards did not agree with the reform coalition on the issue of alcohol and feared that the same sweeping moral judgments might prevent proper consideration of what the Philippine Commission told them was a complicated problem. They regarded Crafts as an extremist and manipulator whose "fine hand" could be detected in every protest.[27] Therefore they chose an investigative committee that would have a moral and religious tone but would serve as a buffer between the government and the utopian aspirations of the reform groups to cleanse government of all sin. For a key committee member, Roosevelt and Root chose Bishop Charles Brent, one of the sternest opponents of opium among the missionaries and yet a man not associated with the evangelical wing of his church. His fellow members were Manila physician Jose Albert and Major E. C. Carter, president of the Board of Health. As an Episcopalian and yet not a low churchman, Brent held views that were more in line with the conservative approach of Root and Taft. The committee studied and absorbed the then current trend among colonial powers in Southeast and East Asia toward introduction of monopoly systems for dispensing opium. Their report closely followed the Japanese system for its colony of Formosa (Taiwan, acquired in 1895) and recommended prohibition after three years except where used for medical purposes; a three-year government opium monopoly in the meantime; registration of addicts for supply by the government on a gradual reduction of dosage over the three years; and a moral and educational campaign on the dangers of drug addiction. In fact, the system proposed was tougher than the one instituted in Formosa, where the reduction of the tightly controlled addict population would be achieved over a much longer period by its dying off over time.[28]

However, the Philippine Commission did not want prohibition at all. It regarded the system as impractical due to smuggling by "ingenious" Chinese, nor did it favor a government monopoly. Opposition to a monopoly came from the Philippines Bureau of Internal Revenue, backed by dissent from within the local community, some of whom were Christians wanting immediate prohibition, while others wanted opium-selling opportunities that would be impossible under a government monopoly. The committee had returned to Manila in February 1904 but, faced with the multiple divisions of opinion, did not report until June.[29] When added to the Republicans' machinations over the presidential election, and Philippine Commission procrastination, nothing was done in Washington for a further six months, with Brent blaming political and administrative intrigue.[30] Now back in the United States as the new secretary of war, Taft prompted the commission for a final recommendation. But Congress preempted the process in March 1905 by passing a law insisting on ultimate prohibition after three years—in line with the sentiment expressed by the moral lobbyists and the investigative report. Congress also required immediate prohibition of opium for Filipinos (allowing continued use for three years only to Chinese in the Philippines) and, except where used by physicians for medical purposes, mandated total prohibition for all subjects in the islands after 1908. Regarding the phase-out period, Congress delegated to the Philippine Commission the right to regulate existing use. Thereby, Taft made a concession to allow the revenue system to adjust. The stopgap system adopted was one of "high licence" for dealers and registration of all adult Chinese "Habitual Users." The latter could get opium but "only on a Physician's Certificate." Addicts' use of the drug would be curbed through gradual reduction of the rations of opium allowed at government dispensaries. With the temporary adoption of high license, the Philippine Commission instituted taxes with the revenue going to treatment for opium addicts. The pressure for action came from Washington through Taft, but it was stimulated by the lobbying of Crafts and his allies, since the evangelical reformers had not been silent while the report was being considered.[31]

The final compromise was accepted with grumbling by the missionaries, who would have preferred immediate prohibition and abhorred any association with high license. As in the attempted abolition of the saloons in the Philippines and the regulation of prostitution, Christian lobbyists had come to an arrangement with the administration in Washington.[32] Crafts told the president that he would support the revised congressional bill as "much better than hitherto proposed" and, indeed, "the best obtainable." He also agreed to "support with public opinion the enactment of the proposed legislation," and he did more still by mediating between the government and the missionaries to get their compliance with this compromise.[33]

There was a quid pro quo for this acquiescence. Crafts obtained a tacit agreement from the government to turn the anti-opium policy into a regional campaign that would set opium prohibition as a goal of U.S. diplomacy. On November 10, 1904, while the decisions were pending on the form of control in the Philippines, Crafts had obtained a second audience for the Native Races Deputation to meet Secretary of State Hay, almost exactly three years after the 1901 meeting on alcohol issues. On this occasion the aim was to get the American government to pressure Britain into releasing China from its obligations to import opium under the treaty of 1858. Sensing the importance of documenting extensive firsthand experience, Crafts arranged for veteran missionaries to speak. Most had more than twenty years of service in China: Esther Baldwin, who, on top of two decades with her husband, Stephen, in Fuzhou, spent a further twenty years as president of the New York branch of the Woman's Foreign Missionary Society of the Methodist Episcopal Church;[34] the Rev. Frank Gamewell, called "the hero of Pekin" from his role in defying the Boxer Rebellion of 1900,[35] who had first arrived in China in 1881; and the Rev. William Ashmore, the Student Volunteer supporter whose fifty-four years of missionary service in China was legendary. The International Reform Bureau, the WCTU, and the major evangelical missionary societies took part, but Crafts made the key presentation. The addresses received a very cordial hearing from Hay, who replied that in order to achieve the aim of international cooperation, the reform lobby should submit petitions reflecting what the Founding Fathers called "a decent respect for the opinion of mankind."[36] In this way, Crafts's petition methods were co-opted for government service.

As part of this agitation, Crafts's job was to engage in his own quasi-diplomatic forays. He wrote to British prime minister Arthur Balfour, calling for joint action between the American and British governments, and coordinated the American campaign with the British Native Races Committee by establishing a "British Council" of the International Reform Bureau in 1906. Crafts then worked along with Margaret and Mary Leitch to attack the production of opium in India. The three argued that because Britain's opium revenue for India was diminishing, it was timely to act before a serious Indian nationalist agitation against British oppression arose. Though the British government responded in bureaucratic style that the American approach would "receive careful consideration," Crafts continued to develop a closer relationship with the British anti-opium movement.[37] He contacted Joseph B. Alexander, secretary of the British Society for Suppression of the Opium Trade, who called Crafts's intervention a "welcome reinforcement."[38] The effort of "no country" was more appreciated, claimed Alexander, but he also feared that nothing would come of this cooperation: "I am afraid your government may feel it a delicate thing to make representations to ours on the subject of the opium trade."[39] Yet Hay "promptly undertook the diplomatic tasks" suggested, Crafts reported.[40]

Crafts spread the tentacles of his own International Reform Bureau in this same period by establishing branches in Canada, Japan, China, and Australia as well as Britain. He arranged for the Rev. Francis Clark of Christian Endeavor, who was on one of his world tours in 1904, to lobby Prime Minister Alfred Deakin to represent the views of the newly federated Australia on the need for the prohibition of opium exports. Clark could easily get a favorable hearing because the issue touched Australian fears of drug-crazed Chinese immigrants posing a "yellow peril" to that new nation.[41] Crafts embarked on his own tour of East Asia and Australasia in 1907, where he lobbied leaders and gathered petitions. Significantly, he went with the encouragement of the State Department, receiving an endorsement from new secretary of state Root. As Crafts departed in late 1906, Root told him, "I am with you and the government is with you" regarding opium in China. "My part is diplomacy, your part is agitation."[42]

Crafts threw himself into petitioning in his own country and used the ideology of the Open Door to further his aims, blending morals and economic foreign policy objectives. This approach followed the China missionaries, who had become by this time a key pillar of the American Open Door policy because they saw the opening of China as a spiritual as well as material process, and one that relied on the free flow of information.[43] This was exactly the position of Crafts and his allies, but the process of lobbying did not always go directly from missionaries to government. Crafts's role in the Open Door agitation was to mobilize the more reluctant constituency of business. In response, the Pittsburgh Chamber of Commerce, the Merchants Association of New York, and the Baltimore and Jacksonville boards of trade petitioned Roosevelt against the opium traffic in China and emphasized that Britain had inflicted this trade upon the Chinese. Businessmen followed Crafts's prompting and told the U.S. government "that the pauperizing of more than one hundred millions [sic] of [China's] people by opium and the antiforeign feeling" (itself "partly caused" by hostility to foreign opium imports) was "one of the largest obstacles to the development of that largest market in the world." The trade and missionary possibilities for the United States in East Asia could be materially enhanced by a vibrant China freed of opium, Crafts's commercial and missionary allies chorused. This argument was completely consistent with official objectives under the Open Door policy and showed how the moral reformers used the opium issue to fashion and support wider American economic foreign policy in the region in ways that legitimized the growth of American world power.[44]

In Crafts's estimate, the International Reform Bureau had moved British opinion. In May 1906, two members of the British Parliament successfully pressed a motion calling for an end to the Anglo-China opium treaty. One of them, the Liberal MP and temperance advocate Dr. V. H. Rutherford, was on Crafts's British Council. Another leading speaker in the debate, Henry J. Wilson, was the "prominent Liberal internationalist and anti-imperialist" who had visited the United States to campaign against legalized prostitution in 1876. Wilson also served on Crafts's British Council.[45] Crafts boasted that he had sent Wilson and his allies materials documenting the reforms in the Philippines.[46] The resolution in the House of Commons reflected in part American lobbying, including that from the chambers of commerce, and John Hay's "outspoken concurrence to the appeal of American missionary and commercial bodies." Crafts also arranged for Sidney Gulick to lecture on the subject across Britain.[47] The American example did have some influence. Secretary of State for India John Morley cited the Philippines Opium Commission report and the fact that "the United States so recognized the use of opium as an evil for which no financial gain could compensate" that the government would not allow its citizens to encourage the business "even passively." Morley hoped the House of Commons would take careful note of this report's recommendation and back the resolution of May 1906 calling on the United Kingdom to bring British involvement in the opium trade "to a speedy close."[48]

To what extent International Reform Bureau correspondence contributed to this debate is less than clear, however. Certainly Crafts's activities should not be seen through his own lens or that of his supporters alone. Morley had stipulated that any action would depend on the Chinese demonstrating a desire to eliminate the traffic. The key consideration was that, by 1906, the Chinese were at last ready to act. As the historian Kathleen Lodwick states, "despite all the energy the missionaries expended, only when the Chinese finally recognized the harm opium did to their people did they take action to suppress it."[49] The achievement of moral reformers was to keep the issue before the public in the metropolitan centers of empire until Chinese nationalists sensed both the possibility of international action and the necessity of internal reform. In 1909 Brent confessed that he was "surprised to find so much vigour" among the Chinese on this point of internal revitalization,[50] but he should not have been. The Philippines Opium Commission report was widely circulated in China by the missionaries; this action had given "a new impetus" to the agitation[51] and became the "immediate cause of the Imperial edict dealing with opium in China," as Brent himself pointed out.[52] Stimulated by this example, the Chinese government had issued its own anti-opium decree of 1906[53] and pushed for concessions from Britain. Under the Anglo-Chinese agreement of 1907, British officials agreed to reduce exports of Indian opium to China annually until they "ceased altogether in 1917." Should the internal Chinese production be "entirely abolished in the meantime," the importation would also be "simultaneously stopped."[54] With imports falling a reputed 80 percent by 1911, the conditions had been set for a definitive Anglo-China Opium Treaty, signed in that year to end the opium trade with India. Whether real reductions could be achieved thereafter remained unclear and the statistical evidence of the traffic's demise was much disputed when domestic producers filled some of the vacuum and opium continued to be imported illegally.[55] China's 1911 revolution further disorganized the grip of the central administration and reversed the reductions in opium poppy production. Archbishop of Canterbury Randall Davidson and Brent were alarmed to discover the *Times* reporting several Chinese provinces were "now aflame with poppy."[56]

Quite apart from the actions of the Chinese themselves, there are other reasons specific to domestic circumstances in the metropolitan countries that limited Crafts's influence. For one thing, the British attitude was shifting because of internal political conditions. The election of a new Liberal government in 1906 under which Morley had served made political circumstances more favorable. Domestic politics in the United States also affected Crafts's lobbying power. His role was bound to diminish once the American opposition to opium had been made official policy. That is, the International Reform Bureau was most useful lobbying the national legislature or international conferences, and marginalized in the arena of intergovernmental diplomacy. As in the canteen issue, policymakers considered Crafts a moralistic gadfly whose interventions were deeply resented because they interfered with the Department of State's own conceptions of American national interests. Alvey Adee, the second assistant secretary of state, had become virtually part of the furniture of the Department of State, so long had he worked there. In 1906 Adee told Root that Crafts and others like him wanted to "butt in" on international agreements and complicated delicate relations with foreign powers.[57] Crafts was important in mobilizing support for the discussions of May 1906 in the House of Commons, but thereafter attention shifted to getting official British agreement. For this, official diplomacy and internal British political circumstances would be more important.

With Roosevelt as president, the government showed an increased interest in the power politics of East Asia but was more concerned with listening to people other than Crafts for advice on opium's international complications. A more effective figure in this process was Brent. The bishop worked through the transnational channels of the Anglican movement by lobbying the archbishops of Canterbury and York, who in turn contacted British politicians to get action.[58] Brent also had vital American political links through Theodore Roosevelt. As early as 1904, Roosevelt developed a friendly relationship that culminated in an attempt to get Brent to give up his Manila mission and become the most important bishop in the United States by taking charge of the national diocese in Washington, D.C., in 1908.[59] All this lay in the future, however, when Brent decided to take advantage of the budding friendship. Believing that the change in Chinese official opinion and the House of Commons resolution of May 1906 offered an excellent opportunity, Brent took a crucial initiative. In July 1906 he wrote the president, "suggesting that in view of the uneasiness which England exhibited touching her method of handling the opium question, it seemed ... worth while to consider the idea of an international commission on the subject." Brent told Roosevelt that such a commission could proceed on the basis of the "manifestly high" position of the United States and that it was the nation's duty to promote international action.[60]

Brent also believed that combined action among the colonial powers and the governments of Asia would enhance, through an international agreement, the prospects for regional peace. In the context of the recently concluded Russo-Japanese War, this statement was fraught with geopolitical significance. If the United States were to supply moral and political leadership in the region, it would need to do more than simply displace the older hegemony of European colonialism. The rising military power of Japan had to be countered morally, economically, and diplomatically. Precisely because Japan had taken a strong stance against opium in its colonies, Americans needed to do the same.[61]

The objectives were thus not merely moral, even from Brent's or Crafts's point of view; they were strategic as well. Brent and Roosevelt wished to use the opium issue to effect regional political change, bringing the "dependencies in the Orient" together in a common goal of colonial uplift. Brent argued that action was "almost our duty" because of the historical record of the nation on the "traffic in opium" in Asia, a position enhanced by the new colonial responsibility "of actually handling the matter" in the Philippines. The president believed that Brent's proposal "would do far-reaching good" and ordered its implementation.[62] He con-

Fig. 11. Bishop Charles Henry Brent. Reproduced from Alexander C. Zabriskie, *Bishop Brent: Crusader for Christian Unity* (Philadelphia: Westminster Press, 1948), frontispiece.

vinced other powers to join with him in holding the Shanghai Opium Commission of 1909. This was a move challenging old-style power politics in the region and heralding their replacement by a new international order led by the United States. China was central to this strategy. When Assistant Secretary of State Robert Bacon gave the commission to Brent as the head of the American delegation, he directed him not only to study the problem of opium from the "foreign and American point of view" but also to give "special attention to practical suggestions for assisting China in her purpose of suppressing the opium evil."[63] Brent needed no such direction. He argued that American intervention was essential to the success of the Chinese reforms against opium addiction. "The sole hope for the Chinese" to overcome the opium scourge as he saw it lay "in concerted action," with diplomatic assistance from the United States.[64]

Related to the interest in China was the issue of the Open Door that missionaries had emphasized.[65] Perhaps Roosevelt hoped to use the meeting to "mollify Chinese resentment" over the treatment of Chinese laborers in the United States that had led to an informal Chinese merchant embargo on American goods in 1905.[66] Yet it is significant that Roosevelt feared the impact of any embargo on American trade. Secretary of State Philander Knox stated at the conclusion of the Shanghai meeting that "the interest of the United States in the opium problem [was] material as well as humanitarian,"[67] and the U.S. chief negotiator Hamilton Wright publicly admitted that it was "not entirely from altruistic motives that the State Department went about this crusade." Rather, "it looked like a good business move, as well as a long stride in the direction of the good of mankind."[68]

More immediate motives were at stake, too. Under "material" interests Knox included the need to consolidate the opium prohibition in the Philippines and protect potential victims of the drug in the United States.[69] The strong connections of Chinese in Manila with those in Hong Kong made it predictable that the United States should move outward from its own decision to ban opium in the Philippines to a regional drive for prohibition. As Alvey Adee emphasized in his directions to consular officials accredited to the governments represented in the Shanghai Opium Commission, the nation's "intimate commercial intercourse with the Orient" and its unrestricted importation of the drug was an American concern. The United States needed international cooperation because the nation was not producing opium but importing it.[70]

An underlying ideological objective, however, was the attempted assertion of an American hegemony in East Asia. That would involve cooperation between the United States and its rivals, but mixed with competition for the ascendant role. The need to maintain a morally superior stance was strongly emphasized by missionaries such as Homer Stuntz, but the ideological objective was taken up in diplomatic maneuvering and public diplomacy as well.[71] Shanghai Opium Commission delegate Hamilton Wright boasted that "the moral uplift of the world" required Americans to stand against Britain and other imperial powers and that they had "won out" in the negotiations.[72] Wright and Brent both expressed satisfaction that the United States had taken the lead and pushed the British to action at the 1909 commission, noting that Calcutta-based British merchant and friend of Bishop Thoburn, Sir Robert Laidlaw, had expressed shame because Roosevelt had embarrassed Britain. Wright told Brent that "there was no doubt considerable chagrin because of the leadership of the United States." However, Wright understood that American objectives needed to be contained within a broader regional consensus. He was glad that the Shanghai commission put the issue on "a broad International basis" rather than a purely American one and thus "enable[d] the State Department to proceed to a logical solution" of the problem through international agreement.[73] U.S. policy would not be old-fashioned imperialism but multilateral cooperation under American leadership.

Hegemony involves vigorous contests over power, and the victory of 1909 was no exception. Indeed, the gains of the Shanghai meeting seem Pyrrhic ones in the light of subsequent developments. When Americans reported that their nation had "won" at Shanghai, they incurred British displeasure and underestimated the difficulties that lay ahead. The colonial powers repeatedly put obstacles in the way of implementing American plans. Americans took heart that the chief powers with an interest in Asia had agreed at the Shanghai meeting to the "gradual suppression" of the opium trade, but that language was a watering down of the original American proposal.[74] Moreover, as a "commission," the meeting could investigate, discuss, and make proposals, but it did not have treaty-making power; it lacked the higher status of a diplomatic "conference." Britain's foreign secretary Edward Grey returned home from the commission meeting and, a newspaper headline screamed, promptly "rebuked" the United States. Because the system of opium regulation in India prevented abuse and because conditions differed, Grey alleged, Britain did not intend to follow the commission's resolutions—and ban opium within British possessions. Yet headlines aside, he had already begun to talk with the Americans about making concessions.[75] His remarks were part of the tough negotiations that preceded the treaty agreement at the International Convention on Opium at The Hague in 1912, where he served as president of the convention, and at every succeeding step when opium diplomacy resumed after World War I.

A negative judgment on the 1909 commission misses the point of the diplomatic anti-drug push. Several American objectives had already been achieved. The United States had taken the moral high ground against the European powers and thus reinforced ideas of American exceptionalism held by the moral reform movements. The nation had also gained the support and gratitude of the Chinese government and thus served the larger aims of American foreign policy. Wright and his allies had attained, too, a lever with which to push at home for stronger anti-opium policies. He used the Shanghai meeting to lobby for internal reform to align domestic policy on opium with the nation's apparently high-minded policy abroad, an objective achieved in the act of 1909 to prohibit opium imports passed just before the holding of the Shanghai commission. The government's chief chemist, Harvey Wiley, argued that opium prohibition within the United States could have been accomplished using the existing Pure Food and Drug Act of 1906, but Wright knew that such a route would not advertise internationally the nation's anti-drug credentials.[76]

Nevertheless, the lobbying had to continue, and it was Hamilton Wright who pressed the debate forward between 1909 and 1912. The forty-four-year-old doctor from Ohio came to the anti-opium crusade not through the pulpit but the hospital, and acquired an ambition to be the first drug czar of the United States. He gave frequent interviews to the press, talked up his achievements, and conducted diplomacy publicly, seeking to shame foes outside and inside the United States into abiding by his moral concerns. These he pursued with evangelical zeal. Even though he rarely mentioned religion, moralism pervaded his thinking. He believed it necessary to ensure that "God reigns" in Washington and in opium policy.[77] With a medical degree from McGill University, he spent two years in China and Japan and a period under a British Medical Association Studentship, and then from 1900 to 1903 studied tropical diseases in India. After 1909, Wright became for a few years the leading negotiator and spokesman for the American position as a Department of State functionary. Wright knew that the 1909 act was only the beginning. Because the act effectively prohibited nothing more than smoking opium, U.S. imports of other opium products continued to rise. Despite the boastful claims of leading the world on the opium poppy's suppression, the United States used the "most habit-forming drugs per capita" of any nation, he told newspapers in 1911, and greater than the six major European countries put together. He called his own country, so the *New York Times* headline blazoned, "The Worst Drug Fiend in the World." Far fewer safeguards surrounded the American use of opium—the "most pernicious drug known to humanity"—than in "any nation in all Europe," claimed Wright in typically hyperbolic style. With imports increasing from 1860 by 351 percent compared to 133 percent for total population growth, usage was also growing rapidly and had far outstripped the quantity used by the Chinese immigrant population.[78]

After the Shanghai meeting, Wright used the meeting's agreement, his capacity for self-publicity, and his insistent lobbying to push for further action. He had the backing of William Jennings Bryan, the secretary of state under Woodrow Wilson and a man with strong evangelical connections. Responding in part to Wright's tireless efforts but also to the lobbying of the legal pharmaceutical industry, Congress passed the Harrison Act of 1914 controlling the use of opium as well as cocaine, a drug that had begun to raise great anxiety in the United States for its use among African Americans and in patent medicines. Taxes and compulsory registration as the vehicles to stop illegal trade outside pharmacological and medical areas made this law's prohibition of narcotics a de facto one, but it enabled the United States to comply with the 1912 International Opium Convention.[79]

By 1914, the involvement of Crafts in the diplomatic struggle had well and truly ended. Increasingly, the problems of opium control were highly technical, extremely complex, and not resolvable through Crafts's petitioning tactics. Emphasis had moved to official diplomatic negotiations, but Crafts already had additional reasons to shift his interests. Crafts had gone from being an antagonist of the government to one of its publicists, acting as an unofficial ambassador to garner support throughout East Asia for official American actions on drugs. He could no longer take an oppositional stance, the area in which he excelled. When Elihu Root succeeded John Hay as secretary of state in 1905, he had publicly sanctioned Crafts's moral diplomacy, even though Root was a man previously scathing of Crafts.[80] In return Crafts now professed mutual admiration for the Roosevelt administration's work. Its diplomatic offensive leading to the 1909 Shanghai commission provided Crafts with "The Greatest News of the Year" and "the greatest act" of the president's life.[81] The evangelical coalition and the government had arrived at a mutual confluence of interests. Political and strategic objectives can make for strange bedfellows, so the expression goes, and opium politics conformed to this time-honored maxim.

In the light of this success, Crafts could turn back to the larger objectives of the International Reform Bureau by working quietly to enhance the "protection of the native races." Indeed, he had already begun to do so at the 1906 Brussels Conference of the colonial powers on Africa. Arriving to lobby for further restriction of alcohol in the region of the Congo and West Africa, Crafts, in characteristic style, presented a great petition on behalf of the British and American missionary bodies. On that occasion the assembled powers raised duties on alcohol exports to Africa to curb "native" drinking. Then Crafts worked with the World's WCTU to influence a further international conference of 1912, but the meeting failed to come to an agreement. As a result, the WCTU affiliate, the British Women's Temperance Association, lobbied the British government to take further action within its own West African colonies. In 1913, Secretary of State for the Colonies Lewis Harcourt met with the World WCTU's superintendent of the Department of Native Races, the Scot Christina Robertson, and assured her of his interest.[82] Thereafter, the British tightened the restrictions in their own colonies to back up the international conventions of 1899 and 1906, though in practice the availability of liquor to African people far exceeded the hopes and expectations of prohibitionists.[83]

If the reform coalition now left opium diplomacy to the experts, it did so mainly to take on such new tasks. Of these the most strategically important was not alcohol prohibition in Africa or Asia but at home. The continued export of alcohol to the underdeveloped world from the United States (and Europe) highlighted chapter and verse the need to change the nation before further temperance reform could be achieved in Africa and the Pacific. This approach was tied to Crafts's idea of a Christian nation-state, whose tasks would include influencing other states through its moral conduct. He believed that once enough individuals were converted to evangelical beliefs in any given nation, it became "a Christian nation." With this status achieved, the nation was "responsible" for all of its acts in any colonies. Christian nations were moving, he argued, on the example of his own government, gradually if unevenly toward the implementation of Christian principles in foreign relations. With "considerably more" than half the world's surface under Christian governments, "and the remainder largely under their control," the world should "soon be Christianized," and thus brought under moral government.[84] The abolition of the canteen showed what could be done within an empire and across the nation-state. Government could be patiently cleansed of sin, issue by issue. National prohibition now beckoned as a goal. The evidence pointed to a growing alliance of moral politics and the state. Insofar as such an alliance meant endorsement of American empire, not all of the moral reformers agreed, however. To the radicals who repudiated such alliances we must now turn.

Chapter 8

IDA WELLS AND OTHERS:

RADICAL PROTEST AND THE NETWORKS

OF AMERICAN EXPANSION

THE LYNCHING VIOLENCE OF THE 1890s was a dark passage in the history of American race relations. Despite the fierce terror of the Ku Klux Klan, the 1870s was not the peak of racial mayhem against the newly freed African American people. That came in the decade of American cultural expansion abroad of the 1890s, when lynching reached historic heights. Was there a connection between this internal oppression and the external projection of American power? An intrepid English Quaker, Catherine Impey, could detect such links, but she did not limit her attack to lynching. Impey targeted all forms of discrimination against African Americans that flourished in late nineteenth-century America. She saw African Americans as a prime example of a worldwide principle exhibited in the British colonial regimes in India, South Africa, and the Pacific. With three trips to the United States and meetings with many African Americans to back her claims, caste was the name she gave to the racial discrimination she witnessed: "Caste is indeed no other than slavery under a new name" and, "as such," people "should be prepared to meet it."[1] In her periodical, *Anti-Caste*, she pronounced in 1889: "Of all oppressions this is the most grinding, the most terrible, the foulest of all we know." That African Americans faced "Intimidation—lynching—terrorising" indicated the thorough dimensions of the problem. Not deterred by the enormity of the prejudice she unearthed, Impey observed consciences stirring among people "whose numbers will grow, for Truth is on their side." One of those spurring change would be the well-known anti-lynching campaigner, the African American Ida Wells (later Wells-Barnett). Wells was one of several activists who probed the networks of Anglo-American reform in order to transform the patterns of American race relations and cultural expansion abroad. Wells and others like her wished to puncture the sometimes self-congratulatory tone of "humanitarianism" and turn the task of social reform inward toward changing the budding American empire at its source.[2]

Criticism of the racial and socioeconomic order was a common thread within the moral reform coalition. Many mainstream reformers were uncomfortable with imperialist schemes and with racial discrimination. Women were prominent among the dissenters in proclaiming a sisterhood of women, but some took the point further to proclaim a brotherhood of humankind. Anti-imperialist and peace campaigner Mary Alderman Garbutt exhibited such tendencies in the WCTU. She served a term as president of the southern California WCTU, was state organizer in the 1890s, and sat on the executive continuously from 1887 until 1924.[3] Garbutt bemoaned workers and other ordinary people who were "crushed" by the capitalist system, and campaigned for the Socialist Party in the 1912 presidential election. A thoroughgoing internationalist, she commended arbitration between nations and advocated building an International Peace Statue at the entrance to the Panama Canal, in order to assert the true message of the canal as "bringing the earth together in closer bands of brotherhood and goodwill." Garbutt also headed the Los Angeles Ramabai Circle and worked to help "that heroic little woman" whose name and mission in India inspired the group.[4]

However, moral reformers who criticized American or European imperialism did not always operate consistently, nor did they see the contradictions of their thought and practice. Their work as bearers of American benevolence entailed contact with, and dependence on, imperialism abroad and compromises over race and gender oppression. Garbutt, for instance, accepted the canal as an instrument of peaceful commerce, even though the project depended on American de facto control of Panama and on the entire machinery of forceful Rooseveltian diplomacy that went into the creation of the Canal Zone. Wilbur Crafts's position was also compromised. He defended the Chinese against immigration restrictions, as did many missionaries. "Plans for restricting immigration must not violate the brotherhood of man," he maintained, and urged Christians not to forget the ancient civilization that flourished in China when Europe remained still "savage."[5] At the same time, Crafts proclaimed the need for European-led benevolence toward not only the "child-races as wards of civilization" but what would be described in the twenty-first century as failed states. He preferred European control over underdeveloped races under transnational protectorates that would serve the interests of all, not individual imperial powers. Inspired by the Hague Peace Treaty of 1907, he proposed a "Hague Executive Commission" to insist that everywhere, "even in South America," there should be "efficient government in accord with civilized conceptions of human rights." Where lacking, the executive commission could intervene forcibly, backed by the great powers, to create "a protectorate to be continued until an adequate native government could be established and neutralized" or the area "annexed to some other Government in the interest, not of that country alone but of the world."[6] Such sentiments in some ways anticipated the idea of a mandates system of allocating protectorates under the League of Nations, but Crafts's proposal was derived from his response to the Chinese Boxer Rebellion of 1900. There the United States had joined European powers in a peacekeeping force to protect American commerce and missionaries against the turbulent forces of dissent and religious re-vitalization among the Chinese people.

Though such sentiments as Crafts offered were flawed and sometimes patronizing, they encouraged others to push the reformers' moral agenda still further. Individuals emerged to draw attention to the hypocrisy of those who preached racial equality and the rights of humankind but did not practice these high ideals consistently. Radical dissenters challenged the attachment of reformers to the colonial state and the international order of European domination, and championed the interests of oppressed groups, including colonial peoples. To varying degrees, these dissenters confronted Christian reformers' role within the transnational world of non-governmental reform by attempting to use the very networks that moral reformers had created. Generally speaking, critics were not suc-cessful in radically altering the orientation of the American moral reform networks abroad, but they highlighted contradictions within them.

Activist challenges fell into several categories. Some began on the mar-gins of the broader Anglo-American imperial networks, as was the case with the campaign of the Englishwoman Impey and the American Wells on lynching. They challenged dominant assumptions of racial superiority and the efficacy of the missionary project. Similar were the radical pro-tests on behalf of oppressed South Asian womanhood coming from the American purity campaigners Kate Bushnell and Elizabeth W. Andrew, who, in the 1890s, denounced the British army's inspection of prosti-tutes for the interests of the Indian colonial government as violations of human rights.[7] Another category was that of indigenous collabora-tors with empire, who tried to build on promises of equality, moderniza-tion, and spiritual uplift that reformers offered in various guises. Pandita Ramabai provides an example of an Indian woman working collabora-tively with the Christian reform movements while trying to adapt them to indigenous purposes. More overt critics began within the missionary project as agents of its agenda, but their colonial and transnational expe-rience reshaped their beliefs and they ended up promoting radicalism at home in the United States. Men as well as women were involved in this radical dissent. Foreign missionary work changed the perspective of the YMCA's traveling secretary, Sherwood Eddy, and conditioned his gradual

disillusionment with domestic liberal reform; similarly, evangelical Episcopalian Mercer Johnston's experience in the Philippines stimulated his
later labor reformism and anti-imperialism.

Ida Wells illustrated the possibilities and limitations of working from outside the leading reform networks. Wells did not know Catherine Impey
in the 1880s when the English Quaker first spoke out against lynching.
Born a slave in 1862, Wells grew up in the era of Reconstruction and its
aftermath, became a teacher, and fought against segregation in her native
Memphis, Tennessee. Driven out of her teaching job because of her civil
rights agitation in 1891, Wells launched a career as an anti-racist journalist when three acquaintances were lynched in Memphis in March 1892.
This was three years after Impey's first attacks on lynching in the pages
of *Anti-Caste*. The Englishwoman did not mention the American at the
time of Impey's 1892 visit to the United States nor, indeed, prior to Wells's
tours of Britain.[8] Then she drew public attention to the significance of
Wells's work.

What did Impey have to gain by involving herself in this American
controversy? By agitating the supercharged issue of lynching as an aspect
of racial oppression, Impey could heighten awareness of racism around
the globe. The circulation of *Anti-Caste* was small, whereas the World's
WCTU with which Wells locked horns over racism claimed a half-million
supporters globally at the time and affiliates in many parts of the British Empire. This interweaving of networks was a critical part of Impey's
strategy as much as it was of Wells's. If the World's WCTU affiliate, the
British Women's Temperance Association, could be converted to Impey's
viewpoint, a heightened sense of the evils of racial oppression could be
spread to the sugar colonies of the West Indies and racism in India exposed.[9] Impey lamented the exploitation of Assam tea workers and its
implications for the character of the British Empire: "We are increasingly
troubled," she wrote, over "the subjected condition of India, under the
conviction that much of our English rule over this great continent is inspired by the spirit of caste rather than that of brotherhood." From her
point of view, campaigning on the execrable extremities of lynching could
crystallize understanding about race prejudice as a general feature of European expansion abroad. Knowledge of the injustice of racial oppression
exposed through lynching could educate Britons as well as Americans by
providing them with something that the new transnational networks did
best—increasing the circulation of knowledge: "Caste prejudice is often
the effect of imperfect knowledge, and we suspect that this is largely so
in this case."[10] By involving Wells and the anti-lynching crusade, Impey
could build upon old British sympathies for African American slaves

to link Wells's endeavor with that of India's downtrodden. Impey also wanted to expose the contradictions in Christian reform abroad. She saw the missionaries as unwitting servants of imperial power when they failed to agitate politically against extreme discrimination: "I feel I should be doing God's service more by circulating this work, than by contributing to the Missionary Society," she stated in a backhand attack on the pros- elytizing of her Christian brethren abroad.[11]

Wells's motivations were similar. Faced with an almost impenetrable wall of racism at home, Wells chose to follow in the steps of anti-slavery abolitionists and stir the conscience of Americans indirectly from abroad. "Miss Ida Wells's voice," wrote Impey in 1895, "has been *better heard in America* from the platform of Exeter Hall, than from any American platform that was previously open to her." Where a whole nation was "under the spell of such a sentiment," any "awakening must come from outside."[12] *Anti-Caste*'s circulation throughout the British Empire and among the Quakers who had led the campaigns against slavery offered Wells sympathetic access to the British reading public, but first she had to make the contacts that would open doors for her.[13] Her trip made sense in the light of strong ties already evident between British and American anti-racist campaigners. British women had begun not only to agitate on the issue of lynching but also to travel to the United States to investigate race relations and evangelical reform. Several had come as early as 1878 and met African American leaders.[14] Impey was one of these. She was a temperance supporter, had attended the National WCTU meeting in Minneapolis in 1886, and had mixed extensively in Quaker and aboli- tionist circles across the Northeast. Impey met anti-slavery abolitionist Frederick Douglass, one of a number of prominent African Americans who subscribed to Impey's paper. In Philadelphia she found impressive a black temperance worker from the WCTU, schoolteacher Frances Cop- pin. These transatlantic friendships allowed the development of a figura- tive information highway along which the ideas of Wells could travel.[15] Wells was encouraged by knowledge of Impey's new transatlantic net- work to journey across the ocean. She was invited by a friend of Impey's, Isabelle Mayo, who visited Douglass in Washington. When Douglass was unable to go to Britain at Impey's request, Wells went instead at his encouragement. She sailed for Britain to conduct a speaking tour on April 5, 1893.

In Britain, Wells immediately began to tap into the networks of British humanitarianism, but squabbling among her Quaker supporters limited her impact. Impey had confessed her love for a black anti-racist worker, and the incident scandalized sections of British society, threatening in the process to detract from the campaign. Wells "aborted her trip" and re- turned to the United States.[16] She could not get easy access to the American press until she returned in 1894, better prepared and armed with evidence for her second tour, when the Rev. Charles Aked befriended her. The British Baptist minister generated concern by voicing his own criticisms of lynching and also helped disseminate her views in the mainstream media.[17]

Since Britain was the South's greatest cotton market, it made sense to appeal to the reform-minded public there, as Douglass had done in the 1840s against chattel slavery. Wells sent back accounts of her meetings and resolutions against lynching to the Memphis press, which "felt compelled to publish these and to respond."[18] As in the Civil War, Britain was now called upon to seek other sources of cotton and thus threaten the foundations of the southern economy. The white elite would, it was hoped, discourage lynchings in response, but the initial effect was to expose through the "coarse" and unapologetically racist replies from elements of the southern press the true extent of prejudice. The anti-lynching cause gained strength internationally as a consequence. Together, Wells and her supporters scored blows not only against the South's greatest crop—cotton—but against the efforts of southern boosters to get British investment for industrial growth.[19]

Yet Wells did more than strike at the purses of cotton planters and New South industrialists. Wells wanted to puncture the growing confidence of American evangelical reformers on their path to overseas expansion. She wished to expose the limits of American "humanitarianism." She wrote in her widely quoted tract, A Red Record, that "Surely the humanitarian spirit of this country which reaches out to denounce the treatment of Russian Jews, the Armenian Christians, the laboring poor of Europe, the Siberian exiles and the native women of India—will no longer refuse to lift its voice." She wanted the "Y.M.C.A.'s, W.C.T.U.'s and all Christian and moral forces" to condemn every example of lynching.[20] When questioned on the subject in Britain, she noted the exploits of "great moral reformers" such as Dwight Moody who had spurred the missionary revivals, yet "had never said a word against lynching." Too many such people were blind to racial oppression.[21] Wells also critiqued the putative civilization that missionaries spread. She asked whether the "precepts and theories of Christianity" were simply "a system of morals to be preached to heathen until they attain to the intelligence which needs the system of Lynch Law."[22] Thus she exposed hypocrisy and predicted the ultimate failure of missions as an instrument of cultural expansion and imperial policy.

A vital part of Wells's campaign involved exploiting the networks of the World's WCTU because that association was manifestly transnational in its influence and aspirations. It not only sent out round-the-world missionaries but also had strengthened its ties to the British Women's

Temperance Association (BWTA) by a formal alliance within the World's
WCTU achieved in 1886. At the annual meeting of that year in Minneapolis, BWTA president Margaret Bright Lucas clasped hands with Frances Willard in symbolic recognition of Anglo-Saxon unity while Impey
looked on. The World's WCTU president was Isabel Somerset, Willard's
great friend. Thereafter, the transatlantic ties in women's temperance
grew critically stronger. From 1893 to 1895 Willard based herself in Britain, where she attempted to use the wealth of Somerset and Britain's strategic position at the center of a great empire to further the ambitions of
the World's WCTU. Wells was aware that Willard led the most important
women's movement of the time. To convert Willard to an unequivocal
anti-lynching stance would be strategically important on both a global
and an American level. Yet Wells did not directly attack the WCTU leader
until her second trip in 1894, when reporters asked questions concerning
Willard's and the WCTU's record on race relations in the United States.
Nevertheless, an acrimonious debate had already spread within the wom-
en's movement and temperance circles across the Atlantic.

Willard first made disparaging remarks to journalists about African
Americans in 1890, when the National WCTU's annual convention was
meeting in the South for the first time. She attempted to explain racist southern attitudes in terms of whites' response to "crazed," illiterate
African Americans. In an off-the-cuff interview in Atlanta she revealed
conventionally prejudiced attitudes toward race: "The colored race mul-
tiplies like the locusts of Egypt," Willard casually claimed, and opined
that African Americans exerted political power through the "grog shop."
Northerners should not judge southerners for their attempts to control
black voting, nor were the good, genteel, sober, and well-educated whites
responsible for racial violence. It was "Half-drunken white roughs" who
murdered African Americans, and then only in response to the latter's
unwarranted attempts to seize political power. "Would-be demagogues"
led "colored people to destruction," said Willard. More controversial still
in the eyes of African Americans was Willard's apportioning of blame for
sexual violence: "The safety of women, of childhood, [and] of the home,
[was] menaced in a thousand localities" by the aspirations of blacks for
political power and social equality. She held African Americans responsible for initiating reprehensible interracial sex. No room was left in this
argument for free sexual relations between white women and blacks, in
which the former actually initiated the interest. To Wells and other African American activists, Willard's prurient view condoned "fraud, violence, murder at the ballot box" and "shooting, hanging and burning."[23]
Willard's compromises became those of her whole national union in a
tepid anti-lynching resolution passed in Chicago at the October 1893
annual meeting.[24]

When Wells returned to Britain in 1894 for a second tour much better covered by the press, she responded to the WCTU's now institutionalized prevarication on race. The African American campaigner asserted that white women initiated sexual relations "as willing victims." Many "cases of 'Assault'" were "simply adulteries between white women and colored men," Wells told a Liverpool audience in March 1894.[25] Since the tour was reported in the *Chicago Inter-Ocean*, a paper for which Willard herself wrote from time to time, Wells's attack could hardly go unnoticed. The deeply offended WCTU leader retorted by having the WCTU accuse Wells of "injudicious speech" on the subject. The African American agitator breached civilized conventions by casting aspersions on the purity of white womanhood.[26] Willard strenuously denied that she was pro-lynching and claimed to have denounced the odious practice. Nevertheless, she became caught in a classic political wedge. She did not want to offend the racially segregated WCTUs in the South, and wished her beloved temperance union to extend its influenced there. At the same time, she promoted WCTU influence overseas where, in Britain, racist policies received a much less favorable view among liberally inclined women who supported temperance. Willard's dilemma was demonstrated at the 1894 annual meeting in Cleveland, when delegates attempted to retrieve the moral ascendency for the WCTU. They resolved against lynching, professing the union as "opposed to all lawless acts."[27] At the same time, they compromised this stance when they denounced in the same resolution "the unspeakable outrages which have so often provoked such lawlessness." Temperance women thereby implied that African American men were, indeed, responsible for the moral outrages of interracial sex that led to their lynching.

Wells's impact grew in 1894–95 because she won support among not only Impey's circle but also a noisy, radical minority of the BWTA. Through the BWTA, Wells could tap into the disquiet among British liberal reformers about imperial rule. This work centered on Florence Balgarnie, who, Impey reported, was "doing valiant service in the Anti-Lynching cause in England."[28] The daughter of a Congregational minister and born and based in Yorkshire, Balgarnie had a temperament and a background in the Protestant culture of English Dissent that caused her to be a thorn in the side of the BWTA's leadership. An activist who had helped secure Somerset's victory as the pro-American, "progressive party" president of the BWTA over the conservative forces in a watershed 1893 split over policy, Balgarnie had become head of a newly created department of politics and women's suffrage within the association. As Balgarnie had also visited the United States in 1894, she was aware of American conditions and had brought home many ideas for the better treatment of women.[29] When Wells visited Britain for the second time,

Balgarnie was stung by the anti-lynching campaigner's charges that the WCTU was a racist organization. In line with her pro-democratic views and her hostility to racial oppression in the British Empire, Balgarnie bitterly criticized Willard's failure to oppose lynching strenuously enough.[30] She told the *Leeds Mercury*: "If Christian women can apologise for injustice in any form or shape, little wonder that rough men hound down their fellows to death."[31]

The ever-gritty Balgarnie proved difficult for Willard and Somerset to handle, especially when she led the attack at the BWTA's annual meeting in 1895. According to the London *Daily News*, the Yorkshire liberal "vindicated Miss Wells, and in an eloquent and impassioned speech, received with some disfavour by the American visitors, gave some account of the horrors of lynching" and called on "American sisters to speak out more boldly in the matter." A resolution supported by sixty-five branches denouncing lynching was carried unanimously. Affirming that "under no circumstances must human life be taken without due process of law," the WCTU was forced to backtrack from its "unspeakable outrages" position in new anti-lynching resolutions at the 1895 World's and National WCTU meetings as well. This reversal came about solely because of the agitation in Britain.[32]

The WCTU's concessions were not the only positive results of Wells's British campaigns. A small party of Britons conducted a fact-finding mission on lynchings in response to her tour and stirred up a veritable hornet's nest. When she first left the United States lynching was not a subject of great controversy. When she returned permanently in 1895, it was.[33] The superintendent of the 1890 U.S. Census reported to the *Chicago Inter-Ocean* that an Englishman told him: "I will not invest a farthing in States where these horrors occur. . . . [W]here life is held to be of such little value there is even less assurance that the laws will protect property."[34] Others protesting in favor of Wells in America included the liberal theologian Lyman Abbott of Brooklyn, and Anti-Lynching Committees on both sides of the Atlantic joined the chorus.[35] William L. Garrison II (son of the famous abolitionist) told the *Times* late in 1894 that "A year ago the South derided and resented Northern protests; today it listens, explains, and apologizes for its uncovered cruelties."[36] With "Governors and Judges in several States" issuing "proclamations against lynching," and with active measures taken in some states to suppress lynching, the outlook seemed to the British Anti-Lynching Committee to be "decidedly encouraging."[37]

Yet Wells's impact was a mixed one. Lynching declined in the mid- to late 1890s, but most historians credit "factors other than Wells's efforts." In any case, the fall was slow and uneven. In the first eight months of 1895, 137 lynchings had already occurred, according to the British Anti-

Lynching Committee set up as a result of Wells's visit.[38] Over the whole of
the 1890s, one American was lynched every two days and 82 percent of
these were non-whites. Lynching decreased more slowly in the South than
elsewhere, and its incidence became more concentrated among African
American victims. Substantial reductions in these figures did not occur
until the second decade of the twentieth century.[39] "Vehement" American opposition stopped further British fact-finding tours, with the *New
York Times* labeling Wells a "slanderous and nasty minded mulatress"[40]
who traded in images of "the unchastity and untruthfulness of Southern
white women."[41] The same paper condemned her "inopportune" theories concerning "negro outrages" and criticized the British for "minding
other people's business."[42] Even African Americans were by no means
united in support for Wells. The New York Cleveland League Democrats,
a "colored" organization, denounced her as a "fraud."[43] She was accused
of going to Britain for an "income," not an "outcome."[44] A meeting of
the National Conference of Colored Women in Boston debated bitterly
whether to endorse the WCTU's work, because Willard had "looked
upon [lynching] in the light of a necessary evil." But the conference nevertheless backed the WCTU "almost unanimously," even though some did
not approve of its temporizing on the race question.[45] Within Britain and
its empire, too, the campaign had its limits. The BWTA had split over the
issue, but a clear majority supported Willard and Somerset, and Balgarnie
was subsequently marginalized within the organization.[46]

   New and unforeseen circumstances curbed the campaign's impact. One
of the chief targets quickly took evasive action. Willard returned to the
United States in 1895 and removed herself from the British scene where
she had been most vulnerable to attack. Further handicapping the movement was the personal scandal enveloping Impey.[47] To her supporters
Impey had compromised the politics of the movement and confirmed
racist judgments that white women who campaigned for racial equality secretly harbored desires for interracial sex. Impey's marginalization
was matched by Wells's voluntarily removal from the international stage
when, in June 1895, she married lawyer Ferdinand L. Barnett and settled
in Chicago to raise a family. This is not say that she failed to oppose race
prejudice thereafter, but she focused for several years on issues concerning her local community. Wells-Barnett's self-denying exit coincided with
a less receptive political and intellectual climate. She and Impey had tried
to tap transnational networks of Quakers and anti-slavery abolitionists,
but these networks proved to be of diminishing strength. The abolitionists of the 1850s and 1860s were dying off, and the equalitarian strain
of thought that Impey represented was increasingly shelved.[48] She and
her American allies had only limited success for this reason. Evangelical
groups developed closer alliances with the state project of imperialism,

and, as they grew in strength, the radicalism of those who sought equality in the temporal world was outflanked.

Wells (and her coworkers in Britain) criticized Anglo-American racial practices by boring away at the moral reform networks emanating from the imperial center. Yet Europeans wishing to project abroad their messages of reform and salvation also had to contend with indigenous activists on the periphery of Euro-American expansion. Most of the cases discussed in this chapter are of Americans, but they interacted with men and women from other countries in their work. People in colonial and quasi-colonial settings both resisted and collaborated with the work of the American reformers. This complicated process was conducted primarily within particular colonies, but occasionally indigenous responses to Westernization reached the heart of the metropolitan effort to organize reform transnationally. Such transitions could come about because a major focus of voluntary organizations' work, especially in the case of the YMCA and the WCTU, was to co-opt indigenous workers for the national and transnational efforts. Indigenous converts to the WCTU sometimes became roving temperance lecturers and broke through conventional gender and race barriers.

One example was Pandita Ramabai Sarasvati, the "high-caste Hindu widow" and author (in Marahti) of *The Peoples of the United States* (1889).[49] Much less known than Alexis de Tocqueville's or James Bryce's tomes as examples of how others saw the nineteenth-century United States, Ramabai's volume is nevertheless instructive of complex colonial-metropolitan relations. She elicited, notes historian Meera Kosambi, "generous support" from the WCTU and the Ramabai Circles formed in American cities as a result of her visit to the United States in 1886–88.[50] Collaboration is an important theme in empires, and people such as Ramabai became collaborators by supporting and helping refashion the WCTU in a multicultural direction; they made the WCTU's work one of intercultural mediation, interpreting Western messages to the indigenous and offering criticisms of as well as comfort to the organization.[51] Ramabai was not an isolated example. The wider missionary enterprise of the Protestant churches had to function in this way if it was to be successful, particularly by being translated into vernacular cultures, spoken idioms, and written languages. Missionary processes both secular and religious relied on collaboration, but the collaborators often modified the meaning of the message.[52] Thus Ramabai sought Western aid for projects that did not conform to orthodox Christianity. In England she resisted supporters' attempts to structure her work in directions consistent with Anglicanism, and questioned the Christian and civilizing rationale for British occupation of India.[53] Sometimes to the despair of the orthodox, both Christian and Hindu, she adopted religious syncretism in her patterns of work and belief.

Fig. 12. Pandita Ramabai and her daughter Manorama. (Author's personal collection.)

The cultural exchange in which she participated occurred on grounds that advantaged the American reformers. Whereas tensions sometimes flared between missionaries and empire conventionally conceived, the WCTU did not stand for formal empire and could more easily present an alternative form of cultural hegemony. Like Wells, Ramabai shared a critical attitude toward American race relations and was by no means unaware of other flaws in American society. Yet Ramabai stressed how the WCTU could profit from its image as the representative of the United States—a "nonimperialist western power." The WCTU's non-denominationalism, which Ramabai praised, also contributed to the reformist nature of its institutions and allowed it to project a different kind of relationship between Europeans and subject peoples than was typically present in British rule. According to Ramabai, "out of all the many unions that exist in the developed countries, this union [the WCTU] is the best and the greatest." Praising its "extraordinary and outstanding organization," she contrasted the WCTU with women's mission societies that "do not have the unity among themselves that they should and do not accomplish as many good things as the temperance union has taken upon itself to do."[54] Ramabai "juxtaposed a staunch anti-British stance with an equally strong pro-American one, as a consciously deployed strategy of resistance" to colonialism. Consequently, Kosambi has aptly stated, Ramabai saw "liberation only through a Western model for India's progress." This remarkable Hindu widow came close to endorsing American modernism and cultural hegemony over stereotypical European empires. She was a culturally syncretic figure who mixed a "Hindu Brahmin mystique" with evangelical Christianity, but she could not openly challenge the process of American cultural expansion.[55]

If Wells lay outside the major evangelical networks, and Ramabai necessarily acted as a collaborator attempting to mediate between the moral reform project and indigenous culture, other critics operated to varying degrees inside the same project. Even though criticism of British and American imperialism was far from unknown among missionaries, by and large American missionaries were more muted in their criticism of their own government. Missionaries sought to take advantage of American colonial acquisitions for their spiritual conquests.[56] Yet the moral imperatives of evangelical reform operated to foment dissent even at the heart of the colonial effort, and the negative experiences of some missionaries had impacts on American domestic society. One critic attacking from the inside was Mercer Johnston.[57]

The Tennessee-educated Johnston was the son of a missionary bishop to west Texas, James Steptoe Johnston. After study at Sewanee's University of the South Theological College, Mercer followed his father's calling in 1903, but he carried his proselytizing much further geographically by heeding the appeal for missionaries for the Episcopal Church in the Philippines and took up duties as an assistant to Bishop Charles Brent. In 1907 he became rector of the new Episcopal Cathedral of Saint Mary and Saint John in Manila. Leaving the Philippines in October 1908 after a five-year stint, he spent a further five years as a missionary on the Texas borderlands and then held a pastorate in Newark, New Jersey, from 1913 to 1916.[58] There, in the industrial turmoil and class divisions of urban

New Jersey, he discovered the Social Gospel, or so it seemed.[59] Yet Johnston continued his interests in East Asia by reading up on the forces of modernization in China and on outspoken critics of Western missions and supporters of the country's new liberal revolution of 1911.[60] Books such as Lin Shao-Yang's *Chinese Appeal to Christendom Concerning Christian Missions*, a work intensely critical of the cultural insensitivities of missionaries, became staples of his thought. He addressed churches and clubs on the Philippines, kept in touch with repatriated Americans, fraternized with old missionary acquaintances, and attended sessions of the annual Lake Mohonk conference "of friends of Indians & other Dependent Peoples."[61] By the 1920s, Johnston had become an inveterate anti-imperialist. As editor of a Progressive magazine, *Good Neighborship*, the bulletin of the National Citizens Committee on Relations with Latin-America, and as secretary of that committee, Johnston organized protests against "the Kellogg-Coolidge strong-arm policy for weak neighbors," railed at U.S. Marines' occupation of Nicaragua, and denounced the American government's attempted intimidation of Mexico.[62] Johnston had become a strident social activist and remained so for the rest of his life. He died in 1954.

Johnston's left-wing sympathies were not obvious in the Philippines, but his time in Manila did, when more closely observed, anticipate and shape the disposition toward corruption, authority, social inequality, and the hierarchies of empire that he later displayed. He took the lead in the campaign of the Manila Evangelical Union to stop gambling and drinking, but it was cockfighting that he raged against most vociferously in a controversial intervention. Among a number of anti-cockfighting initiatives, the campaign against the colonial political establishment in the Manila Carnival Association affair of 1908 stands out as highly revealing of his growing anti-imperialist sentiments. The annual carnival included well-publicized cockfighting accompanied by widespread gambling. American officials dominated the committee that sponsored the carnival, and the Philippine Commission licensed the practice of cockfighting there. Leading the charge on this issue was Vice-Governor William Cameron Forbes, who also served as president of the Carnival Association and regarded cockfighting as harmless and colorful recreation.[63] Even though Philippine Commission officials considered the tearing apart of animals unseemly to European sensibilities, they believed it better to focus on modifying what they regarded as the truly serious racial and social defects of the Philippine people. They refused to waste time on matters of taste. In parallel with its preferences on opium policy, the commission favored adapting to Asian ways. Governor-General Henry Ide conceded in 1906 that cockfighting had a "demoralizing effect" from the European point of view, and he shared Johnston's "sense of humiliation that many

Americans should have pandered to that kind of vice which prevails so extensively among the Filipinos." But as a local "vice," it needed to "be looked upon with a certain degree of consideration" because a majority of complaints against the practice came from Americans and "there would be a great outcry against the interference with the long established customs of the people."[64]

Prior to this time, Johnston had not quite resolved his conflict over the American empire. He came from the American South and was well aware of and influenced by ideas of racial hierarchy that colonial officials shared. Mercer saw the duty of the U.S. government to be one of uplift and civilizing, and had scoffed at the establishment of an elected assembly for the Filipino people.[65] As late as August 1907 Johnston argued that the Stars and Stripes were "the Bread and Wine of America: the outward and visible sign of the inward and spiritual grace of patriotism." This "no demagogue, no fanatic, no opportunist" should forget.[66] He praised the military efforts of brave soldiers to subdue Filipino rebels and pondered the impossibility of escaping the heavy burden of imperial rule and its costs to the American people. He mourned the loss of Major General Henry Ware Lawton, killed by rebels in 1899, and turned this sacrifice into homage for the American white man's burden. Speaking at the memorial to the fallen soldier in 1906, Johnston proclaimed: "A dignified escape from the responsibility our nation has assumed in this Archipelago [was] impossible." If the flag were withdrawn before it had "worked its perfect work," the United States would "lose countenance in the presence of half a billion people [of East Asia] among whom perdition is less feared than loss of face."[67] For this reason, he maintained "Loyalty" to Lawton. Though Johnston was not opposed to Philippine independence when the time was ripe, then was not the time.[68]

In 1908, however, his dissatisfaction with the low moral conduct of some Americans in the colony became clear. Wishing to see restored "the good name of America throughout the world," Johnston urged Americans to rise to the nation's nobler standards.[69] This attitude allowed Johnston to develop a thinly veiled moral critique of American imperialism. He preached a series of fire and brimstone sermons that became his hallmark. Swift and vehement denunciation of hypocrisy marked *A Covenant with Death, an Agreement with Hell*, in which Johnston pronounced it "far worse for Americans" than for native people to support the traditional Filipino pastime of cockfighting. Because Americans had shouldered the white man's burden, countenancing immoral behavior was "unpardonable" in an American official.[70] Johnston drew on the thinking of Filipino nationalist Emilio Aguinaldo, quoting him that "gambling more than anything else in the Philippines is the mother of crime." Johnston stated that using the name of Aguinaldo in this connection "ought to bring the blush of shame to the faces of those Americans who have had it in their power to do so much more to deliver the Filipino from his inveterate enemy." According to Johnston, national hero José Rizal was of like mind; he compared the sport's ravages "among his own people to the use of opium among the Chinese." Johnston appealed to the sense of humanitarian uplift in the American administration, noting the anti-cockfighting protest of students of the Philippines Normal School "who are, in a peculiar sense, the hope of our American experiment in these Islands."[71]

All this and more he expounded in front of the congregation of the Episcopal Cathedral, with leading members of the American community present. No wonder there was offense when Johnston pronounced that the official who presided over the Manila Carnival Association would be "seen by many eyes through the filthy atmosphere of a native cockpit." No wonder there was offense when Johnston claimed that to go ahead with the event would be "placing upon our American escutcheon the blackest blot that has yet appeared on it in connection with our venture in the Philippines." The message for Filipinos was also clear: Do not accept the moral hegemony of the American rulers, since the standards of the nationalist elite were higher: "Were I a Filipino, I would hate or despise the American who trafficked in the vices of my people, and withstand him to the face, at all hazards." If Americans were permitted to "exploit the vice of gambling among our wards in these Islands, either permanently, or to meet any emergency, . . . the God of Nations ought to send some overflowing scourge to wash her heart clean of its despicable hypocrisy."[72] When the Carnival Association insisted that it could not break its contract with the cockfight licensee, Johnston exclaimed that this stance was a form of the "business morality" that "oftentimes makes socialists, sometimes anarchists, and once in a great while a French Revolution."

Through the Philippine Commission's attitude toward cockfighting, Johnston was able to crystallize his growing anti-imperial sentiment. Bishop Brent did not support his fiery assistant's assault on the American establishment, and Johnston resigned his position as a result of pressure from parishioners. As a final broadside he called Brent a lazy and ineffective missionary and one who loves "a fellow with a good deal of toady in him"—someone quite unlike Johnston.[73] Almost immediately Johnston returned to the United States to seek "prophetic," not "parish," work and wanting to "live my Christ" in such a way "that the most radical labor leader or socialist will be compelled, if he has any honesty in him, to take my Christian life seriously."[74] His subsequent career in the United States revisited the themes established in the Philippines. As rector of the fashionable Trinity Episcopal Church in Newark, Johnston harangued his congregation over its hypocrisies. Once again parishioners called for his resignation because of "his refusal to suppress passages in his sermons which were calculated to make sinners feel uncomfortable."[75] He specifically announced his Social Gospel credentials in 1916 on resigning from his church, but the roots of these ideas lay far away, in the insular possessions of the Philippines where they were first revealed.[76] The colonial world had a habit of striking back through the experiences of empire's contradictions.

George Sherwood Eddy (1871–1963) was another affected by the experience of American mission work abroad and swayed in the direction of radicalism. As in the case of Johnston, the seeds of the Social Gospel lay not in American cities but among the restive masses of Asia. Born in Leavenworth, Kansas, in 1871, Eddy graduated from Yale University and the Princeton Theological Seminary. Though identified with the YMCA, Eddy first embarked for India in 1896 as traveling secretary for the Student Volunteer Movement for India and Ceylon, then almost immediately took on the closely associated role of college secretary for YMCA work there.[77] In 1911 John Mott tapped him to be traveling secretary for the whole of Asia in line with the YMCA leader's transnational approach to evangelism, but India continued to be Eddy's most important base. *Time* portrayed Eddy in the 1920s as an impassioned orator and deeply committed to the Social Gospel. "[P]reeminent among the exhorters of Americans and others," Eddy was said to speak with clenched fist, contracted brow, and tightly drawn lips. "He bullies men's consciences, he stirs their emotions. In almost every land, he has exhorted for peace, brotherhood, personal purity," and for "taking Christ seriously."[78]

It was the Social Gospel as preached by fellow Kansan Charles M. Sheldon in the 1880s and 1890s that reportedly influenced Eddy's generation to campaign on the social implications of their Christianity. Yet neither Eddy nor the larger YMCA was an early and easy convert. In his own words, Eddy had to undertake a "Pilgrimage of Ideas." In this odyssey of "the Re-Education of Sherwood Eddy," the major scene for transformation lay in Asia.[79] Eddy showed little sign of the Social Gospel when he first traveled through India after his appointment in 1896. The famine of 1897 he could hardly help but notice, yet Eddy continued to treat the spiritual task of saving souls as far more important. His fervent evangelicalism left little room for contemplation of the cultures he encountered.[80] Eddy saw the means of uplift quite conventionally as the progress of the Christian word but married his beliefs to a sense of Darwinian selection and Anglo-Saxon superiority that was common in an age of imperialism. He told Christians that Hinduism displayed "the dregs of a heredity of centuries of heathenism, while you have the heredity and environment which is the product of centuries of Christian civilization."[81]

Not until 1903 did he begin to appreciate India's nationalism and cultural revitalization.[82] Even then, he remained broadly supportive of British rule and of the American effort in the Philippines. When Eddy visited the Philippines in 1911, he followed the official American line that colonialism there was different from European empires and beneficent in its anti-imperial trajectory. He was most impressed that there was "No army canteen" in the American colony to make soldiers intemperate and that the "moral tone of the soldier" was "better in consequence." Moreover, the Filipino people needed the helping hand of Americans. The United States would, he predicted, "probably make discoveries and establish precedents which will be of service throughout the tropics."[83] Keeping the colony was necessary because, though "progressive, bright and keenly interested in politics," the people of the insular possessions were "no more ready for complete self government than the inmates of an orphanage would be to establish a self governing republic and develop its resources and industries." Eddy actually feared that "America [had] gone too fast in attempting to give freedom" to the Filipinos.[84] It is telling that his *New Era in Asia* (1913) discussed the growth of nationalism in the region and the European response without touching on the Philippines at all. American colonialism was a great absence in his thought at the time because he could not confront the idea that the United States might be like other empires whose days he now saw as numbered.[85]

The change in Eddy's position toward a socially radical Christianity had roots in these early experiences. In more than a decade as a YMCA traveling secretary he learned about the social and economic causes of conflict in India and became strongly attached to the country and its people. But the political and social implications were not noticeable until the second decade of the twentieth century. Touring India again in 1915–16, he responded to new droughts and the rise of Indian nationalism by advocating the pouring of funds into social programs in the Indian rural economy. In this period, the YMCA had created a rural department that would "begin to grapple with the terrific economic and social needs of the down-trodden outcast masses of the poor."[86] Indian Christians had started banks that loaned money to cooperative societies organized by the YMCA. With a friend Eddy sunk $10,000 in the Christian Central Bank of Madras, stating that, for the uplift of the Indian people, "I know of no better investment to-day."[87] This was a definite shift toward a Social Gospel approach, and it occurred on the frontiers of American intellectual development, not at the metropolitan center.

World War I's impact hastened but did not mark the beginning of his embrace of Asian nationalism. He noted in 1913 a "growing sense of nationality" in India stimulated by British rule, the English language, Western education, "and Christian ideals." This concoction of forces was "drawing the peoples of India increasingly toward political unity."[88] Eddy expressly downplayed the 1909 political reforms of Lord Morley and emphasized "the changes which are taking place under Indian leader-

ship in the Indian social structure itself." He even found encouraging the
"eclectic systems which are a combination of Christian truth and Hindu
tradition."[89] Further developing this view in the aftermath of World War
I, he became by the early 1920s a vocal supporter of the Indian nationalist movement. Conceding that British rule in India was "the finest instance I know in history of the governing of one people by another,"
he nevertheless maintained that self-determination was "desirable, inevitable and just."[90] Like Mercer Johnston, Eddy now opposed American as
well as British colonialism, attacked racism in South Africa, and agitated
against U.S. military intervention in the Caribbean.[91] By the mid-1920s
he had become a controversial figure on the American Left. Eddy toured
Europe, including Soviet Russia in 1926, and then annually from 1929 to
1938, conducting a non-denominational "American Seminar" in which
intellectuals, business leaders, and politicians as well as evangelists and
bishops took part. All wished to see the new Europe after World War I
and to promote American internationalist sentiment.[92] From his tours
Eddy came to praise the new Soviet state's socialist advances. He could
write Joseph Stalin in 1932 that "I want to see this daring undertaking of
a classless society under a new social order succeed, and it is succeeding."
Despite the communist system's obstacles and flaws (he did not dwell on
the human toll of the great agricultural collectivization of the period),
Eddy proclaimed that the "great Five Year Plan" was "magnificently succeeding."[93] This progress Eddy saw not as godless communism but as
equivalent to the social and economic reform that he had advocated for
Indian agriculture on the local level in the years before the Russian Revolution. At home in the United States, he worked to combat racism in the
South, which he equated with the racism he had experienced in his tours
of the British Empire in earlier decades.[94] He served on the committee
of the American Civil Liberties Union in the 1930s and opposed war
alongside socialist Norman Thomas. Eddy rightly denied that he was a
communist, but this did not stop the American Legion from attacking
him for his radical views.[95]

Notwithstanding his social activism, Eddy remained a Christian and
an advocate of missions. John Mott defended him in the 1920s against
anxious complaints from "Judge" Elbert Henry Gary of the U.S. Steel
Corporation and John D. Rockefeller Jr., who funded so much of the
YMCA's overseas work.[96] A Mott telegram endorsement of January 9,
1928, stressed Eddy's progressive version of Christianity as being within
the YMCA's orbit: He was an "earnest advocate of the Christian religion
which he is preaching today as consistently as when he spent fifteen years
as a missionary in India."[97] Eddy's views were indeed in line with the
Social Gospel he had begun to develop as a YMCA envoy throughout
Asia before World War I. When journalist Katherine Mayo attacked, in

Mother India (1927), the capacity of the Indian social structure to engage in progressive change, Eddy insisted on the roles of missionaries
as agents of that progress and resented the way Mayo played down the
significance of Christian work. Unlike many of the Westerners who reviewed the book, Eddy joined nationalists to defend India against Mayo's
charges. Mayo should, Eddy insisted, go out to help in "relieving present
need and actual misery."[98] He also had advice for missionaries in this
squabble because they "should go in a spirit that is teachable, ready to
be taught [by Indians] the much that they have to teach and that we need
to learn." His Christianity had taken an inter-religious, intercultural, and
ecumenical stance in which missionaries must "welcome every value in
the religion and culture of the people to whom we go." For this reason,
Eddy professed to be eager for "great messages" from Gandhi. Whereas
Mayo's view denied the fitness of colonial peoples for self-government,
to Eddy imperialism and militarism were the key problems, not flawed
indigenous capacities.[99]

Eddy's trajectory was spectacular, but it was not entirely unusual.
American missionary groups defended India against Mayo and, with the
World's WCTU, spoke favorably about the rising nationalist sentiment.
They all built upon their prewar critique of the British Raj's role in the
licensing of alcohol and opium in India to do so.[100] Other moral reformers changed in more spectacular fashion. In the 1920s, African American
YMCA worker Max Yergan shifted from evangelical religion to revolutionary socialism, with the "critical role" being played by "his residence
in South Africa."[101] More broadly, the Social Gospel thrived in many missionary settings where the YMCA worked. Its non-denominationalism
and creative adaptation to local cultures became common. In China,
the YMCAs moved in the 1910s and 1920s toward social service. They
helped Chinese leaders or took over leadership in "starting schools, planning opium-control campaigns, providing famine relief, assisting students
overseas, and organizing youth activities."[102] They sought to "indigenize
the organization" and stressed education's role in the achievement of a
moral society. These policies served the YMCA well in China for a time.
By 1922 the organization had fifty-four thousand members in thirty-six
Chinese cities.[103]

Eddy approved of this modernizing; he saw Asian societies as irrevocably set upon a course toward transformation by Western influence,
and looked forward to a new cultural and social synthesis in which the
Christian Social Gospel would play a central role. These were views espousing a liberal-developmentalist approach to missions, in which the
United States could stimulate material as well as spiritual change.[104] Yet
Eddy's hopes first outlined in 1913 for a Christian and Western-oriented
"renaissance of Asia" were premature.[105] In the 1920s the YMCA faced

Fig. 13. Sherwood Eddy and the YMCA cultivated Asian nationalism in the 1920s. Here he is pictured with Chinese Nationalist leader Sun Yat-sen. Reproduced with permission of Sidney D. Gamble Photographs, Archive of Documentary Arts, Duke University; Item 140-791.

cascading "organized hostility" from the Chinese Communist Party (founded 1921) toward Christian missions as agents of "imperialism and capitalism."[106]

The permutations of radical dissent from the mainstream of American reform and missionary endeavors abroad in the decades before World War I were legion. Yet some generalizations can be ventured from these individual cases. Not only were the critics of American cultural expansion's blind spots in a minority; those who worked from without found it difficult, as in Ida Wells's case, to penetrate key transnational organizations and make an impact, though they did unsettle a self-congratulatory humanitarian consensus. Those who worked from within were often, like Johnston, minority dissenters. Meanwhile the indigenous who were collaborating with elements of the American reform program oscillated uneasily between cultures. Dissenting views on U.S. colonialism were certainly far from absent among the evangelical reformers. At the time of the Spanish-American War many women in the WCTU exhibited discomfort about American empire. During the 1899 annual meeting of the National WCTU held in Seattle, patriots complained in the press that they found in the women's deliberations that year "no word of praise for the peaceful expansion . . . no praise for the government that has gone before the missionary" and "no tracing of God's signs in the path of nations."[107] The weakness of the Seattle resolutions reflected the divided opinion in the organization on the efficacy of colonies and the criticism from radical opponents of empire such as Mary Garbutt. Nonetheless, Garbutt represented only one strand of thought within the WCTU, which mounted no consistent campaign against the occupation of the Philippines. In their thoughts and actions on American imperialism, most reformers were closer to the position of Eddy before World War I, who lacked a clear critique of American empire at all and viewed American cultural expansion in the form of the YMCA as a liberating, transnational force based on its Christian missions.

Eddy's optimism on the eve of World War I matched the prospects of the Christian moral reformers. Evangelicals had achieved much toward creating Wilbur Crafts's dream of a moral government. Working alongside voluntary groups the state would, reformers hoped, aid the global spread of Christian standards. Personal links with high policymakers were vital for projecting the influence of the reform networks in this way. The alliance of "soft" and "hard" power that architects of strategic policy and leading moral reformers jointly forged masked many tensions and compromises, but it also presented grand opportunities amid the changed circumstances of American power in the era of World War I. If 1886 was the decisive moment for the revitalization of American missions, 1917–19 was equally decisive for the new form of American empire, as moral reformers used the war in the march toward the zenith of their power.

PART IV

The Era of World War I and the Wilsonian New World Order

Chapter 9

STATES OF FAITH:

MISSIONS AND MORALITY

IN GOVERNMENT

ON APRIL 27, 1911, William Howard Taft addressed a Methodist Social Union dinner in New York, full of praise for missionaries. Recalling his time in the Philippines, the portly American president waxed eloquent: "I found Methodist brethren and missionaries at my back ready to furnish all the assistance I needed."[1] He became "so fond of one of the Methodist brethren, the Rev. Homer C. Stuntz," that, Taft claimed, "I have been running him for Bishop ever since." A year later Stuntz was indeed elected a bishop of the Methodist Episcopal Church on the first ballot. The endorsement of Taft may not have hurt.[2] At the Methodist dinner, the mutual back-scratching continued through dessert and coffee. Carl H. Fowler, the toastmaster, referred to Taft's efforts for international arbitration with Britain; he was "a Christian statesman whose victories of peace were as important as many of our victories in war." Remarkably, Taft himself was a Unitarian whose theological views came under attack by evangelical Americans at the time of the presidential election campaign in 1908,[3] yet he felt obliged to pay homage to the strength of the missionary lobby, and the lobby felt obliged to praise him.[4] Taft attached the same importance to the vast auxiliary machinery of the missionary enterprise in the form of Christian moral reform societies. In a 1911 speech to Christian Endeavor's international convention in Atlantic City, New Jersey, Taft cultivated support for his views on peace and arbitration. He reviewed the history of Christian Endeavor as having "the most beneficent effect upon the citizenship of a nation like this." Moral reform groups were a vital part of a social order, he noted, because they led to betterment of the individual and became "a leaven of the whole community" that uplifted the "righteousness" of a nation.[5]

Taft's praise was far from remarkable. The missionary lobby was one to be feared or respected by politicians, statesmen, and other policymakers, even if the homage-payer did not agree fully with its sentiments. Theodore Roosevelt and Woodrow Wilson, not to mention William McKinley, all cultivated positive relations with the benevolent empire of missionary groups. They addressed evangelical reform conferences, in which statements of mutual admiration abounded, and received deputations from them. Within the foreign policymaking elite, similar ties existed. Noted geopolitical strategist Alfred Thayer Mahan and Secretary of State Elihu Root exemplified these views. Policymakers could not completely ignore Protestant evangelicalism. To be sure, evangelical groups had long beaten a path to the White House on domestic political issues. William T. Sherman lamented that Abraham Lincoln faced too long a line of "preachers" and "Grannies" seeking to impart wisdom. From the turn of the twentieth century onward, the change was the scope of the moral interventions and their highly sophisticated, organized nature. The evangelical lobby became a factor of growing importance in American international relationships and part of the landscape of politics.[6]

Friction, however, marked relations between reformers and imperial strategists as much as agreement did. Stuntz, for example, was hardly at one with Governor Taft's policies on opium in 1903 and had proven a source of annoyance to the Philippine Commission on other occasions. Moreover, political leaders used the reformers more effectively than the latter influenced political leadership, with evangelicals becoming more and more the unwitting agents of the nation-state. While moral reform networks and missionaries did contribute at times to specific policy outcomes, these were usually determined by realpolitik. Rather than determine statecraft, the Christian coalition contributed to a missionary and reformist *Weltanschauung* within the higher echelons of American politics. The focus of this chapter is not, therefore, policy impacts but personal connections and commonalities of thought.

The solicitude of politicians toward the Christian reform coalition was rooted in one plain fact: an expansion of American moral reform and missionary work abroad so impressive that it could not be ignored. "America Leads in Giving," shouted one headline, while other commentators noted the vast expansion of the ancillary organizations as the "great progress of Christian missions."[7] Americans could boast upon the stages of international conferences abroad, as in the International YMCA meetings as early as 1894, that "America leads the world" in YMCAs' influence, numbers, and funding.[8] To media, politicians, and strategists, it seemed that the power of the United States was not based on military or economic muscle alone. The softer possibilities of persuasion were equally vital to American national purposes.[9] Ex-president Taft called the Student Volunteer Movement "another world power working in behalf of America" with results comparable to the ascension of American military power at the time of the Spanish-American War.[10] He and Woodrow Wilson were equally happy to use this "power" to further American material interests. When missionaries reported on the importance of their work to the growth of American commerce through the Open Door policy, the connection was obvious, but the relationship was broader than that. Strategists recognized the importance of ideas and their free exchange as being integral to the new world order of which American politicians dreamed.[11]

Architects of American empire such as Alfred Thayer Mahan and Theodore Roosevelt were tough realists but they had a thoroughly religious as much as strategic view. Mahan served ten years on the Board of Missions of the Protestant Episcopal Church and told Roosevelt in 1901 that it was important for the European powers to provide, in East Asia, "simple, entire liberty of entrance for European thought as well as European commerce."[12] This was not empty rhetoric. At precisely that time, Mahan took an active part as a parishioner in the moves to establish a Protestant Episcopal diocese in Philippines, the position to which Bishop Brent was appointed. The aim was to promote a "higher form of Christianity in the islands," as Mahan put it, to underpin American civil authority in the new colonies with the "enlightened public opinion" appropriate to a civilized society.[13] Mahan became a contributor to the World Missionary Conference in Edinburgh in 1910, advising New York politician and Mugwump reformer Seth Low, who headed the American advisory group attending the conference. Mahan influenced the conference's deliberations, and its *Report VII* on missionaries' relations to government used Mahan's work as a "verbatim source for substantial sections of the report."[14]

According to Mahan, missionaries had their own sphere, using the power of ideas to further the kingdom of Christ in an "act of Christian benevolence," but Mahan saw missionaries' work as more than that.[15] It was a key force in "the progress of the change which the impact of Christianity on the world produces."[16] Some countries, such as Japan, could be voluntarily "drawn into the movement of moral forces" with their common international standards of ethical and legal conduct. Vital therein was the leavening role of the Christian churches.[17] In Mahan's eyes, Christian work was akin to a form of soft power in the interests of the state and the expansion of Western civilization. Yet soft power could not be divorced from hard power. Mahan saw the progress of Christianity and the material expansion of American civilization as inextricably linked. At bottom, this was because God worked through material power to achieve spiritual ends. In 1909 Mahan published *The Harvest Within: Thoughts on the Life of the Christian*, arguing for "the parallelism" between "the occupation of Canaan by the Israelites and the occupation of America by the English race." Mahan could see "the finger of God" in the American westward movement.[18] Somewhat like the Jewish people, the English had been authorized to redeem a wilderness for a "distinctive mission of universal salvation." Mahan saw the American annexation of the Philippines as a "divine strategy" for extending this project to the whole of East Asia.[19]

For all this, Mahan was not securely in the camp of moral reform. He was a conservative and realist thinker who deplored perfectionist and utopian strains in evangelical thinking. While Mahan favored the evangelicals' spiritual efforts, he wanted them to stick to their missionary work—undertaken in the spiritual realm. He chided their attempts to intervene directly in international politics, especially where they sought to create a higher moral law above the law of nations and in contravention of national interests. In particular, he alluded to peace reformers who would deny the underlying reliance on force as justifiable for the Christian state. Missionaries did not, in his view, understand precisely how their own spiritual work depended on the physical power of Western military might. In an article in the *North American Review* published after the Edinburgh conference, he set out the ideal relationship between missionaries and government, and summarized the convictions he expressed in his influential advice to the conference. Force was "inoperative" in regard to "Christianity as a religious system," but this was not Mahan's realm, nor those he advised as a member of the foreign policy elite. That realm he called "Christianity as a political system," or "the Christian state." Christianity as a state-oriented power was the force that realized God's will, and hence was essential to spiritual and intellectual power. "Without man's responsive effort, God Himself is—not powerless—but deprived of the instrument through which alone He wills to work."[20] In this way, Christianity itself relied on the force of the state, and Mahan deplored the tendency of Christian churches to think or act otherwise.

While force was an essential element of U.S. and European relations with the colonial and quasi-colonial world, force had to be "used for the benefit of the community, of the commonwealth of the World." In this process "aggression" was inevitable. Japan might willingly accede to Western standards, but other colonial or quasi-colonial dependencies, such as Egypt, India, and the Philippines, "must be brought despite themselves into external conditions favorable to their welfare and the general good." For Christianity as a political system, force—"the sword if necessary"—was incumbent to "amend external conditions" just as the force underlying American law was used domestically to ameliorate social evils.[21] Mahan's arguments reflected widely shared Anglo-American views that made Protestant Christianity and the progress of Western imperial domination coterminous.

Mahan was not the only member of the foreign policy elite who endorsed missionary and moral reform abroad and yet wished those actions to respect the primacy of state political power. Elihu Root, who served successive administrations as secretary of war (1899–1904) and secretary

Fig. 14. Alfred Thayer Mahan, military strategist and Episcopalian missionary advisor. Reproduced from Charles Carlisle Taylor, *The Life of Admiral Mahan, Naval Philosopher* (London: John Murray, 1920), frontispiece.

of state (1905–9) before becoming an influential senator from New York (1909–15), had an evangelical past. A Presbyterian religious revival at Hamilton College during the Civil War had swept him up, and he served as a delegate to the Cleveland National Convention of the YMCA in 1866. Many years later, he acknowledged to John Mott the "old friendship and comradeship" he found in the YMCA. Yet Root, like Mahan, went out of his way to distance himself from evangelical meddling in foreign affairs; he intimated that he had traveled far from his youthful religious experience: "There have been very great changes in the world," he told Mott.[22] Root became a corporate lawyer of conservative inclination and an Episcopalian, and he was not, as we have already seen, sympathetic to Wilbur Crafts's brand of evangelical reform. The *New York Times* stated of Root that there was "nothing of the professed preacher" in his attitude toward public affairs, nor was he a "moralist" in the regard of "his fellow-citizens."[23] Nevertheless, he stressed the need for ethical standards to underwrite international law and acknowledged the role of the YMCA as an agent for the dissemination of those standards and for the progress of international cooperation. In 1909, he was invited to the YMCA International Committee's annual dinner. Guests at the Waldorf-

Astoria meeting listened to the triumphal boasting of YMCA leaders on "the Growth of the Association in Many Lands." Root was the principal speaker, and he added to the chorus of praise, but in ways that reflected his estimate of the evangelicals. He declared that the reason for the great success of the YMCA was its capacity to keep out of politics and doctrinal theology.[24] Christianity must know its place as an auxiliary to the power of the state in improving the international system, not as a substitute for national interests. Four years earlier as secretary of state, he had praised the upcoming meeting of the World Student Christian Federation in Tokyo (1907) and noted "the mingling of the young men of the Occident and Orient to discuss questions pertaining to the highest life of men" that "must result in much good to all countries." As with Mahan, Root saw Christianity as an aid to diplomatic efforts in promoting "good understanding and cordial relations between the different countries and races."[25]

Only in two cases did close personal relations develop between missionary leaders and the influential policymakers of the time, but the examples are instructive. Bishop Brent and John Mott had remarkable access to presidents, and each served as an advisor, Brent primarily to Roosevelt but also to Taft, and Mott to Woodrow Wilson. Of these two cases, Brent's personal contact with political power was the more superficial but nevertheless significant. Brent had performed an important role in the development of U.S. anti-opium policy from 1903 to 1909 and as a result had become acquainted with both Roosevelt and Secretary of War Taft while the latter was governor-general of the Philippines (1901–3). As a Republican, Brent supported Roosevelt's presidency and GOP policies on the Philippines. Like the Republican leadership, he favored retention of the "insular possessions" for as long as possible, but found Taft's creation of an elected assembly in the Philippines in 1907 irritating and argued that this sop to democratic opinion was designed purely to further Taft's presidential ambitions in 1908.[26]

Roosevelt was not tainted by this immediate policy connection and so did not suffer in his relations with Brent until after his presidency had ended. Even as Brent occasionally criticized Roosevelt's style and his political maneuverings, the two had much in common through their religious beliefs and practices. Roosevelt grew up within the Dutch Reformed Church, but he was ecumenical and non-doctrinal in his religious views, and took communion at Christ Church Episcopal at Oyster Bay, a church he regarded in later life as his home parish.[27] Roosevelt's religious worship gave him links with Brent, who had been influenced in his youth and early parish work by Anglo-Catholicism but moved as a bishop to a more middle-of-the-road theological position within Anglicanism. While Roosevelt had many ways of learning about missions, one of them was through Brent during the latter's frequent visits to the United States to confer with bishops, when he often trod the path to Oyster Bay or the White House. Oyster Bay itself was a congenial setting for reminders about the history of missions. Its rector was the Rev. George E. Talmage, who also had a Reformed Church background and was one of the original Student Volunteers of 1886.[28]

Brent was both impressed and mildly irritated by Roosevelt's high-octane style. Roosevelt "talks too much," the bishop complained, but he affirmed that the president had "done a great deal that will endure to the benefit of the country." As an anti-Jeffersonian and believer "in centralization," Brent was highly susceptible to the version of Progressivism that Roosevelt preached with its heavy doses of American nationalism and its aspirations to flex American muscle on the world stage.[29] The bishop supported Roosevelt in the 1904 presidential election[30] and pronounced the result a "great victory" that ensured "a future for the Filipinos" under protracted American tutelage. In turn Roosevelt approved of Brent as a man whose candid advice was always "directed to doing good, not merely to cause unpleasant feelings."[31]

At their meetings, Roosevelt confided with Brent about strategic policy in East Asia, and Brent opined on Japan's introduction to the role of a Westernized and civilizing power in the region as vital to the stability of the world.[32] Brent told the wife of American ambassador Whitelaw Reid in London about these conversations, and argued that the United States must wake up to its "unique opportunities in the Orient to influence life and manners." No longer was the world "divided into two political halves." The globalized twentieth-century world was "a close-wrought unity in which oriental countries hold quite as important a place as the countries of the western hemisphere." Japan's "victorious course" in the Russo-Japanese War of 1904–5 showed the way toward modernization through Christian influence that would "become equally manifest before many years pass away in the adjacent nations." He and Roosevelt discussed former secretary of state John W. Forster's book on American diplomacy in East Asia, a work said to open "a vista of what lies beyond today."[33] Forster praised the role of missionaries in Hawaii in favoring the American annexation of the islands in 1898, and emphasized the importance of the China missions as "useful to the government and society in many ways" because of the "service they have rendered in diplomacy" and "the benefits of education and medicine" that they had brought.[34]

Partly because Brent impressed presidents, he impressed his fellow bishops. The rumor spread among clerics that "More than any other Bishop, Bishop Brent has influence with the civil authorities at Washington."[35] It came as no surprise, then, that in May 1908 Brent was elected bishop of the District of Columbia, the most important diocese in the country.[36] Both Roosevelt and Taft tried to get Brent to accept the offer, and Taft argued that the Washington position would bring the bishop "closely in touch with the leaders of political thought in the Nation," enabling him to "exercise an influence much more widespread than the comparative number of churches under your pastoral guidance."[37] Roosevelt wanted as bishop someone with "the intense zeal of a missionary" and yet "the practical judgment of a cool-headed reformer" to advise him on problems afforded "by the slums" of the nation's capital and throughout the nation, and he saw Brent as such a man. The lessons of Manila could be applied in a new missionary setting at home.[38] Yet Brent was not susceptible to such entreaties or thoughts of vanity. He favored the cause in East Asia as a sacred, uncompleted task of uplifting the non-white races and did not take the Washington job. Telling Taft that he had "never been dependent upon the prestige of position," Brent nevertheless assured him that "You can always depend upon me during my life in the Philippines to serve the interests of my country in every way possible."[39] Both Taft and Roosevelt were disappointed but acquiesced and continued the friendship.[40]

By 1912, Brent's political stance changed. He was peeved with Roosevelt over the third-party Bull Moose split from the Republicans that gave the election to the Democrats. Not only was he fed up with Roosevelt's incessant politicking; he was also disillusioned with Taft and claimed that he would vote for Wilson if he were in the United States at the time of the election.[41] The erosion of Progressivism within the Republican Party under Taft's leadership made Brent vulnerable to the new progressive currents within Wilson's ranks, but he worried that the historic shift of power to the Democrats might "mean a very serious crisis in Philippine affairs."[42] The Democrats' determination to hasten Philippine independence drove him back to the Republicans, where he supported the unsuccessful Charles Evans Hughes in the 1916 election. Brent despaired at the views of his fellow voters: "If there were any hope of [Wilson's] changing and becoming what one desires a political leader to be, it would be different." He feared, however, "that a leopard cannot change his spots."[43] Yet this is precisely what Wilson did in Brent's estimation. Soon, Brent would be a staunch ally and advocate of Wilsonian idealism. John Mott would not have been surprised, since his own relationship with Wilson had always been positive. By 1917, Brent and Mott thought alike in praise of Wilson, but in the years before, it was Mott who became allied with Wilson and whose views were brought into greater prominence by the coming of World War I.

John Mott's background was Presbyterian, so, like Roosevelt's relationship with Brent, religious sympathies smoothed the path to presidential cooperation and even friendship. Wilson's father was a clergyman in the Southern Presbyterian Church, a church with four mission stations in China from the 1860s and forty in foreign fields by 1900.[44] Mott first met Wilson at a Wesleyan University campaign of the Student Volunteer Movement in 1889 while Mott was associate secretary of that organization and Wilson a professor.[45] Over the course of the next fifteen years, the friendship grew to one of mutual admiration founded in similar worldviews of evangelicalism, non-denominational cooperation in moral reform, and the global spread of Protestant Christianity's influences. Theologically their positions were similar. Wilson sided with Mott's view of the primary importance of evangelicalism over social service among the Student Volunteers. Reading Mott's lectures on "the problem of securing able men for the ministry" suggested to Wilson the importance of the pastor's "spiritual" role. Churches had perhaps diverted their attention "from the effectual preaching of the Word." To Wilson the danger seemed to be "that individual churches will become great philanthropic societies" rather than "organizations from which go forth the spiritual stimulation which should guide all philanthropic effort."[46] Mott professed to be in "full and hearty agreement."[47] They were also personal friends. Mott even received a handwritten invitation to the wedding of Wilson's daughter to William Gibbs McAdoo in 1914.[48]

Because of their contacts and affinities, Mott was able to secure the future president as a speaker at Christian conferences during Wilson's years as president of Princeton University and governor of New Jersey. One was at the highly significant Northfield meetings. At the Seventeenth Annual Conference of the American and Canadian Student YMCAs in 1902, Wilson gave the Fourth of July oration. He stressed religion as an energizing force of moral character that focused an individual's life upon higher patriotic service. "How a religious man can fail to have the fine impulse of patriotism I cannot conceive," he remarked.[49] Wilson also addressed the Inter-Church Conference on Federation in a speech titled "The Mediation of Youth in Christian Progress" on November 19, 1905.[50] There he used the example of the YMCA as a successful story of non-dogmatic, interdenominational cooperation in the "mighty task" of making the United States "a mighty Christian nation," and thus aid its efforts "to Christianize the world."[51] Many times Wilson spoke at YMCA meetings and heartily supported the organization of which Mott was the leading light.

The future president's alliance with Mott was not merely theological. It fit Wilson's geopolitical ambitions for America. He saw the YMCA as the most successful Christian organization not only for sharpening an American moral purpose but also as a lever to open China and Japan to Western influence. In Wilson's view, missionaries tended to penetrate only the marginalized in societies they touched. He credited the YMCA

rather than regular missionaries with reaching the elites who were making the decisive changes in China's political and social systems under the
new republic established in 1911. The Chinese Revolution he regarded
positively as a progressive change. Behind the superficial movements of
politics, Wilson detected the hand of God working through the forces
of moral reform that underlay political freedom. No doubt the YMCA
had contributed to political change in China because nothing, in Wilson's
estimate, was "so revolutionary as the light; nothing . . . so revolutionary as those rays that disclose the moral relationships of men."[52] He also
believed that the YMCA served successfully as a modernizer and civilizer
in Japan for just one reason. It used a minimum of dogma in comparison
with regular missionaries.[53] His views were thus similar in this respect to
Mahan's, who saw Christianity as part of the exertion of Euro-American
hegemony to promote peaceful progress in East Asia.

Wilson championed the interests of Mott because he saw the Volunteers' leader as an architect of global evangelism, an agent of American
cultural expansion abroad, and a figure with foreign policy significance.
Just as Roosevelt supported Brent for the position of Bishop of the District of Columbia, Wilson as president of Princeton University lauded
Mott's reputation and conferred honors upon him by granting him a
doctor of laws degree. Wilson saw this as a "tardy recognition" of the
"great work you have been doing for the advancement of the deepest
human interests."[54] The citation listed Mott's role as a Christian crusader in the conquering of the world. Wilson's opinion of Mott was so
high that he regarded him as a candidate for high office, perhaps as a
university president. But he joked that "Mr. Mott can't afford to take
the presidency of a great university," as Wilson had done, because "Mr.
Mott occupies a certain spiritual presidency in the spiritual university of
the world."[55]

Mott had no hesitation in using his friendship with Wilson to lobby for
changes that would facilitate missionary work abroad or improve life in
the lands to which missionaries had gone. In February 1913, the YMCA
leader called on Wilson to recognize the Chinese republic. Prompt action
would, he urged a Wilson confidante, "enormously enhance our prestige
in the East."[56] This request received a favorable response; historians cannot say that Mott's influence was a determining factor in achieving U.S.
recognition, though it probably reinforced the impression Wilson already
had.[57] But Mott's own lobbying had another effect. It brought him to
Wilson's attention as a possible American ambassador to China. With
the concurrence of the evangelically inclined Secretary of State William
Jennings Bryan, Wilson was keen to have Mott as his diplomatic representative in Peking in order to signal the importance he attached to the
missionaries' role. Acknowledging "the influence which American mis-

sions and religious institutions have had in the regeneration of China," Wilson boosted Mott as a conduit for the "harmonious discharge" of those missionary views and as integral to the administration's recognition of the new republic.[58] Wilson's entreaties to accept the offer were conveyed by their mutual friend Cleveland H. Dodge. The evangelical businessman Dodge had been Wilson's classmate at Princeton and was an important benefactor of the YMCA. Though Mott was resistant, Wilson enlisted Dodge and others to pressure the YMCA leader because "the interests of China and of the Christian world" were so "intricately involved."[59] "I have set my heart on you" as "eminently fitted" for the post, Wilson explained to Mott, and begged him to accept the mission.[60] In a separate piece of pleading, Wilson even promised that Mott would be allowed to continue his private activities with the Student Volunteers and the YMCA. He would be given leave while still ambassador to undertake missionary assignments: "It would help rather than interfere with your work as representative of this government if you retained your posts" for "guidance in your present work."[61]

Underpinning the offer was Wilson's merger of morality and American statecraft, a move that won missionary approval. Wilson wished to send a signal that American policy in East Asia was anti-imperialist and directed toward the strengthening of the moral forces that he believed underpinned the revolutionary changes in China. Missionaries sensed Mott's political skills, contacts, and worth to their cause, and endorsed the appointment in a meeting with the president.[62] Yet Mott saw things differently because he accepted Wilson's own view of Mott's global rather than national role. Though he deeply regretted having to turn down the president, he declined such a "truly great opportunity" because he could "not fulfill serious obligations already assumed and do justice to [the] new position."[63] God was more important to him than any narrow view of patriotism. While Wilson professed despair at Mott's rejection, the friendship remained intact.[64] Like Brent, Mott had refused an offer from a president to serve in a national capacity, but the parallel did not end there. Both men were swayed to reconsider their obligations to the nation in time of war, though they did so in different ways.

Once war was declared between Britain and Germany in August 1914 Brent sprang to the defense of what he saw as Anglo-American civilization against German aggression and autocracy. These were themes congenial to Wilson, but Brent took his stance from his Canadian birth and his religion more than anything else. Friendship with leading Anglican dignitaries, including the Archbishop of Canterbury, gave him the intellectual backing for his increasingly pro-British views.[65] He quickly became pro-war, and his opinion of Wilson waxed and waned depending on the president's variable diplomatic stance toward Germany. While visiting

London in a show of Anglo-Saxon solidarity in late 1916, Brent urged Wilson to break off diplomatic relations with Germany and objected to a drive designed to achieve what Brent called a premature and unfair peace settlement.[66] He claimed that there was already cause enough for war and not to fight would be "cowardice." Wilson's vacillation made the nation itself potentially a collection of cowards in Brent's view, but as Wilson moved steadily toward war in early 1917 Brent depicted the United States as newly "unified in the direction of a great purpose."[67] Once the nation was committed to the struggle, Brent argued for Wilsonian idealist objectives, not a territorial war of aggression or reprisal.[68] He accepted an appointment as senior chaplain in the General Headquarters of the American Expeditionary Force, worked in close cooperation with Mott's YMCA, and lectured the troops in Europe on the "great moral and spiritual significance" of the "entry of America into the War."[69]

By 1919 he was a committed Wilsonian internationalist. So much so that in the 1920s, he named Wilson as one of the four greatest men of the twentieth century alongside Gandhi, Lenin, and anti-German Cardinal Désiré Joseph Mercier of Belgium.[70] He told parishioners in Buffalo, New York, "No more can America move back to her aloof position; no more can [we] busy ourselves with mere petty nationalism; all that we think and all that we do must be colored by the fact that our nation is related to all the nations of the world and is, in a measure, responsible for their wellbeing." This change in status he believed was true not only of national affairs but of missions.[71] Brent had become a convinced internationalist, but he was also able to keep his internationalism compatible with growing respect for the United States through support for Wilsonian statecraft. Brent now lost his sense of being different, of being a Canadian. "I was a foreigner, but I was never treated as such," he reminisced of his arrival in the United States thirty-two years earlier, and there came a time when "it would be impossible for me ever to leave." The American people had accepted him and he was at their service.[72] These were postwar reflections on a much earlier time, but only the American commitment to the European struggle allowed this reconciliation for him. The crusading nation spilling blood on the battlefield for human liberty and right conduct had aligned his personal intellectual and spiritual journey with both the American nation and the new internationalism of Woodrow Wilson.

Mott's personal political odyssey was similar though starting from a different point since he had always been a supporter of Wilson. His relations with the president did not cool as a result of his rejection of the China post in 1913. He expressed to Wilson in 1914 "profound appreciation of the remarkable way in which you are bringing to bear the principles of righteousness and unselfishness in all your relations to national and international affairs. My world-wide travels have enabled me to see that you are lifting our nation into a high and large place in the thought of those whose opinions we must value."[73] Wilson returned the compliment, depicting Mott's work with the YMCA as an element of this same extension of righteousness, and agreed to provide an endorsement for the opening of the new YMCA headquarters building in the Philippines.[74] Nor did the mutual respect decline during the war, though the two inevitably became distant as the pressures of office on Wilson grew. Occasionally Mott could still see Wilson, but White House staff increasingly shielded the president from further close interaction.[75] Yet this did not undermine the relationship on ideological, political, or moral levels.

Deepening world conflict made Mott even more inclined to align the YMCA with Wilson's efforts to achieve reform in the international order. Turmoil within Mexico after the revolution of 1911 set faction upon faction, and the instability could not be contained within national boundaries. In 1916, cross-border tension with Mexico rose when the United States sent a punitive expedition to Mexico, led by General John J. Pershing, to quell bandit raids on American territory by Francisco "Pancho" Villa's rebel forces. Wilson depicted this conflict as one of protecting American property and citizens and as consistent with high standards of international law. As a committed Wilsonian, Mott agreed. So too did the Federal Council of Churches judge the Mexican incursion ethical. Protestant churchmen sought an "ethics for an international policeman" with the nation on the brink of war with Mexico. "Jesus never condemned national self-protection," ventured the council's *Biblical World*. "A policeman protecting social ideals from maniacs and thugs is an exponent of more efficient social service than a Good Samaritan licking up the wounds of victims of social neglect."[76] Here the Social Gospel underwrote the nation's exercise of hard power.

Wilson selected Mott to serve as one of three commissioners to discuss with the commissioners of the Mexican government the settlement of questions arising out of the "Mexican situation."[77] The outcome of the Joint High Commission was an agreement that did not meet with Mexico's approval because it did not provide for the immediate removal of Pershing's troops. Yet it did, historian Arthur Link has argued, stave off war until after the 1916 presidential election, a time when any U.S. military retreat would have been politically difficult. With the election over, Wilson was able to engineer a withdrawal.[78] Dutifully Mott performed his assigned role in these proceedings, but the issues were technical, diplomatic, and economic, and did not in any substantial way include the moral ones that Mott made his own. Mott's participation was interesting chiefly in the fact that Wilson actually chose him—a Protestant evangelical—over Catholic opposition within the United States.[79] Mexico was a Catholic country, a fact that made Mott's selection symbolically important. It reflected Wilson's determination to press his foreign strategic and political objectives welded together with a missionary-like ethical dimension. The Federal Council of Churches chorused that an "appeal to police methods" could be "justified only when free of any policy of aggrandisement."[80] This, the council and Mott believed, the United States was doing. The subsequent American entry into World War I would soon raise similar ethical issues, and Mott could not avoid these either.

More significant than the Joint Commission appointment was the choice of Mott as a member of ex-senator Elihu Root's Special Diplomatic Mission to Russia.[81] Conducted after the collapse of the tsarist state and its replacement by the liberal-democratic Kerensky government early in 1917, the mission was designed to stimulate a continuing Russian commitment to the war as an ally of the United States. William Sloane, chairman of the War Council of the YMCA, claimed that Mott was chosen because he was "so thoroughly acquainted with Russian conditions, as a result of his student talks and other association activities there in the last eighteen years."[82] Indeed, Mott had already visited Russia three times as part of Student Christian Federation work and had contacts in the Orthodox Church through his prominence at ecumenical Christian conferences in Europe before the war. Wilson also knew that Mott was one of his strongest supporters and could be relied on to put a case similar to that which he himself would have made. The choice of Mott also signaled the importance Wilson assigned to the YMCA in the war effort, work that the president frequently endorsed.[83]

In Russia, Mott's tasks were to maintain the morale of the Russian troops so that they would continue to fight. He addressed meetings of the Orthodox Church and interviewed its individual leaders as a way of influencing opinion, began the process of extending the YMCA's war work in providing moral guidance, material relief, and recreation for soldiers returning from the front, and delivered speeches urging the Russian people to "stand firmly behind the Provisional Government."[84] Mott did not focus on Russia's continued military effort in the war. These political and diplomatic aspects were left to Root. Rather, issues of the "democratization of the Orthodox Church" preoccupied the YMCA leader. If civil society were to develop in Russia, Mott argued, the strengthening of "democratic forces" would be vital. He emphatically concluded that one of the most critical problems facing Russia was "ensuring an able leadership of the Christian forces of the nation."[85] Mott's role in Russia and his focus on moral questions were entirely consistent with the new international order that Wilson proclaimed. Wilsonian diplomacy preached open commerce, the rights of democracy, self-determination, and the rule of law. These ideals depended on peaceful economic interactions between peoples but also presumed ideological and religious freedom.[86]

Not only was Mott's personal career now closely nailed to the mast of Wilsonianism; the entire institution of the YMCA joined in the effort to win the war. On the Western Front, the YMCA ministered to American troops by staffing their own military canteens. Though other American and foreign groups such as the Knights of Columbus and the Salvation Army assisted the work for soldiers, for the United States the YMCA was the dominant partner. To a considerable degree, the YMCA became a semi-official arm of the U.S. government. Mott had Wilson's support for his work. The president spoke of the YMCA's vitally important mission "to carry the generous message of an unselfish America to the soldiers and prisoners" in Europe and to "lighten the burdens of the men who carry our colors."[87] He acceded to the demand for $4 million of government money to aid the work in Russia, Italy, and France after Mott's recommendation upon his return from Moscow.[88] Under Mott's leadership, the YMCA also established a campaign to raise $35 million from the private sector for war work. Within just one month it had gleaned $3 million, often from small donations, but also including the usual large business contributions. Later, YMCA secretaries introduced relief work to the prisoner-of-war camps in Germany as well as Russia, where they aimed to "remove the misery of idleness" among prisoners that could lead to "viciousness."[89] A remarkable outpouring of the humanitarianism that had been seen before World War I in aid of famine victims was now displayed on the battlefields of Europe. Harold Ickes, the future secretary of the interior, portrayed in his reports as an agent of the YMCA a "vivid picture of middle-aged, business and professional men suddenly called from sedentary lives," sleeping out, marching with the soldiers but on less rations, and "anxious only to be of service."[90] The work meant supplying suitable reading material, operating canteens, providing moral counseling, and attempting to combat sexual license.

A good deal of the YMCA effort took place within the United States, before the departure of troops, yet the enterprise was truly transnational. Even within American territory, it covered the far-flung outposts of the Philippines and Hawaii, and in Europe mingled workers and recipients from many countries in a cooperative program designed to enhance international understanding. It did not operate purely within American lines, and its efforts concerned not only Allied soldiers and prisoners of war but also the transnational migration of laborers. The YMCA carried out a program of great magnitude in moving and caring for over 130,000 Chinese non-combatants sent to the Western Front as part of the Allies' logistical requirements. These poor workers were recruited by the YMCA of China to serve as exemplars to Europeans of the uplifting work going on in the mission schools and YMCAs in East Asia. Recruits would showcase the new China that the missionaries and the Chinese

republican government were forging together. They would also contribute to the new international world order of peace and progress when
they returned from the war zone. Peking-based missionary Charles Ewing
aimed to "get them to give a great impetus to the new China, the most important thing at which we may aim."[91] Fearing, however, that the Chinese
would be unimpressed by the incidence of "vice" and racism among soldiers on the Western Front, the YMCA leadership sent agents to smooth
the laborers' paths, provide them with suitable recreations to avoid the
temptations of sex and drink, and aid their return to China at the war's
end. The organization received international funding for this enterprise.
The Chinese government gave $1.3 million, mostly to the YMCAs but
also to the Salvation Army. Among those who joined the enterprise were
Scottish and American missionaries, but Christian Chinese converts were
also prominent. By 1919, seventy-four Chinese student secretaries served
the YMCA in France; over forty came from the United States but others
directly from China. Their command of the Chinese language gave them
a great advantage over workers from the United States. As one Scottish
missionary accompanying the laborers stated, "The Chinese Secretaries
have been a good deal of the backbone in this movement. . . . What could
you do without the Chinese[?]"[92]

After the war the YMCA faced criticism back home for its overreaching program, as the nation shrank back from its wartime commitment.
Brigadier General John J. Bradley, inspector general of the army, argued
that the military could have done a better job with the canteens on such
matters as their variable opening hours. It was alleged that the canteen
work took up too much time at the expense of Christian duties and that
a disproportionate number of YMCA secretaries remained in Paris rather
than at the front where they were vitally needed.[93] Critics also charged
that the YMCA's educational programs in the military camps were necessarily ephemeral in impact because of the rapid deployment and constant
movement of troops.[94] Within the YMCA, too much attention had been
paid to advertising its own plans and too little to the actual delivery
of services. Ickes stated that "enlisted men became antagonistic toward
us" because of indiscreet publicity. In both the United States and France,
"over-claiming" tarnished the effort of the rank-and-file workers. This
"real and justifiable cause of complaint" was compounded by the fact
that the YMCAs charged for canteen goods while other welfare organizations often gave theirs away.[95]

Despite the criticism, the humanitarian impulse did not stop at the
war's end. Alongside the Red Cross and other bodies, the YMCA channeled food and clothing to the war-torn populations of central and eastern
Europe. Prewar voluntarist traditions of humanitarian giving founded in
the 1890s continued with the missionary-inspired American Committee

for Armenian and Syrian Relief (later renamed the Near East Relief Committee). Formed in September 1915 at the beginning of a new round of Armenian massacres within the Ottoman Empire, the scale of the committee's relief operations vastly increased from the war's end in November 1918. A key responsibility was dealing with the human consequences of the upheaval in the Ottoman territories, where the prewar Protestant missionary effort had been so strong. As with prewar humanitarianism, this relief had religious and moral freight; it served American ideological purposes. The committee's food aid aroused "a sincere regard and even affection for America," wrote Calvin Coolidge. "Our country was the good Samaritan that did not pass them by."[96]

The postwar philanthropy differed from that before 1914, however, in the extent of the public-private partnership. In the case of the Indian famine of the 1890s, hesitant government involvement had incurred the displeasure of the missionaries. Now, the magnitude of the crisis in Europe and the Middle East gave voluntarism even greater importance but in a closer partnership with an interventionist government. The Near East Relief Committee was incorporated under an act of Congress in 1919, but from its very inception in 1915 upon the news of the Armenian slaughter of that year, the "entire files" of the Department of State were placed at the committee's "disposal" for intelligence and reconnaissance purposes, while government and private philanthropy worked hand in hand with assistance from the U.S. Navy and other agencies.[97] The government's American Relief Administration established early in 1919 under Herbert Hoover's direction was centrally important in this work. In partnership with the YMCA, the Red Cross, and the Near East Relief Committee, Hoover worked with other private agencies and the remains of his wartime U.S. Food Administration to distribute food aid in Europe. Under Hoover's leadership, American "ambassadors, ministers, consuls," and other government officials "carried a generous share of the responsibilities for the actual administration of the relief funds."[98] Hoover became involved in food diplomacy to combat the spread of the Russian Bolshevik Revolution, especially in Poland, Hungary, and Austria where, the future president himself put it, "the food operation was indeed a race against both death and Communism." Hoover warned that food shipments would be suspended if public order were disturbed and claimed that "fear of starvation held the Austrian people from Revolution."[99]

Humanitarianism was now harnessed to the interests of American foreign policy in ways that broke with the more transnational formulations of the 1880s and 1890s by directly serving American strategic and diplomatic objectives. Not that the missionaries could achieve their own political aims. The old Protestant missionary lobby in the Ottoman Empire could not get Congress to endorse demands for a U.S. mandate over the

Armenian part of Turkey. The missionaries were not able to determine events on the larger world stage, where great power politics, the rapidly changing events in Turkey itself, and the assertion of Bolshevik control in the Caucasus region undermined Armenian hopes to create an independent state.[100]

The greatest symbol of evangelical entanglement with the postwar politics of the state was Mott himself. The leading figure in the YMCA and the Student Volunteers had become involved in government diplomacy, and the outcome was especially seen in his work in Russia, where the YMCA implemented Woodrow Wilson's projected role for nongovernmental organizations in the new world order. These would bypass governments, serve on a people-to-people level, and express the highest ideals of American foreign policy.[101] The YMCA work was ambitious in regard to Russia, reaching "a peak" with $8 million spent and over four hundred workers in the field from 1917 to 1920, but this program had to be gradually curtailed as a result of the Bolshevik Revolution. When Russia divided between anti-communists and Bolsheviks in the great civil war, and the United States intervened in Siberia alongside allies to protect anti-communist forces, Mott continued to support the president. He believed Wilson had been "providentially guided from the beginning ... with reference to Russia."[102] As a result of the intervention, however, the YMCA's role as a neutral force in the conflict was compromised and its last workers were forced to leave by 1923. The Bolsheviks viewed Mott's men as an extension of both American power and foreign policies antagonistic to the survival of socialist revolution.[103] Already Wilson's diplomacy was dead, with both the Siberian intervention and the League of Nations ratification failing, but the missionaries and their allies still had one last millenarian scheme in hand. They were determined to capitalize on the heightened sense of American power and internationalist sentiment to push moral reform campaigns upon Europe and the world. Prohibition of alcohol would be the vehicle for one last extension of the moral reform networks bequeathed by the transnational expansionism of the Progressive Era.

Chapter 10

TO MAKE A DRY WORLD:

THE NEW WORLD ORDER OF

PROHIBITION

THE EARLY 1920s was an era of great hope but also one of equally great potential for disillusionment. World War I upset dreams of peaceful evolution and cooperation and, with the controversial peace settlement and rejection of the League of Nations, many American internationalists despaired.[1] Protestant evangelical values also faced new challenges within the United States. Religious fundamentalism rent the churches, while the growth of sexual freedom and secularism seemed to go together as new generations flouted Victorian decorum, leaving Americans deeply divided over morals and manners. Among the hopes unsettled were those of the expansive prewar missionary campaigns, but amid doubts over the best course of action for Christian reform, dreams of a better future persisted. The true disillusionment and decline for the Christian moral reformers had not yet arrived because the war paved the way for their greatest single effort to change the world. For daring and sheer overreaching, few plans could outdo those of the prohibitionists who dreamed of a dry world, made so by American example and missions.

Moral reform's disillusion was effectively delayed until the second half of 1920s by the onset of national prohibition and the possibilities it opened up for global regeneration. Passage of the Eighteenth Amendment to the Constitution and its legislative implementation through the Volstead Act in 1919 achieved the national victory that could be the perfect platform for an international campaign. Rather than being deterred by the experience of World War I, evangelical reformers saw Wilsonian democratic idealism (itself influenced by connections to the missionaries, YMCAs, and other Christian organizations) as a model for the extended moral influence of the United States. The struggle "over there" to defeat German autocracy and bring victory to the democracies would be duplicated in a struggle against drink. The WCTU's *Union Signal* proclaimed "world prohibition" as essential to "worldwide democracy."[2] Anti-Saloon League of America cofounder Howard Russell called prohibition "the world-wide campaign to carry this blessing of freedom throughout the world."[3] And the evangelical responsibility would rest upon the United States because "God has brought America into the Kingdom for such a time as this," proclaimed Methodist bishop James Cannon.[4]

The breathtaking ambitions of the World League Against Alcoholism (WLAA) are the subject of this chapter. The grasp for global moral hegemony clashed with the new modernist culture abroad as well as at home but at the same time carried elements of American modernity with it. While these American religious and moral values attracted like-minded social groups and reformers abroad who contributed to the new movement, the direction of reform had changed. Whereas in its earlier manifestations the experience of other empires and events in the quasi-colonial world had influenced reformers in the United States, the post–World War I movement was a projection outward of newfound American power. Internal American reform was now the sole model for the world. American reform's relations with the world were still transnational, involving the reciprocal movement of ideas, institutions, and personnel across national boundaries, but the relationship had become profoundly unequal. War had accentuated the moral imbalance, spurring a highly charged and triumphant patriotism that distinguished the new campaign. Characteristically, the *Union Signal*'s front-page headline calling for world prohibition now carried a border of American flags as embellishment.[5]

The ink was scarcely dry on the Wartime Prohibition Act of November 1918 when the leaders of the preeminent temperance societies intensified their calls for world prohibition. Results came quickly. At a June 1919 meeting in Washington, prominent Anti-Saloon League (ASL) official Ernest H. Cherrington formed, through joint action of the ASL of America and the Dominion Temperance Alliance of Canada, the World League Against Alcoholism. Cherrington himself took the job of secretary. The new organization opened an office in Britain and held its first international conference in Toronto in 1922, where over a thousand delegates attended. To coordinate European work the league appointed Henry Beach Carre, a Tennessee clergyman, as overseas manager based in London; and it sent a variety of ASL officials on international missions. The WLAA tapped preexisting reform networks of the period before 1914 to extend this work abroad. A delegation of prohibitionists led by Cherrington hurried to Europe at the war's close to lobby the Versailles Peace Conference, after which he boldly claimed that the ASL was responsible for the provisions against the supply of alcohol to African colonial peoples agreed to in a convention attached to the Treaty of St. Germaine-en-Laye (September 10, 1919).[6] At the same time, the delegation held several conferences in European cities to curry support and initiate new networks. Of four presidents initially chosen for the WLAA, three were foreigners: Leif Jones, Emil Vandervelde, and Robert Hercod.[7] The Welshman Jones was president of the United Kingdom Alliance, the main temperance group in Britain, and a Liberal Party MP.[8] Vandervelde, a Belgian Democratic Socialist and Cabinet minister, was the author of the Vandervelde Law, which prohibited the sale of distilled spirits in liquor shops, later modified to prohibit on-premises consumption only. To prohibitionists too far away to appreciate local complexities, Vandervelde represented the closest equivalent to an Anti-Saloon League approach on the European continent. Hercod they knew better from before the war, since he was director of the International Bureau against Alcohol based in Lausanne, Switzerland. Hercod's organization had been founded at the Eleventh International Congress on Alcoholism in 1907 and was established as a Bureau of the International Congress, but after 1919 he received funding from the World League.[9] Officials of the Scientific Temperance Federation and International Order of Good Templars joined the executive along with a variety of groups in other countries that modeled their activities on the ASL. The WCTU cooperated as did the YMCA, though each maintained its own missionary programs abroad. Beginning initially with twelve countries affiliated, the World League grew in the 1920s to representation in thirty-four countries, with sixty-one partner organizations.[10]

This aspiration for a dry world went back to the 1880s, but not until the world war and its aftermath were circumstances promising. Prohibitionists had long viewed national victory as the path to global victory. When Cherrington explicitly announced the goal of world prohibition for the Anti-Saloon League in 1913, the WCTU had already done so—in 1911. The WCTU's then president Lillian Stevens called "for a great crusade to carry the vital truth to the people of all lands, and through them to place prohibition in the organic law of all nations and ultimately in the organic law of the world."[11] But just a few years later, reformers seized the possibility to effect their dreams by capitalizing on changing attitudes toward drink revealed abroad in World War I. An important early architect of a constitutional prohibition amendment, Democratic congressman Richmond P. Hobson, told Anna Gordon of the WCTU in 1915 that "The action of the governments in Europe[,] far more drastic than anything we are dreaming of, has prepared the public mind for being focused in this way."[12] Wartime enthusiasm had wrought its effect on liquor and anti-liquor forces in many parts of Europe. Even the French had banned the highly potent absinthe, "the sole case of prohibition of a drink in France."[13] In a much-publicized statement British prime minister David Lloyd George declared drink a greater enemy of the British nation than the Kaiser's hordes, while his foe, Germany, had also restricted brewing.[14] Some countries went much further. Iceland had enacted prohibition as early as 1912, and Finland would soon do so in 1921. Norway had established a partial prohibition by outlawing liquors over 12 percent alcohol in content in 1917; a pro-prohibition vote was taken by plebiscite in 1919 and the wartime change enacted in permanent legislation in 1921.[15] Canada enacted wartime prohibition in 1916, and wartime liquor restrictions continued in Britain and Australasia. Local option sentiment was growing in New Zealand, four of the six Australian states enacted six o'clock closing during the war, and another introduced nine o'clock closing, partly as a measure to restrict heavy drinking among the troops but also as an opportunistic drive that would lay the groundwork for future prohibition.[16] Concern over liquor consumption was not a purely American aberration: it was part of an international movement seeking greater national efficiency during the world crisis.

To be sure, other motives mingled with an idealism born of the rising international interest. This was an era of xenophobia in the United States, and the movement was undoubtedly tinged with these intellectual currents. In a period characterized by bouts of radical, labor, and ethnic conflict stirred by the war, prohibitionists became, like many Americans, concerned with preempting problems of cultural diversity. Immigrants trained in principles of Americanism that included sober behavior would pose no threat when they reached the United States, argued leading WCTU official Ella Boole.[17] Allied to this concern was the issue of smuggling. Since porous national borders could challenge the effectiveness of U.S. prohibition, drys added practical to ideological reasons for imposing American-style prohibition on the world. According to Cherrington, international prohibition would "free this great international boundary line of ours from the Rum Row and the Smuggling Row" and take the fight to the enemy "in order that we may keep this rapidly developing international liquor traffic truly defending itself in the many countries of Europe . . . instead of permitting that international battle line to concentrate its power and its money and its influence to break down prohibition right here in America."[18]

Yet xenophobia was only one element in the prohibitionist repertoire, and smuggling did not come to the fore as an issue until after the World League had been well and truly launched. Prohibitionists did not fear the outside world precisely because they believed the outside world was on their side and heading in the same direction.[19] Even in 1925, as smuggling seriously threatened the dry heartland of prohibition, long-term ideological goals remained of critical importance. Cherrington stressed the inherent concept of altruism, with which prohibition was allegedly suffused. The anti-alcohol crusade was "a movement with one specific purpose, and that to help the other fellow." Global benevolence in this interpretation required American moral and material support for prohibition abroad. This campaign drew strongly upon the inherited tradition of Christian evangelical reform. The WLAA message was a "gospel of prohibition" that followed in the steps of American missionaries and backed up their work; prohibition must be carried abroad as "the torch" of salvation to be borne by the saintly "to the rest of the world." Saving the world from alcohol would help save it from sin and would rebound to the glory of the "Christian politics" of the United States. Just as the Christian churches had gone abroad in part to save America, so too would the prohibition cause revitalize evangelicalism at home against its secular enemies.[20] Cherrington also reiterated the evangelical imperative to work against the spread of liquor in the colonial world, which "threatened to debauch these people who have been under the influence of the missionaries."[21] In this as in so many other ways, world prohibition represented the apogee of the prewar moral reform movements.

The World League has been overlooked because its claims were so ambitious and yet its achievements so relatively insubstantial.[22] This estimate misses the degree to which foreign temperance reformers at first embraced the cause of world prohibition, and it also misses the vigor with which WLAA agents pursued their campaign in the first few years of the movement's existence. Prohibitionist efforts were broader and more intense than appears at first inspection because they did not depend on the WLAA alone but on a wider circle of interlocking reform networks.

Because of its worldwide links, the most important cooperating institution was the World's WCTU. Initially WCTU officials appeared annoyed that their organization's pioneering role as a promoter of global temperance reform was being usurped, and the WCTU maintained its own parallel campaign for prohibition abroad. WCTU president Anna Gordon told her national convention in 1922 that "Our international program preceded by forty years the world temperance movement"—a point she repeated to WLAA officials such as Southern Methodist bishop James Cannon. Nevertheless, she had come to recognize the importance of concerted action and elimination of inefficiencies in the campaign, announcing that "today we are gladly cooperating."[23] Within the WLAA leadership Gordon replaced the Belgian Vandervelde as one of the four presidents in an admission of the WCTU's importance for the dry world strategy. Courting the WCTU was essential for the WLAA because the WCTU had by the 1920s developed an international network of organizational affiliates and bodies of loyal supporters in more than forty countries. In the Anglo-Saxon world, its support levels were impressive, with 136,000 dues-paying members in England in 1918–19 at the start of the world campaign, 348,593 in the United States, 9,385 in the relatively small country of Australia, and sizable affiliates in Scotland, Canada, New Zealand, South Africa, India, and Sweden.[24] Cherrington himself acknowledged the role of the World's WCTU in providing a model for—and the very inspiration behind—his drive for world prohibition.[25]

Just as the ASL and the WCTU had methodically prepared the way for a legislative fight in the United States between 1907 and 1917, world prohibitionists conceived their task systematically. Maps of global expansion such as the "Wet and Dry Map of the World" depicted, sometimes very optimistically, the temperance view of the dry, damp, and wet areas of the planet. This approach was meant to hearten faithful followers in the United States and to identify the enemy abroad. Prohibitionist publications gave great space to international events, providing copious information on how other countries depicted and allegedly endorsed the Volstead Act. The WLAA sought comprehensive information, attained by the scouting expeditions of its agents and from foreign informers. Judging by the quantity of material on foreign issues presented in the prohibition press, the sincerity of the push for world prohibition cannot be denied. International material in the years immediately after World War I was ubiquitous in prohibition papers such as the ASL's *American Issue* and the WCTU's state and national organs.

The primary foreign target of American prohibitionists was Europe because of the huge wine industry there as well as the Scottish and Irish whiskey interests.[26] ASL worker William E. "Pussyfoot" Johnson toured European countries extensively between 1919 and 1924 in his role as "organizing secretary" for the World League. Former Prohibition Party presidential candidate and celebrated orator John G. Woolley made a special investigative European tour in 1922, while George W. Henry went from a wartime position in Britain in the Overseas Young Men's Christian Association to spend more than a year working for prohibition in Scotland, Ireland, and England before returning to ASL work in the United States.[27] Bishop Cannon was honorary chairman of the ASL's National Legislative Committee but in the 1920s led the charge abroad, particularly in Britain where he lectured widely and informed the readers of the London *Times* on what the editor called "Prohibition at Work: The American Lesson to England" in 1920.[28] The Rev. Frederick MacMillan went from being head chaplain of the U.S. Army rest camp at Winchester, England, to "take the war path" for temperance among the British public.[29] Anna Gordon and *Union Signal* editor Julia Deane participated along with Henry Beach Carre, Howard Russell, George Henry, and Pussyfoot Johnson in the campaign for no-license in Scotland in 1920. Gordon and Deane then took a tour of war-devastated Europe in connection with the same trip. In 1922, the WLAA sent ten pastors associated with the Swedish American temperance movement to Sweden to fight for prohibition in the referendum of August 23. The most prominent was the Rev. David Ostlund, who coordinated the activities of the Swedish temperance groups and founded the Anti-Saloon League of Sweden.[30]

The Swedish campaign was of particular importance because of the country's long tradition of regulation rather than prohibition of the liquor trade. In the 1890s, American prohibitionists had rejected the plan of public management of licensed premises established in the 1850s in Gothenburg.[31] This Swedish form of municipal ownership had won support from anti-prohibitionist temperance reformers in the United States in the elitist social reform group, the Committee of Fifty, formed in 1895, and American prohibitionists continued to view any variant of the Gothenburg System as a threat to the progress of prohibition and especially to its spread throughout Europe.[32] As an alternative, Sweden adopted in 1917 a grim plan for government-controlled passbooks and liquor permits called the Bratt System, named for the Stockholm doctor who devised it. The scheme carefully allocated permissible purchases to registered individuals on the basis of character, health, and other factors. Though draconian in comparison with the Gothenburg System, this concession was still not prohibition. As WLAA official Carre wrote, Sweden was "the most important of the Scandinavian Countries," with a population "greater than that of Norway and Denmark combined." As the home of the Gothenburg and Bratt systems, it was "the most formidable [rival] of prohibition in Scandinavia, Finland and the British Isles. Rejection of these systems in favor of prohibition would be a body blow" to the European liquor traffic.[33]

Other important prohibitionist audiences were in the British dominions. The WLAA lauded Canada's wartime prohibition. Until the backsliding of the provinces became clear by the mid-1920s, the northern neighbor of the United States was treated as a province successfully conquered.[34] Partly for this reason, more effort went into places that had never had prohibition, such as South Africa. The South Africa Temperance Alliance tried to get a local option law passed during 1922 and 1923, and it encouraged WLAA and WCTU officials to help. To the Cape Province came Bishop Cannon from a missionary trip in the Belgian Congo. In Cape Town he addressed a public meeting in which, according to the *American Issue,* Cannon "held his audience [including the Chief Justice of the Cape Province] spellbound." The WCTU's Deborah Knox Livingston also joined the same campaign to "a series of ovations" at rallies. At the same time, Eva C. Wheeler went to Australia and Mary Harris Armor to New Zealand, both on behalf of the WCTU.[35]

A third area stressed was the colonial and developing world. WCTU president Anna Gordon went to South America in 1921 along with Julia Deane and declared optimistically that Brazil could be dry as early as 1922.[36] However, much more campaigning took place in India, China, and Japan, with emphasis on Scientific Temperance Instruction in missionary and government schools. Nowhere was the prohibitionist cause to receive a better welcome than in India, where it blended with nationalist currents stirring against British rule.[37] There, moral reformers of various stripes had begun well before World War I to flirt with anti-colonialist themes, and this activity reached a peak in 1920–22, when Pussyfoot Johnson saw an opportunity for asserting American influence by encouraging the Indian struggle for self-rule. Johnson was vividly aware of the nationalist unrest and its link with the liquor question. "The situation in India at this time is very acute and disturbed," he wrote from London in the course of organizing his trip to the subcontinent. Despite the addition of six million voters to the rolls for the November 1920 Legislative Council elections, the nationalists were "sore at the British Government" largely because it had "not gone farther or faster in the matter of self-government."[38]

Even so, Johnson planned to enter this tumultuous fray to take advantage of it for the sake of world prohibition. Johnson's tour was planned at the time of widespread unrest and the implementation of M. K. Gandhi's boycott of liquor shops. Rumors swept the subcontinent that the British authorities opposed the celebrated American agitator because his message would be subversive.[39] Johnson denied the charge that he wished to unsettle British authority, pointing out that Britons in the Anglo-Indian Temperance Association had organized his visit.[40] Johnson claimed that he sided with the more moderate party "made up mostly of Indians whose theory is to accept what has been given by the British government" in the electoral reforms of 1919 "and to holler for more." Yet these words actually encouraged anti-colonial sentiment. Johnson set himself against the "whites, particularly Britishers" who "want their rations of whiskey and soda."[41] Statements such as this were bound to be interpreted as hostile to British rule, and the unsettling implications of the tour, which finally took place in the autumn of 1921, shone through in his highly charged symbolic actions. Nowhere was this clearer than in Johnson's visit to the site of the Amritsar massacre of 1919, where British troops gunned down a large crowd of demonstrators, and in his laudatory correspondence with Gandhi. By these actions Johnson indicated a willingness to exploit the power of the non-cooperation movement for the benefit of world prohibition and at the expense of British power. Gandhi had done "more for temperance reform in two years," Johnson concluded, "than any other man has been able to accomplish in that time, in the history of the world."[42]

Aided in India and in other places by the efforts of the WCTU, the prohibitionists carried on the anti-colonial form of American moral hegemony that they had forged out of older American traditions and in the struggles over American acquisition of the Philippines. To readers back home Johnson emphasized that while Britons faced "grievances, real and imaginary," from the Indian people, American missionaries, their schools, and their support for prohibition all won high regard: Indians "know all about the work of America in the Philippines" and "all about what we did for Cuba in setting her free." The United States had "befriended China" and "saved" Latin America from "monarchial aggression," making the nation "synonymous with political freedom."[43] American prohibition would by implication be a highly successful moral export to the colonial world.

This moral proselytizing was not simply an imposition of American cultural imperialism. In host countries, the WLAA's efforts found allies among indigenous supporters, who frequently asked Americans to participate. The Indian non-cooperationists conducting pickets against liquor shops implored his support and, despite chaperoning from more moderate nationalist hosts, Johnson broke away to visit Gandhi's home and attend the anti-liquor picket lines.[44] The nationalists' appropriation of Johnson's message showed how foreigners selected what they wanted from American speakers, often dealing independently with the visitor outside the formal WLAA program. In Europe as much as in Asia, this process was one of collaboration rather than one-sided American penetration. The Scottish Permissive Bill and Temperance Association asked Johnson to help in the 1920 plebiscite, against opposition from WLAA leaders.[45] In a similar fashion, Swedish Good Templars had invited anti-liquor lecturers to come to Scandinavia, and Mary Armor's visit to New Zealand was at the invitation of the New Zealand WCTU president.[46] A clear example of non-Americans' influence came after early negative reaction to the World League's campaign in Britain tempted WLAA officials to curtail British operations late in 1919. On behalf of the Scottish prohibitionists, W. J. Allison objected "strongly" to "the proposal to withdraw Mr. Johnson and close ... the London office." This, Allison argued, would deprive Scottish temperance forces of Johnson's "services at a time when they needed them most in challenging and in repudiating the vile assertions of the liquor press." Allison claimed that the Americans were "taking far too gloomy a view of the situation here, . . . and far too pessimistic a view of the noble stand taken by the Anti Saloon League in support of our Scottish campaign."[47] In their objections the Scottish prohibitionists were successful; the WLAA left the London office open and continued to employ Johnson.[48]

Foreign travelers to the United States supplemented the efforts of American speakers. Coming from countries such as Sweden, Australia, the United Kingdom, and India, they often returned to their home countries to report on the benefits of the Volstead Act. Some were committed reformers such as Tarini Prasad Sinha from India and Alexis Björkman, the director of the Swedish Temperance Societies' Information Bureau. Björkman returned to tell Swedes that American women would never let the country drop prohibition, while Sinha journeyed to the United States in 1922 from Benares to spend six months working with the ASL. Sinha praised Pussyfoot Johnson's efforts and solicited further aid for India's own anti-liquor struggles.[49] Foreign journalists flocked to the United States to report; in 1925 the *Dundee Advertiser*'s correspondent crossed the ocean and the North American continent in a tour ostentatiously titled "Fifteen Thousand Miles of Prohibition."[50] Still others were tourists and incidental visitors like the group of English Rotarians who told the *Christian Science Monitor* in 1925 that "in the main" prohibition was "a great success" in the United States, and then had their opinions publicized around the world by prohibition journals.[51]

Foreign sympathizers often acted on their own initiative and did not always agree with the thrust of the American campaign. They were receptive toward the WLAA's general objective of a dry world but dissented over means. Both themes were evident in the case of the World Prohibition Federation (WPF), led by Guy Hayler. Closely allied with the Independent Order of Good Templars, Hayler's group was founded in London in 1909 as the International Prohibition Confederation, more than a decade before the WLAA burst upon the scene. Hayler was a prominent English teetotaler who from 1889 to 1907 had been general secretary of the North of England Temperance League. Reorganized as the WPF in 1919, the group had representation in twenty-five countries and published a quarterly *International Record* to register the global march of temperance legislation. The WPF believed that the ultimate solution to the alcohol problem was "total suppression of the traffic in intoxicants," and this goal tied its efforts to the propaganda war over the Eighteenth Amendment. In keeping with this objective, the WPF adopted the slogan of "a dry Europe by 1930."[52]

Friction between the WLAA and Hayler's WPF raised important issues concerning the limits to the attempted American hegemony over moral reform. Relations between the two groups were sometimes "acrimonious" because of personality conflicts and antagonism over the WPF's inferior financing.[53] An Australian Methodist newspaper announced that "the honour of giving vitality to the idea" of "world-wide prohibition" belonged to Hayler, a statement indicating some jealousy over the WLAA's role as a usurper.[54] Behind these petty conflicts lay tactical and policy differences. The WPF was in the United States closer to the old Prohibition Party, whereas the American Anti-Saloon League adopted a non-partisan policy giving votes to the driest candidates, whatever party they represented. While Hayler supported the goal of world prohibition, he did not subordinate his efforts to those of the WLAA. Hayler organized his own European committee that competed with the WLAA's affiliates and drew in part on the same personnel. The WPF also had a broader agenda that included all drugs of addiction, not just alcohol. Hayler took advantage of the fact that the United States was not a member of the League of Nations to seize a role in agitating in Geneva the issue of narcotic trafficking and the smuggling of alcohol in Europe from non-prohibitionist to prohibitionist countries.[55] Rivalries such as this one did not become open warfare, and a degree of cooperation continued, but the WLAA wished to get its way; it represented the bold, brash face of American cultural expansionism centered on prohibition as the panacea for global regeneration. In reality, the Americans had the prestige as well as the organizing clout, and the WPF was forced to work in the shadow of the WLAA, which received far more publicity. In 1927 talks over a merger faltered because the WLAA refused to create a "reasonable position" for the son of the WPF leader in the merger proposal, and the smaller organization limped along as an ancillary group in the global coalition.[56]

Differences also arose from frank awareness among the allies of the WLAA in Europe that prohibition was not for them a realistic stance for the immediate future. In France, the Ligue Nationale Contre Alcoolisme, a federation of French temperance societies, joined the WLAA and declared that "henceforth antialcoholism would be waged on the international level," but that group was not wedded to total abstinence principles. Most French temperance reformers saw American prohibition simply as an inspiration or "an encouragement."[57] Even the more radical WLAA supporters in continental Europe, such as Paul-Maurice Légrain, the French Good Templar and total abstainer, and the Swiss head of the International Temperance Bureau, Hercod, were far from sanguine about the short-term prospects for European prohibition.[58]

Rather than accept the advice of foreigners urging caution, American drys preferred to highlight the claims of supporters abroad who emphasized the chances of quick success.[59] American prohibitionists tended as the 1920s went on to become more dogmatic in their pronouncements of the imminent worldwide triumph. As Canada's provinces repealed prohibition laws one by one in the 1920s, the Canadian prohibitionists' shrill defense of the policy of "our ally—the United States" became more noticeable. In the midst of a series of provincial setbacks, Canadian WCTU president Sara Rowell Wright stridently reaffirmed in 1925 that "the world is going dry."[60] Foreign collaboration of this type was a trap for the American prohibition movement. Weaker groups abroad tended to encourage illusions of global advance. The WLAA listened to the non-American temperance reformers who told the American architects of a dry world what they wanted to hear.

The years 1919 to 1922 marked the high tide of this international organizing in electoral terms. In every country U.S. prohibitionists and their foreign allies exerted a mighty effort, but they were rebuffed at the polls, in some cases easily but in others only narrowly. In New Zealand, prohibition had very nearly succeeded in 1919; the loss came by 1,000 votes out of 540,000. As one modern historian concluded, only the vote of the nation's troops still in Britain "saved New Zealand from national prohibition in 1919."[61] In the succeeding poll in 1922, the anti-prohibitionist margin (20,000 votes) was only slightly more comfortable. Meanwhile, the pressure for extending prohibition began to ebb away in many other countries. The Swedish prohibition plebiscite of 1922 went down by a 42,000 "no" majority out of 1.8 million votes. Women voted dry by a large margin, but their votes were overcome by a male plurality in favor of the existing Bratt System.[62] The local-option poll in Scotland had been lost in 1920 in an election spread over two months in various localities. The wets conceded only a few districts that they had previously controlled. Of 253 voting areas discussed in a contemporary report, 206 had voted not to change. Yet the actual voting revealed a respectable anti-liquor sentiment. The dry vote in heavily working-class Glasgow, for example, was 142,328 compared to 6,449 for limitation of license, and 182,860 for no change.[63] Perhaps the most serious defeat from the point of view of drys in the United States was the gradual adoption of government liquor control in Canada from the Quebec legislation of 1921 through to the defeat of prohibition in Ontario in the 1926 provincial election. These losses enhanced the opportunities for smuggling to the United States.[64] After 1925 prohibitionists shifted toward defense of the American heartland and gave increasing emphasis to the issue of international smuggling. This preoccupation on the part of American drys with internal enforcement accelerated with the collapse of the partial prohibition measure in Norway in 1926 and the abandonment of prohibition in Finland in 1931. Iceland had modified its prohibition law in 1921, though the law was not completely rescinded until 1933.[65]

The reasons for rejection abroad were varied. In essence, the long tradition of wine production and drinking in Europe made that continent a barren field for American drys, who insisted on eliminating both spirits and wine.[66] European wine producers banded together in an international anti-prohibition alliance in 1922. Wine merchants in France were concerned not merely with the effects on their home market but with their ability to sell in other markets, such as Finland and Iceland where the WLAA encouraged prohibition. These same producers and merchants circulated anti-prohibitionist literature in the United States threatening European trade retaliation. Édouard Barthe, president of the International Bureau of Wine, pointed out that eighteen million Frenchmen earned a living from the grape and claimed that the ability of the French to buy American products would be greatly reduced by the curtailment of this major industry. In this way French (as well as other European) objections to prohibition were brought into the domestic American debate.[67] In addition, resentment against interference in national and class-based drinking cultures stood as a powerful obstacle to prohibition in many European countries. The beer halls of Germany, the restaurants and cafés of France, and the pubs of Britain all served as important social institutions deeply imbedded in popular culture. As in the United States, resistance was most indelibly shown through drinking.[68]

A further obstacle was an anti-Americanism expressed through irritation at the growth of American political and economic power in Europe. This was especially clear in the British case. Prohibition became, for the British press, an example of American interference and the equation found an almost perfect metaphor in the "meddling" of Pussyfoot Johnson. In the words of a popular English ditty of the time:

> Who are you, who are you,
> Pussyfoot?
> Don't you know we hear your meow,
> Why don't you stay in the U.S.A.
> And wail in your own backyard?
> Though you've got the public puzzled
> The Bull-Dog isn't muzzled,
> Keep away, keep away,
> Pussyfoot![69]

Pussyfoot's reception in England made him a figure of controversy from the very start of the WLAA offensive abroad. He was burned in effigy on Guy Fawkes night, and students attacked him in an ugly confrontation at a meeting in November 1919 that resulted in his losing sight in one eye.[70] American newspaperman Kenneth Roberts concluded that Johnson was "the best anti-Prohibition argument in the Wets' bag, and a constant irritant to the British."[71] Henry Beach Carre agreed, claiming that the heckling by British audiences was "particularly noticeable when Americans are speaking because the opposition claims that we are intruders and meddlers in their affairs."[72]

Johnson was a formidable tactician and publicist, however, who inspired loyalty and admiration among foreign prohibitionists. He gained a more sympathetic reaction from the British press for his bravery when he devoted a medical fund raised on his behalf to blind, returned British soldiers. Prohibitionists exploited the British tradition of "fair play" by focusing on the violence that led to Johnson's lost sight. Noted anti-prohibitionists such as the chairman of the Wine and Spirit Defence Fund

Fig. 15. Anti-prohibition poster showing the strong reaction against William E. "Pussyfoot" Johnson and the World League Against Alcoholism campaign in Britain, 1920. Reproduced from Kenneth L. Roberts, *Why Europe Leaves Home* (New York: Arno Press, 1977), 276.

were forced to apologize and prohibitionists rallied in a packed meeting under a banner titled "Pussyfoot's Eye Will Make England Dry."[73] After this incident, British wets took more careful tactical action against the WLAA. Prominent British accountant Sir William Barclay Peat, the chairman of Allsopps Brewery, claimed that the Americans were "possessed of considerable financial support" and identified Johnson as "a real danger to the brewing industry." Fearing Johnson's talent for publicity, brewers and distillers stepped up the wet campaign.[74] As the reaction to Pussyfoot Johnson showed, prohibition faced the obstacle of association with an "American invasion," an idea already popularized in journalistic accounts of U.S. economic penetration before World War I.[75] After prohibition's rise to prominence on the American scene, the literature of non-American total abstinence societies became dominated by the debate over the drive toward U.S.-style national prohibition. Those who campaigned for prohibition in Europe and the Asia-Pacific could not avoid being tied to the "made in America" tag.[76]

Anti-American sentiment was by no means the only obstacle in Europe, to be sure. Economic pressures impinged on prohibition in Scandinavia, just as they would after 1930 in the United States. Norway, Iceland, and Finland dropped prohibition more quickly and more easily than did the United States because of these practical constraints.[77] The small size of these Scandinavian countries made them vulnerable to international trade retaliation from wine-producing countries. In Finland in 1931 these economic considerations prevailed. The Finns caved in under the pressure of threats to exclude their fish products from southern European markets unless wines were allowed freely into Finland. The same pressure had forced Iceland to admit Spanish wines in 1921, even though its Parliament was unwilling to abandon prohibition completely as a statutory law.[78]

In still another variation, the alternative of governmental control of the trade was significant in blunting the temperance vote in some countries where prohibition sentiment was strong. Academics, politicians, and reformers tempted the undecided with more moderate policies that claimed to achieve the same results with less acrimony. Sweden's Bratt System drew off some temperance support after its introduction in 1917.[79] In Canada, too, the decline of prohibition in the 1920s was matched by the rise of government-controlled liquor outlets, but the country's regional and cultural differences also contributed to prohibition's demise. Canadian prohibition was province-based and was initially undermined by the opposition of the populous, poorer, Catholic, and French-speaking Quebec and by the financial temptation of smuggling alcohol across the border to the American republic and to other provinces.[80] The ebbing of prohibitionist sentiment outside the United States was in part the result of factors peculiar to each country or group of countries, but it also reflected a great irony. American influence abroad did not necessarily favor the dry argument. Through its diverse networks of activists, the nation sent out mixed messages.

The increasing resistance to prohibition in the United States blunted the message of prohibitionist lecturers abroad, since the flouting of the Volstead Act was amply reported in the foreign media. In New Zealand, the WCTU's guest American campaigner in the 1922 license poll, Mary Armor, blamed anti-prohibitionists for the failure of the dry vote to keep pace with the wet vote's expansion. "Never was a crime committed in America but it was heralded from one end of the Dominion to the other, as being the result of prohibition," Armor lamented. She concluded, however, that more American influence on other nationalities, not less, was required: "they [the New Zealanders] could not have been deceived" if "the masses could have been made to understand our mode of government."[81] Anti-prohibitionist literature and arguments drawn from American experience had also been useful to the wets in Scotland in 1920 and Sweden in 1922. When John Koren, the American advocate of liquor regulation and a member of the Committee of Fifty, called American prohibition "horrible" his indictment was widely published in the Swedish press during the 1922 campaign.[82] In the Scottish campaign, too, anti-prohibitionists such as Charles A. Windle of Chicago, the editor of *Brann's Iconoclast*, were employed to show what was wrong with the Volstead Act. Writing in the *Chicago American*, Windle worked on behalf of the (Liquor) Manufacturers and Dealers Association of America, and he carried out the same task in Britain, contesting both the economic and health benefits of prohibition and drawing attention to extensive liquor violations in Chicago.[83] Ironically, this use of American agents and material coexisted with the strong theme of anti-Americanism. The debate testified deftly to the expansion of American cultural influence even though the prohibitionists were roundly defeated. As the *Chicago Tribune*'s correspondent put it in his account of the Scottish campaign: "whether Scotland goes dry, wet, or merely moist, Americans on either side will bear much of the responsibility."[84]

The new medium of film developed by Hollywood into a mass entertainment did not help the prohibitionists in their international campaigns either. Images of an American people racked by sexual immorality, divorce, crime, and gangster violence proliferated abroad. Moral reformers outside the United States did not like what they saw, and American visitors to foreign countries reported home the negative impact that Hollywood had on support for prohibition around the world. An Uruguayan editor backed such claims by telling an American journalist in 1928 that movies were the "main obstacle to the proper understanding and esteem" between South American countries and the United States.[85] Maude Aldrich, director of the Motion Pictures Department of the WCTU, had no trouble agreeing. In 1925 she had raised the alarm that "American motion pictures" were "presenting lawlessness, crime, theft, murder, highway robbery, broken homes, . . . and free love as typical of American life." This "misrepresentation" was "severely crippling our work for world prohibition."[86] Aldrich was extremely active in promoting this view of film's subversive nature, including to missionary societies, though even the conspiratorially minded had to concede that liquor interests did not directly control foreign outlets for Hollywood movies.

Despite the reverses, the WLAA did not die. As long as national prohibition survived so too would the league. Throughout the 1920s it continued to fund or supply personnel and propaganda to foreign campaigns. Bishop Cannon continued his hectic round of overseas trips to keep up the spirits of international colleagues. The organization advertised its international role in 1927 by holding another "World's Congress," this time in prohibition's midwestern heartland, at Winona Lake, Indiana, where the roll call of delegates again passed the one thousand mark.[87] Supporters came from Japan, Germany, Britain, Denmark, Canada, and Australia, among other countries. The WLAA could even boast a Turkish feminist delegate, Saffie Hussein, who gained great publicity because of her progressive views on women's suffrage for her home country and her support for the modernizing policies on controlling Islamic influence of Turkish nationalist Kemal Atatürk. Her refusal to wear a veil surprised Americans but delighted prohibitionists because of the way it identified the American crusade with the global spread of Western modernity. This was precisely how the WLAA and its allies portrayed prohibition.[88]

The apparent cosmopolitanism and international commitment was misleading, however. The WLAA's evangelical connections were emphasized by the site of the congress in Winona Lake, a popular religious Chautauqua meeting place of the early twentieth century. The township was the home of the famous fundamentalist evangelist Billy Sunday, whose Billy Sunday Tabernacle seated over seven thousand people. The location and its cultural associations underlined a growing conservatism and fundamentalism in the prohibition crusade and the erosion of linkages with social service and social justice movements. The prohibition movement was on the defensive in the United States, though it was to be another six years before the repeal of the Eighteenth Amendment.[89]

Behind the scenes, the evidence suggested that the show of international force at Winona Lake was thin and that deep divisions existed in the movement. Several foreign delegates disputed Pussyfoot Johnson's characterization of impending world victory for the dry crusade and urged the more moderate policy of local option to be adopted in Europe.[90] More candid than Johnson was Ernest Cherrington, who reportedly acknowledged that "the stupendous undertaking of a world movement against alcoholism appears all but impossible." Obtaining worldwide representation at Winona Lake was, he confided, an "uphill job."[91] Within the ASL's leadership, divisions threatened the very survival of the WLAA as an organization. The dominant faction led by Wayne Wheeler, general counsel and national legislative superintendent, disagreed with Cherrington. Wheeler was less interested in the international work, which he called "too grand a scheme" and "impractically idealistic."[92] In contrast, Wheeler wanted to focus on enforcement in the United States. Always inadequate to the vast needs, financial support from the ASL began to dwindle beginning in 1924, partly as a result of Wheeler's attitudes. Efforts to get alternative funding, notably from John D. Rockefeller Jr., failed soon after. Rockefeller's enthusiasm for the prohibition cause, to which he had given ample funding in earlier years, was fading, and in 1925 Cherrington had been forced to cut appropriations to Robert Hercod's European Bureau in Lausanne.[93]

The WLAA struggled on nevertheless; indeed, even on the eve of the final collapse, Cherrington greeted the new decade in 1930 with an optimistic press release. He claimed that "marked progress" around the world had been made toward greater restriction in the use of liquor, with "Italy abandoning wine." Cherrington was especially heartened to report that Afghanistan had gone dry. The changing modern civilization, the increasing intensity of international economic rivalries, and a growing appreciation of the "needless ravages" of alcohol were the "most significant factors" in his cheerful estimate.[94] This brave front finally collapsed with the repeal of the Eighteenth Amendment in 1933. That date also marked the virtual termination of the wider spectrum of Protestant religious and moral crusades that had begun in the 1880s, but a mixed legacy remained, one that went far beyond the issue of alcohol prohibition and extended all the way to the very contest over international hegemonic leadership into which the United States had first been thrust during World War I. The wider context of the 1920s remains a story to be told, as individual reformers looked back on several decades of the struggle for the expansion of a moral American "empire."

Conclusion

THE JUDGMENTS OF HEAVEN:

CHANGE AND CONTINUITY IN MORAL REFORM

PROHIBITION'S DEMISE was a critical blow to the Christian moral reform enterprise that had flourished for more than thirty years because the dry crusade had become the flagship of evangelical reform. Even the WCTU had, despite its continuing commitment to progressive causes such as peace and social justice, put a good deal of its eggs in the one (dry) basket in the 1920s. Reforming the world seemed to have come to an end at the hands of a particularly quixotic, wrongheaded crusade. Yet the moral reform movement also suffered from longer term, adverse trends, including growing secularization that affected the religiously minded as much as it did the wider society. Christian Endeavor continued to function as a major church-related organization internationally but had lost its sense of moral urgency. Its international and national conventions advertised convention experiences abroad as a secular tourist activity rather than as an opportunity to assist missions or save souls. Meanwhile, the YMCA and YWCA in the 1920s had increasingly accepted social service as their raison d'être rather than evangelizing. The Student Volunteers experienced "intense theological controversy" between fundamentalists and liberals, as well as conflict over the direction that missions should take between a focus on social service and evangelizing. Unselfconscious righteousness had faltered.[1] At the 1924 Quadrennial Convention the Volunteer delegates debated "the problems of race and war," and questioned the "right to impose our western civilization and Christianity upon foreign people."[2] Within the larger mission movement, the 1928 Jerusalem Conference of the International Missionary Council, the first to be held of this organization formed in 1921, became preoccupied with interfaith issues and social policies rather than Christian evangelism. The energizing influences of the women's mission movement also began to fade as amalgamation of mission boards "inevitably diluted the power formerly wielded by women in foreign missions."[3] Both ecumenical and denominational fund-raising drives for missions fell below expectations within five years of the war's end.[4]

Changing fortunes came partly from external challenges. The older moral reform movements suffered from new competitors for influence abroad. No longer were America's "missionaries" mainly Protestant clergy and temperance reformers. Rotary International, a novel movement fusing service and economic efficiency, promoted American business culture internationally. Founded in Chicago in 1905 as a businessmen's club, Rotary quadrupled in size and businessmen soon introduced their clubs in Canada and then Europe by 1913, and other parts of the world in the 1920s, when major expansion occurred. By 1929, the club had about a quarter of its affiliates overseas. Rotary International also spawned through its example a number of competing organizations such as the Kiwanis clubs (founded in 1915) and foreign rivals such as Britain's Round Table and Australia's Apex that, although less restrictive on rules of membership, were closely modeled on Rotary's business ethics and community service programs. Women contributed their own businesswomen's club, the Soroptimist Club of Oakland, California, which spread to Great Britain and Canada by 1923 and to continental Europe by 1934.[5] Service clubs matched the earlier reformers in missionary enthusiasm, propensity for specialized work, and, especially in the Rotary case, global aspirations. Rotary's role in American hegemony became significant as a promoter of a new internationalism through peace and mutual exchanges of ideas but also through a common commitment of businessmen across different nationalities to capitalist, market values.[6] Espousing social service, internationalism, and a common culture of progress, Rotary took key messages of the prewar reformers and put them into a religiously neutral framework.[7]

Another competitor came in the form of the Rockefeller Foundation. Though the Rockefeller family fortune continued to fund the International Committee of the YMCA, from its beginnings in 1913 the foundation secularized the mission enterprise. It bankrolled efforts to improve the health of people in the developing world. Already active in the treatment of hookworm in the United States, in 1913 the foundation established the International Health Commission. This commission (changed in name to "Board" in 1916) set out to control yellow fever, malaria, tuberculosis, and other diseases across the tropical world. Especially important in the health field was the separate China Medical Board (founded in 1913) that established the Peking Union Medical Hospital. It became commonly known as the Johns Hopkins of the "Far East" because the hospital was modeled on the famous university's medical school facility. Through this agency, the Rockefeller Foundation applied the latest approaches in scientific medicine and took a critical stance toward the older missionary medical colleges' adaptation to local traditions and circumstances.[8]

At the same time, this challenge to the ascendancy of missions was in many ways an extension of the missionaries' work. The continuity is not surprising, as the Rockefeller family's links with the Baptist Church went deep. Though the Rockefeller Foundation championed the "progress of western medicine," its chief architect was the Rev. Frederick Gates, a Baptist minister and wily financial advisor. Gates was "the man most responsible for shifting the Rockefellers from denominational charity to international philanthropy," and the China Medical Board was one of his favorite projects.[9] The foundation had taken over the Peking facility from Protestant missionaries in 1915 and, at the dedication ceremony upon the hospital's completion in 1921, James L. Barton of the American Board of Commissioners for Foreign Missions and other missionaries were present. The foundation copied here and elsewhere in its enterprises the approach of the moral empire. The Peking hospital was not designed simply to provide medical services for China. It was to give "stimulation and support" to "medical missionaries." As a model "not only in China, but throughout the Far East," it would generate an ambitious transnational network of medical personnel. Doctors and researchers would come from American and European hospitals to spread the latest technologies among one another and across the Asia-Pacific region.[10] In a parallel fashion, the International Health Board mimicked transnational organizing by focusing not on particular areas in which the United States had acquired formal colonies but on providing services on a global basis. The approach, historian Warwick Anderson has shown, utilized the experience of the American colonial regime in the Philippines, including its personnel, but deterritorialized the application of that experience.[11] As in the strategy of the Student Volunteers, the American (medical) missionary presence was to be mobile, adaptable, and potentially located everywhere, not territorially fixed.

If some of the new organizations extended or complemented the earlier work, the decline of the older moral reform and missionary coalitions in the 1920s should not be exaggerated either. Even the controversial prohibition crusade survived the decade politically intact in the United States. The 1928 election saw the victory of a presidential candidate who preached prosperity and professed enforcement of the Volstead Act; Herbert Hoover was happy to be endorsed by the WCTU and the Anti-Saloon League.[12] In missions, too, the 1920s witnessed soul-searching, infighting, and attrition, but not evidence of steep decline. In proportional terms, the American influence actually reached a temporary statistical zenith in this decade with "slightly less than half" of the global Protestant missionary force. Though the numbers of new Student Volunteers dwindled between 1920 and 1928 by a third, the movement's finances peaked in 1924, and most of the decline in Volunteers actually sailing for foreign posts occurred after 1925.[13] A more serious falling off came with the Great Depression, when financial constraints sharply curbed activity. The stock market crash of 1929 and its aftermath also "produced the greatest period of retrenchment in the history of YMCA service."[14] Then, in the crucial China missionary field, thousands were forced to curb their work as the country plunged into civil war and faced the intensified Japanese occupation after 1937.[15]

What did begin to ebb in the 1920s was the old evangelical influence, as the growing number and extent of faith missionaries began to challenge the SVM's central role. Faith missionaries operated without financial support from mission boards or drives for subscriptions, trusting instead that God would provide. They often preempted the premillennial part of the old evangelizing cause; focused purely on spreading the Gospel; and yet borrowed from the SVM's and YMCA's non-denominational tactics.[16] Though some of these bodies had been established in the nineteenth century, they grew stronger from the second decade of the twentieth onward. Adding to the diversity of the American presence, they expanded the zones within which major missionary initiatives took place. An important faith-oriented mission grew in Kenya beginning in 1901, when Charles E. Hurlburt of Coatesville, Pennsylvania, took charge of the British-founded Africa Inland Mission and expanded into the Belgian Congo after 1910. New ground was broken with the Latin America Evangelization Crusade beginning in Costa Rica in 1921, which anticipated Protestant organizing in Latin American countries such as Colombia.[17] In line with the growing fundamentalist-modernist split, these faith missions advanced in the interwar period but often fractured the precarious unity of the evangelical churches. A feather in the wind was the shift of former Baptist missionary official Lucy Peabody, who attacked the criteria for training missionaries as too liberal and modernist. She withdrew from the existing Baptist Missionary Board in 1927 to found her own Association of Baptists for World Evangelism, "which concentrated its efforts in new mission fields in the Philippines." This enterprise she labeled "Adventures of Faith."[18]

Belying arguments of absolute decline in moral reform, new crusades of the 1920s were born out of the tempestuous experience of alcohol prohibition. The export of prohibition was not the only effort to inculcate American values across the globe in the 1920s, but others modeled themselves after the earlier moral campaigns. As prohibition began to face political and social resistance, the baton began to pass to an anti-narcotic campaign that mimicked the tactics and strategies of the dry forces. One key instigator had strong links with temperance organizations. Richmond Hobson was the naval hero from the Spanish-American War who, as a congressman from Alabama in 1914, had attempted to introduce a national alcohol prohibition amendment.[19] Though he did not get the required support for the amendment to proceed at that time, Hobson won through this legislative move a reputation as a sterling supporter of the cold-water crusade. Becoming convinced of the need for new educational organizations to reinforce alcohol prohibition, in 1922 he founded the American Alcohol Education Association.[20] Alcohol was, he argued, a "racial poison, entailing as the generations pass, the decline of nations." Unless checked, the demon drink threatened a reversion to "barbarianism or the extinction of the race." Hobson aired these views wherever he could, including at the International Congress Against Alcoholism that met in Washington in 1920 to celebrate the passage of the Eighteenth Amendment.[21] Though the naval hero worked initially for the Anti-Saloon League, he differed with that body over methods and, furthermore, wished to pursue a separate endeavor that would highlight his own contribution. No longer a member of Congress, he still harbored ambitions to be politically influential within the Democratic Party (he tried to broker a compromise in the famously deadlocked 1924 Democratic National Convention) and in 1923 saw the opportunity to extend his educational work to other drugs in ways that would be politically visible.[22]

His interest settled on the world trade in narcotics, though his position unmistakably derived from his eugenicist beliefs forged before World War I that alcohol was a racial poison. Hobson founded the International Narcotic Education Association in 1923 and organized the World Conference on Narcotic Education in Philadelphia in 1926. Attending were representatives of the American Red Cross, the American Legion, Rotary International, and other civic and professional bodies. A Wilsonian who believed that the League of Nations should be used for moral defense against drugs as well as for collective security, Hobson gravitated naturally toward international action and established affiliates in Britain, continental Europe, and Australia. Using these networks in ways that consciously imitated the earlier moral reform patterns of transnational contact, he attempted, states one historian, to "globalise America's anti-drug crusade."[23] In reality, others within the evangelical reform coalition had been trying to do what Hobson boasted of since the days of the Shanghai Opium Commission chaired by Bishop Brent, and Hobson merely complemented rather than overthrew these earlier endeavors.

Though the aim was at first educational, Hobson quickly pressured governments for stronger anti-narcotic laws. In 1927 he established the World Narcotic Defense Association and appeared on radio frequently, exploiting in the process his status as a military hero. Hobson emphasized linkages between a strong military defense, particularly a powerful navy, and moral defense against the more insidious threat of social decay. Making "reverent reference to Bishop Brent" and his work, Hobson also began to network with Elizabeth Washburne Wright, the widow of Hamilton Wright, the State Department official who had agitated for the 1914 Harrison Act that created narcotic prohibition in the United States. Elizabeth Wright had become an indefatigable lobbyist for the anti-narcotic cause and worked with Wilbur Crafts on this issue prior to his death in 1922.[24] Hobson's organization cultivated both American and international donors but especially relied on Hobson's friendship with the wealthy pharmaceutical manufacturer Josiah K. Lilly.[25] The World Narcotic Defense Association established headquarters in Geneva, the most strategic location for influencing decisions on opium policy, and its representatives met to lobby delegates to the International Opium Conference. From that body came the Convention for Limiting the Manufacture and Regulating the Distribution of Narcotic Drugs, signed at Geneva on July 13, 1931. Official delegates to the conference were among those that attended the parallel Narcotic Association meeting. In reporting on the proceedings, Hobson conceded that tracing the actual impact of his organization would be difficult: "Naturally, the extent of this influence cannot be accurately calculated but, when the future is taken into account, it would be difficult to overestimate its value," he claimed. "The official delegates consciously or unconsciously felt that our unofficial organization would take a dominant part in the future enforcement of the Convention provisions."[26]

To be sure, Hobson received plaudits from Pope Pius XI himself, but despite self-obsessed claims of influence, Hobson was only one actor in a much larger picture.[27] Even within the American context, his work did not match in terms of policy implementation that of Harry Anslinger, who became commissioner of the newly formed U.S. Bureau of Narcotics in 1930, but Anslinger too had anti-alcohol links. He was a former enforcer of national prohibition within the Federal Bureau of Investigation and had attended the 1928 International Congress Against Alcoholism held in Antwerp, Belgium.[28] The bureau chief quickly overshadowed Hobson, yet the naval hero's views did carry some political weight and Herbert Hoover endorsed Hobson's group, just as an earlier generation of American presidents had given support to the YMCA, the WCTU, and the Student Volunteers. The idea of an exportable moral state backed by the activities of voluntary organizations did not die in the 1920s but persisted, albeit with temporarily diminished force in the years of the Great Depression. As historian Frank Ninkovich has pointed out in the case of the China Medical Board, American internationalism evidenced a continuing role of voluntary organizations in "the marriage of national interest and private policymaking."[29]

The moral reformers also remained a force to be reckoned with in the larger scheme of social change. They contributed their own version of a new style internationalism that had distinctive American roots in the evangelical, voluntarist tradition. The new internationalism that moral reformers supported turned on the exchange of ideas, norms, and values among like-minded individuals in voluntary organizations across national boundaries. Ordinary people would work together in non-state relationships to enhance international understanding, to foster ethical conduct, and to promote moral reform. Peace between nations would flow from the activities of clubs and reform organizations. Rotary International promoted this idea, as did the WLAA and the WCTU. The WCTU, for example, was a member of the Committee on the Cause and Cure of War founded by suffragist Carrie Chapman Catt in 1925. Yet the men and women of these organizations contributed to a process that went far beyond these intentions and encompassed an attempted American international hegemony. This effort occurred on a broad cultural front, and the work of prohibitionists and other moral reformers was simply one controversial part.

Intrinsic to this assertion of a new cultural hegemony, the supporters of alcohol and drug prohibition had conveyed cultural values deeply rooted in American circumstances. Prohibitionist efforts jelled with the spread of American technology and economic influence. Despite its putative association by the 1920s with American fundamentalism, the WCTU pushed a modernist ideology that emphasized the values of Henry Ford and mechanized civilization. Symbolically, the WCTU held its 1925 convention in the "Motor Capital of [the] World," which it depicted as the epitome of modernity, competition, and industrial efficiency. Discounting widespread violation of prohibition in Detroit, the WCTU emphasized instead a "Speed Up Convention," in which prohibitionists everywhere would "step on the gas" to promote world prohibition.[30] They also praised Ford for seeking dry jurisdictions around his overseas automobile plants in Copenhagen, Denmark, and Melbourne, Australia.[31] Ford had argued in the *Dearborn Independent* that "modern civilization wants increased speed because it increases efficiency, but a high standard of efficiency cannot be attained ... without clear thinking and quick action. Prohibition is one of the means by which clear thinking is accomplished."[32] The possible impact of the automobile in encouraging sobriety won the enthusiastic support of prohibitionists abroad who stressed the incompatibility of driving and drinking.[33] Not just cars but the whole paraphernalia of machinery, Frederick Taylor's system of industrial time management, and the wonders of electric power appealed to foreign prohibitionists. They embraced the iconography associated with modern technology in the form of enthusiastic press reports on the sober values of Thomas Edison and Ford.[34] Such cultural hegemony did not rely purely on the initiative of individual states and the assertion of their power. Rather, the new hegemony would be system based and would draw on positive foreign valuations of American cultural products.

The significance of such foreign endorsements escaped many commentators, but not the Italian communist Antonio Gramsci. From his prison cell in Italy, Gramsci explored, in a cryptic article that examined American cultural influence abroad, the importance of the ideology and practice of "Fordism" and its cultural paraphernalia, including prohibition. Gramsci was one of the few intellectuals able to step beyond the immediate, superficial reaction against Americanization in Europe among cultural conservatives to see how American cultural expansion, not through diplomacy and state power but through a range of voluntary organizations, might contribute to a new system of international hegemony that did not equate the power of modern capitalism with the conventional imperial domination of a single state.[35] Gramsci was impressed by the way Ford praised prohibition, and he judged the anti-liquor laws to be intrinsic to an efficient, rationalized system of mass production. Such a system would attempt to locate hegemonic power in the factory itself and its accompanying culture.

The problem for moral reformers lay in the contradictory impacts of this moral muscle flexing. Prohibitionists who identified with an American moral and cultural hegemony actually disrupted the social order without achieving their aims. The export of American values convinced some people abroad but enraged others. The reaction to Pussyfoot Johnson in Britain was a case in point. Linked to anti-Americanism, "Pussyfootism" became a code word for American meddling even as some nationalist groups in India and other foreign supporters such as Turkey's Saffie Hussein saw prohibition as a means of national and social revitalization.[36] This attempted new hegemony was also unstable because of the foreign diplomatic turmoil that prohibition provoked. Not only were Pussyfoot Johnson's Indian interventions upsetting for British diplomats and colonial officials; many a diplomat's tranquility in continental Europe suffered from the complications of American domestic policy on booze.[37] The mere phenomenon of prohibition itself, as well as the occasional disregard for established international law in the American pursuit of smugglers, suggested to British authorities that the United States was "not prepared to assume its position as a respected member of the international community."[38] The United States was forced to undertake discreet diplomatic activity to smooth ruffled feathers in Europe and to ensure that American cultural expansion through prohibition did not shatter friendly relations with important trading partners. As Swiss temperance reformer Robert Hercod noted in 1926, "It is significant that such a world power as the United States has found it impossible to defend itself effectively against alcohol smuggling ... without entering into special agreements with nine sea Powers."[39] Even then, the 1924 Anglo-American Liquor Treaty was the subject of "endless controversy" over how to interpret it.

British diplomatists repeatedly protested "overzealous enforcement" by the U.S. Coast Guard.[40]

Prohibition in the 1920s logically required a global vision and a global politics that both extended American power and yet complicated it through such foreign resentment and resistance. If the moral reformers provided one model for a new U.S. hegemony in an age of "independent internationalism," these reformers could not shape the terms of debate on the moral issues that they canvassed; they could not command sufficient allegiance abroad to effect the form of moral hegemony that they sought, and the wider American hegemony of a non-territorial form of empire through trade in goods and services remained incomplete as well.[41]

Apart from the Pacific islands such as Hawaii, the Mariana Islands, and other places where the ABCFM went and Protestantism's influence was profound, evangelical Christian *conversions* among indigenous peoples in non-Western countries were quite limited. Marginal populations such as low-caste groups and Eurasians were the most common converts for American missionaries and moral reformers alike in India and Ceylon, and Orthodox Christians were the favored target in the Ottoman Empire. In China and Japan, the evangelical impact was demographically small, even in comparison with the much longer work of European Catholics. The Philippines was already nominally Catholic when Americans took command and the material impact of Bishop Brent's work was restricted mainly to European expatriates, the Chinese community, and "savage" peoples such as the Igorot and Moro. The Methodists under Homer Stuntz went further and had greater conversion "success" because they were less inhibited about trespassing on the territory of other Christian churches.[42]

But for all denominations, Christian contributions in the area of schools and medical assistance were far more enthusiastically taken up than conversion. The Leitch sisters' anecdote mentioned earlier in this study is apt: "I will become a Christian if you will tell me where I will get something for my children to eat."[43] Sherwood Eddy discovered that the YMCA in China and India from 1911 to 1917 did better where plows were provided and rural credit banks assisted than where a hard-line gospel message was stressed. That stated, the achievements of the men and women studied in this book were substantial. They had established missionary institutions that continued to function over several genera-tions and brought schools and hospitals as well as the Bible to potential converts. They had built a network of transnational non-governmental organizations to support moral reform work in a wide variety of coun-tries. Some of these organizations continued to be influential in later decades where, as in the case of the Christian Endeavor, YMCA, and

YWCA in many countries, they had adapted to local conditions and to changing times.

Because the "regular" missionaries lived for longer periods in particular non-Western societies, they were more likely to be changed by the experience of missionary work than were those studied in this book who, through the YMCA traveling secretaries, Christian Endeavor visitors like Francis Clark, and touring WCTU workers such as Mary Leavitt circulated "above the ground" offering plans to be implemented, often by locals. Yet, as this study shows, missionaries such as Mercer Johnston and YMCA figures such as Sherwood Eddy were profoundly altered by confrontation with different cultures that influenced the transnational reform projects with which these emissaries were aligned. "Regular" missionaries on the ground also felt, as the case of the Leitch sisters shows, the Protestant presence of other nations and saw themselves as members of *both* a transnational Christian community and an American evangelical culture. A transnational circulation of ideas occurred both within the colonial missions and across missionary fields as transnational reform organizations spread. The consequent mixture of ideas from all of these influences fed back to the United States. The evangelical moral reform groups shaped policies on manners and morals abroad that anticipated legal and administrative changes within the United States. Sometimes, as in their opposition to narcotic drugs, they bequeathed a policy to the American state that politicians maintained long after the high point of the moral expansionism of the Progressive Era. Their experiences in the course of transnational campaigns and contact with foreign coworkers had many feedback effects on home supporters. One of the most important sources of popular knowledge about foreign places and cultures came from the missionary and moral reform lobbies—in magazines, newspaper articles, exhibitions, lecture tours, and fund-raising campaigns. American knowledge of—as well as ignorance about—the wider world reflected in part the structures of the reformers' foreign encounters.

The impact on American politics and diplomacy was less. Missionaries and moral reformers were not servants of state power conventionally conceived. Statesmen and missionaries often thought alike on issues of morality and religion, but they also quarreled over detail and Christian reformers criticized state power. What the missionaries and accompanying moral reformers did do was provide a model for—and contribute to—the development of a new form of hegemony that went beyond the assertion of crude state power, whether political or military.

Ideologically, these groups had a particularly important function when they worked outside colonial structures. They obscured any potential metropolitan focus on the American formal empire by situating it within a larger field—the informal empire of Christian conquest that knew no geographical boundaries. This strategic choice unconsciously helped blur the idea of the United States as a colonial power, but in the very act of creating a different kind of empire. Allegiance to an evangelical Christian crusade could occlude the national allegiance and power structures of that empire. In a far more general sense, moral reformers had bequeathed to the American nation a tradition of entanglement with the wider world; this tradition included the urge to be part of the world and yet at the same time superior to other countries. This experience imparted a streak of moral interventionism that cast the United States as an exception to the norms of empire and that urged higher moral standards on Americans. Paradoxically, this spirit of moral particularism encouraged a mission to change the world. The United States was seen to be both in the world and yet not of it. The tension between this sense of difference and the sense of opportunity in and obligation to a global society powered the uneven American engagement with the wider world.[44] A heady, dynamic, unstable brew of ideas and experiences it was.

To be sure, a newer, more genuinely ecumenical and politically engaged style of liberal Protestantism had gained ascendancy by the 1930s and 1940s. For many of the survivors of older-style Protestant evangelicalism, this new world of missions and reform lacked the spiritual certainties of the past. Yet the newer liberal Protestantism showed in its emphasis on economic and social modernization of the developing world that its leaders had their own moral certainties and strategies that still exerted, in more subtle ways than in earlier decades no doubt, power on and over other peoples. A good many of the intellectual descendants of the 1880s upheaval took part in this refashioning of religion and American empire without losing sight of the missionary goal of individual conversion. Indeed, even some surviving leaders of the earlier phase, such as Sherwood Eddy and John Mott, adjusted and assumed supportive roles. Others did not. The kaleidoscope of individual experience illustrates this complex denouement.

The perspectives of hindsight provide ways of assessing the achievements of the moral reform movements discussed in this book. Historians must observe the "span" of history but also history's "depth"; the past needs empathy as much as contextual analysis. The individuals who participated in the empire of reform saw the denouement of their efforts in the 1920s from a kaleidoscope of perspectives. Their stories reflect the subjective histories of insiders. Their own assessments mixed satisfaction over achievements and regret that more had not been done. The fates of four of the major actors of the moral crusades before 1920 illustrate an inevitably jumbled picture of dreams and memories. Nowhere was the story more poignant than in the lives of the Leitch sisters, who had undertaken the long journey to the mission fields of British Ceylon and then back again to the centers of imperial power and the corridors of the U.S. Congress. By the 1920s, these heady days were long gone for them, and the outcome was ambiguous indeed. They reflected the turmoil in the mission enterprise but also pride in achievement.

The declining years of Mary Ann and Margaret Winning Leitch were not happy ones. After retiring from missionary work at the end of World War I, the two sisters and their brother George had settled in Claremont, California, far from the scenes of their Vermont youth. By 1925 they were in a state of near penury living on a meager pension from the ABCFM. Mary, who was then seventy-six, could not lift her younger bedridden sister and desperately needed a nurse. She petitioned the Prudential Committee of the board, hoping for an increase in her family's "monthly allowance."[45] The $83 a month received "barely covers the living and incidental expenses of my brother, sister and self," she complained. To back her claim for an increased payment to $100, Mary documented in copious detail the lessons of the sisters' epic missionary endeavors and their sacrifices for the cause of the board and for Christ.[46] Mary reminded church officials that they ought to be grateful because the sisters did not quibble on the need for money when the ABCFM was in debt in 1896–97 but flew to its rescue by providing their own money and starting their own fund-raising drive. By 1920, the sisters had spent their modest inheritance entirely to fund mission work. By implication, the ABCFM should now reciprocate.

Yet no increases came, and though Margaret died in 1926, Mary's travail did not end. This time it was not money for sick relatives that she sought. Now, the changing policies of the board offended the forthright woman. In 1927, she wrote Dr. Enoch F. Bell, editor of the *Missionary Herald*, attacking the Rev. William E. Strong's advocacy of "Getting Away from Missions," which signaled "serious reductions" in the funding for the work that she had nurtured.[47] Invoking the memory of her sister, she appealed for aid in saving the Jaffna venture. Margaret, she felt, "seems to be standing by my side and wishing to give a message to you. She says: 'Oh dear Dr. Bell: I beseech of you, do not let the mission work in Ceylon suffer. Do not let the work in any of the mission fields of the American Board suffer.'" A long typewritten account of her missionary life detailed evidence for her case. This cry for help received even less sympathy than the earlier appeal. Board corresponding secretary Cornelius H. Patton noted "the fertility of her mind." She "must have paid a pretty sum of money to have all that type-writing done and it does not strengthen her appeal for a stipend from the Board," observed Patton. Mary's view he considered old-fashioned. Rationalization of ABCFM activities must occur to eliminate competition between missions. "Of course," Patton continued, "she is living in a former world denominationally, when the American Board was free to go out independently and appeal to anybody under heaven." As a result of consolidating and rationalizing under the Commission on Missions of the National Council of Congregational Churches, no such "denomination-wide appeal for the relief of the Board, based upon a dollar per member, would be allowed ... nor should it be. That is a worn-out method." Mary had not done her further calls for extra financial help any good. To the board, she simply had "plenty of leisure on her hands."[48]

The bickering between Mary and the board did not stop there. In the 1930s, ABCFM officials wrote to retired missionaries asking them to alleviate its financially weakened position by taking a pension cut. Leitch replied: "I can just manage comfortably on the allowance that the Board is now giving me." Now past eighty-four years of age and the family's lone survivor, she observed, "I have an impression that I am getting pretty near the end of my journey here." Not only was she losing eyesight, but she was also "badly crippled with rheumatism. I cannot walk across the floor without considerable pain, but, nevertheless, I can sit here at my typewriter and write large letter[s] for an hour at a time without much discomfort." This time Leitch tried to ignore the friction of previous correspondence and played for sympathy by praising the board: "All through these past years I have felt the deepest gratitude to the American Board for the honor they conferred on me when they made me a missionary."[49] Perhaps Mary's thoughts had mellowed as she looked back on her career and her achievements and recalled the positive aspects of her relationship with missions. Certainly her last letters reveal a woman content with her life of denial and suffering. The next to last document in the file, dated 1936, took her thoughts back to Ceylon. She received a letter from the Rev. John Bicknell, president of Jaffna College. The Yale-educated Bicknell expressed "gratitude" for Mary's service to the college.[50] But Mary left her earthly life in full knowledge that her work was inevitably incomplete. In May 1937, in her eighty-seventh year, she wrote to the Archbishop of Canterbury, "very concerned regarding the drink and drug traffic in British India." She called upon the Christian churches in Britain to "compel the British Government to put an end to that traffic."[51] This was Mary Leitch's last surviving testimony. She died on January 2, 1940, having lobbied transnational networks in the interests of moral reform to the end.

By the time of Leitch's death, many of those whose work she supported had already passed away. Wilbur Crafts died of pneumonia in December 1922. World War I had greatly troubled him, undermining his sense of an evolving international order in which the ideas behind transnational reform organizations could prosper. In 1908 he had written a laudatory study of the prospects for moral internationalism as a progressive "Science" and rejoiced at the development of "an increasing group of international men."[52] He sent the book, *A Primer of the Science of Internationalism with Special Reference to University Debates*, to the representatives of many national governments, missions, and other associations asking them to have it translated into French, German, Spanish, Arabic, Urdu, Esperanto, and other languages. But the book only won favor with a small minority of old friends. By 1920, it had been translated into just two languages: Arabic and Japanese. Disconsolately Crafts recalled that neither the "Near East" nor the "Far East" nor the English-speaking countries "had enough interest in the subject to undertake a comprehensive study of this new science of 'right relations' among nations."[53] The impact of the war contributed to the slackening interest though, in Crafts's mind, war was only the proximate cause of the backsliding. "When the World War got into full blast in 1915," Crafts "urged that both soldiers and civilians should study the new geography and the new sociology which everybody expected would follow the war." But "little if any heed was given to this unofficial warning" and scarcely more attention was paid to those of such leaders as Britain's prime minister Lloyd George. A "tragic illustration" of the erosion of internationalism was the Senate's failure to ratify the Versailles Treaty. Enough politicians attacked the treaty to "wreck it"; their voting constituents were "manifestly careless" in not opposing with petitions the action of isolationist senators. The public had not given the subject enough study "to render a verdict on the most important question then or ever before the nation and the world." For Crafts the lesson was plain. The study of internationalism was now more critical in the United States than ever because Crafts's own country was the only nation in which delegates to international conferences did not have the authority to guarantee their government's agreement on treaties. The world had to wait while the American public and its representatives educated themselves on international subjects.[54]

The fate of international cooperation was not the only concern gnawing at Crafts. His last years had been increasingly preoccupied with a more concrete objective than worldwide cooperation on drugs and war. Crafts and his wife, Sara, had acquired a home at 206 Pennsylvania Avenue SE, Washington, across from the Jefferson Building of the Library of Congress and conveniently situated symbolically and practically for the International Reform Bureau's lobbying.[55] In 1911, Wilbur hit upon the idea of turning his home on Pennsylvania Avenue into a permanent center for the moral reform movement. He started a drive to raise funds for the project. He envisaged a new building something like the Australian "people's palaces" that provided temperance refreshments and accommodation for young people and Christian travelers. The International

Reform Bureau headquarters would be "essentially" like the sumptu-
ous "Coffee Palace" in Melbourne, Victoria, which Crafts had visited in
1907, but also like a YMCA. It would be a "Library Hotel" for students
and government workers. The building fund began with a promised contribution of $50,000 from Wilbur and Sara,[56] but the Crafts needed to
raise $30,000 more. Though $12,000 was collected,[57] the extra money
remained out of reach. The war intervened, and attention turned to financing the fight for national prohibition.[58] By 1916 the Anti-Saloon
League's needs eclipsed those of the International Reform Bureau. Some
years after Crafts's death, the federal government resumed the property
for the Adams Building of the Library of Congress.[59] Crafts's organization continued, but funding and public attention had long shifted to the
Anti-Saloon League and, on the global stage, to the WLAA. None of these
organizations survived as serious competitors for the hearts and minds of
Americans after national prohibition's demise in 1933.

Crafts's passing barely rated a mention in the major dailies, whereas
Bishop Charles Brent's life ended with greater recognition of his influence, as befitted a man who had advised presidents. In the 1920s Brent
continued his international involvement of the type that Crafts admired.
He became closely associated with the search for global Christian unity.
Though texts cite the influence of the 1910 World Missionary Conference
at Edinburgh on him, Brent's Christian ecumenicalism also reflected the
impact of his time in the Philippines. As a result of that experience, Brent
found it "little short of absurd to try to bring into the Church of Christ
the great nations of the Far East unless we can represent an undivided
front."[60] Non-Christians simply did not understand the smorgasbord of
Christian faiths and doubted the efficacy of such a disordered message.
He worked with the Continuation Committee of the Edinburgh conference after 1910 to press the importance of this point.

World War I's slaughter reinforced his conviction of Christianity's
shortcomings and the need for concerted action. In 1920 he spoke at a
preliminary church meeting on the global "failure of Christianity" that
stemmed from disunity.[61] In 1925 he attended the Protestant churches'
Life and Work Conference at Stockholm "devoted to delivering ways of
mutual cooperation ... in the area of social and political life."[62] But Brent
believed that theology and doctrine needed to be tackled, too, and lobbied for the holding of the first World Conference on Faith and Order in
Lausanne where these issues were seriously discussed in 1927. As president of the conference, Brent returned to his East Asian experience to
argue that "the 100 Missionary Societies in China" were "suicidal for
Christianity."[63] Predictably, no unity was achieved despite Brent's urg-
ings, and Catholics did not attend. Indeed, one American Catholic cleric
was reported as proclaiming that the failure to achieve unity served

the long-term interests of Rome in regaining formal acknowledgment of its supreme authority in Christendom.[64] Even Protestant ministers could do little more than profess a commitment among themselves to keep alive the dialogue that Brent advocated. Brent had not achieved the victory he hoped, but he had spurred the processes of formal Christian ecumenicalism.

Perhaps taken with the scene of his last great international intervention, Brent returned in March 1929 to Lausanne with friends, where he died suddenly. He had undertaken a long life's journey, from Newcastle, Ontario, in the land of his birth, to the University of Toronto for college studies and theological training. Then Boston and a slum parish in the 1890s had become his home, from whence he was drawn to serve the Episcopal Church in Manila. World War I saw him in Paris as senior chaplain to the U.S. Army on the Western Front, where he believed he had truly become a patriotic American. Almost simultaneously, declining health had forced him to resign his Philippines' post to accept election as the bishop of western New York in Buffalo, near his Canadian origins. Provincialism was not to be his fate, however, and Geneva and Lausanne drew him into the whirlwind of 1920s internationalism and the assertion of American political and moral power.[65]

Brent's transnational Christian activism led him to advocate international cooperation in moral and social reform as well as Christian principles. The 1920s saw him still vigorous on this front. Secretary of State and old political ally Charles Evans Hughes had Brent appointed to the U.S. observer delegation sent to the Advisory Committee on Opium within the League of Nations in 1923, and Brent took part as an American delegate to the 1924–25 International Opium Conference that tried to build upon prewar American initiatives.[66] But when European nations resisted American actions aimed at effecting prohibition in the use of narcotics, the American delegation withdrew and did not adhere to the new convention. As a member of the delegation, Brent claimed to be "disgusted" with the result and, joining in the withdrawal, denounced European stonewalling of efforts to realize the substance of the 1912 International Opium Convention at The Hague whose outcome he had worked so hard to secure. An effective prohibition on the production and sale of opium outside bona fide medicinal use remained a still distant prospect.[67]

John Mott also walked the world stage in the 1920s as a representative of both American internationalism and Christian universalism. Problems of refugee relief and prisoner-of-war repatriation in eastern Europe took his time in the immediate postwar years. In 1920, he aided the establishment in Vienna of European Student Relief as a social service to students displaced by the war. Student Christian groups from all over the world contributed to this program that, after the initial crises of the postwar period subsided, became the International Student Service.[68] This effort was part of his attempts to rebuild the international student community through the World's Student Christian Federation and the World's YMCA, of which he became president in 1926. Mott had been on the Continuation Committee of the Edinburgh Conference on Missions after 1910, where he toiled tirelessly for the cause of international missionary cooperation alongside his Scottish coworker Joseph Oldham.[69] From its founding in 1921, Mott also headed the International Missionary Council, born out of the Continuation Committee, which aimed to coordinate global Protestant missions in the interwar years.[70]

From being the confidante of an American president, Mott became a figure of world stature and a Nobel Laureate in 1946, shared with another American, Emily Green Balch. He fulfilled the vow he reputedly averred at the time of signing as one of the first hundred Student Volunteers at Northfield in 1886: his mission would be "the world."[71] Mott's Nobel Prize citation noted that he had "crossed the Atlantic over one hundred times and the Pacific fourteen times, averaging thirty-four days on the ocean per year for fifty years." Decorations from China, Czechoslovakia, Finland, France, Greece, Hungary, Italy, Japan, Poland, Portugal, Sweden, and the United States came his way; among six honorary degrees were those from Edinburgh, Princeton, and Yale.[72] As befitted his worldly acclaim, Mott remained an optimist. In his acceptance speech to the Nobel committee on the occasion of the award of the prize in Oslo, Mott commented: "If I were to add a word it would be a word of abounding hope. The present new generation across the breadth of the world, and whose representatives are planning to assemble here in Norway ... are responsive to the Nobel Peace ideal, and are planning, as no previous generation, for a great united advance in the furtherance of peace and good-will throughout the world."[73] Mott viewed these matters as causes beyond nation, beyond ideology. As Crafts had also hoped, the free flow of information and the voluntary association of like-minded, moral individuals would produce an improved society.

These four people—Leitch, Crafts, Brent, and Mott—represented a range of religious and moral reform movements that distinguished the American contribution to transnational organizing in the period before World War I. That record was one of defeat as much as victory. By the 1920s, Leitch and Crafts were marginalized figures. Brent and Mott were far more successful and built upon the achievements of many other more obscure soldiers in the armies of reform. Whether their work be relatively effective, remembered, or forgotten, the pattern of the four's involvement left moral footprints, enmeshing the United States unmistakably in the affairs of the wider world. The nation had become more deeply connected to international networks conceived in the era of European empire, and these connections shaped the drive for American influence in the 1920s and beyond.

Like Brent's, Mott's work represented the realization of American international cooperation in the 1920s. Despite the "legend of isolationism,"[74] the United States took a vigorous part in international negotiations, and not just in the field of economic foreign policy. Though the nation was still wary of alliances in European politics, outside Europe the United States did not remain politically aloof. The American government convened the 1921–22 Washington Naval Conference aimed at the limitation of armaments in the Pacific. Globally the United States was also active in ways that had strong implications for European politics. In 1928, the United States cosponsored the Kellogg-Briand Pact that renounced war as an instrument of national policy. Non-governmental organizations also expanded their reach in the 1920s, as the examples of the World League Against Alcoholism, Rotary, and many others show.[75] Equally important, the activities of transnational organizations and governments fused in that decade. Wilbur Crafts had not lived to see this internationalism prosper, but it followed in his footsteps and conformed to his aspirations, just as it did those of Brent. The case of narcotics control demonstrated this pattern. While the United States had not joined the League of Nations, its leading role in the events leading up to the 1912 International Opium Convention signed at The Hague made it difficult to avoid the League entirely. After that convention came into effect in 1919, League officials sought to assist the 1912 agreement's implementation with American cooperation. It established the advisory committee to which Brent was sent as part of the observer delegation of 1923 and from whose deliberations came the subsequent International Opium Conference.[76] In such ways, what happened before World War I inevitably influenced American approaches to international cooperation in the 1920s.

The new internationalism of that era still operated amid the realities of nation-states and their interests. American economic foreign policy quite ruthlessly favored the growth of the nation's economic power. Legislation promoted American exports, while high tariffs in the 1920s discriminated against foreign imports. Notably the Webb-Pomerene Act of 1918 allowed U.S. exporters to collude through cartels that remained off limits to foreign exporters to the United States.[77] Whether emanating from the American government or voluntary organizations, international policy initiatives risked being seen as part of an American attempt to capture greater power on the international stage. A subtle dialectic took place between American power and the extension of the nation's moral influence. From the point of view of outsiders, organizations such as the YMCA were too closely associated with the ideology of American capitalism. American relief groups in Russia coordinated by Mott between

1918 and 1923 were forced to leave because Soviet officials were suspicious of their teachings.[78] Similarly, for many western Europeans the export of American prohibition had the air of unwanted Americanization. Other more secular endeavors such as Rotary International faced parallel resentments. Rotary raised the hackles of the Catholic Church as a covert version of a secular religion, before temporarily succumbing in central Europe to the totalitarian political controls of Nazi Germany after 1933.[79] In these and other cases, American internationalism carried strong political freight, but the moral reformers of the 1920s and their predecessors before World War I did not acknowledge these political realities limiting their influence.

Men such as Brent, Crafts, and Mott did not see the export of American-based reform and service organizations as the assertion of a specifically American form of hegemony. Rather, moral reformers believed that their efforts were beyond nation. All had worked, as Mary Leitch did, through an overarching allegiance to varieties of Protestant Christianity. This conflation of Americanism, Christianity, and internationalism applied to Charles Brent who, in 1924, told an American religious magazine that "Moral Questions have no boundaries. The world today is steadily revealing itself to be a world of identical moral interests. If we exploit abroad where we defend at home, the downfall of the exploited will eventually be our downfall."[80] But to realize this noble goal, he needed the diplomatic power of the United States in the case of the opium trade, and he supported American objectives for the suppression of that trade through prohibition, a strategy that many other countries did not accept. Other nations in the opium controversy were not prepared to go so far as to create the "world of identical moral interests" that Brent desired. Brent died in Lausanne confident of his faith, but the example of the Opium Conference showed his work to be dependent on fallible earthly power to realize his moral goals.[81] An admirer has written: "His body was dressed in a purple cassock, placed in a plain oak casket and buried in Bois de Vaux cemetery in Lausanne.... The tree lay where it fell. There was no home to which to take his body: No one place could claim him—be it New Castle [sic], Boston, Manila, Paris or Buffalo. Though a man for all nations, he only sojourned in this world he served: The courts of heaven for him seemed always only a step away."[82] Mott would surely have agreed that this could count as a judgment on himself, and Mary Leitch would not have quibbled to be described as a woman of all nations who awaited only the judgment of heaven. Yet the world they left behind was more complicated than that.

NOTES

INTRODUCTION

1. For example, Robin Winks, ed., *British Imperialism: Gold, God, Glory* (New York, 1963).

2. Louis Stanley Young, *Life and Heroic Deeds of Admiral Dewey* (Philadelphia, 1899), 446; *New York Times*, 22 April 1900, p. 17; Marjorie Balge, "The Dewey Arch: Sculpture or Architecture?" *Archives of American Art Journal* 23, no. 4 (1983), 2–6.

3. Bernard Porter, *Empire and Superempire: Britain, America and the World* (New Haven, 2006), 1; this exact expression does not, however, appear in an official State Department transcript as given in Niall Ferguson, *Colossus: The Rise and Fall of the American Empire* (London, 2005), 1. See also Donald Rumsfeld quoted in "Empire Snaps Back," *The Progressive*, June 2003: "We don't seek empire," he snapped. "We're not imperialistic. We never have been. I can't imagine why you'd even ask the question." http://findarticles.com/p/articles/mi_m1295/is_6_67/ai_102750158/pg_1 (accessed 1 March 2007).

4. See, for example, Ferguson, *Colossus*; Max Boot, *The Savage Wars of Peace: Small Wars and the Rise of American Power* (New York, 2002); Lloyd Gardner and Marilyn B. Young, eds., *The New American Empire: A 21st Century Teach-In on U.S. Foreign Policy* (New York, 2005); Porter, *Empire and Superempire*, 2; Andrew Bacevich, *American Empire: The Realities and Consequences of U.S. Diplomacy* (Cambridge, MA, 2002).

5. Charles S. Maier, *Among Empires: American Ascendancy and Its Predecessors* (Cambridge, MA, 2006); Porter, *Empire and Superempire*; David Abernethy, *The Dynamics of Global Dominance: European Overseas Empires, 1415–1980* (New Haven, 2000).

6. Fernand Braudel, *The Mediterranean in the Ancient World* (London, 2001), 307 (quotes); Ferguson, *Colossus*, 8–13; for insistence on formal political domination, see Abernethy, *Dynamics of Global Dominance*, 19–20.

7. See, especially, William Appleman Williams, *The Tragedy of American Diplomacy*, rev. ed. (New York, 1961); Williams, *Empire as a Way of Life* (New York, 1980).

8. Ian Tyrrell, *Woman's World/Woman's Empire: The Woman's Christian Temperance Union in International Perspective, 1880–1930* (Chapel Hill, 1991); Nancy Boyd, *Emissaries: The Overseas Work of the American YWCA, 1895–1970* (New York, 1986). Emily S. Rosenberg, *Spreading the American Dream: American Economic and Cultural Expansion, 1890–1945* (New York, 1982), provides a short introduction to American cultural "expansion." The role of missionaries in China and the Open Door has been the subject of interesting analysis, for which see James Reed, *The Missionary Mind and American East Asia Policy, 1911–1915* (Cambridge, MA, 1983), but the interaction between different moral

reform organizations of the period has not been studied, even though this cluster of institutions constituted an important presence in the formal and informal empire that Americans created. Moreover, that empire was not located in any one sphere of influence but was conceived of as a global enterprise.

9. *Chicago Daily*, 9 February 1897, 12.

10. A. G. Spalding, *America's National Game: Historic Facts Concerning the Beginning, Evolution, Development and Popularity of Base Ball... .* (New York, 1911), 252, 253 (quote); Sayuri Guthrie-Shimizu, "For Love of the Game: Baseball in Early U.S.-Japanese Encounters and the Rise of a Transnational Sporting Fraternity," *Diplomatic History* 28, no. 5 (2004), 637–62; Mark Lamster, *Spalding's World Tour: The Epic Adventure That Took Baseball around the Globe— And Made It America's Game* (New York, 2006); Thomas W. Zeiler, *Ambassadors in Pinstripes: The Spalding Baseball Tour and the Birth of American Empire* (Lanham, MD, 2006); Frank Ardolino, "Missionaries, Cartwright, and Spalding: The Development of Baseball in Nineteenth-Century Hawaii," *NINE: A Journal of Baseball History and Culture* 10, no. 2 (2002), 27–45; Rob Kroes and Robert Rydell, *Buffalo Bill in Bologna* (Chicago, 2005).

11. On soft power, see Joseph S. Nye, *Soft Power: The Means to Success in World Politics* (New York, 2004). On hegemony, see James Joll, *Gramsci* (London, 1977), 108–9; Antonio Gramsci, "Americanism and Fordism," in Quintin Hoare and Geoffrey Nowell, eds., *Selections from the Prison Notebooks* (New York, 1971), 279–318, 350; T. L. Jackson Lears, "The Concept of Cultural Hegemony: Problems and Possibilities," *American Historical Review* 90 (June 1985), 567–93; Ian Tyrrell, "Prohibition, American Cultural Expansion, and the New Hegemony in the 1920s: An Interpretation," *Histoire Sociale/Social History* 27 (November 1994), 413–45.

12. For a brief survey, see Ian Tyrrell, *Transnational Nation: The United States in Global Perspective since 1789* (Basingstoke, Eng., 2007).

13. On "moral imperialism," see Berta Esperanza Hernandez-Truyol, ed., *Moral Imperialism: A Critical Anthology* (New York, 2002).

14. Kenneth Scott Latourette, "Missionaries Abroad," *Annals of the American Academy of Political and Social Science* 368, Americans Abroad (November 1966), 28–29.

15. E.g., Manuel Castells, *The Rise of the Network Society* (Cambridge, MA, 1996); Margaret Keck and Kathryn Sikkink, *Activists beyond Borders: Advocacy Networks in International Politics* (Ithaca, NY, 1998); Sidney Tarrow, *The New Transnational Activism* (New York, 2005); Richard Price, "Transnational Civil Society and Advocacy in World Politics," *World Politics* 55 (July 2003), 579–606.

16. E.g., Tyrrell, *Woman's World*.

17. Price, "Transnational Civil Society."

18. For older studies, see William R. Hutchinson, *Errand to the World: American Protestant Thought and Foreign Missions* (Chicago, 1987); Paul Varg, "Motives in Protestant Missions, 1890–1917," *Church History* 23 (March 1954), 68–82; Valentin H. Rabe, *The Home Base of American China Missions, 1880–1920* (Cambridge, MA, 1978); James C. Thomson Jr., Peter Stanley, and John Curtis Perry, *Sentimental Imperialists: The American Experience in East Asia* (New York, 1981); Kenneth M. Mackenzie, *The Robe and the Sword: The Methodist*

Church and the Rise of American Imperialism (Washington, DC, 1961); Paul Varg, *Missionaries, Chinese, and Diplomats: The American Protestant Missionary Movement in China, 1890–1952* (Princeton, 1958); John K. Fairbank, ed., *The Missionary Enterprise in China and America* (Cambridge, MA, 1974). For reassessments, see Patricia R. Hill, *The World Their Household: The American Woman's Foreign Mission Movement and Cultural Transformation, 1870–1920* (Ann Arbor, MI, 1985); Jane Hunter, *The Gospel of Gentility: American Women Missionaries in Turn-of-the-Century China* (New Haven, 1984); Ann White, "Counting the Cost of Faith: America's Early Female Missionaries," *Church History* 57 (March 1988), 19–30; Dana L. Robert, ed., *Converting Colonialism: Visions and Realities in Mission History, 1706–1914* (Grand Rapids, MI, 2007).

19. For recent discussions, see Ryan Dunch, "Beyond Cultural Imperialism: Cultural Theory, Christian Missions, and Global Modernity," *History and Theory* 41 (October 2002), 301–25; Carol C. Chin, "Beneficent Imperialists: American Women Missionaries in China at the Turn of the Twentieth Century," *Diplomatic History* 27 (June 2003), 327–52. See also Hutchinson, *Errand to the World*, chap. 4; Arthur Schlesinger Jr., "The Missionary Enterprise and Theories of Imperialism," in Fairbank, *Missionary Enterprise*, 336–73; Mrinalini Sinha, *Specters of Mother India: The Global Restructuring of an Empire* (Durham, NC, 2006).

20. Ussama Makdisi, *Artillery of Heaven: American Missionaries and the Failed Conversion of the Middle East* (Ithaca, NY, 2008).

21. Robert E. Lang, Deborah Epstein Popper, and Frank J. Popper, "'Progress of the Nation': The Settlement History of the Enduring American Frontier," *Western Historical Quarterly* 26 (Autumn 1995), 289–307.

22. Cf. William Appleman Williams, "The Frontier Thesis and American Foreign Policy," *Pacific Historical Review* 24 (November 1955), 379–95; Williams, *The Roots of the Modern American Empire: A Study of the Growth and Shaping of Social Consciousness* (New York, 1969); Walter LaFeber, *The New Empire: An Interpretation of American Expansion* (Ithaca, NY, 1963), 11, 71, 72–80; Richard Slotkin, "Nostalgia and Progress: Theodore Roosevelt's Myth of the Frontier," *American Quarterly* 33, no. 5, special issue: American Culture and the American Frontier (Winter 1981), 663–35. Josiah Strong, the oft-cited expansionist clergyman, did not adopt formal imperialism as a policy prior to U.S. rule in the Philippines. Cf. LaFeber, *New Empire*, 72–80. See Josiah Strong, *Our Country, Its Possible Future and Its Present Crisis* (1885; New York, 1891), 220, 226; Strong, *Expansion under New World-Conditions* (1900; New York, 1971), 278.

23. For the sociological theme of transnational spaces, see Thomas Faist, *The Volume and Dynamics of International Migration and Transnational Social Spaces* (Oxford, 2000). For further discussion, see chap. 1.

24. Alfred W. McCoy and Francisco Scarano, eds., *Colonial Crucible: Empire in the Making of the Modern American State* (Madison, WI, 2009).

25. The literature on the "transnational turn" is growing rapidly. Especially useful from a historiographical viewpoint are Pierre-Yves Saunier, "Learning by Doing: Notes about the Making of the *Palgrave Dictionary of Transnational History*," *Journal of Modern European History* 6 (2008), 159–80; and Kiran Klaus Patel, "'Transnations' among 'Transnations'? The Debate on Transnational His-

tory in the United States and Germany," Center for European Studies Working Paper Series, no. 159 (2008). A different and more comprehensive terminology of "crossed" (or "entangled") history is proposed by Michael Werner and Bénédicte Zimmermann, "Beyond Comparison: Histoire Croisée and the Challenge of Reflexivity," *History and Theory* 45, no. 1 (2006), 30–50. But the latter is not concerned with topics crossing specifically national borders. For further discussion, see Ian Tyrrell, "Reflections on the Transnational Turn in United States History: Theory and Practice," *Journal of Global History* 3 (November 2009), 453–74.

26. The World's YWCA is in need of serious historical analysis, goals not fulfilled in Boyd, *Emissaries*.

27. However, see the important but neglected pioneering work, Merle Curti, *American Philanthropy Abroad: A History* (New Brunswick, NJ, 1963).

28. Cf. Richard Hofstadter, "Cuba, the Philippines, and Manifest Destiny," in Hofstadter, *The Paranoid Style in American Politics and Other Essays* (New York, 1965), 145–87.

CHAPTER 1. WEBS OF COMMUNICATION

1. Joseph O. Baylen, "Stead, William Thomas (1849–1912)," *Oxford Dictionary of National Biography*, http://www.oxforddnb.com/view/article/36258 (accessed 26 June 2007).

2. *New York Times*, 23 April 1912, p. 8.

3. W. T. Stead, "The Twentieth Century Is the Century of Internationalism," in *Review of Internationalism* 1, no. 1 (April 1907), cited in Madelaine Herren, "Governmental Internationalism and the Beginning of a New World Order in the Late Nineteenth Century," in Martin H. Geyer and Johannes Paulmann, eds., *The Mechanics of Internationalism: Culture, Society, and Politics from the 1840s to the First World War* (London and Oxford, 2001), 121; Baylen, "Stead"; Frederic Whyte, *The Life of W. T. Stead*, 2 vols. (London, 1925).

4. William T. Stead, *The Americanisation of the World, or, The Trend of the Twentieth Century* (1901; London, 1902), repr. as *The Americanization of the World, or, The Trend of the Twentieth Century*, Garland ed. with a new intro. by Sandi E. Cooper (New York, 1972). For the Lake Mohonk conferences, see Calvin D. Davis, *The United States and the First Hague Peace Conference* (Ithaca, NY, 1962).

5. The growth of internationalism did not mean all nations were treated equally. Sanitation conferences displayed marked desires to exclude the contagion of "Oriental" disease, and proponents of internationalism among the European powers were themselves not all treated equally. Martin H. Geyer and Johannes Paulmann, "Introduction: The Mechanics of Internationalism," in Geyer and Paulmann, *The Mechanics of Internationalism*, 22–23; Herren, "Governmental Internationalism," 127.

6. Charles Denby Jr., "America's Opportunity in Asia," *North American Review* 166 (January 1898), 37.

7. Jonathan T. R. Hughes, *American Economic History*, 2nd ed. (Glenview, IL, 1987), 368–69.

8. Eileen Scully, *Bargaining with the State from Afar: American Citizenship in Treaty Port China, 1844–1942* (New York, 2001).

9. *New York Times*, 31 August 1858, p. 5.

10. For the expansion of cable, see Daniel R. Headrick, *The Invisible Weapon: Telecommunications and International Politics, 1851–1945* (New York, 1991), 28–49; Donald Murray, "How Cables Unite the World," *World's Work* 4 (July 1902), 2298–2309.

11. Christopher Endy, "Travel and World Power: Americans in Europe, 1890–1917," *Diplomatic History* 22 (Fall 1998), 567.

12. Andrew Aird, *Glimpses of Old Glasgow* (Glasgow, 1894), 361–62.

13. Bernard A. Weisberger, "Elizabeth Cochrane Seaman," *NAW*, 3:253–55; Lynne Withey, *Grand Tours and Cook's Tours: A History of Leisure Travel, 1750–1915* (New York, 1997).

14. [Elizabeth Cochrane Seaman], *Nellie Bly's Book: Around the World in Seventy-Two Days* (New York, 1890); Weisberger, "Seaman," 3:253–55.

15. Tyrrell, *Transnational Nation*, chap. 8; Tyrrell, *Woman's World*, chap. 5.

16. *The Poetical Works of Reginald Heber*, new ed. (Boston, 1857), 86 (quote); Geoffrey Cook, "'From India's Coral Strand': Reginald Heber and the Missionary Project," *International Journal of Hindu Studies* 5 (August 2001), 131–64; Tyrrell, *Woman's World*, chap. 5; Joan Jacobs Brumberg, "Zenanas and Girlless Villages: The Ethnology of American Evangelical Women, 1870–1910," *Journal of American History* 69 (September 1982), 347–71.

17. Kristin Hoganson, *Consumers' Imperium: The Global Production of American Domesticity, 1865–1920* (Chapel Hill, 2007), 190–91.

18. Mary Schriber, *Writing Home: American Women Abroad, 1830–1920* (Charlottesville, VA, 1997), 4; Mary Louise Pratt, *Imperial Eyes: Travel Writing and Transculturation* (New York, 1992).

19. Philip Pauly, "The World and All That Is in It: The National Geographic Society, 1888–1918," *American Quarterly* 31, no. 4 (1979), 532; Hoganson, *Consumers' Imperium*, esp. chap. 2.

20. Howard Mumford Jones, *The Age of Energy: Varieties of American Experience, 1865–1915* (New York, 1971), 263–65, 280–81, 291 (quote), 292.

21. Justin Willis, "Brussels Act and Conventions, 1890–1912," in Jack S. Blocker Jr., David Fahey, and Ian Tyrrell, eds., *Alcohol and Temperance in Modern History: An International Encyclopedia*, 2 vols. (Santa Barbara, 2003), 1:118–19; Suzanne Miers, *Slavery in the Twentieth Century: The Evolution of a Global Problem* (Walnut Creek, CA, 2003), 20–22 (quote at 20); Adam Hochschild, *King Leopold's Ghost: A Story of Greed, Terror, and Heroism in Colonial Africa* (New York, 1998), 92–93, 111–12; Gil Gott, "Imperial Humanitarianism: History of an Arrested Dialectic," in Hernandez-Truyol, ed., *Moral Imperialism*, 19–39.

22. Frederick T. Frelinghuysen, quoted in Peter Duigan and L. H. Gann, *The United States and Africa: A History* (New York, 1984), 134.

23. Randolph Bourne, "Trans-National America," *Atlantic Monthly* 118 (July 1916), 86–97; Pierre-Yves Saunier, "A Texans' Universe? First Drafts of a History of Universals," *New Global Studies* 2, no. 1 (2008), http://www.bepress.com/ngs/vol2/iss1/art8 (accessed 12 April 2008).

24. F.S.L. Lyons, *Internationalism in Europe, 1815–1914* (Leyden, 1963), 215–22; Herren, "Governmental Internationalism," 126–27.

25. Simeon E. Baldwin, "The International Congresses and Conferences of the Last Century as Forces Working toward the Solidarity of the World," *American Journal of International Law* 1 (July 1907), 565-78.

26. Lyons, *Internationalism in Europe*, 209, 214; Warren Kuehl, *Seeking World Order: The United States and International Organization to 1920* (Nashville, 1969), 38–41ff.

27. Lyons, *Internationalism in Europe*, 14; Leila Rupp, "The Making of Women's International Organizations," in Geyer and Paulmann, *The Mechanics of Internationalism*, 208.

28. Paul S. Reinsch, "International Unions and Their Administration," *American Journal of International Law* 1 (July 1907), 579–623.

29. Herren, "Governmental Internationalism," 121–44.

30. Lyons, *Internationalism in Europe*, 14.

31. George Snow, "International Congresses on Alcoholism," in Blocker, Fahey, and Tyrrell, *Alcohol and Temperance in Modern History*, 1:318.

32. Reinsch, "International Unions," 609.

33. Valeska Huber, "The Unification of the Globe by Disease," *Historical Journal* 49, no. 2 (2006), 453–76.

34. Herren, "Governmental Internationalism," 137; George M. Sternberg, "The International Sanitary Conference at Rome in 1885," *Science* 6, no. 131 (August 1885), 101–3; Huber, "Unification of the Globe"; Lyons, *Internationalism in Europe*, 240; "International Exhibition and Congress of Public Health and Safety, to Be Held in Brussels in 1876," *Journal of the Statistical Society of London* 38 (June 1875), 249–52.

35. Huber, "Unification of the Globe."

36. Reinsch, "International Unions," 609; Enoch C. Wines, *Report on the International Penitentiary Congress of London, held July 3–13, 1872* ... (Washington, DC, 1873), 179.

37. Mark Lawrence Schrad, "The Prohibition Option: Transnational Temperance and National Policymaking in Russia, Sweden and the United States" (Ph.D. diss., University of Wisconsin–Madison, 2007), 465.

38. Snow, "International Congresses on Alcoholism," 318–19.

39. Ernest R. Sandeen, "The Distinctiveness of American Denominationalism: A Case Study of the 1846 Evangelical Alliance," *Church History* 45 (June 1976), 222–34; Philip Schaff and Samuel Prime, eds., *History, Essays, Orations, and Other Documents of the Sixth General Conference of the Evangelical Alliance, held in New York, October 2–12, 1873* (New York, 1874).

40. Anne Summers, "Which Women? What Europe? Josephine Butler and the International Abolitionist Federation," *History Workshop Journal* 62, no. 1 (2006), 214–31.

41. David J. Pivar, *Purity Crusade: Sexual Morality and Social Control, 1868–1900* (Westport, CT, 1973), esp. 69–70; Henry J. Wilson and James Gledstone, *Report of a Visit to the United States, as Delegates from the British, Continental, and General Federation for the Abolition of Government Regulation of Prostitution* (Sheffield, Eng., 1876), 13–26.

42. William Lloyd Garrison to Henry J. Wilson, 29 May 1876, in Walter Merrill and Louis Ruchames, eds., *To Rouse the Slumbering Land, 1868–1879: The Letters Of William Lloyd Garrison* (Cambridge, MA, 1981), 6:408; Millicent G. Fawcett and E. M. Turner, *Josephine Butler: Her Work and Principles, and Their Meaning for the Twentieth Century* (London, 1927), 117; E. Moberly Bell, *Josephine Butler: Flame of Fire* (London, 1963), 132–33; Aaron M. Powell, *State Regulation of Vice: Regulation Efforts in America* (New York, 1878).

43. Wines, *International Penitentiary Congress*, 147.

44. Aaron M. Powell, *Personal Reminiscences of the Anti-Slavery and Other Reforms and Reformers* (New York, 1899), 237–54; see also Powell, *The National Purity Congress: Its Papers, Addresses, Portraits* (1895; New York, 1976), vi, regarding the New York Committee for the Prevention of the State Regulation of Vice.

45. Ruth Bordin, *Frances Willard: A Biography* (Chapel Hill, 1986), 132–33; Tyrrell, *Woman's World*, 200–202.

46. Margaret E. Parker, *Six Happy Weeks among the Americans* (Glasgow, 1876), 55; Eliza D. Stewart, *The Crusader in Great Britain: Or, the History of the Origin and Organization of the British Women's Temperance Association* (Springfield, OH, 1893), xiii–xv.

47. David Fahey, *Temperance and Racism: John Bull, Johnny Reb, and the Good Templars* (Lexington, KY, 1996).

48. Robert W. Rydell, *World of Fairs: The Century-of-Progress Expositions* (Chicago, 1993); Olive Checkland refers to this phenomenon as a "movement." See Checkland, *Japan and Britain after 1859: Creating Cultural Bridges* (London, 2003), 17; Merle Curti, "America at the World's Fairs, 1851–1893," *American Historical Review* 55 (July 1950), 837–38.

49. *Centennial Temperance Volume: A Memorial of the International Temperance Conference, held in Philadelphia, June, 1876. With the specially-prepared essays, addresses of foreign delegates, deliberations … etc.* (New York, 1877), 49; Jun Xing, *Baptized in the Fire of Revolution: The American Social Gospel and the YMCA in China, 1919–1937* (Bethlehem, PA, 1996), 26.

50. Quoted in Douglass Kellner, "Habermas, the Public Sphere, and Democracy: A Critical Intervention," http://www.gseis.ucla.edu/faculty/kellner/papers/habermas.htm (accessed 28 January 2008); Jürgen Habermas, *The Structural Transformation of the Public Sphere: An Inquiry into a Category of Bourgeois Society*, trans. Thomas Burger (1962; Cambridge, MA, 1991). This "space" came to fuller fruition with new institutions such as the Permanent Court of Arbitration at The Hague (1907), which gave a model of a new world order. Herren, "Governmental Internationalism," 142–43.

51. "Internationalism: The Characteristic of the 20th Century," *Twentieth Century Quarterly* 8 (June 1908), 8.

52. Wilbur Crafts, *A Primer of the Science of Internationalism with Special Reference to University Debates* (Washington, DC, 1908), 9 (quotes); "Pneumonia Is Fatal to Reformer," *Los Angeles Times*, 28 December 1922.

53. Letter No. 1, 15 November 1896, in India, Eddy, G. Sherwood, Report Letters, 1896–1903, National Committee, 1891–1926, Y-57-1, KFYMCAA.

54. Crafts, *Primer*, 86.

55. Arthur Tappan Pierson, *The Crisis of Missions: Or, the Voice Out of the Cloud* (New York, 1886), 76–77.

56. James Mills Thoburn, *The Christian Conquest of India* (New York, 1906).

57. Diary, 8 July 1873, book 3, Wilbur Crafts Notebooks, BHLM (hereafter Crafts Notebooks).

58. Journal 1867, Paris, 3 June 1867, box 1, Adee Family Papers, LC.

59. Frances Willard, *Glimpses of Fifty Years* (Chicago, 1889), 422.

60. G. W. Leitch to Dr. N. G. Clark, 6 January 1880, reel 456, American Board of Commissioners for Foreign Missions Papers, Houghton Library, Harvard University (hereafter ABCFM Papers).

61. Letter No. 1, 15 November 1896, in India, Eddy, G. Sherwood, Report Letters, 1896–1903, National Committee, 1891–1926, Y-57-1, KFYMCAA.

62. *Union Signal*, 20 December 1883, 8.

CHAPTER 2. MISSIONARY LIVES, TRANSNATIONAL NETWORKS:
THE MISSES MARGARET AND MARY LEITCH

1. Mary and Margaret Leitch to Rev. N. G. [Dr. Nathaniel George] Clark, 17 May 1890, reel 459, ABCFM Papers; for the intellectual inheritance of their South Ryegate church, see Randolph A. Roth, "The First Radical Abolitionists: The Reverend James Milligan and the Reformed Presbyterians of Vermont," *New England Quarterly* 55 (December 1982), 540–63.

2. Edward Miller and Frederic Wells, *History of Ryegate, Vermont, From Its Settlement by the Scotch-American Company of Farmers to Present Time. With Genealogical Records of Many Families* (St. Johnsbury, VT, 1913), 406; Mary Leitch and Margaret Leitch, *Seven Years in Ceylon: Stories of Mission Life* (New York, 1890), 152 (quote); Mary Leitch to unknown recipient, 15 August 1883, reel 456, ABCFM Papers.

3. On women and the Reconstruction effort in the postbellum South, see James M. McPherson, *The Abolitionist Legacy: From Reconstruction to the NAACP* (Princeton, 1975), 194–99, 56; Carol Faulkner, *Women's Radical Reconstruction: The Freedmen's Aid Movement* (Philadelphia, 2004).

4. George W. Leitch to N. G. Clark, 6 June 1880, reel 456, ABCFM Papers.

5. *Seventy-Second Annual Report of the American Board of Commissioners for Foreign Missions* (Boston, 1882), 52–53; *Seventy-Third Annual Report of the American Board of Commissioners for Foreign Missions Presented at the Meeting Held in Detroit, Michigan, October 2–5, 1883* (Boston, 1883), 65; *Seventy-Fourth Annual Report of the American Board of Commissioners for Foreign Missions Presented at the Meeting Held at Columbus, Ohio, October 7–10, 1884* (Boston, 1884), 49.

6. Leitch and Leitch, *Seven Years in Ceylon*, 90–93.

7. George W. Leitch to N. G. Clark, 14 April 1881, reel 456, ABCFM Papers; Leitch and Leitch, *Seven Years in Ceylon*, 158.

8. George W. Leitch to N. G. Clark, 14 April 1881, reel 456, ABCFM Papers. However, the Shaivites did not oppose all of the Leitch sisters' work. In [Mary

and Margaret Leitch], *Annual Report for 1886* (n.p., n.d. [1886]), the sisters explained that donors to the Oodooville School included "Sivites, who were yet glad to show that they appreciated the good work which all confessed the educational institutions of our mission were doing" (9). Copy in the British Library.

9. George W. Leitch to N. G. Clark, 23 June 1882, reel 456, ABCFM Papers: "none of which are on a social equality."

10. Gerald Carson, *Cornflake Crusade* (New York, 1957), 114.

11. "Temperance Notes," *Chicago Inter-Ocean*, 3 March 1888, in book 34, p. 100, WCTU Scrapbooks, WCTUHQ.

12. Mary C. Leavitt, *Report of the Hon. Sec. of the World's Woman's Christian Temperance Union* (Boston, 1891), 39, 40.

13. Leitch and Leitch, *Seven Years in Ceylon*, 101–12.

14. Ibid., 136 (first quote); "Our Experience in Collecting Funds: Some Lessons Learned," p. 3, Leitch 1, biographical file, box 43, WBMHL; "Occasional Letter, No. 7, Seven Months in Ceylon,—A Retrospect," from the Misses Leitch, 15 February 1894, p. 26, Leitch 1, biographical file, box 43, WBMHL (second quote).

15. Margaret W. Leitch to N. G. Clark, 13 April 1886, reel 456; Mary Leitch to Clark, 10 June 1887, reel 456, ABCFM Papers.

16. Helen Root, comp., *A Century in Ceylon: A Brief History of the Work of the American Board in Ceylon, 1816–1916* (n.p., 1916), 59–60.

17. Margaret Leitch to N. G. Clark, 10 July 1893, reel 459, ABCFM Papers.

18. Mary and Margaret Leitch to N. G. Clark, 27 January 1894, reel 459, ABCFM Papers; *Abkari*, no. 20, January 1895, 2.

19. *Ceylon Observer*, quoted in *Abkari*, no. 15, October 1893, 177.

20. Ibid.; *Abkari*, no. 20, January 1895, 2; "Occasional Letter, No. 7, Leitch and Leitch, Seven Months in Ceylon,—A Retrospect."

21. Lord Kinnaird to James L. Barton, 4 October 1895, reel 459, ABCFM Papers.

22. *New York Times*, 16 June 1900, p. 11.

23. Ibid., 26 April 1900, 10.

24. *Abkari*, no. 15, October 1893, 177.

25. Mary and Margaret Leitch to Dr. [Charles H.] Daniels, 5 June 1897, reel 459; Mary Leitch to Louis Klopsch, with Mary to Margaret Leitch, 26 March 1897, reel 459, ABCFM Papers; Gaines M. Foster, "Conservative Social Christianity, the Law, and Personal Morality: Wilbur F. Crafts in Washington," *Church History* 71 (December 2002), 799–819.

26. Wilbur Crafts et al., *Protection of Native Races against Intoxicants & Opium* (New York, 1900); Wilbur Crafts, Sara Crafts, Mary Leitch, and Margaret W. Leitch, *Intoxicating Drinks and Drugs in All Lands and Times*, 10th rev. ed. (Washington, DC, 1909).

27. "Statement of Miss Margaret W. Leitch," U.S. Congress, House, Committee on Insular Affairs, 56th Cong., 1st and 2nd Sess., 1900–1901, *Committee Reports, Hearings, and Acts of Congress Corresponding Thereto* (Washington, DC, 1904), 131–42.

28. Mary Leitch to Anna Gordon, 21 February 1914, Frances Willard Papers, WCTUHQ.

29. *Report of the Forty-Third Annual Convention of the National Woman's Christian Temperance Union, held in the Murat Temple, Indianapolis, Indiana, November 17–22, 1916* (n.p., n.d.), 333.

30. For discussion of methodological problems in the study of missionary history, see David Arnold and Robert A. Bickers, introduction to Robert A. Bickers and Rosemary Seton, eds., *Missionary Encounters: Sources and Issues* (Richmond, Surrey, 1996), 1–10; for historiography, see Andrew Porter, "Church History, History of Christianity, Religious History: Some Reflections on British Missionary Enterprise since the Late Eighteenth Century," *Church History* 71 (September 2002), 555–84, esp. 555–56; William R. Hutchinson, "Missionaries on the 'Middle Ground' in China," *Reviews in American History* 25, no. 4 (1997), 631–36.

31. See, for example, John R. W. Smail, "On the Possibility of an Autonomous History of Modern Southeast Asia," *Journal of Southeast Asian History* 2, no. 2 (1961), 72–102.

32. Fairbank, *Missionary Enterprise*. A good summary, influenced by the Fairbank School, of U.S.-East Asian relations is Thomson, Stanley, and Perry, *Sentimental Imperialists*.

33. Hill, *The World Their Household*; Hunter, *The Gospel of Gentility*; Patricia Grimshaw, *Paths of Duty: American Missionary Wives in Nineteenth-Century Hawaii* (Honolulu, 1989); White, "Counting the Cost of Faith," 19–30.

34. Barbara Welter, "'She Hath Done What She Could': Protestant Women's Missionary Careers in Nineteenth-Century America," *American Quarterly*, special issue: Women and Religion, 30 (Winter 1978), 624–38.

35. Leitch and Leitch, *Seven Years in Ceylon*, frontispiece (quote, regarding brothers); Mary and Margaret W. Leitch to N. G. Clark, 20 April 1888, reel 456 ("our sisters"), ABCFM Papers. For genealogy, see Miller and Wells, *History of Ryegate, Vermont*, 406.

36. According to Paul Varg, the expansion of missionary work abroad came from a rising spirit of nationalism ("Motives in Protestant Missions," 81) and was shaped in humanitarian terms by the "climate of opinion at home" (77). Hutchinson, *Errand to the World*, 92, stressed civilizing and Westernizing impulses within the American churches and the outward projection of a "spiritual imperialism." Michael Parker, *The Kingdom of Character: The Student Volunteer Movement for Foreign Missions, 1886–1926* (Lanham, MD, 1998), unpaginated introduction, credited the YMCA, revivalism, and premier nineteenth-century American evangelist Dwight Moody for the Student Volunteer Movement; more generally, see Rosenberg, *Spreading the American Dream*, 29.

37. Makdisi, *Artillery of Heaven*, 214–16.

38. Chin, "Beneficent Imperialists," 342.

39. Ibid., 327–29.

40. Ibid., 329, 351.

41. On cultural imperialism, see especially Schlesinger, "The Missionary Enterprise and Theories of Imperialism."

42. Dunch, "Beyond Cultural Imperialism," 320.

43. Margaret W. Leitch to N. G. Clark, 17 November 1881 (first two quotes); Mary Leitch to Clark, 22 May 1889; Mary Leitch to Clark, 20 January 1889, all in reel 456, ABCFM Papers.

44. Brian C. Hosmer, "Reflections on Indian Cultural 'Brokers': Reginald Oshkosh, Mitchell Oshkenaniew, and the Politics of Menominee Lumbering," *Ethnohistory* 44 (Summer 1997), 493–509; Ilana Gershon, "When Culture Is Not a System: Why Samoan Cultural Brokers Can Not Do Their Job," *Ethnos* 71 (December 2006), 533–55.

45. Leitch and Leitch, *Seven Years in Ceylon*, 72.

46. Ibid.; Eliza F. Kent, "Tamil Bible Women and the Zenana Missions of Colonial South India," *History of Religions* 39 (November 1989), 147, 149.

47. The episode is summarized in Mary and Margaret W. Leitch to Charles H. Daniels, 22 January 1900, in Letters and Papers from Mary and M. W. Leitch, February 17, 1900, bound file, Leitch 2, biographical file, box 43, WBMHL. See, for examples of a voluminous correspondence, Mary and Margaret Leitch to Daniels, 7 April 1899, and 30 September 1897, reel 459, and Mary Leitch to Daniels, 16 October 1899, reel 459, ABCFM Papers.

48. Mary and Margaret W. Leitch to "Mrs. Smith" (née Emily Maria Fairbank, of Tillypally, Ceylon), 19 April 1890, reel 459, ABCFM Papers (emphasis in original).

49. Margaret W. Leitch to N. G. Clark, 3 April 1882, reel 456, ABCFM Papers. The sisters report that the presence of a "good speaker" from "the Wesleyan or Church mission" "attracts a larger audience and encourages our workers." They repay speakers with "Sciopticon" presentations.

50. Margaret W. Leitch to N. G. Clark, 20 October 1887, reel 456, ABCFM Papers.

51. Mary Leitch to N. G. Clark, 4 January 1890, reel 459, ABCFM Papers; Samuel W. Howland to N. G. Clark, 2 October 1890, Leitch 1, biographical file box 43, WBMHL.

52. Mary Leitch to N. G. Clark, 29 November 1890, reel 459, ABCFM Papers.

53. Margaret W. Leitch to N. G. Clark, 5 January 1889, reel 456, ABCFM Papers.

54. Margaret W. Leitch to N. G. Clark, 17 November 1881, ibid.

55. Leitch and Leitch, *Seven Years in Ceylon*, 24–25.

56. Varg, "Motives in Protestant Missions," 75.

57. Mary Leitch to N. G. Clark, 17 May 1888, reel 456, ABCFM Papers.

58. Judson Smith, "The Evangelization of Africa," *Seventy-Ninth Annual Report of the American Board of Commissioners for Foreign Missions, Presented at the Meeting Held at the City of New York, October 15–18, 1889* (Boston, 1889), xvi.

59. Leitch and Leitch, *Seven Years in Ceylon*, 153.

60. Castells, *The Rise of the Network Society*; Keck and Sikkink, *Activists beyond Borders*; Price, "Transnational Civil Society."

61. Tarrow, *The New Transnational Activism*, 163–64.

62. Leitch and Leitch, *Seven Years in Ceylon*, 111–12.

63. "Statement of Miss Margaret W. Leitch."

64. Leitch and Leitch, *Seven Years in Ceylon*, 101–12; "Statement of Miss Margaret W. Leitch."

65. Headrick, *The Invisible Weapon*; Dwayne R. Winseck and Robert M. Pike, *Communication and Empire: Media, Markets, and Globalization, 1860/1930* (Durham, NC, 2007).

66. Margaret Leitch to Miss [Abbie B.] Child, 27 October 1890, Margaret Leitch file, box 3, WBMHL.

67. Leitch and Leitch, "Seven Months in Ceylon,—A Retrospect."

68. Richard Hofstadter, "Manifest Destiny and the Philippines," in Daniel Aaron, ed., *America in Crisis: Fourteen Crucial Episodes in American History* (New York, 1952), 173–200; Hofstadter, "Cuba, the Philippines, and Manifest Destiny," in Hofstadter, *The Paranoid Style in American Politics and Other Essays* (New York, 1965), 145–87. On humanitarianism and social movements, see Thomas L. Haskell, "Capitalism and the Origins of the Humanitarian Sensibility," *American Historical Review* 90 (April and June 1985), 339–61, 547–66. The best general account for the United States in the 1890s is still Curti, *American Philanthropy*.

69. Mary and Margaret Leitch to N. G. Clark, 17 May 1890, reel 459, ABCFM Papers (emphasis in original).

70. Mary and Margaret W. Leitch to G. Henry Whitcomb, 2 January 1899, in "Our Experience in Collecting Funds."

71. See chap. 5.

72. Leitch and Leitch, *Seven Years in Ceylon*, 159–60 (italics in original).

73. Justin Abbott to editor, *New York Times*, 25 August 1901, p. 5.

74. Margaret and Mary Leitch to Dr. Charles H. Daniels, 5 June 1897 ("standpoint"); Mary Leitch to Louis Klopsch, 26 March 1897; Margaret Leitch to Dr. Daniels, 1 March 1897, all in reel 459, ABCFM Papers; Charles M. Pepper, *Life-Work of Louis Klopsch: Romance of a Modern Knight of Mercy* (New York, 1910); *New York Times*, 7 March 1910, p. 9 and 10 March 1910, p. 9.

75. "Our Experience in Collecting Funds," 17. See chap. 5.

76. "Statement of Miss Margaret W. Leitch," 140–42; "The Crowning Infamy of Imperialism" (Philadelphia, [1900]), http://www.boondocksnet.com/ai/ailtexts/infamy.html, in Jim Zwick, ed., *Anti-Imperialism in the United States, 1898–1935*, http://www.boondocksnet.com/ai/ (accessed 23 December 2006).

77. Letters, n.d. [1899], box 4, Luella (Mrs. F. T.) McWhirter Papers, Lilly Library, Indiana University, Bloomington.

78. Luella McWhirter to the White Ribboners of Converse, Indiana, 30 May 1901, ibid.

79. Luella McWhirter, "President's Address," *Twenty-Fifth Annual Meeting of the Indiana Woman's Christian Temperance Union, Lafayette, October 3 to 11, 1898* (n.p., n.d.), 13.

CHAPTER 3. THE MISSIONARY IMPULSE

1. *New York Times*, 24 March 1886, p. 2; Lawrence C. Goodwyn, *Democratic Promise: The Populist Moment in America* (New York, 1976), 77–82; Henry David, *The History of the Haymarket Affair: A Study in the American Social Revolutionary and Labor Movements* (New York, 1936); Elias Nason, *A Gazetteer of the State of Massachusetts, with Numerous Illustrations*, revised and enlarged by George J. Varney (Boston, 1890), 515–18.

2. Quoted in William H. Beahm, "Factors in the Development of the Student

Volunteer Movement for Foreign Missions" (Ph.D. diss., University of Chicago, 1941), 74, 7.

3. J. Wilbur Chapman, *The Life and Work of Dwight L. Moody, Presented to the Christian World as a Tribute to the Memory of the Greatest Apostle of the Age,* ... (Philadelphia, [1900]), 220, 34 (quotes); Beahm, "Factors," 55.

4. Parker, *The Kingdom of Character,* unpaginated introduction [p. 2]. A superior account is Clifton J. Phillips, "The Student Volunteer Movement and Its Role in China Missions," in Fairbank, *Missionary Enterprise,* 110–34.

5. John Mott, *The American Student Missionary Uprising: or, The History and Organization of the Student Volunteer Movement for Foreign Missions* (n.p., 1892); Bradley J. Longfield, *The Presbyterian Controversy: Fundamentalists, Modernists, and Moderates* (New York, 1991), 18; John Pollock, "Studd, Charles Thomas (1860–1931)," *Oxford Dictionary of National Biography,* http://www .oxforddnb.com/view/article/38027 (accessed 14 March 2008).

6. For social movements, see Nick Crossley, *Making Sense of Social Movements* (Philadelphia, 2002); John Wilson, *Introduction to Social Movements* (New York, 1973); Charles Tilly, *Social Movements, 1768–2004* (Boulder, CO, 2004); Sidney Tarrow, *Power in Movement: Collective Action, Social Movements and Politics* (New York, 1994); Bert Klandermans and Suzanne Staggenborg, eds., *Methods of Social Movement Research* (Minneapolis, 2002); Bryan R. Wilson, ed., *Patterns of Sectarianism: Organisation and Ideology in Social and Religious Movements* (London, 1967).

7. Ben J. Wattenberg, *Statistical History of the United States* (New York, 1976), 383.

8. Robert T. Handy, *A Christian America: Protestant Hopes and Historical Realities* (New York, 1971), 140–41; Sydney E. Ahlstrom, *A Religious History of the American People,* 2nd ed. (New Haven, 2004), 867 (quote); Varg, "Motives in Protestant Missions," 68.

9. George M. Marsden, *Fundamentalism and American Culture: The Shaping of Twentieth-Century Evangelicalism, 1870–1925* (New York, 1980), 72–85; Richard Carwardine, *Trans-Atlantic Revivalism: Popular Evangelicalism in Britain and America, 1790–1865* (Westport, CT, 1978), chap. 1.

10. Timothy L. Smith, *Revivalism and Social Reform in Mid-Nineteenth-Century America* (New York, 1957), 104, 112–13; James F. Findlay, *Dwight L. Moody: American Evangelist, 1837–1899* (Chicago, 1969), 342–43 (quote at 343); Marsden, *Fundamentalism,* 80.

11. See Marsden, *Fundamentalism,* 48–71, for premillennialism and post-millennialism.

12. Stephen L. Baldwin, *Foreign Missions of the Protestant Churches* (New York, 1900), 143; George M. Stephenson, *The Religious Aspects of Swedish Immigration* (Minneapolis, 1932), 108–13.

13. Robert Wilder, *The Student Volunteer Movement: Its Origin and Early History* (New York, 1935), 8.

14. "Cables under the Ocean," *New York Times,* 10 July 1892, p. 17.

15. Dana L. Robert, *Occupy Until I Come: A. T. Pierson and the Evangelization of the World* (Grand Rapids, MI, 2003), 103–9; Arthur T. Pierson, *George Müller of Bristol: His Life of Prayer and Faith* (New York, 1899), 246–56.

16. William G. McLoughlin Jr., *Modern Revivalism: Charles Grandison Finney to Billy Graham* (New York, 1959), 265; Rosemary Chadwick, "Spurgeon, Charles Haddon (1834–1892)," *Oxford Dictionary of National Biography*, http://www.oxforddnb.com/view/article/26187 (accessed 28 July 2007). Findlay notes that Spurgeon's preaching "was simple, direct, and full of vivid imagery, in many ways paralleling Moody's peculiar abilities as a popular preacher" (*Moody*, 146). Yet he claims "the ties between the two men were never strong" (145).

17. Ronald Rompkey, "Grenfell, Sir Wilfred Thomason (1865–1940)," *Oxford Dictionary of National Biography*, http://www.oxforddnb.com/view/article/33565 (accessed 29 July 2007).

18. Ian M. Randall, "Meyer, Frederick Brotherton (1847–1929)," *Oxford Dictionary of National Biography*, http://www.oxforddnb.com/view/article/35006 (accessed 29 July 2007).

19. *The Mildmay Conference, 1894: Reports of the Addresses, Corrected by the Speakers* (London, [1894]), viii–ix, xiii–xviii.

20. Pollack, "Studd"; Chapman, *Life and Work of Dwight L. Moody*, 216–17; Randall, "Meyer"; Findlay, *Moody*, 342–43; Harold H. Rowdon, "Edinburgh 1910, Evangelicals and the Ecumenical Movement," *Vox Evangelica* 5 (1967), 49–71, http://www.biblicalstudies.org.uk/pdf/vox/vol05/edinburgh-1910_rowdon.pdf; D. W. Bebbington, "Moody, Dwight Lyman (1837–1899)," *Oxford Dictionary of National Biography*, http://www.oxforddnb.com/view/article/53842 (accessed 29 July 2007).

21. Mott, *American Student Missionary Uprising*, 11 (quote); Ruth Rouse, *The World's Student Christian Federation: A History of the First Thirty Years* (London, 1948), 26–29.

22. Chapman, *Life and Work of Dwight L. Moody*, 219.

23. Mott, *American Student Missionary Uprising*, 12 (quote); Charles K. Ober, *Luther D. Wishard: Projector of World Movements* (New York, 1927), 78, 94.

24. Letter of Dr. A. P. Harper, Presbyterian Board of Missions, in James Johnston, ed., *Report of the Centenary Conference on the Protestant Missions of the World, held in Exeter Hall (June 9th–19th), London, 1888*, 2 vols. (London and New York, 1888), 2:573; Will Johnston to "My Dear Uncle and Aunt," 18 December 1871, in Barbara Mitchell Tull, ed., *Affectionately, Rachel: Letters from India, 1860–1884* (Kent, OH, 1992), 256; White, "Counting the Cost of Faith," 28; Dana L. Robert, "The Influence of American Missionary Women on the World Back Home," *Religion and American Culture* 12 (Winter 2002), 59, 61, 67; "A Missionary Nurse Needed for Turkey," *American Journal of Nursing* 13 (May 1913), 612–13; "Thoburn, James Mills," in James Grant Wilson and John Fiske, eds., *Appletons' Cyclopaedia of American Biography*, 6 vols. (New York, 1887–89), 3:70; Maina Chawal Singh, "Gender, Thrift and Indigenous Adaptations: Money and Missionary Medicine in Colonial India," *Women's History Review* 15 (November 2006), 701–17.

25. *Springfield Republican*, 2 August 1886, p. 1, folder 5234, box 449, Archives of the Student Volunteer Movement for Foreign Missions, Record Group 42, YDSL; Parker, *Kingdom of Character*, 2 (quote); C. Howard Hopkins, *John R. Mott, 1865–1955: A Biography* (Grand Rapids, MI, 1979), 27 (Ashmore "fanned the fire"); "William Ashmore, D.D.," in William Cathcart, ed., *The Baptist Ency-*

clopedia (1881; rpt. 1988), p. 45, http://www.geocities.com/baptist_documents/ashmore.wm.china.missnry.html (accessed 1 October 2007).

26. *Springfield Republican*, 2 August 1886, p. 4 (quote), 6, 7, in folder 5234, box 449, Archives of the Student Volunteer Movement for Foreign Missions, Record Group 42, YDSL.

27. Beahm, "Factors," 62–63.

28. *Springfield Republican*, 16 July 1888, p. 4; Robert A. Schneider, "Royal G. Wilder, New School Missionary in the ABCFM, 1846–1871," *American Presbyterian* 64 (Summer 1986), 73–82; Ruth Wilder Braisted, *In This Generation: The Story of Robert Wilder* (New York, 1941), 8–19.

29. Quoted in Beahm, "Factors," 72 (underlining in original).

30. *Springfield Republican*, 16 July 1888, p. 2.

31. Judson Smith, "The Future Work of the American Board," *Seventy-Fifth Annual Report of the American Board of Commissioners for Foreign Missions, Presented at the Meeting held at Boston, Mass. October 13–16, 1885* (Boston, 1885), xxxvi (quotes); Henry M. Stanley, *The Congo and the Founding of Its Free State* (New York, 1885).

32. Smith, "Future Work of the American Board," xxxvii.

33. James T. Campbell, *Middle Passages: African-American Journeys to Africa, 1787–2005* (New York, 2006), 142.

34. Ober, *Wishard*, 162–67.

35. Judson Smith, "The Appeal of the Hour," *Seventy-Seventh Annual Report of the American Board of Commissioners for Foreign Missions, Presented at the Meeting held at Springfield, Mass., October 4–7, 1887* (Boston, 1887), xlix.

36. N. G. Clark, "Missionary Comity: Methods and Means for Carrying Forward the Work in the Foreign Field," *Seventy-Sixth Annual Report of the American Board of Commissioners for Foreign Missions, Presented at the Meeting held at Des Moines, Iowa, October 5–8 1886* (Boston, 1886), xxvi; E. K. Alden, "The Home Department—A Brief Review," *Seventy-Fifth Annual Report of the American Board of Commissioners for Foreign Missions*, xxii–xxiii.

37. Strong, *Our Country*, 251.

38. Smith, "Future Work of the American Board," xxx.

39. *Springfield Republican*, 2 August 1886 (first quote); Delavan Leonard Pierson, *Arthur T. Pierson: A Spiritual Warrior, Mighty in the Scriptures: A Leader in the Modern Missionary Crusade* (New York, 1912), 197 (second quote).

40. Pierson, *Crisis of Missions*, 298, 293 (last quote).

41. Jacob Chamberlain to Cephas Brainard, 6 October 1887, folder Correspondence and Papers October 1887, n.d. 1888, India Correspondence and Papers 1887–90, box 356, Y.63-4, KFYMCAA.

42. Samuel H. Kellogg, *The Light of Asia and the Light of the World* (London, 1885), 371; Thomas A. Tweed, *The American Encounter with Buddhism, 1844–1912* (Chapel Hill, 1992).

43. George W. Leitch to N. G. Clark, 14 April 1881, reel 456, ABCFM Papers; D. Denis Hudson, "Tamil Hindu Responses to Protestants: Nineteenth-Century Literati in Jaffna and Tinnevelly," in Steven Kaplan, ed., *Indigenous Responses to Western Christianity* (New York, 1995), 95–123; Geoffrey A. Oddie, *Hindu and Christian in South Asia* (London, 1991), 189, 191, 192.

44. *Report of the Executive Committee of the Student Volunteer Movement for Foreign Missions Presented at the Third International Convention held at Cleveland, Ohio, Feb. 23–27, 1898* (n.p., n.d.), 4; *Report of the Executive Committee of the Student Volunteer Movement for Foreign Missions Presented at the Second International Convention held at Detroit, Mich., February 28 to March 4, 1894* (Detroit, n.d.), 19 (quote).

45. Pierson, *Crisis of Missions*, 42, 368.

46. Diary, e.g., 26–30 March 1892, 9 February 1892, folder 141, box 13, Robert Parmelee Wilder Papers, YDSL (hereafter Wilder Papers); Braisted, *In This Generation*, 51–65, 87–99; Luther Wishard to Charles K. Ober, 28 June 1888, box 105, Miscellaneous Personal Papers Collection, RG 30, YDSL.

47. Rouse, *World's Student Christian Federation*, 25.

48. Braisted, *In This Generation*, 30; Longfield, *Presbyterian Controversy*, 18.

49. Charles Cardwell McCabe (Methodist Episcopal Church Mission) to Luther Wishard, 5 October 1886, folder 3, box 1, Wilder Papers.

50. Robert, *Occupy Until I Come*, ix, 322.

51. Arthur Tappan Pierson, "Can This World Be Evangelized in Twenty Years?" *Missionary Review* 4 (November–December 1881), 437.

52. Pierson, *Arthur T. Pierson*, 143.

53. Frederick Coan, *Missionary Life in the Middle East: Or Yesterday in Persia and Kurdistan* (1939; Piscataway, NJ, 2006), 60, 71, 224.

54. [Mrs.] Chas. W. Shelton, "The Santee Normal Training School and Indian Missions," *American Missionary* 42, no. 1 (January 1888), http://infomotions. com/etexts/gutenberg/dirs/1/1/7/6/11762/11762.htm (accessed 4 November 2007); Richard E. Jensen, ed., *Voices of the American West*, vol. 1: *The Indian Interviews of Eli S. Ricker, 1903–1919* (Lincoln, NE, 2005), 251; "*Abraham Lincoln Toni Kin Qa Aesop Towoyake Kin* by James W. Garvie," http://webpages. charter.net/lincolnbooks/ToniKin.html (accessed 4 November 2007).

55. *New York Times*, 28 July 1944, p. 13; 13 November 1938, p. 45.

56. Beahm, "Factors," 128, 234; of the many thousands who enrolled from 1893 to 1912, 26.5 percent of volunteers actually served as foreign missionaries. Parker, *Kingdom of Character*, 200.

57. "The Volunteer Movement's Possible Peril," *Student Volunteer*, March 1895, p. 3.

58. For example, W. W. Smith to Robert Wilder, 31 January 1889; Mary Gibson to Wilder, 18 February 1889, folder 10, box 1, Wilder Papers.

59. In the case of Bishop Charles H. Brent, opinion on his appointment as a missionary was very divided. For example, Algernon Crapsey (St. Andrews Rectory, Rochester) to Brent, 15 October 1901, urged Brent not to "throw yourself away on those islands," but others stressed: "the God-given errand of the reformed church has been not only to enlighten the heathen but as well to exert a leavening influence which should purge and quicken demoralized Latin Christianity." Clipping in folder "Another Letter on Philippine Diocese," box 5, Charles Henry Brent Papers, LC (hereafter Brent Papers).

60. "The Volunteer Movement's Possible Peril," 2.

61. Arthur Mitchell to Robert Wilder, 1 October 1886, folder 3, box 1, Wilder Papers.

62. William R. Moody, *The Life of Dwight L. Moody, by his Son, William R. Moody* (New York, 1900), 380.

63. *Report of the Executive Committee of the Student Volunteer Movement ... 1894*, 8.

64. Mott, *American Student Missionary Uprising*, 17.

65. *Report of the Executive Committee of the Student Volunteer Movement ... 1894*, 8.

66. See, for example, John Mott, *The Evangelization of the World in This Generation*, rept. ed. (London, 1900), 6–12.

67. Others called Speer a "Christian missionary statesman." John F. Piper Jr., *Robert E. Speer: Prophet of the American Church* (Louisville, KY, 2000), 113–14, 138, 146, 184 (quotes).

68. Hopkins, *Mott*, 206–7, 426, 677.

69. Barbara Welter, "Feminization of American Religion," Welter, *Dimity Convictions: The American Woman in the Nineteenth Century* (Athens, OH, 1976), 83–102.

70. N. G. Clark, "A Review of Twenty-Five Years—A.B.C.F.M.," *Seventy-Fifth Annual Report of the American Board of Commissioners for Foreign Missions*, xxv; Alden, "The Home Department," xxii–xxiii.

71. *Sixth Annual Conference of the Young People's Society of Christian Endeavor, held at Saratoga Springs, N.Y., July 5, 6 and 7, 1887* (Boston, 1887), 32 (quote); Parker, *Kingdom of Character*, 25; Clark, "A Review of Twenty-Five Years," xxv; Clifford Putney, *Muscular Christianity: Manhood and Sports in Protestant America, 1880–1920* (Cambridge, MA, 2001), 18–30.

72. John D. Rockefeller Jr. to John Mott, 12 November 1901, folder 1359, box 74, John R. Mott Papers, YDSL (hereafter Mott Papers).

73. Johanna M. Selles, "The Role of Women in the Formation of the World Student Christian Federation," *International Bulletin of Missionary Research* 30 (October 2006), 189–94, esp. at note 8.

74. Leitch and Leitch, *Seven Years in Ceylon*, 120.

75. Parker, *Kingdom of Character*, 44.

76. Ibid., 60.

77. No author, "List of College Leaders," 24 April 1894, folder 5241, box 449, Archives of the Student Volunteer Movement.

78. Robert Speer, "The Student Volunteer Movement: Its Hopeful Features," *Sunday School Times*, 12 March 1892, pp. 1–2.

79. Ibid.

80. Beahm, "Factors," 234; Parker, *Kingdom of Character*, from the unpaginated introduction.

81. Calculated from Baldwin, *Foreign Missions*, 260; Latourette, "Missionaries Abroad," 25; Parker, *Kingdom of Character*, unpaginated introduction. For 1894–95, the American figure was listed as 30.3 percent (*Almanac of Missions for 1894* [Boston, n.d.]), 36, based on Rev. Jens Vahl's statistics from the Danish Mission Society, but these did "not give the wives of missionaries as ours do." The ABCFM admitted that "summaries can only be approximately correct." German missions scholar R. Grundemann's statistics for 1885 yield a figure of 27.8 percent American. See *Almanac of Missions for 1886* (Boston, n.d.), 28. For

1889, the figure was 39 percent, a similarly suspect figure. *Almanac of Missions for 1889* (Boston, n.d.), 38. Figures for 1909–10 were 6,452 Americans out of a global total of 16,824 missionaries. *Almanac of Missions for 1911* (Boston, n.d.), 30, 33–35.

82. Johnston, *Report of the Centenary Conference on the Protestant Missions.*

83. W.H.T. Gardiner, *"Edinburgh 1910": An Account and Interpretation of the World Missionary Conference* (Edinburgh, 1910), 59, 63. A Baptist World Congress met in 1905 in London, but that was not ecumenical nor specifically missionary in focus. It was also instigated by Americans, who had the largest representation. See Joe Early Jr., *Readings in Baptist History: Four Centuries of Selected Documents* (Nashville, TN, 2008), 131–32.

84. William R. Hogg, *Ecumenical Foundations: A History of the International Missionary Council and Its Nineteenth-Century Background* (New York, 1952), 144–56.

85. Joseph Oldham to the Rt. Rev. Bishop of Southwark, 23 February 1909, folder 3374, box 214, Mott Papers.

86. Sherwood Eddy, "J. H. Oldham," in *Pathfinders of the World Missionary Crusade* (Freeport, NY, 1945), 279–86; Kathleen Bliss, "Oldham, Joseph Houldsworth (1874–1969)," rev. Andrew Porter, *Oxford Dictionary of National Biography*, http://www.oxforddnb.com/view/article/35301 (accessed 2 June 2008); Harlan Beach, *Findings of the Continuation Committee Conferences, Held in Asia, 1912–13* (New York, 1915), 8–14, 407–16 (quote at 407); Baldwin, *Foreign Missions*, 255–60; Hogg, *Ecumenical Foundations*, 144–56; Hutchinson, *Errand to the World*, 135–36. The statistical emphasis was not noticeable at the 1888 conference. See Johnston, *Report of the Centenary Conference on the Protestant Missions.*

87. Hopkins, *Mott*, 61.

88. *Report of the Executive Committee of the Student Volunteer Movement for Foreign Missions Presented at the Third International Convention held at Cleveland, Ohio, February 23–27, 1898* (n.p., 1898), 9.

89. John Mott, "Seven Years Contrast in Australasia," Report Letter No. 1, 1903, folder 1937, box 117, Mott Papers.

90. "Executive Committee of the Student Volunteer Movement ... April 23, 1901," folder 5251, box 449, Archives of the Student Volunteer Movement.

91. Mott, *American Student Missionary Uprising*, 33.

92. Quoted in Hopkins, *Mott*, 238; John D. Rockefeller Jr. to John Mott, 25 April 1901, and 12 November 1901, folder 1359, box 74, Mott Papers.

93. William T. Ellis, *Men and Missions: With a Foreword by John B. Sleman, Jr., Founder of the Laymen's Missionary Movement and With a Statistical and Historical Appendix Compiled by Abigail J. Davies* (Philadelphia, 1909), 74–75.

94. Quoted in David McConaughy, *Pioneering with Christ: Among the Young Men of India and the Churches of America ...* (New York, 1941), 88; *Boston Daily Globe*, 10 March 1907; *Washington Post*, 12 February 1907, 3; J. Campbell White to John Mott, 7 May 1907, folder 35, box 3, Wilder Papers.

95. *New York Times*, 16 January 1910, p. 6.

96. Ben Primer, *Protestants and American Business Methods* (Ann Arbor, 1979), 96–98; Gail Bederman, "'The Women Have Had Charge of the Church

Work Long Enough': The Men and Religion Forward Movement of 1911–1912 and the Masculinization of Middle-Class Protestantism," *American Quarterly* 41 (September 1989), 432–65; Ellis, *Men and Missions*, 75; J. Campbell White, "Laymen's Missionary Movement," in *The New Schaff-Herzog Encyclopedia of Religious Knowledge* (New York, 1908–14), 8:33–34; *New York Times*, 9 January 1910, p. C5.

97. *Boston Daily Globe*, 22 February 1896, p. 3; Mary and Margaret Leitch to "Dear Friend," in "Letters and Papers from Mary and Margaret W. Leitch, Feb. 17, 1900," and "Address delivered by Miss Margaret W. Leitch of Ceylon, at the Denominational Rally of the Congregational Denomination, held in one of the large tents, on Sabbath afternoon, July 12th, in connection with the Fifteenth International Christian Endeavor Convention, Washington, D.C." [1896], Leitch 2, biographical file, box 43, WBMHL.

98. McConaughy, *Pioneering with Christ*, 88.

99. "World Laymen's Crusade On," *New York Times*, 20 December 1909, p. 6.

100. Hunter, *The Gospel of Gentility*, 31, 46, 191.

101. *Ecumenical Missionary Conference, New York, 1900 ...*, 2 vols. (New York, 1900); "Last Day of the Conference," *New York Times*, 2 May 1900, p. 6; "Women's Great Conference Day," *New York Times*, 27 April 1900, p. 5; "India's Last Suttee; Scotch [sic] Missionary's Proofs of the Decline of Pagan Rites," *New York Times*, 23 April 1900, p. 2.

102. Julia C. Emery, *Century of Endeavor, 1821–1921: A Record of The First Hundred Years of the Domestic and Foreign Missionary Society of the Protestant Episcopal Church in the United States of America* (New York, 1921), 275–76; Reed, *Missionary Mind*, 16.

103. Hill, *The World Their Household*, 161.

104. *New York Times*, 6 August 1906, p. 7.

105. "Ten Thousand People to Portray Missionary Life; Great Exhibition in Boston Will Give Vivid Reproductions of How Natives Live in Foreign Lands Where Church Work Is Carried On," *New York Times*, 22 January 1911, SM 14.

106. Frank O. Erb, "The Development of the Young People's Movement," *Biblical World* 48 (September 1916), 173.

107. Wilson S. Naylor, *Daybreak in the Dark Continent* (New York, 1905).

108. James Mills Thoburn, *The Christian Conquest of India* (New York, 1906), map, facing 108, vi (quote).

109. Emery, *Century of Endeavor*, 275.

CHAPTER 4. THE MATRIX OF MORAL REFORM

1. Theda Skocpol and Morris Fiorina, eds., *Civic Engagement in American Democracy* (Washington and New York, 1999), 9; Arthur M. Schlesinger, "Biography of a Nation of Joiners," *American Historical Review* 50 (January 1944), 1–25; Evan Schofer and Marion Fourcade-Gourinchas, "The Structural Contexts of Civic Engagement: Voluntary Association Membership in Comparative Perspective," *American Sociological Review* 66 (December 2001), 806–28.

2. Theda Skocpol, Marshall Ganz, and Ziad Munson, "A Nation of Organizers: The Institutional Origins of Civic Voluntarism in the United States," *American Political Science Review* 94 (September 2000), 527, restricts the concept of voluntarism to the structure of the nation-state and lobbying within it.

3. Tyrrell, *Woman's World*.

4. "Miles on Miles of Names," *New York Times*, 10 February 1895, p. 21.

5. Norman Clark, *Deliver Us from Evil: An Interpretation of American Prohibition* (New York, 1976), 84–88, at 88.

6. Frances Willard, "History of the Woman's National Christian Temperance Union," in *Centennial Temperance Volume: A Memorial of the International Temperance Conference, held in Philadelphia, June, 1876. With the specially-prepared essays, addresses of foreign delegates, deliberations ... etc.* (New York, 1877), 687.

7. *Minutes of the National Woman's Christian Temperance Union, at the Tenth Annual Meeting, held in Detroit, Michigan, 31 October–3 November, 1883* (Chicago, 1883), 66; *Union Signal*, 8 November 1883, p. 6; 17 May 1883, 13; Willard, *Glimpses of Fifty Years*, 430; Tyrrell, *Woman's World*, chap. 1; Francis Clark, *Christian Endeavor in All Lands: A Record of Twenty-Five Years of Progress* (Boston, 1906), 266.

8. Reported in *Sixth Annual Conference of the Young People's Society of Christian Endeavor held at Saratoga Springs, N.Y., July 5, 6 and 7, 1887* (Boston, 1887), 39.

9. Christopher Lee Coble, "Where Have All the Young People Gone? The Christian Endeavor Movement and the Training of Protestant Youth, 1881–1918" (Th.D. diss., Harvard University, 2001), 153.

10. Primer, *Protestants and American Business Methods*, chaps. 4–5.

11. *Sixth Annual Conference of the Young People's Society*, 43.

12. *New York Times*, 6 July 1905, p. 8.

13. *Fifth Annual Conference of the Young People's Society of Christian Endeavor, held at Saratoga Springs, New York, July 6, 7 and 8, 1886* (Lynn, MA, n.d.), 42.

14. Coble, "Christian Endeavor Movement," 173.

15. *Fifth Annual Conference of the Young People's Society*, 3.

16. "Secretary Baer's Report; Wonderful Increase of the Christian Endeavor Societies," *New York Times*, 11 July 1892, Christian Endeavor Extra, p. 3; Coble, "Christian Endeavor Movement," 172 (quote), 175, 174 (quote).

17. Coble, "Christian Endeavor Movement," 158, 159.

18. Ibid., 159, 157, 158.

19. *Sixth Annual Conference of the Young People's Society*, 29.

20. Ibid, 45.

21. Coble, "Christian Endeavor Movement," 162.

22. Clark, *Christian Endeavor in All Lands*, 438: "because of its size and importance and advancement in Christian Endeavor," Australia "deserves the first place."

23. "Secretary Baer's Report."

24. *New York Times*, 19 July 1900, p. 6, 12 December 1909, SM 3.

25. *Report of the Second Annual Conference of the Young People's Societies of Christian Endeavor in Connecticut, held in the South Church, Bridgeport, Oct. 28, 1886* (New Haven, 1887), 23, copy in box 33, Religious and Benevolent Societies and Organizations, RG 34, YDSL.

26. Hopkins, *Mott*, 115.

27. Clark, *Christian Endeavor in All Lands*, 266–67.

28. *Union Signal*, 31 January 1907, p. 9.

29. Francis E. Clark, *Our Journey around the World: An Illustrated Record of a Year's Travel of Forty Thousand Miles through India, China, Japan, Australia, New Zealand, Egypt, Palestine, Greece, Turkey, Italy, France, Spain, etc., with Glimpses of Life in Far Off Lands As Seen through a Woman's Eyes by Mrs. H. E. Clark* (Hartford, CT, 1897).

30. Robert Anderson, *Christian Endeavor in Every Land* (Boston, 1931), 258; Erb, "Development of the Young People's Movement," 149–54, 159–60, quote at 152.

31. Clark, *Christian Endeavor in All Lands*, 443–44.

32. *Union Signal*, 12 December 1901, p. 5.

33. Ibid., 21 January 1904, p. 4.

34. William Shaw, *The Evolution of an Endeavorer: An Autobiography* (Boston, 1924), 361.

35. Francis Clark, "Some International Delusions," *North American Review* 163 (July 1896), 36.

36. Shaw, *Evolution*, 249; see also Francis Clark, "The Relation of Congregational Young People and Their Societies of Christian Endeavor to the American Missionary Association," *American Missionary* 48 (January 1894), 41.

37. Cf. Shaw, *Evolution*, 254; "Seattle Disgraced by Drawing Color Line," *Seattle Republican*, 24 May 1907, in "To the Memory of Horace Roscoe Cayton (1859–1940) Whose Courage, Forcefulness, Dedication and Determination Helped Make Our Lives Better," http://aaahrp.org/Research_Sources/Horace_Cayton/body_horace_cayton.html (accessed 18 July 2007).

38. Shaw, *Evolution*, 201, 202.

39. Francis Clark, "The Empire of the Dead," *North American Review* 171 (September 1900), 379 (first two quotes), 386, 387 (last two quotes).

40. "The King's Daughters in Session," *New York Times*, 11 August 1888, p. 1; "The King's Daughters," *New York Times*, 22 October 1888, p. 8; "Work among the Poor," *New York Times*, 10 April 1895, p. 8; Jacob Riis, *The Making of an American* (1901; New York, 1970), 186–87; Riis, *How the Other Half Lives: Studies among the Tenements of New York* (New York, 1890), 221.

41. Margaret Leitch to (Miss) A. B. Child, 16 June 1891, Margaret Leitch file, box 3, WBMHL; Charles Richmond Henderson, "The Influence of Jesus on Social Institutions," *Biblical World* 11 (March 1898), 172; "The Red Cross," *American Journal of Nursing* 12 (September 1912), 1021.

42. Erb, "Development of the Young People's Movement," 166.

43. Frank Thistlethwaite, *America and the Atlantic Community: Anglo-American Aspects, 1790–1850* (1959; New York, 1963), 85.

44. Root, *Century in Ceylon*, 70; L. D. Wishard, folder History of India and Ceylon: After 1899, Ceylon box 2 A and B, KFYMCAA.

45. David McConaughy to Missionary Sub-committee, International Committee of the Young Men's Christian Association, 22 January 1890, stated that the Bombay Association was formed by "Dr. Somervaille" (Rev. Dr. Alexander Neil Somerville), a Scotsman who "had been stirred by Moody's meetings in London" in April 1875. Folder January 1890, India Correspondence and Papers 1887–90, box 356, Y.63-4, KFYMCAA. On Somerville, see Aird, *Glimpses of Old Glasgow*, 361–62.

46. Ober, *Wishard*; *New York Times*, 8 January 1894, p. 9. Wishard also toured Europe in 1888. Luther Wishard to Charles Ober, 28 June 1888, box 105, Miscellaneous Personal Papers Collection, RG 30, YDSL.

47. Jacob Chamberlain to R. C. Morse, 20 March 1888, folder Correspondence and Papers 1888, India Correspondence and Papers 1887–90, box 356, Y.63-4, KFYMCAA.

48. Charles H. Brent to John Mott, 30 April 1909, folder Philippines Correspondence and Reports, 1909, Philippines, box 1, KFYMCAA.

49. Jacob Chamberlain to Cephas Brainard, chair, International Committee YMCA, 6 October 1887, folder Correspondence and Papers October 1887, n.d. [1888], India Correspondence and Papers 1887–90, box 356, Y.63-4, KFYMCAA.

50. Jacob Chamberlain to Cephas Brainard, 6 October 1887; extract from the minutes of the Madras [Missionary] Conference of date 12th of March 1888, with Richard Morse minute, 6 April [1888]; Jacob Chamberlain to Morse, 20 March 1888; Chamberlain to Luther Wishard, 19 May 1888, folder Correspondence and Papers 1888, India Correspondence and Papers 1887–90, box 356, Y.63-4, KFYMCAA.

51. "Work in Foreign Lands, from Year Book of 1890," and Richard C. Morse to Pastor Trophel, 23 September 1889, folder Correspondence and Papers, February–September 1889, India Correspondence and Papers 1887–90, box 356, Y.63-4, KFYMCAA.

52. "Main Facts Connected with the Beginning of the Foreign Work" and "Main Points by Elbert Munrow [Monroe] of New York and John Trumbull Swift," folder Correspondence and Papers 1888, India Correspondence and Papers 1887–90, box 356, Y.63-4, KFYMCAA.

53. Boyd, *Emissaries*, 3–6, 27, 33–34, 56–57.

54. *Annual Reports of Foreign Secretaries of the International Committee, October 1, 1903 to September 30, 1904,* Reports of Foreign Secretaries, 1904, box 29, Y-24-50, KFYMCAA.

55. But see C. Howard Hopkins, "The Kansas-Sudan Missionary Movement in the Y.M.C.A., 1889–1891," *Church History* 21 (December 1952), 314–22.

56. Pierson, *Crisis of Missions*, 64–65, 95.

57. Reports of Foreign Secretaries, box 29, Y-24-50, KFYMCAA.

58. Hopkins, "The Kansas-Sudan Missionary Movement," 314.

59. Putney, *Muscular Christianity*, 144–45, 147; Boyd, *Emissaries*, 30–31, 40–41.

60. Robert Wilder to no correspondent, 9 February 1890, folder February 1890, India Correspondence and Papers 1887–90, box 356, Y-63-4, KFYMCAA.

61. Report of George Gleason, 1 October 1904, *Annual Reports of Foreign Secretaries of the International Committee, October 1, 1903 to September 30, 1904*, 229, Reports of Foreign Secretaries, box 29, KFYMCAA (underlining in original).

62. Sherwood Eddy, "Mr. Meyer's Tour of India," Report Letter No. 16, March 1899, India, Eddy, G. Sherwood Report Letters 1899–1900, National Committee, 1891–1926, Y-57-1, KFYMCAA.

63. David McConaughy to Richard C. Morse, 14 May 1890, folder May 1890, India Correspondence and Papers 1887–90, box 356, Y-63-4 (underlining in original). See also more generally on McConaughy, folder India, David McConaughy, Association News, the Young Men of India, 1890, 1896, India. Histories, Reports, David McConaughy, Papers and Publications, box 340, Y-56-4, KFYMCAA.

64. Report of A. H. Grace, 31 October 1902, folder Annual and Quarterly Reports (B-Gr, 1902), India. Correspondence and Quarterly Reports, n.d. [1892–1912], Annual and Quarterly Reports, 1893–1906, Y-57-2, KFYMCAA; John Mott to Robert Wilder, 17 March 1900, and Mott to Wilder, 10 July 1900, folder 104, box 10, Wilder Papers.

65. David McConaughy to My Dear Friend [Richard C. Morse], 3 June 1890, folder March 1890, India Correspondence and Papers 1887–90, box 356, Y-63-4, KFYMCAA.

66. Johnston, *Report of the Centenary Conference*; William R. Hutchison, "Innocence Abroad: The 'American Religion' in Europe," *Church History* 51 (March 1982), 71–84, at 79 (quote). On the foundations of the American revivalist methods in Britain, see Carwardine, *Trans-Atlantic Revivalism*.

67. Warneck, quoted in Hutchison, "Innocence Abroad," 79.

68. Quoted in Parker, *Kingdom of Character*, 73.

69. Hutchison, "Innocence Abroad," 80.

70. Quote in ibid., 79; see Stephenson, *The Religious Aspects of Swedish Immigration*, 48; *Almanac of Missions for 1893* (Boston, 1893), 24.

71. Luther Wishard, *A New Program of Missions* (New York, 1895), 15–16.

72. Rouse, *World's Student Christian Federation*, 58.

73. Mott, quoted in ibid., 54.

74. Sherwood Eddy, "Lecturing to Educated Hindus," Report Letter No. 32 [n.d., 1903], folder Report Letters October 1902–December 1903, India, Eddy, G. Sherwood, Report Letters, 1896–1903, National Committee, 1891–1926, Y-57-1, KFYMCAA.

75. Report of J. N. Farquhar, Bengal, *Annual Reports of Foreign Secretaries of the International Committee, October 1, 1902 to September 30, 1903*, 102, Reports of Foreign Secretaries, 1903, box 29, Y-24-50, KFYMCAA (quotes); see also Eric J. Sharpe, *Not to Destroy But to Fulfill: The Contribution of J. N. Farquhar to Protestant Missionary Thought in India before 1914* (Lund, Sweden, 1965), 188–89.

76. Eddy, "Lecturing to Educated Hindus"; on missionaries' reactions to theosophy, see Carl T. Jackson, *Vedanta for the West: The Ramakrishna Movement in the United States* (Bloomington, IN, 1994), 5–6 (last two quotes, 5).

77. Chamberlain to Brainard, 6 October 1887; Chamberlain to Morse, 20 March 1888.

78. Meera Kosambi, "Introduction: Returning the American Gaze: Situating Pandita Ramabai's American Encounter," in Kosambi, ed., *Pandita Ramabai's American Encounter: The Peoples of the United States (1889)* (Bloomington, IN, 2003), 15–16; "Row Sattay's Folly," *New York Times*, 30 August 1886, p. 4.

79. Martin E. Marty, "World's Parliament of Religions," *Encyclopedia of Chicago*, http://www.encyclopedia.chicagohistory.org/pages/1387.html (accessed 1 September 2008 [quote]); Richard H. Seager, ed., *Dawn of Religious Pluralism: Voices from the World's Parliament of Religions, 1893* (Peru, IL, 1993); Seager, *The World's Parliament of Religions: The East/West Encounter, Chicago, 1893* (Bloomington, IN, 1995).

80. Jackson, *Vedanta*, 16–37; Carl T. Jackson, *The Oriental Religions and American Thought: Nineteenth-Century Explorations* (Westport, CT, 1981), 250; Robert Frykenberg, "Introduction: Dealing with Contested Definitions and Controversial Perspectives," in Frykenberg, ed., *Christians and Missionaries in India: Cross-Cultural Communication since 1500, with Special Reference to Caste, Conversion, and Colonialism* (Grand Rapids, MI, 2003), 21.

81. Quoted in Jackson, *Vedanta*, 27.

82. "The Truth about India," *Christian Herald*, 19 June 1895.

83. Sherwood Eddy, "The Indian Student Conference of 1897," Report No. 4, April 1897, folder Report Letters, 1896–98, India, Eddy, G. Sherwood, Report Letters, 1896–1903, National Committee, 1891–1926, Y-57, KFYMCAA.

84. Hopkins, *Mott*, 264.

85. Report of J. N. Farquhar [1903], 101.

86. Hopkins, *Mott*, 264.

87. Report of J. N. Farquhar [1903], 101.

88. J. N. Farquhar to Mott, 19 December 1923, folder India 1912–64 Misc. print, India. Histories, Reports, box 340, Y-56-4, KFYMCAA (underlining in original).

89. Shirley S. Garrett, *Social Reformers in Urban China: The Chinese Y.M.C.A., 1895–1926* (Cambridge, MA, 1970), 49 (first quote); *Annual Reports of Foreign Secretaries of the International Committee, October 1, 1902 to September 30, 1903*, Reports of Foreign Secretaries (second quote).

90. Garrett, *Social Reformers*, 81.

91. Ibid., 79, 80.

92. Ibid., 77.

93. Hopkins, *Mott*, 335.

94. Report of Galen Fisher, Japan, *Annual Reports of Foreign Secretaries of the International Committee October 1, 1902 to September 30, 1903*, 148.

95. Jon Thares Davidann, *A World of Crisis and Progress: The American YMCA in Japan, 1890–1930* (Bethlehem, PA, 1998), 37.

96. David McConaughy to Dear Friend [Richard C. Morse], 22 April 1890, folder April 1890; McConaughy to Morse, 19 August 1890, folder August 1890, India Correspondence and Papers 1887–90, box 356, Y-63-4, KFYMCAA.

97. Report to the International Committee of the YMCA's ... by City Department, ... by Alfred T. Morrill, Exec. Sec., n.d. [29 September 1916], received 28

October 1916, folder Administrative Reports 1914–16, Philippines Administrative Reports, box 5, KFYMCAA.

98. Report of Louis Hieb (general secretary, Ceylon), 12 October 1904, *Annual Reports of Foreign Secretaries of the International Committee, October 1, 1903 to September 30, 1904*, 23.

99. "The social gospel never became an organized 'movement'. Rather it was a network of movements operating in different contexts." Ronald C. White Jr. and C. Howard Hopkins, "What Is the Social Gospel," in White and Hopkins, eds., *The Social Gospel: Religion and Reform in Changing America* (Philadelphia, 1976), xviii; Henry May, *The Protestant Churches and Industrial America* (New York, 1949); C. Howard Hopkins, *The Rise of the Social Gospel in American Protestantism, 1865–1915* (New Haven, 1940).

100. Janet F. Fishburn, "The Social Gospel as Missionary Ideology," in Wilbert R. Shenk, ed., *North American Foreign Missions, 1810–1914: Theology, Theory, and Policy* (Grand Rapids, MI, 2004), 218–42.

101. C. Howard Hopkins, *History of the Y.M.C.A. in North America* (New York, 1951), 532.

102. Paul T. Phillips, *A Kingdom on Earth: Anglo-American Social Christianity, 1880–1940* (University Park, PA, 1996) xx, 139–41, 147; William R. Hutchison, "The Americanness of the Social Gospel: An Inquiry in Comparative History," *Church History* 44 (September 1975), 367–81; Mina Carson, *Settlement Folk: Social Thought and the American Settlement Movement, 1885–1930* (Chicago, 1990).

103. Eddy, "The Indian Student Conference of 1897"; Report of J. N. Farquhar, *Annual Reports of Foreign Secretaries of the International Committee, October 1, 1902 to September 30, 1903*, 102.

104. Report of Robert E. Lewis, *Annual Reports of Foreign Secretaries of the International Committee, October 1, 1902 to September 30, 1903*; report of B. R. Barber, ibid., 271–72.

105. A. F. Grimm, "Report of the Physical Director of the San Juan Young Men's Christian Association, the Year October 1st, 1915 to September 30th, 1916," 13, Reports 1908–15, Puerto Rico Correspondence and Report Letters 1908–69, box 557, Y-34-22, KFYMCAA.

106. Sherwood Eddy, *The New Era in Asia* (1913; Edinburgh, 1914); Lian Xi, *The Conversion of Missionaries: Liberalism in American Protestant Missions in China, 1907–1932* (University Park, PA, 1997), 155–61.

CHAPTER 5. BLOOD, SOULS, AND POWER:
AMERICAN HUMANITARIANISM ABROAD IN THE 1890S

1. Kosambi, *Pandita Ramabai's American Encounter*, 16, 243; Padmini Sengupta, *Pandita Ramabai Saraswati: Her Life and Work* (London, 1970), 154–55, 162–63; Uma Chakravarti, *Rewriting History: The Life and Times of Pandita Ramabai* (New Delhi, 1998), 333–34; Ramabai Sarasvati, *The High-Caste Hindu Woman*, new ed. (New York, 1901); Antoinette Burton, *At the Heart of the Empire: Indians and the Colonial Encounter in Late-Victorian Britain*, 1st Indian ed. (New Delhi, 1998).

2. Hopkins, *Mott*, 39.

3. Kumari Jayawardena, "Going for the Jugular of Hindu Patriarchy: American Women Fund Raisers for Ramabai," in Vicki L. Ruiz and Ellen Carol DuBois, eds., *Unequal Sisters: A Multicultural Reader in U.S. Women's History*, 3rd ed. (New York, 2000), 199.

4. Clara Barton, *The Red Cross in Peace and War* (Washington, DC, 1904), 175–78; George S. Queen, "American Relief in the Russian Famine of 1891–1892," *Russian Review* 14 (April 1955), 140–50.

5. *Washington Post*, 7 April 1892.

6. Curti, *American Philanthropy*, 115–16.

7. Cf. Foster Rhea Dulles, *The American Red Cross: A History* (New York, 1950).

8. Quoted in *Emporia Weekly Gazette*, 21 January 1897.

9. Williams, *Roots of the Modern American Empire*; "Last Year's Grain Exports," *New York Times*, 15 January 1900, p. 8.

10. Malcolm Falkus, "Russia and the International Wheat Trade, 1861–1914," *Economica*, n.s., 33 (November 1966), 416.

11. *Weekly Bea and Courier* (Charleston, SC), 19 May 1897.

12. Curti, *American Philanthropy*, 119.

13. Williams, *Roots of the Modern American Empire*.

14. H. F. Smith, "Bread for the Russians: William C. Edgar and the Relief Campaign of 1892," *Minnesota History* 42 (Summer 1970), 54–62; William C. Edgar, "Russia's Conflict with Hunger," *American Review of Reviews* 5 (July 1892), 691–700, at 699–700; Edgar, *The Story of a Grain of Wheat* (New York, 1903); "Wheat; William C. Edgar's Interesting Story of Its History and Development," *New York Times*, 20 June 1903, BR 5.

15. Edgar, *Story of a Grain of Wheat*.

16. *Union Signal*, 10 December 1891, p. 1; Queen, "American Relief in the Russian Famine," 141–42, 143.

17. "The Famine in Russia," *Review of Reviews* 5 (June 1892), 577–78; "Relieving the Russian Starvelings: The Gift of the American Millers," *Review of Reviews* 5 (April 1892), 407–9; Edgar, "Russia's Conflict with Hunger," 576–79.

18. "*AHR* Forum: Entangled Empires in the Atlantic World," *American Historical Review* 112 (June 2007), 610–799; Werner and Zimmermann, "Beyond Comparison."

19. *Union Signal*, 11 February 1892, p. 9.

20. American missionary penetration was still of "relatively small size," mainly Baptist and Pentecostal, before World War I. David S. Foglesong, *The American Mission and the "Evil Empire"* (New York, 2007), 34.

21. *Union Signal*, 7 January 1892, p. 1.

22. Ibid., 14 January 1892, p. 1.

23. Cf. Smith, "Bread for the Russians," 54, 55.

24. George Kennan to Frances Willard, 29 August 1888, folder 47, Correspondence, 1888, July–September, reel 15, Woman's Christian Temperance Union Series, Temperance and Prohibition Papers, microfilm, MHC-OHS.

25. *Union Signal*, 10 March 1892, p. 1.

26. W. Joseph Campbell, *Yellow Journalism: Punctuating the Myths, Defining the Legacies* (Westport, CT, 2001), 7–8; Delos F. Wilcox, "The American Newspaper: A Study in Social Psychology," *Annals of the American Academy of Political and Social Science* 16 (July 1900), 56–92.

27. Pepper, *Life-Work of Louis Klopsch*, 4, 321–22.

28. "A Famous Divine," *Milwaukee Daily Journal*, 7 April 1890.

29. *Georgia Weekly Telegraph and Georgia Journal and Messenger* (Macon, GA), 12 March 1878 (italics in original).

30. Pepper, *Life-Work of Louis Klopsch*, 6; "Thomas De Witt Talmage," *Dictionary of American Biography*, 18:287–88.

31. *Christian Herald*, 23 March 1892, p. 181; Curti, *American Philanthropy*, 112; *Galveston Daily News*, 24 May 1896, p. 10; Pepper, *Life-Work of Louis Klopsch*, 21.

32. *Christian Herald*, 23 March 1892, p. 182 (quotes), 4 May 1892, p. 296.

33. *Union Signal*, 19 May 1892, p. 1.

34. Ibid., 16 October 1896, p. 8.

35. Ibid., 9 January 1896, p. 1, 16 January 1896, p. 1, 19 December 1895, p. 9.

36. Edwin Munsell Bliss, *Turkey and the Armenian Atrocities: A Reign of Terror* (Philadelphia, 1896), 512.

37. *Union Signal*, 17 October 1895, p. 9.

38. Jessie Ackermann, reported in "From a Bloody Text," *Washington Post*, 13 January 1896, p. 4.

39. *Union Signal*, 12 December 1895, p. 8; James A. Field, *America and the Mediterranean World, 1776–1882* (Princeton, 1969), 358–59 (quote at 359).

40. *Union Signal*, 12 December 1895, p. 8.

41. *Time*, 26 October 1925; *New York Times*, 21 February 1935, p. 8; Moses Gulesian, "The Armenian Refugees," *The Arena*, March 1897, in Arman Kirakossian, ed., *The Armenian Massacres, 1894–1896: U.S. Media Testimony* (Detroit, 2004), 236–47.

42. *Union Signal*, 19 December 1895, p. 9.

43. Ibid., 16 July 1896, p. 5.

44. *New York Times*, 14 January 1895, p. 5; *Union Signal*, 22 October 1896, p. 1.

45. *New York Times*, 14 January 1895, p. 5.

46. *Union Signal*, 18 June 1896, p. 9, 16 April 1896, p. 9, 30 April 1896, p. 9.

47. Ibid., 6 February 1896, p. 8.

48. Frederick Davis Greene, *Armenian Massacres, or The Sword of Mohammed containing a complete and thrilling account of the terrible atrocities and wholesale murders committed in Armenia by Mohammedan fanatics ...* (Philadelphia and Chicago, 1896); Greene to Clara Barton, 31 July 1896, Armenia and Turkey Correspondence, December 1895–June 1896, Clara Barton Papers, microfilm, LC.

49. Frederick Davis Greene, *The Armenian Crisis in Turkey: The Massacre of 1894, Its Antecedents and Significance* (New York, 1895); *New York Times*, 20 March 1895.

50. Curti, *American Philanthropy*, 123; "John Crosby Brown Dead," *New York Times*, 26 June 1909, p. 7; Edwin J. Perkins, *Financing Anglo-American*

Trade: The House of Brown, 1800–1880 (Cambridge, MA, 1975); "Gives Presbyterians Advice; Preach Gospel in the Streets and Win Sinners, Says John H. Converse," *New York Times*, 23 May 1909, p. 9; *New York Times*, 13 April 1918, p. 13.

51. *Union Signal*, 19 November 1896, p. 4; on Lovell, see *Union Signal*, 2 May 1895, p. 2.

52. Thomas Bonner, "Sarah Ann Hackett Stevenson," *NAW*, 3:375; *Chicago Tribune*, 27 December 1895.

53. Mary Leitch and Margaret Leitch to Charles H. Daniels, 6 March 1897, reel 459, ABCFM Papers.

54. Alice Blackwell, *Armenian Poems* (Boston, 1896), http://armenianhouse .org/blackwell/armenian-poems/armenian-intro.html (accessed 19 October 2007).

55. "Introduction," in ibid.

56. Tyrrell, *Woman's World*, 141, 143 (quote).

57. *Washington Post*, 13 January 1896, p. 4.

58. *Union Signal*, 16 April 1896, 9, 7 May 1896, p. 4.

59. Curti, *American Philanthropy*, 130.

60. *Union Signal*, 10 December 1896, p. 8.

61. Curti, *American Philanthropy*, 131; Rebecca K. Krikorian, *Jerusalem: The Life Sketch of Miss Rebecca Krikorian and Her Nephew Rev. Samuel Krikorian, Together with Their Divine Call to Open a Field of Work in Jerusalem* (Kansas City, 1919); "'Bon Voyage' to Miss Willard," *New York Times*, 20 April 1896, p. 5.

62. *Union Signal*, 12 December 1895, p. 1, 16 June 1896, p. 1.

63. Ibid., 6 February 1896, p. 8.

64. Bliss, *Turkey and the Armenian Atrocities*, 551.

65. Ibid., 514.

66. Clara Barton, *America's Relief Expedition to Asia Minor under the Red Cross* (Meriden, CT, 1896), 3–5; *New York Times*, 26 August 1896, p. 9; Clara Barton to Stephen Barton, 10 March 1896, Barton Papers.

67. *Union Signal*, 24 December 1896, p. 9.

68. Edward Mead Earle, "American Missions in the Near East," *Foreign Affairs: An American Quarterly Review* 7 (April 1929), 409–10.

69. Cyrus Hamlin, "America's Duty to Americans in Turkey: An Open Letter to the Hon. John Sherman, United States Senator from Ohio," *North American Review* 163 (September 1896), 276–81; *Union Signal*, 17 September 1896.

70. *Union Signal*, 9 January 1896, p. 1.

71. *Washington Post*, 13 January 1896, p. 4.

72. Petition to the Senate, reprinted in *Union Signal*, 30 January 1896, p. 9.

73. *Washington Post*, 13 January 1896, p. 4; *Union Signal*, 6 February 1896, p. 8; "To Annihilate Turkish Empire," *New York Times*, 14 January 1896, p. 5; *Washington Post*, 15 January 1896 (quote).

74. Curti, *American Philanthropy*, 131.

75. Ibid., 133.

76. *Union Signal*, 19 November 1896, p. 4; Josiah W. Leeds, *The Help of Armenia* (Philadelphia, 1896).

77. Margaret and Mary Leitch to James L. Barton, 6 March 1897, reel 459, ABCFM Papers.

78. Joseph L. Grabill, *Protestant Diplomacy and the Near East: Missionary Influence on American Policy, 1810–1927* (Minneapolis, 1971), 46–47.

79. *Union Signal*, 24 September 1896, p. 1.

80. Curti, *American Philanthropy*, 115.

81. "The Grosvenor House Committee and Armenian Relief Work," *The Times*, 3 October 1898, p. 6.

82. Dulles, *Red Cross*, 38–39.

83. Curti, *American Philanthropy*, 125.

84. Ibid., 133.

85. *Atchison Daily Globe*, 1 January 1897, n.p.

86. Ibid.

87. "Our Experience in Collecting Funds."

88. Ibid.

89. Curti, *American Philanthropy*, 136; Pepper, *Life-Work of Louis Klopsch*, 68.

90. Pepper, *Life-Work of Louis Klopsch*, 351.

91. Ibid., 356–57.

92. Mary and Margaret Leitch to James Barton, 6 March 1897 (quote); Mary and Margaret Leitch to George Leitch, 26 February 1897, reel 459, ABCFM Papers.

93. Ramabai, *The High-Caste Hindu Woman*, 22–23, 24 (quote), 52.

94. *New York Times*, 15 January 1900.

95. Mary and Margaret Leitch to "Dear Friend," 14 May 1897, reel 459, ABCFM Papers.

96. Justin Abbott to editor of the *New York Times*, 25 August 1901, p. 5.

97. Mary and Margaret Leitch to Charles H. Daniels, 5 June 1897, reel 459, ABCFM Papers.

98. "The Scourges of India," Letter No. 5, May 1897, India, Eddy, G. Sherwood, Report Letters, 1896–1903, National Committee, 1891–1926, Y-57-1, KFYMCAA.

99. *Union Signal*, 3 March 1897, p. 9.

100. "Our Experience in Collecting Funds," 17.

101. "Indian Appreciation of American Generosity," clipping, folder misc. print, India. Histories, Reports, David McConaughy, Papers and Publications, box 340, Y-56-4, KFYMCAA (quotes); Pepper, *Life-Work of Louis Klopsch*, 86.

102. *Morning Oregonian*, 4 December 1896, p. 4 (quote); *Rocky Mountain News*, 2 November 1897.

103. *Denver Evening Post*, 4 November 1897, p. 6.

104. *Irish World and American Industrial Liberator*, 22 October 1898, n.p.

105. *Macon (Ga.), Telegraph*, 2 November 1897, p. 5.

106. "Famine," Report No. 21, March 1900, India, Eddy, G. Sherwood, Report Letters, 1896–1903, National Committee, 1891–1926, Y-57-1, KFYMCAA.

107. John Gerardus Fagg, *Forty Years in South China: The Life of Rev. John Van Nest Talmage, D.D.* (New York, [1894?]).

108. "Our Experience in Collecting Funds," 15.

109. "Women Battle with Famine," *Rocky Mountain News*, 2 November 1897, p. 6.

110. Baldwin, *Foreign Missions*, 209–11; *Almanac of Missions for 1893*, 32.

111. *Wisconsin State Register*, 8 May 1897, n.p.

112. Mary and Margaret Leitch to James L. Barton, 6 March 1897, reel 459, ABCFM Papers.

113. Campbell, *Yellow Journalism*, chap. 4.

114. *Union Signal*, 19 March 1896, p. 8.

115. Clara Barton, *The Red Cross: A History of This Remarkable International Movement in the Interest of Humanity* (Washington, DC, 1898), 520–22; Curti, *American Philanthropy*, 204; Elizabeth Brown Pryor, *Clara Barton: Professional Angel* (Philadelphia, 1987), 303.

116. *Union Signal*, 7 April 1898, p. 9.

117. Pepper, *Life-Work of Louis Klopsch*, 110–11.

118. Ibid., 115 (quote); "Mr. Moody's Last Services; ... Prayers and Aid for Suffering Cubans," *New York Times*, 17 January 1898, p. 7.

119. *New York Times*, 17 January 1898, p. 7.

120. Pepper, *Life-Work of Louis Klopsch*, 116.

121. Ibid., 119.

122. *Chicago Daily Tribune*, 28 March 1898, p. 1.

123. "Dr. Louis Klopsch Returns," *Washington Post*, 31 March 1898.

124. Pepper, *Life-Work of Louis Klopsch*, 119.

125. Ibid., 119–20.

126. "Sure of Freedom," *Chicago Daily Tribune*, 4 April 1898, p. 1.

127. *Chicago Daily Tribune*, 3 April 1898, p. 6.

128. "Cubans and an Armistice," *New York Times*, 5 April 1898, p. 4.

129. Curti, *American Philanthropy*, 202.

130. Quoted in Hopkins, *Mott*, 243.

131. *Washington Post*, 30 May 1898, p. 10.

132. Minutes of the Synod of Pennsylvania, October 20th to 24th, A.D. 1898, pp. 18, 29 in file 201601 with D, box 1263, Records of the Adjutant General, RG 94, National Archives, Washington, DC.

133. *Atlanta Constitution*, 22 July 1900, p. 5.

134. Curti, *American Philanthropy*, 207.

135. *New York Times*, 1 August 1916, p. 9, 10 March 1909, p. 9.

CHAPTER 6. REFORMING COLONIALISM

1. *New York Times*, 5 November 1898, p. 2; "Our Country's New Responsibilities: Call for a National Christian Citizenship Convention at Washington, D.C., Dec. 13–15, 1898," folder 11 (quotes), and Crafts form letter, 18 February 1902, folder 13, box 1, reel 2, Scientific Temperance Federation Series, Temperance and Prohibition Papers, microfilm edition, MHC-OHS.

2. *Washington Post*, 14 December 1898.

3. Foster, "Conservative Social Christianity."

4. *Los Angeles Times*, 12 September 1902, p. 10.

5. Foster, "Conservative Social Christianity," 809.

6. "Fifteenth Anniversary Edition, 1910," *Twentieth Century Quarterly* 10, no. 4 (March 1910), 17.

7. Strong, *Our Country*, 251.

8. Also spelled Katherine Lente Stevenson in some publications.

9. *New York Times*, 5 November 1898, p. 2.

10. Gaines M. Foster, *Moral Reconstruction: Christian Lobbyists and the Federal Legislation of Morality, 1865–1920* (Chapel Hill, 2002); Foster, "Conservative Social Christianity."

11. Crafts, "National Perils and Hopes," *Washington Post*, 30 May 1898, p. 10.

12. *Union Signal*, 31 October 1901, p. 6.

13. Major Louis L. Stevenson, "Why the Army Canteen Should Be Restored," *North American Review* 176, no. 554 (January 1903), 80–82; David M. Delo, *Peddlers and Post Traders: The Army Sutler on the Frontier* (Helena, MT, 1998), 199–206; Edward M. Coffman, *The Regulars: The American Army, 1898–1941* (Cambridge, MA, 2004), 118–19; *Chicago Daily Tribune*, 29 May 1890, p. 9; *New York Times*, 5 April 1890, p. 4; *Los Angeles Times*, 29 May 1890, p. 5; *Union Signal*, 27 April 1899, p. 8.

14. Brian M. Linn, "The Long Twilight of the Frontier Army," *Western Historical Quarterly* 27 (Summer 1996), 143; Linn, *The Philippine War, 1899–1902* (Lawrence, KA, 2000); "The Anti-Canteen Law," *Harper's Bazaar*, 9 June 1900, in Wilbur Crafts, *Patriotic Studies of a Quarter Century of Moral Legislation in Congress for Men's Leagues, Young People's Societies and Civic Clubs … 1888–1911* (n.p., [1911]), 141–42.

15. *Annual Report of the National Woman's Christian Temperance Union* (Chicago, 1901), 318.

16. Richard Hamm, *Shaping the Eighteenth Amendment: Temperance Reform, Legal Culture, and the Polity, 1880–1920* (Chapel Hill, 1995).

17. Rev. Robert Hunter, Presbyterian Church in the United States of America, to Secretary of War, and accompanying resolution on the canteen, n.d., and Minutes of the Synod of Pennsylvania, October 20th to 24th, A.D. 1898, 18, file 201601 with D, box 1263, Records of the Adjutant General's Office, Record Group 94, National Archives, Washington (hereafter RG 94, NA).

18. Diary, 1902, box 1, Brent Papers; see also Speech of Sen. Jacob H. Gallinger, M.D., *Congressional Record*, 11 January 1901, in Crafts, *Patriotic Studies*, 143.

19. Mrs. M. Hansel to William McKinley, 11 February 1900, file 311420, box 1263, RG 94, NA.

20. Index to petitions, Adjutant General's Office Files, reel 936, microfilm series 698, NA; see also resolutions requesting that they [canteens] be done away with forwarded by Epworth League, 24 November 1898 (102053); and petition of WCTU of Winthrop, Mass., requesting that intoxicating liquors be not sold at post or camp exchanges, 24 November 1898 (162100), all with file 201601 with D, box 1263, RG 94, NA.

21. *Union Signal*, 16 February 1899, p. 5, 13 April 1899, p. 16, 9 March, 1899, p. 2.

22. "Beverages in Army Canteens," *Union Signal*, 27 April 1899, p. 8; "Let Attorney-General Griggs Be Nullified," *Union Signal*, 28 December 1899, p. 8. The law was enacted on 2 April 1899 and declared unconstitutional by Griggs on 3 April.

23. C. V. Culver to William McKinley, 20 January 1900, file 1333-1, box 189, entry 5, RG 350, Records of the Bureau of Insular Affairs, National Archives, College Park, MD (hereafter RG 350, NA).

24. Delo, *Peddlers and Post Traders*, 212; "U.S. Army 'Prohibition,' 1890–1953," http://www.druglibrary.org/schaffer/alcohol/prohibit.htm (accessed 10 December 2006).

25. Mrs. E. Johnson to William McKinley, 19 January 1901, file 1580-9, box 207, RG 350, NA.

26. *New York Times*, 3 May 1900, p. 6.

27. *Union Signal*, 11 January 1900, p. 6.

28. Truman R. Clark, "Prohibition in Puerto Rico, 1917–1933," *Journal of Latin American Studies* 27 (February 1995), 77–97.

29. J.A.C. Gray, *Amerika Samoa: A History of American Samoa and Its United States Naval Administration* (Annapolis, MD, 1960), 135–36; Crafts et al., *Intoxicating Drinks*, 219–20. A Samoan alcohol prohibition was implemented in 1921. Ernest H. Cherrington, "World-Wide Progress toward Prohibition Legislation," *Annals of the American Academy of Political and Social Science* 109 (September 1923), 221.

30. *New York Times*, 1 May 1900, p. 7, 3 May 1900, p. 6.

31. *Chicago New Voice*, 30 August 1900; Crafts et al., *Protection of Native Races*, 201.

32. *Leslie's Weekly*, 27 January 1900, quoted in Crafts et al., *Protection of Native Races*, 190.

33. Survey of fourteen petitions, 1900–1901, file 1580-6, box 207, RG 350, NA.

34. Quoted in Crafts et al., *Protection of Native Races*, 199.

35. *Union Signal*, 11 June 1903, p. 11; W. F. Etter (New Castle, PA) to William Howard Taft, 26 August 1904, file 1580-21; Major W. Lassiter to Adjutant General, Manila, 22 September 1910, file 1580-33 and E. E. Gilbert to Secretary of War, 30 August 1910, file 1580-32, provided evidence of illegal alcohol sale in Los Banos; W. A. McVean to Major J. A. Goodin, 3 September 1909, and R. F. Smith to Major James A. Goodin, 3 September 1909, file 1580-34, all in box 207, RG 350, NA; Coffman, *The Regulars*, 118–19.

36. Petition of George Howe and others, 29 March 1901, regarding a "mass meeting" in Warrensburg, Missouri, 25 November 1900, file 1580-6, box 207, RG 350, NA.

37. Ibid.

38. Paul A. Kramer, *The Blood of Government: Race, Empire, the United States, & the Philippines* (Chapel Hill, 2006).

39. Petition and resolution against "Island Saloons and Canteens," signed by three hundred members of the United Presbyterian Church of Bloomington, Indiana, 1 April 1900; resolutions unanimously passed by Methodist and United Presbyterian Preachers' meetings of Pittsburgh, 19 February 1900, file 1580-3,

box 207, RG 350, NA. See also petition of Rev. A. E. Thomson of Cincinnati, 23 January 1901, file 1580-7, ibid.

40. Arthur J. Brown, *The New Era in the Philippines* (New York, 1903), 111, 113; *Fourth Annual Report of the Philippine Commission, 1903*, part 1 (Washington, 1904), 49.

41. Brown, *New Era*, 111 (quoted); for the practical working of the policy, see Major W. A. Duvall to [Clarence Edwards?], 17 October 1910; minutes by Clarence Edwards, 5 December 1910, file 1580-31, box 207, RG 350, NA.

42. Cf. Hochschild, *King Leopold's Ghost*, 92–93, 111–12.

43. William T. Hornaday, *Free Rum on the Congo and What It Is Doing There* (Chicago, 1887), i–iii.

44. Leavitt, *Report of the Hon. Sec. of the World's Woman's Christian Temperance Union*, 44–45, 48.

45. Ernest H. Cherrington, ed., *Standard Encyclopedia of the Alcohol Problem*, 6 vols. (Westerville, OH, 1925–30), 4:1866 (hereafter *SEAP*).

46. *New York Times*, 12 January 1892; A. B. Keith, *The Belgian Congo and the Berlin Act* (Oxford, 1919).

47. Crafts et al., *Intoxicating Drinks*, 56–57. On Paton, see *Union Signal*, 12 November 1901, p. 5; David Hilliard, "Paton, John Gibson (1824–1907)," *Oxford Dictionary of National Biography*, http://www.oxforddnb.com/view/article/35411 (accessed 5 July 2007).

48. Crafts et al., *Intoxicating Drinks*, 210.

49. John G. Paton, "The Drink Traffic as an Anti-Christian Force," in *Ecumenical Missionary Conference: New York, 1900 ... ,* 2 vols. (New York, 1900), 1:381–83; Hilliard, "Paton."

50. Crafts et al., *Intoxicating Drinks*, 210. Leitch and Crafts had this item placed on the 1900 meeting agenda; it was not present on the first draft (p. 218). Leitch was not listed as speaking at the official proceedings of the actual conference but was a delegate, *Ecumenical Missionary Conference*, 2:406.

51. Crafts et al., *Intoxicating Drinks*, 157, 160–61.

52. Ibid., 218–19; [Wilbur Crafts], "Memorandum Concerning International Restraint of the Traffic in Intoxicants and Opium among Aboriginal Races," 1, 8, in Subject File International Opium Conference, Printed Matter, 1860–1931, box 41, Brent Papers.

53. Crafts et al., *Intoxicating Drinks*, 53 (first quote), 59–60 (second quote), 219.

54. Ibid., 51, 57; Bernard Porter, *Critics of Empire: British Radicals and the Imperial Challenge* (London, 2008), 51.

55. See, for example, Justin Willis, *Potent Brews: A Social History of Alcohol in East Africa, 1850–1999* (Oxford, 2002), 119; Charles H. Ambler, "Drunks, Brewers, and Chiefs: Alcohol Regulation in Colonial Kenya, 1900–1939," in Susanna Barrows and Robin Room, eds., *Drinking: Behaviour and Belief in Modern History* (Berkeley, CA, 1991), 166–67, 172.

56. Crafts, *Patriotic Studies*, 199.

57. *Leslie's Weekly*, 27 January 1900, printed in Crafts et al., *Intoxicating Drinks*, 191. For a copy of the petition submitted, see *Union Signal*, 21 November 1901, p. 9.

58. *Union Signal*, 12 December 1901, p. 5.

59. Lyman (1843–1913) of Connecticut was a Republican Mugwump, and Civil Service Commissioner (1886–93). He was later employed in the appointments division of the Secretary of the Treasury.

60. Crafts, *Patriotic Studies*, 184.

61. *Congressional Record*, vol. 35, part 2, 57th Cong., 1st Sess., 1 February 1902, 1202-3.

62. *Union Signal*, 11 June 1903, p. 11.

63. Crafts undated letter with Theodore Roosevelt to Elihu Root, 6 June 1903, file 1023-14, box 157, RG 350, NA.

64. Brown, *New Era*, 111.

65. *Union Signal*, 31 March 1901, 4.

66. Patricio Abinales, "Progressive-Machine Conflict in Early-Twentieth-Century U.S. Politics and Colonial-State Building in the Philippines," in Anne L. Foster and Julian Go, eds., *The American Colonial State in the Philippines* (Durham, NC, 2003), 148–82.

67. Diary typescript, 2:312, October 1907, William Cameron Forbes Papers, LC; Forbes to Mercer Johnston, 27 January 1908; and "Extracts from Minutes of Meeting of the Evangelical Union held in the Methodist Church, February 15th, 1908" with secretary, Evangelical Union, to James Smith (governor-general), 29 February 1908, box 18, Mercer Green Johnston Papers, LC (hereafter Johnston Papers).

68. Elihu Root to Rev. S. B. Dexter, 27 August 1901, box 175, part 1, Elihu Root Papers, LC.

69. Brown, *New Era*, 109, 110.

70. Kenton J. Clymer, "Religion and American Imperialism: Methodist Missionaries in the Philippine Islands, 1899–1913," *Pacific Historical Review* 49 (February 1980), 44–45; "Extracts from Minutes of Meeting of the Evangelical Union held in the Methodist Church, February 15th, 1908."

71. Paul A. Kramer, "The Darkness That Enters the Home: The Politics of Prostitution during the Philippine-American War," in Ann Laura Stoler, ed., *Haunted by Empire: Geographies of Intimacy in North American History* (Durham, NC, 2006), 366–403.

72. This was not a Philippines issue only. See comments in A/G/1873215/F 19 March 1902, index to petitions, Adjutant General's Office Files, reel 936, microfilm series 698, NA, regarding widespread and unregulated prostitution in Puerto Rico and recommending that civil authorities take corrective action. The Americans had inherited a policy in which commercialized sex was regulated there, too. Eileen Findlay, *Imposing Decency: The Politics of Sexuality and Race in Puerto Rico, 1870–1920* (Durham, NC, 1999), 176.

73. Kramer, "Darkness," 379.

74. David J. Munro to Theodore Roosevelt, n.d., file 2039-27, box 246, RG 350, NA.

75. Allan M. Brandt, *No Magic Bullet: A Social History of Venereal Disease in the United States since 1880* (New York, 1985), 97.

76. Kramer, "Darkness," 377.

77. *Philadelphia Press* clipping of 25 March [1902], with file 2039-21, box 246, RG 350, NA; see also special order no. 10, Carroll J. Potter, Major 14th Infantry, 3 November 1899, file 2039-10, box 246, ibid., regarding "invalid" females at San Lazaro Hospital.

78. Arthur McArthur to Adjutant General, 4 February 1901, file 2039-5, box 246, RG 350, NA.

79. Kramer, "Darkness," 372.

80. Charles Lynch (major and surgeon, U.S. Volunteers) to President, Board of Health, 18 May 1901, file 2039-13, box 246, RG 350, NA.

81. Ira C. Brown (acting president, Board of Health, and surgeon, U.S. Volunteers) to Acting Adjutant General, 16 May 1900, file 2039-11, box 246, RG 350, NA.

82. Summaries of petitions in index to petitions, Adjutant General's Office Files, reel 936, microfilm series 698, NA.

83. Crafts, *Primer*, 69.

84. Senator Joseph R. Burton to Roosevelt, 5 June 1903, file 1023-41, box 246, RG 350, NA; Perl W. Morgan, ed. and comp., *History of Wyandotte County Kansas and Its People*, 2 vols. (Chicago, 1911), http://skyways.lib .ks.us/genweb/archives/wyandott/history/1911/volume1/243.html (accessed 10 February 2008).

85. W. Cary Sanger to Henry Cabot Lodge, 21 April 1902, after file 2039-21, box 246, RG 350, NA.

86. *New York Times*, 28 March 1901, p. 8.

87. *Union Signal*, 5 December 1901, p. 5; "Mothering in Manila," *Union Signal*, 4 July 1901, p. 9.

88. *Union Signal*, 28 November 1901, p. 11, 5 December 1901, p. 6, 13 February 1902, p. 1.

89. Joseph R. Burton to Theodore Roosevelt, 5 June 1903, file 1023-41, box 246, RG 350, NA; *Manila Times*, 26 January 1900. W. A. Kinkaid to Mercer Johnston, 8 July 1906; William H. Donavan to Johnston, 3 July 1906; "An Amigo" to Johnston, 21 May 1906, all in box 38, Johnston Papers.

90. "State Regulation of Vice at Manila," *Woman's Journal*, 1 September 1900, reprinted from *Chicago New Voice*, file 2039-1, box 246, RG 350, NA.

91. Henry Browne Blackwell, editorial, *Woman's Journal*, 1 September 1900, in file 2039-3, box 246, RG 350, NA.

92. *The Crowning Infamy of Imperialism* (Philadelphia, [1900]), http://www .boondocksent.com/ai/ailtexts/infamy.html (accessed 15 August 2005).

93. Mary Livermore, "Remarks at the Annual Meeting of the New England Anti-Imperialist League," *Report of the Fifth Annual Meeting of the New England Anti-Imperialist League* (Boston, 1903), http://www.boondocksent.com/ai/ ailtexts/livermore.html (accessed 1 June 2005).

94. For Britain, see Judith Walkowitz, *Prostitution and Victorian Society: Women, Class and the State* (New York, 1980).

95. John D. Long to Elihu Root, 5 September 1900, file 2039-2, box 246, RG 350, NA.

96. Henry Browne Blackwell to John D. Long, 1 September 1900, with file 2039-3, box 246, RG 350, NA.

97. Editorial, *Woman's Journal,* 1 September 1900, file 2039-3, box 246, RG 350, NA.

98. Kramer, "Darkness," 387.

99. Clarence Edwards to Senator Chester Long, 15 June 1903, file 1023-31, box 157, RG 350, NA; George Courtelyou to Elihu Root, 6 February 1902, file 2039-17, box 246, RG 350, NA.

100. Arthur McArthur to Adjutant General, Washington, 4 February 1901, file 2039-5, box 246, RG 350, NA.

101. General Order No. 101, 21 May 1901, file 2039-26, box 246, RG 350, NA.

102. Clarence Edwards to Hon. E. J. Hill, 16 October 1901, file 2039-8, box 246, RG 350, NA.

103. *Union Signal,* 7 October 1909, p. 3.

104. For Ellis's biographical details, see *Union Signal,* 17 January 1901, p. 8, 30 July 1925, p. 7; *New York Times,* 14 July 1925, p. 21.

105. Margaret Ellis, "Relating to the Regulation of Vice in the Philippines," n.d. [1902], file 2039-18, box 246, RG 350, NA.

106. Elihu Root to Luke Wright, 18 February 1902, file 2039-18.1/2, box 246, RG 350, NA; Tyrrell, *Woman's World,* 213–17.

107. Circular No. 10, 18 March 1902, Order of the Secretary of War, file 1333-24, box 189; Elihu Root to Margaret Ellis, 3 April 1902, file 2039-20, box 246, RG 350, NA.

108. "Disobedience of Lt. Col. Louis M. Maus, Medical Department in that he did not discontinue the issuance of certificates of inspection to prostitutes in Philippine Islands," 18 October 1902, 456918, index to petitions, Adjutant General's Office Files, reel 936, microfilm series 698, NA.

109. Wilbur Crafts to Robert Shaw Oliver, 25 November 1907, file 2039-29, box 246, RG 350, NA.

110. D. W. Egner, memorandum to Louis Vernon Carmack, 25 May 1908, file 2039-30, box 246, RG 350, NA.

111. *Union Signal,* 1 May 1902, p. 8, 7 October 1909, p. 3.

112. Index to petitions, Adjutant General's Office Files, reel 936, microfilm series 698, NA, for example, from Wilbur Crafts, 21 January 1902; "State Regulation of Vice at Manila," (Boston) *Woman's Journal,* 1 September 1900; Tyrrell, *Woman's World,* 213–17.

113. Kramer, "Darkness," 396.

114. Elihu Root to Margaret Ellis, 3 April 1902, file 2039-20, box 246, RG 350, NA.

115. Margaret Ellis to Clarence Edwards, 26 April 1902, file 2039-24, box 246, RG 350, NA.

116. On the ideal Christian state, see Wilbur Crafts's Theological Index "The State," box 1, Crafts Notebooks; Foster, "Conservative Social Christianity," 807; Crafts, *Practical Christian Sociology: A Series of Special Lectures before Princeton Theological Seminary and Marietta College ...* (New York, 1895), 23; *Los Angeles Times,* 12 September 1902, p. 10 (quote).

CHAPTER 7. OPIUM AND THE FASHIONING OF THE
AMERICAN MORAL EMPIRE

1. William C. Dix to Elihu Root, 1 June 1903, file 1023-11; Memorandum for Secretary of War, 4 June 1903, regarding the protest of William C. Dix, file 1023-1, both in box 157, entry 5, RG 350, NA.

2. "An Act to Suppress the Sale of Opium to the Filipino People, to Confine its Use to People of the Chinese Race, and to Restrict and reduce its consumption by Chinese within the Philippine Islands," file 1023-13, box 157, RG 350, NA; Memorandum for Secretary of War, 4 June 1903, file 1023/29, RG 350, NA (quote); *Fourth Annual Report of the Philippine Commission 1903*, part 1 (Washington, DC, 1904), 96; Anne L. Foster, "Models for Governing: Opium and Colonial Policies in Southeast Asia, 1898–1910," in Foster and Go, *The American Colonial State in the Philippines*, 92–117.

3. Clarence Edwards to John D. Long, 15 June 1903, file 1023-31, box 157, RG 350, NA (quote); "Report of the Commissioner of Public Health," *Sixth Annual Report of the Philippine Commission, 1905*, part 2 (Washington, 1906), 86–87.

4. Clarence Edwards to Major Gen. Elwell S. Otis, 16 April 1900, file 1023-3, box 157, RG 350, NA, regarding complaints from Dr. H. C. DuBose; G. Thompson Brown, "Hampton Coit Dubose," in Gerald H. Anderson, ed., *Biographical Dictionary of Christian Missions* (New York, 1998), 187.

5. Kathleen L. Lodwick, *Crusaders against Opium: Protestant Missionaries in China, 1874–1917* (Lexington, KY, 1996), 6.

6. William H. Park, *Opinions of over 100 Physicians on the Use of Opium in China* (Shanghai, 1899).

7. *Report of the International Opium Commission, Shanghai, China, February 1 to February 26, 1909, Vol. 2, Reports of the Delegations* (Shanghai, 1909), 7; Davis Edwards, "Opium a Greater Menace to New York Than Liquor," *New York Times*, 20 October 1912, SM4 (quote); "6,000 Opium Users Here; Dr. Hamilton Wright Thinks Five-Sixths of Them Are White," *New York Times*, 1 August 1908, p. 6.

8. Park, *Opinions of over 100 Physicians*; Lodwick, *Crusaders against Opium*, 39–49. Crafts was influenced by Park's work. William H. Park to Theodore Roosevelt, 18 June 1907, in *Twentieth Century Quarterly* 7, no. 4 (21 June 1908), 15.

9. Crafts, *Patriotic Studies*, 245 (quote); Arthur Bonner, *What Brought Thee Hither? The Chinese in New York, 1800–1950* (Madison, NJ, 1997), 49.

10. Clarence Edwards to Major Gen. Elwell S. Otis, 16 April 1900, file 1023-3, box 157, RG 350, NA; extract from H. DuBose letter, 1023-1, ibid. (quote); Arnold H. Taylor, "American Confrontation with Opium Traffic in the Philippines," *Pacific Historical Review* 36 (August 1967), 307–24.

11. Chester Long to Clarence Edwards, 9 June 1903, file 1023-31, box 157, RG 350, NA; J. R. Bishop to Theodore Roosevelt, 5 June 1903, file 1023-41, box 158, ibid.

12. Among numerous protests, see Petition of J. W. Magruder, Methodist Episcopal Church, Portland, Maine, n.d., referring to Senate Resolution of 4 June

1901, file 1023-30, box 157, RG 350, NA; Lillian Stevens and Suzannah M. D. Fry (WCTU) to Theodore Roosevelt, 10 June 1901, ibid.; John H. Converse, telegram, 12 June 1903, ibid.; James A. Amerman telegram to Roosevelt, 11 June 1903, ibid.

13. Wilbur Crafts to Elihu Root, 18 June 1903 (quote), Root to Crafts, 30 June 1903, file 1023-42; Crafts to Root, 8 July 1903, file 1023-43; and "Brief of Arguments of Thoburn and Crafts," 9 July 1903, file 1023-44, all in box 158, RG 350, NA.

14. Theodore Roosevelt to Elihu Root, 6 June 1903, file 1023-14, box 157, RG 350, NA; William Loeb (secretary to president) to Root, 8 June 1903, transmitting papers as submitted by Crafts, ibid.

15. Elihu Root to William Howard Taft, 5 June 1903, file 1023-10, box 157, RG 350, NA.

16. Root to Taft, 10 July 1903, box 165, Elihu Root Papers, LC.

17. McGruder petition, 4 June 1903; John Converse's telegram, 3 June 1903; Elisha K. Kane to Root, 14 July 1903, all in file 1023-30, box 157, RG 350, NA.

18. Crafts, *Patriotic Studies*, 239.

19. Crafts, *Primer*, 10.

20. "Brief of Arguments of Thoburn and Crafts," 9 July 1903, file 1023-44, box 158, RG 350, NA.

21. See, for example, John Mott to Woodrow Wilson, 4 April 1913, folder 1760, box 100, Mott Papers.

22. [Wilbur Crafts], "Memorandum Concerning International Restraint of the Traffic in Intoxicants and Opium among Aboriginal Races," Subject File International Opium Conference, Printed Matter, 1860–1931, box 41, Brent Papers.

23. Sandra C. Taylor, *Advocate of Understanding: Sidney Gulick and the Search for Peace with Japan* (Kent, OH, 1984); Jennifer C. Snow, "A Border Made of Righteousness: Protestant Missionaries, Asian Immigration, and Ideologies of Race, 1850–1924" (Ph.D. diss., Columbia University, 2003).

24. Senator Chester Long to Clarence Edwards, 9 June 1903, file 1023-31, box 157, RG 350, NA; Edwards to Long, 15 June 1903, ibid.

25. Theodore Roosevelt to Elihu Root, 6 June 1903, with letters from Wilbur Crafts, "who transmits protest of Methodist Episcopal Mission in Manila against opium traffic in P.I. Govt. licensing etc," file 1023-14; Homer Stuntz, 2 May 1903, to "Dear Fellow-Worker" [Crafts]: he had no luck with Taft yet he "hope[d] you will lift your voice against its enactment," Crafts letter, n.d. [c. 3 May 1903], file 1023-14; Stuntz to Crafts, 2 May 1903, file 1023-17, all in box 157, RG 350, NA.

26. Roosevelt to Root, 6 June 1903, file 1023-14, box 157, RG 350, NA; Root to Taft, 10 August 1903, file 1023-103, box 159, ibid.

27. Clarence Edwards to Chester Long, 15 June 1903, file 1023-31, box 157, RG 350, NA (quote); [Elihu Root] to William Howard Taft, 10 August 1903, file 1023-103, ibid.

28. "Opium in the Orient: Report of the Philippines Commission," 19–21, in file 1023-13, box 157, RG 350, NA, published as *Report of the Committee Appointed by the Philippine Commission to Investigate the Use of Opium and the Traffic Therein* (Washington, DC, 1905); Westel W. Willoughby, *Opium as an International Problem* (1925; New York, 1976), 117–22.

29. Foster, "Models for Governing," 109; Theodore Roosevelt to Charles Brent, 19 October 1904, folder 1904, box 6, Brent Papers.

30. Charles Brent to Frederick G. Morgan (Kasr el Dubara, Cairo), 13 May 1905, folder May–December 1905, box 6, Brent Papers.

31. "Filipinos Stop Opium," *Washington Post*, 10 March 1906; "Stop Sale of Opium: Filipinos Adopt Drastic Measures to Stamp It Out," *Washington Post*, 13 March 1906, p. 5 (quotes); David F. Musto, *The American Disease: Origins of Narcotic Control*, 3rd ed. (New York, 1999), 28; Willoughby, *Opium as an International Problem*, 18–20; Taylor, "American Confrontation with Opium Traffic," 321; Anne L. Foster, "Prohibition as Superiority: Policing Opium in South-East Asia, 1898–1925," *International History Review* 22, no. 2 (2000), 253–73.

32. Crafts accepted the temporary high license in a tacit compromise over a (temporary) monopoly, as in Japanese policy, that he would have preferred. Wilbur Crafts to William Howard Taft, 27 August 1904, file 1023-106, box 159, RG 350, NA. See also Clarence Edwards to Crafts, [31?] August 1904, and Edwards to Crafts, 23 December 1904, file 1023-106, Edwards to Crafts, 4 February 1905, and Crafts postcard, 2 February 1905, file 1023-108; and James B. Rodgers to Civil Commission, 15 July 1904, file 1023-102, all in box 159, RG 350, NA.

33. Wilbur Crafts to Theodore Roosevelt, 20 December 1904, file 1023-108, box 159, RG 350, NA.

34. Esther Baldwin (née Jerman, 1840–1910) married Stephen Livingstone Baldwin, a missionary in Fuzhou, in 1858. *New York Times*, 1 March 1910; Bonner, *What Brought Thee Hither?*, 48–49.

35. Mary Porter Gamewell, *Mary Porter Gamewell and Her Story of the Siege in Peking*, ed. A. H. Tuttle (New York, 1907), 190.

36. Crafts, *Patriotic Studies*, 248; *Union Signal*, 24 November 1904, p. 15 (quote), 22 June 1905, p. 14.

37. Wilbur Crafts to Arthur J. Balfour, 12 October 1904, in *Patriotic Studies*, 235.

38. Crafts's words, ibid., 249.

39. Joseph B. Alexander to Wilbur Crafts, 1 November 1904, in *Patriotic Studies*, 251; see also "A Plea for China" [Speech of the Lord Bishop of Durham, 9 December 1904], in ibid., 252–56.

40. Crafts et al., *Intoxicating Drinks*, 51.

41. The bureau had a British Council headed by V. H. Rutherford, MP. The Australian Council had the reformer W. H. Judkins as district secretary for "Australasia" and the "South Seas." Tokyo Bureau councillors included the pro-temperance Sho Nemoto, MP. The Rev. Charles Eby was district secretary for Toronto but also for Tokyo. See Crafts, *Internationalism*, 90.

42. Crafts, *Patriotic Studies*, cover endorsement (quote); *Union Signal*, 5 December 1907, p. 7.

43. Reed, *Missionary Mind*, 100.

44. Crafts, *Patriotic Studies*, 247.

45. "The Opium Traffic," *The Times*, 26 May 1906, p. 16. Wilson had been sent the Philippines opium report and referred to it; M. Hewitt, "Wilson, Henry Joseph (1833–1914)," *Oxford Dictionary of National Biography* (quote), http://www.oxforddnb.com/view/article/50958 (accessed 20 December 2007).

46. Crafts et al., *Intoxicating Drinks*, 223.

47. *Union Signal*, 12 July 1906, p. 15 (quote); Crafts, *Internationalism*, 62.

48. Hamilton Wright, "The International Opium Commission," *American Journal of International Law* 3 (July 1909), 668 (first two quotes), 671 (last quote); *The Times*, 31 May 1906, pp. 6, 9 (editorial).

49. Lodwick, *Crusaders against Opium*, 182.

50. Charles Brent to Mercer Johnston, 9 February 1909, folder Feb. 1909, box 8, Brent Papers.

51. Wright, "The International Opium Commission," 670, 668 (quote); *The Times*, 31 May 1906, pp. 6, 9 (editorial).

52. Brent to F. C. Shattuck, 27 May 1907, folder January–June 1907, box 6, Brent Papers.

53. For the text of the decree and its constituent regulations, see *White Ribbon Signal*, 1 February 1907, p. 5. See also J. F. Scheltema, "The Opium Question," *American Journal of Sociology* 16 (September 1910), 216.

54. *New York Times*, 28 May 1911 (quotes); for the broader context of British policy, see R. K. Newman, "India and the Anglo-Chinese Opium Agreements, 1907–14," *Modern Asian Studies* 23, no. 3 (1989), 525–60.

55. "Opium Trade Growing," *New York Times*, 25 June 1910, p. 4.

56. Randall Davidson to Charles Brent, 2 August 1912; Brent to Davidson, 22 October 1912, folder July–December 1912, box 10, Brent Papers; *The Times*, 3 June 1912, 9 (quote).

57. Alvey Adee to Elihu Root, 5 October 1906, 721/4, M862, R. 101, RG 59, Numerical and Minor Files of the Department of State, 1906–1910, NA.

58. Charles Brent to Archbishop of York, 30 July 1906, and other letters in folder January–December 1906, box 6, Brent Papers.

59. Theodore Roosevelt to Charles Brent, 29 June 1908, folder July 1908, box 7, Brent Papers.

60. Reported in Brent to Shattuck, 27 May 1907; Brent to Theodore Roosevelt, 24 July 1906, folder January–December 1906, box 6, Brent Papers (last quote).

61. Brent to Roosevelt, 24 July 1906; Brent to Leonard Wood, 17 February 1910, folder January–February 1910, box 9, Brent Papers; *Twentieth-Century Quarterly* 7, no. 2 (21 December 1907), 21, and 8, no. 2 (21 December 1908), 1; Crafts, *Patriotic Studies*, 239.

62. Brent to Roosevelt, 24 July 1906; Roosevelt to Brent, 28 August 1906, folder January–December 1906, box 6, Brent Papers (last quote).

63. Robert Bacon to Charles Brent, 3 August 1908, box 8, Brent Papers.

64. Brent to Roosevelt, 24 July 1906.

65. Reed, *Missionary Mind*, 100.

66. Musto, *American Disease*, 31 (quote); Howard K. Beale, *Theodore Roosevelt and the Rise of America to World Power* (Baltimore, 1956), 191–223; C. F. Remer, *A Study of Chinese Boycotts with Special Reference to Their Economic Effectiveness* (Baltimore, 1933), 29–39.

67. Philander Knox to William Howard Taft, 11 February 1910, folder January–February 1910, box 9, Brent Papers.

68. *New York Times*, 25 July 1909, SM4 (quotes); Foster, "Prohibition as Superiority."

69. Foster, "Prohibition as Superiority."

70. Alvey Adee to Diplomatic Officers of the United States accredited to the governments represented in the Shanghai Opium Conference, 1 September 1909, with Knox to Taft, 11 February 1910 (quote); see also Bacon to Brent, 3 August 1908.

71. Homer C. Stuntz, *The Philippines and the Far East* (New York, 1904), 508.

72. *New York Times*, 25 July 1909, SM4.

73. Hamilton Wright to Charles Brent, 9 February 1910, folder January–February 1910, box 9, Brent Papers.

74. Taylor, *American Diplomacy and the Narcotics Traffic*, 84; Foster, "Prohibition as Superiority," 264–65.

75. "America Rebuked," *New York Times*, 27 November 1909, p. 16.

76. An Act to prohibit the importation and use of opium for other than medicinal purposes, 5 Public Law No. 221, 1909, in "Opium Problem; Message from the President of the United States," *Senate Documents*, 61st Cong., 2nd Sess., Doc. No. 377, 2–53; Charles Brent to Mercer Johnston, 9 February 1909, folder Feb. 1909, box 8, Brent Papers; H. W. Wiley to Robert Bacon, 29 October 1908, folder Oct. 1908, ibid.

77. Hamilton Wright to Charles Brent, 25 November 1916, folder November 1916, box 13, Brent Papers.

78. *New York Times*, 12 March 1911, SM12.

79. Musto, *American Disease*, 53, 54.

80. *Patriotic Studies*, cover endorsement; *Union Signal*, 5 December 1907, p. 7.

81. *Twentieth-Century Quarterly* 8, no. 1 (21 September 1908), 3.

82. *Report of the Ninth Convention of the World's Woman's Christian Temperance Union, 1913* (Brooklyn, 1913), 140.

83. Simon Heap, "'We Think Prohibition Is a Farce': Drinking in the Alcohol-Prohibited Zone of Colonial Northern Nigeria," *International Journal of African Historical Studies* 31, no. 1 (1998), 23–51; H. A. Wyndham, "The Problem of the West African Liquor Traffic," *Journal of the Royal Institute of International Affairs* 9 (November 1930), 801–18; Willis, *Potent Brews*, 96–97; Willis, "Brussels Act and Conventions," 118–19; Lewis Harcourt, "The Crown Colonies and Protectorates and the Colonial Office," *Journal of the Society of Comparative Legislation*, n.s., 13, no. 1 (1912), 36.

84. Crafts et al., *Intoxicating Drinks*, 16–17.

CHAPTER 8. IDA WELLS AND OTHERS: RADICAL PROTEST
AND THE NETWORKS OF AMERICAN EXPANSION

1. Editorial, *Anti-Caste* 2 (March 1889), 2.

2. Ibid.

3. *Los Angeles Times*, 14 August 1924, p. A1.

4. Mary Garbutt to Caroline Severance, 15 September 1890, box 17, Caroline Severance Collection, 1875–1919, Huntington Library ("heroic"), 29 December 1890 ("crushed"), 13 January 1912, 7 June 1911, "Peace Statue," "Brotherhood"; Mary Alderman Garbutt, *Victories of Four Decades: A History of the*

Woman's Christian Temperance Union of Southern California, 1883–1924 (Los Angeles, 1924), 105. See also Mary E. Garbutt to Elizabeth Boynton Harbert, 24 March 1912, box 4, Elizabeth Boynton Harbert Collection, Huntington Library.

5. "An Outline for Study of Public Questions, Prepared by the International Reform Bureau, Washington, D.C.," in Crafts, *Patriotic Studies*, 12. The *Union Signal*'s corresponding editor similarly urged repeal of the restrictive immigration laws for the sake of the missionaries in China and the "equality of which we boast." *Union Signal*, 3 April 1902, p. 1.

6. Crafts, *Primer*, 36.

7. For extensive coverage, see Tyrrell, *Woman's World*, chap. 9.

8. E.g., see the reports of Impey's 1892 tour, *Anti-Caste* 5 (October 1892), 1.

9. "Letters from Our Sugar Colonies, No. 1—British Guiana," *Anti-Caste* 3 (June 1890), 1–2; editorial, p. 3.

10. *Anti-Caste* 3 (July/August 1890), 1.

11. Quoted in Vron Ware, *Beyond the Pale: White Women, Racism and History* (London, 1992), 188; editorial, *Anti-Caste* 3 (June 1890), 3.

12. *Anti-Caste* 7 (March 1895), 2.

13. Caroline Bressey, "A Strange and Bitter Crop: Ida B. Wells' Anti-Lynching Tours, Britain 1893 and 1894," *Centre for Capital Punishment Studies: Occasional Papers* 1 (December 2003), 8–28; Caroline L. Karcher, "Ida B. Wells and Her Allies against Lynching: A Transnational Perspective," *Comparative American Studies* 3, no. 2 (2005), 131–51.

14. See Impey's account, *Anti-Caste* 7 (March 1895), 1.

15. On these networks and changes within them over time, see Sandra Stanley Holton, "Segregation, Racism and White Women Reformers: A Transnational Analysis, 1840–1912," *Women's History Review* 10 (2001), 1, 5–25.

16. Patricia A. Schechter, *Ida Wells-Barnett and American Reform, 1880–1930* (Chapel Hill, 2001), 93.

17. Sarah Silkey, "Redirecting the Tide of White Imperialism: The Impact of Ida B. Wells's Transatlantic Antilynching Campaign on British Conceptions of American Race Relations," in Angela Boswell and Judith N. McArthur, eds., *Women Shaping the South: Creating and Confronting Change* (Columbia, MO, 2006), 97–119.

18. Jacqueline Jones Royster, ed., *Southern Horrors and Other Writings: The Anti-Lynching Campaign of Ida B. Wells, 1892–1900* (Boston, 1997), 36.

19. Ibid.; Alfreda M. Duster, ed., *Crusade for Justice: The Autobiography of Ida B. Wells* (Chicago, 1970), 183 (quote); Silkey, "Redirecting the Tide," 112.

20. Ida B. Wells, *A Red Record* ... (Chicago [1895], reprinted as "A Red Record," in Royster, *Southern Horrors*, 154.

21. Royster, *Southern Horrors*, 140; Ida B. Wells, "Mr. Moody and Miss Willard," *Fraternity*, May 1894, 16–17, scrapbook 69, reel 41, Woman's Christian Temperance Union Series, Temperance and Prohibition Papers, microfilm, MHC-OHS; Duster, *Crusade for Justice*, 111–12.

22. Wells, "Red Record," 155.

23. "The Race Problem: Miss Willard on the Political Puzzle of the South," *New York Voice*, 23 October 1890, p. 8, quoted in Wells, "Red Record," 142 (first quote); ibid. (last quote); Wells, "Mr. Moody and Miss Willard."

24. Bordin, *Frances Willard: A Biography*, 216.

25. *Chicago Inter-Ocean*, 9 April 1894, p. 8, reprinted in Duster, *Crusade for Justice*, 137 ("Assault"), 71 ("victims").

26. Gail Bederman, *Manliness and Civilization: A Cultural History of Gender and Race in the United States, 1880–1917* (Chicago, 1995), 66.

27. Quoted in *Fraternity*, 58, in scrapbook 13, reel 32, WCTU Series.

28. "Miss Balgarnie, the *Daily News* & the B.W.T.A.," *Anti-Caste* 7 (June–July 1895), 6.

29. Ian Tyrrell, "Transatlantic Progressivism in Women's Temperance and Suffrage," in David Gutzke, ed., *Britain and Transnational Progressivism* (Basingstoke, Eng., 2008), 137–38.

30. *Chicago Daily Tribune*, 13 December 1895, p. 7; *The Nursing Record and Hospital World*, 15 June 1895, pp. 428–29; Lilian Lewis Shiman, "Balgarnie, Florence (1856–1928)," *Oxford Dictionary of National Biography*, http://www .oxforddnb.com/view/article/55095 (accessed 25 June 2007); Florence Balgarnie, *A Plea for the Appointment of Police Matrons at Police Stations* (London, 1894).

31. *Leeds Mercury*, [22] March 1895; see also *Indian Messenger* (Calcutta), 10 November 1895, in scrapbook 13, reel 32, WCTU Series.

32. *Lady Henry Somerset's Statement Concerning Accusations of Miss Florence Balgarnie, June 1895–May 1896*, 6–7, in scrapbook 13, reel 32, WCTU Series.

33. Gail Bederman, "'Civilization,' the Decline of Middle-Class Manliness, and Ida B. Wells's Antilynching Campaign (1892–94)," *Radical History Review*, no. 52 (1992), 20–21.

34. Quoted in Wells, "Red Record," 136.

35. *New York Times*, 11 December 1894, p. 6.

36. *The Times*, 9 November 1894, p. 15.

37. *The Times*, 20 December 1895, p. 4.

38. Bederman, "Decline of Middle-Class Manliness," 21 (quote); *The Times*, 20 December 1895, p. 4.

39. C. Vann Woodward, *Origins of the New South: 1877–1913* (Baton Rouge, 1951), 351.

40. Bederman, "Decline of Middle-Class Manliness," 21; *New York Times*, 2 August 1894, p. 4 (quote).

41. *New York Times*, 27 July 1894, p. 4.

42. Ibid.; *New York Times*, 2 August 1894, p. 4.

43. *New York Times*, 4 September 1894, p. 1.

44. *New York Times*, 27 July 1894, p. 4.

45. *New York Times*, 1 August 1895, p. 14.

46. (Edinburgh) *Evening Despatch*, 15 July [1896] and 3 August 1896 in scrapbook 13, reel 32, WCTU Series.

47. Ware, *Beyond the Pale*, 190–92; Duster, *Crusade for Justice*, 105; Holton, "Segregation," 5–25.

48. Holton, "Segregation," 16–17.

49. Robert E. Frykenberg, ed., *Pandita Ramabai's America: Conditions of Life in the United States* (Grand Rapids, MI, 2003); Kosambi, *Pandita Ramabai's American Encounter*; Ramabai, *The High-Caste Hindu Woman*.

50. Kosambi, *Pandita Ramabai's American Encounter*, 23.

51. On Ramabai's career, see Frykenberg, *Pandita Ramabai's America*; Sengupta, *Pandita Ramabai Saraswati*, 154, 155, 162–63; Chakravarti, *Rewriting History*; Burton, *At the Heart of the Empire*, 89, 93, 105.

52. Dunch, "Beyond Cultural Imperialism," 322.

53. Frykenberg, *Pandita Ramabai's America*, x, 24; Burton, *At the Heart of the Empire*, 104–5.

54. Frykenberg, *Pandita Ramabai's America*, 273.

55. Kosambi, "Returning the American Gaze," 38; Sengupta, *Pandita Ramabai Saraswati*, 166, 24 (last quote).

56. Clymer, "Religion and American Imperialism," 29–50; Clymer, *American Protestant Missionaries in the Philippines, 1898–1916: An Inquiry into the American Colonial Mentality* (Urbana, IL, 1986); Clymer, "The Methodist Response to Philippine Nationalism, 1899–1916," *Church History* 47 (December 1978), 421–33.

57. "A Strange Item from Manila," *Washington Post*, 30 January 1905. "We get from Manila, P.I., by way of Springfield, Mass., and through the columns of the *Republican* of the latter city, chief organ of the anti-imperialists, a bit of scurrility credited—or shall we say debited?—to Rev. Mercer Johnston."

58. "Rector in Newark Assails His Vestry," *New York Times*, 15 May 1916, p. 3; Jeremy Bonner, "'An Account of My Stewardship': Mercer Green Johnston, the Episcopal Church, and the Social Gospel in Newark, New Jersey, 1912–1916," *Anglican and Episcopal History* 72 (September 2003), 298–321.

59. Diary, 8 April 1913, 17 April 1913, and 20 May 1913, box 1, Johnston Papers.

60. Ibid., 22 April 1913.

61. Lin Shao-Yang, *A Chinese Appeal to Christendom Concerning Christian Missions* (New York, 1911); "A Chinaman on Missionaries," *New York Times*, 2 July 1911, BR417; Arthur Judson Brown, *New Forces in Old China: An Inevitable Awakening* (London, 1904); Diary, 23 April, 28 September, and 29–30 September, 1913; on 15 October 1913, Johnston attended a reception organized by Bishop Lines and the Woman's Auxiliary of Newark to "missionary workers"; on 23 October 1913 he attended the Lake Mohonk conference and "met many old acquaintances from Philippine Islands." Diaries, box 1, Johnston Papers.

62. *Good Neighborship* 1, no. 2 (August 1927), 4 (quote); 1, no. 1 (July 1927), 3.

63. Mercer Johnston, *A Covenant with Death, an Agreement with Hell: A Sermon Preached in the Cathedral of St Mary and St John, Manila, P.I., Sunday, February 23, 1908* (n.p., n d.), 5.

64. Henry Ide to Mercer Johnston, 15 May 1906, regarding Johnston to Ide, 9 May 1906, box 38, Johnston Papers.

65. Mercer Johnston to James S. Johnston, 15 November 1907; see also James S. Johnston to Mercer Johnston, 10 April 1908, both in box 17, Johnston Papers.

66. Mercer Johnston, *Plain American Talk in the Philippines* (Manila, 1907), 195.

67. Mercer Johnston, "The Devil's Auction: An Address Delivered at the Monument of Major General Lawton in the Valley of the San Mariquina River, near San Mateo, Memorial Day, 1906," in *Plain American Talk*, 130.

68. Mercer Johnston, "Loyalty to Lawton," in Johnston, *Plain American Talk*, 25–26.

69. Johnston, *Covenant*, 10.

70. Ibid., 4.

71. Ibid., 3, 6 (last quote).

72. Ibid., 5–6.

73. Ibid., 9; Mercer Johnston to James S. Johnston, 17 August 1908, folder June–August 1908, box 17, Johnston Papers (last quote).

74. Mercer Johnston to James S. Johnston, 13 August 1908, folder June–August 1908, box 17, Johnston Papers.

75. *New York Times*, 15 May 1916, p. 3.

76. Bonner, "'Account of My Stewardship'"; "The United Front of the Workers against the United Front of the Bosses," *Textile Strike Bulletin* 1, no. 14 (28 May 1926), http://www.weisbord.org/BulletinsTwo.htm (accessed 1 August 2007); *New York Times*, 16 May 1916, p. 24; Mercer Johnston, *Patriotism and Radicalism* (Boston, 1917); *Biblical World* 51 (May 1918), 310.

77. Report Letter No. 1, 15 November 1896; and "First Impressions of India," Report Letter No. 3, March 1897, both in folder Report Letters, 1896–1898, India, Eddy, G. Sherwood, Report Letters, 1896–1903, National Committee, 1891–1926, Y-57-1, KFYMCAA; Rick L. Nutt, *The Whole Gospel for the Whole World: Sherwood Eddy and the American Protestant Mission* (Macon, GA, 1997).

78. *Time*, 23 February 1925.

79. Hopkins, *Mott*, 532, 622; Sherwood Eddy, *A Pilgrimage of Ideas, or the Re-Education of Sherwood Eddy* (New York, 1934).

80. Report Letters for 1901, e.g., "A Hindu Festival," Report Letter No. 25, September 1901, India, Eddy, G. Sherwood, Y-57-1, KFYMCAA.

81. Report Letters for May 1902, September 1902; "A Great Opportunity," Report Letter No. 28, July 1902, India, Eddy, G. Sherwood, Y-57-1, KFYMCAA.

82. "The national consciousness is awakening," Report Letter No. 32 [early 1903], "Lecturing to Educated Hindus," India, Eddy, G. Sherwood, Y-57-1, KFYMCAA.

83. Sherwood Eddy, "First Impressions of the Philippines," 10 April 1911, in Correspondence 1910–1911, in Philippines Correspondence and Reports, box 1, KFYMCAA.

84. Report Letter No. 6, n.d., India Correspondence and Reports n.d. 1892–1912, Y-57-1, KFYMCAA.

85. Eddy, *The New Era in Asia*, 150.

86. Sherwood Eddy, "Famine Stricken India," typescript [1919], folder 63, box 3, George Sherwood Eddy Papers, YDSL. For Eddy and the Social Gospel, see also Phillips, *A Kingdom on Earth*.

87. Nutt, *Whole Gospel*, 96–98; Sherwood Eddy, "Famine Stricken India," *Rural Manhood*, June 1919, n.p., folder 138, box 7, Eddy Papers (quote).

88. Eddy, *New Era in Asia*, 150; "Amazing Renaissance Is Now Sweeping All Asia," *New York Times*, 23 November 1913, SM14.

89. Eddy, *New Era in Asia*, 154, 158.

90. Sherwood Eddy, "Gandhi: An Interpretation," *Christian Century*, 19 April 1923, p. 490.

91. Sherwood Eddy, "Why Missions?" *The World Tomorrow*, January 1928, p. 20, in folder 107, box 6, Eddy Papers.

92. Nutt, *Whole Gospel*, 211.

93. Sherwood Eddy to Joseph Stalin, 29 July 1932, folder 27, box 2, Eddy Papers.

94. Eddy, "Why Missions?" 18.

95. Regarding one visit to Russia with a party of twenty-four, Eddy wrote: "We unsparingly condemned the glaring evils of their system for a dictatorship," their "atheism," and "world revolution by violence." Eddy, "Sherwood Eddy & Free Speech," folder 107, box 6, Eddy Papers.

96. Hopkins, *Mott*, 621–22; John Mott telegram, 9 January 1928, folder 107, box 6, Eddy Papers.

97. Mott telegram, 9 January 1928.

98. Katherine Mayo, *Mother India* (London, 1927); Eddy, "Why Missions?" 20 (quote); Liz Wilson, "Who Is Authorized to Speak? Katherine Mayo and the Politics of Imperial Feminism in British India," *Journal of Indian Philosophy* 25, no. 2 (April 1997), 139–51; Sinha, *Specters of Mother India*.

99. Eddy, "Why Missions?" 20.

100. Sinha, *Specters of Mother India*, 130–36; Tyrrell, *Woman's World*, 165.

101. David H. Anthony III, "Max Yergan in South Africa: From Evangelical Pan-Africanist to Revolutionary Socialist," *African Studies Review* 34 (September 1991), 27.

102. Garrett, *Social Reformers*, 78.

103. Ibid., 79 (quote), 81.

104. Rosenberg, *Spreading the American Dream*, 8, 13, 28.

105. Eddy, *New Era in Asia*, 17.

106. Garrett, *Social Reformers*, 173.

107. *Chicago Daily Tribune*, 28 October 1899, p. 2.

CHAPTER 9. STATES OF FAITH: MISSIONS AND MORALITY IN GOVERNMENT

1. *New York Times*, 28 April 1911, p. 3.

2. Ibid., 17 May 1912, p. 9.

3. Edgar Albert Hornig, "The Religious Issue in the Taft-Bryan Election of 1908," *Proceedings of the American Philosophical Society* 105, no. 6 (15 December 1961), 530–37.

4. The missionaries were, Taft proclaimed in 1913, "the outposts of civilization in all that sea of paganism, and they are having upon China a profound effect." William Howard Taft, *The World-wide Influence of the Y.M.C.A. Address by Hon. William Howard Taft Delivered at the Bedford Branch of the Young Men's Christian Association in Brooklyn, N.Y., on Sunday, December 21, 1913* (Brooklyn, NY, 1913), 23 (quote); Taft to John Mott, 31 December 1906, regarding the "great and practical and non-sectarian good accomplished by this Asso-

ciation," folder 1586, box 90, Mott Papers; *New York Times*, 22 April 1908, p. 5, and 4 March 1914, p. 7.

5. "Taft Talks Peace to Endeavorers; Says There Is No Doubt That Anglo-American Arbitration Treaty Will Be Signed," *New York Times*, 8 July 1911, p. 2.

6. Quoted in Richard Carwardine, *Lincoln: A Life of Purpose and Power* (New York, 2006), 277.

7. "America Leads in Giving," *New York Times*, 16 January 1914, p. 14; Baldwin, *Foreign Missions*, 240–41, 243 (second quote), 260; James S. Dennis, *Centennial Survey of Foreign Missions: A Statistical Supplement to Christian Missions and Social Progress, being a Conspectus of the Achievements and Results of Evangelical Missions in All Lands at the Close of the Nineteenth Century* (New York, 1902).

8. *New York Times*, 5 June 1894, p. 9.

9. Nye, *Soft Power*.

10. *New York Times*, 4 March 1914, p. 7.

11. Reed, *Missionary Mind*, 100.

12. R. N. Leslie Jr., "Christianity and the Evangelist for Sea Power: The Religion of A. T. Mahan," in John B. Hattendorf, ed., *The Influence of History on Mahan: The Proceedings of a Conference Marking the Centenary of Alfred Thayer Mahan's "The Influence of Sea Power Upon History, 1660–1783"* (Newport, RI, 1991), 138 (quote); Brian Stanley, "Church, State, and the Hierarchy of 'Civilization': The Making of the 'Missions and Government' Conference, Edinburgh, 1910," in Andrew Porter, ed., *The Imperial Horizons of British Protestant Missions, 1880–1914* (Grand Rapids, MI, 2003), 61.

13. "An Episcopal Diocese in the Philippines," *New York Times*, 28 March 1901, p. 8.

14. Joseph H. Oldham to Rev. George Robson, 9 April 1909, folder 3374, box 214, Mott Papers; Stanley, "Church, State, and the Hierarchy of 'Civilization,'" 62 (quote).

15. Alfred T. Mahan, *The Harvest Within: Thoughts on the Life of the Christian* (London, 1909), 75.

16. Alfred T. Mahan, "The Place of Force in International Relations," *North American Review* 195 (1 January 1912), 39.

17. Ibid., 38.

18. Mahan, *Harvest Within*, 120.

19. Stanley, "Church, State, and the Hierarchy of 'Civilization,'" 62 (quote); Mahan, *Harvest Within*, 118–24.

20. Mahan, "The Place of Force in International Relations," 38, 39.

21. Ibid.

22. Elihu Root to John Mott, 19 May 1916, folder 1385, box 76, Mott Papers; Philip C. Jessup, *Elihu Root*, 2 vols. (New York, 1938), 1:39, 57, 59–60.

23. "Mr. Root Discusses International Problems," *New York Times*, 9 July 1916, BR276; Elihu Root, *Addresses on International Subjects: Collected and Edited by Robert Bacon and James Brown Scott* (Cambridge, MA, 1916). See also Richard W. Leopold, *Elihu Root and the Conservative Tradition* (Boston, 1954).

24. *New York Times*, 12 November 1909, p. 4.

25. Elihu Root to John Mott, 31 December 1906, folder 1385, box 76, Mott Papers.

26. Charles Brent to Bishop William Lawrence, 30 December 1908, folder Dec. 1908, box 8, Brent Papers.

27. Robert Bolt, "Theodore Roosevelt: Dutch Reformed Stalwart in the White House," *Theodore Roosevelt Association Journal* 17, no. 1 (1991), 12–14; Bolt, "The Religion of Theodore Roosevelt," *Theodore Roosevelt Association Journal* 19, no. 1 (1993), 4–7; Edward H. Cotton, *The Ideals of Theodore Roosevelt* (New York, 1923), 39–60, 137–76.

28. Eugene C. Bianchi, "The Ecumenical Thought of Bishop Charles Henry Brent," *Church History* 33 (December 1964), 448–61; *New York Times,* 28 July 1944, p. 13 (Talmage). Brent and Roosevelt met at the White House in 1904. Charles Brent to Gen. Henry T. Allen, 12 October 1904, box 6; Theodore Roosevelt to Brent, 3 October 1908, folder Oct. 1908, box 8, Brent Papers.

29. Charles Brent to Arthur C. Hall, "Epiphany," [6 January] 1908, folder January–February 1908, box 7, Brent Papers (quote); Richard Collin, *Theodore Roosevelt, Culture, Diplomacy, and Expansion: A New View of American Imperialism* (Baton Rouge, 1985).

30. Diary, 8 November 1904, box 1, Brent Papers.

31. Theodore Roosevelt to Charles Brent, 19 May 1905, folder January–December 1906, box 6, Brent Papers.

32. Theodore Roosevelt to Charles Brent, 19 October 1904, folder January–December 1904, box 6, Brent Papers.

33. Charles Brent to Elizabeth [Mrs. Whitelaw] Reid, 21 July 1905, folder May–December 1905, box 6, Brent Papers.

34. John W. Foster, *American Diplomacy in the Orient* (Boston and New York, 1903), 109, 411–12 (quote at 411).

35. H. Allen Griffith to Charles Brent, 3 May 1908, folder January–February 1908, box 7, Brent Papers.

36. *New York Times*, 7 May 1908, p. 7.

37. William Howard Taft to Charles Brent, 4 August 1908, folder August 1908, box 8, Brent Papers.

38. Theodore Roosevelt to Charles Brent, 29 June 1908, folder June 1908, box 7, Brent Papers.

39. Charles Brent to William Howard Taft, 8 August 1908, folder August 1908, box 8, Brent Papers.

40. Roosevelt to Brent, 29 June 1908.

41. Charles Brent to Arthur C. Hall, 20 July 1912, folder July–December 1912, box 10, Brent Papers.

42. Charles Brent to J. T. Addison, 3 February 1913, folder January–June 1913, box 10, Brent Papers.

43. Charles Brent to W. Cameron Forbes, 10 November 1916, box 13, Brent Papers. Brent claimed that "President Wilson had debauched the United States." Quoted in Anson Phelps Stokes to Brent, 13 November 1916, ibid.

44. Baldwin, *Foreign Missions*, 190–91; Samuel H. Chester, *An Administrative History of the Foreign Work of the Presbyterian Church in the United States* (Austin, TX, 1928), 9–10.

45. Hopkins, *Mott,* 74. See also Hopkins, *History of the Y.M.C.A. in North America.*

46. Woodrow Wilson to John Mott, 1 May 1908, box 100, folder 1760, Mott Papers.

47. John Mott to Woodrow Wilson, 5 May 1908, box 100, folder 1760, Mott Papers.

48. Woodrow Wilson to John Mott, 7 May 1914, box 100, folder 1761, Mott Papers.

49. "Religion and Patriotism," in Arthur S. Link, ed., *The Papers of Woodrow Wilson,* vol. 12, *1900–1902* (Princeton, NJ, 1972), 474–78, quote at 476; "Conference at Northfield," *New York Times,* 15 June 1902, p. 5; "Student Conference Ends," *New York Times,* 7 July 1902, p. 2.

50. Wilson to Mott, 1 November 1905 (quote), Mott to Wilson, 20 November 1905, folder 1760, box 100, Mott Papers; Arthur S. Link, ed., *The Papers of Woodrow Wilson,* vol. 16, *1905–1907* (Princeton, NJ, 1973); see also Arthur S. Link, ed., *The Papers of Woodrow Wilson,* vol. 17, *1907–08* (Princeton, NJ, 1974), 621–22; *New York Times,* 20 November 1905, p. 5.

51. Wilson to Mott, 1 November 1905; Mott to Wilson, 20 November 1905; Link, *Papers of Woodrow Wilson,* 16:230 (quote); *New York Times,* 20 November 1905, p. 5.

52. "An Address in Nashville on Behalf of the Y.M.C.A." [24 February 1912], Arthur S. Link, ed., *The Papers of Woodrow Wilson,* vol. 24, *1912* (Princeton, NJ, 1977), 208.

53. *New York Times,* 20 November 1905, p. 5; Wilson to Mott, 1 November 1905; Mott to Wilson, 20 November 1905 and 25 January 1910, folder 1760, box 100, Mott Papers; Link, *Papers of Woodrow Wilson,* 16:230.

54. Wilson to Mott, 25 January 1910; Mott to Wilson, 21 January 1910, folder 1760, box 100, Mott Papers.

55. "An Address in Nashville on Behalf of the Y.M.C.A."

56. John Mott to Cleveland H. Dodge, [1] March 1913, in Arthur S. Link, ed., *The Papers of Woodrow Wilson,* vol. 27, *1913* (Princeton, NJ, 1978), 145.

57. Michael V. Metallo, "American Missionaries, Sun Yat-sen, and the Chinese Revolution," *Pacific Historical Review* 47 (May 1978), 274. See also Jerry Israel, "For God, for China and for Yale: The Open Door in Action," *American Historical Review* 75 (February 1970), 796–807.

58. *New York Times,* 23 March 1913, p. 2.

59. Hopkins, *Mott,* 399.

60. Woodrow Wilson to John Mott, 24 February 1913, folder 1760, box 100, Mott Papers.

61. Woodrow Wilson to John Mott, undated [1913], folder 1760, box 100, Mott Papers. See also Wilson to Mott, 21 March 1913, ibid.

62. *New York Times,* 20 March 1913, p. 1; "President Hopes J. R. Mott Will Take China Post," *Christian Science Monitor,* 27 March 1913; cable, Rev. Robert Gailey et al. (Peking) to John Mott (Tokyo), 9 April 1913, folder 1760, box 100, Mott Papers.

63. John Mott to Woodrow Wilson, 1 April 1913, folder 1760, box 100, Mott Papers.

64. Metallo, "American Missionaries," 275; Woodrow Wilson to Cleveland H. Dodge, 7 April 1913, in Link, *Papers of Woodrow Wilson*, 27:263.

65. Charles Brent to Rev. A. E. Frost (formerly Diocese of Riverina, Australia), 22 November 1916, and attachment, 10 September 1916, folder November 1916, box 13, Brent Papers.

66. Newspaper clipping, 31 December 1916, scrapbook, p. 45, box 43, Brent Papers; "A Voice from America," *London Evening News*, 13 February 1917.

67. Charles Brent to Constance B. Holt, 9 February 1917; see also Brent to Private W. B. Wallie Smith (Canadian Expeditionary Force), 9 February 1917, both in folder February 1917, box 13, Brent Papers.

68. *London Daily Telegraph*, 21 April 1917, in scrapbook, p. 48, box 43, Brent Papers.

69. Ibid., 41–42; E. C. Carter, quoted from Carter to Charles Brent, 19 April 1917, box 13, Brent Papers.

70. Clipping from *Boston Herald*, n.d., in scrapbook, p. 35, box 43, Brent Papers.

71. *Buffalo Express*, 7 February 1919, in scrapbook, p. 52, box 43, Brent Papers.

72. Ibid.

73. John Mott to Woodrow Wilson, 30 May 1914, folder 1761, box 100, Mott Papers.

74. J. M. Groves to John Mott, 20 March 1914, regarding a presidential message that would give "significance" to the ceremonies for the dedication of the Manila "Filipino YMCA" building; Mott to Woodrow Wilson, 23 June 1914; Wilson to Groves, 26 June 1914, hoping "that God will bless its work in every respect." All in folder 1761, box 100, Mott Papers.

75. Joseph Tumulty to John Mott, 11 October 1913; Tumulty to Mott, 2 September and 1 December 1914; Woodrow Wilson to Ambassadors, Ministers, and Consular Agents, 14 October 1913, all in folder 1761, box 100, Mott Papers.

76. "Ethics for an International Policeman," *Biblical World* 48 (July 1916), 2.

77. Woodrow Wilson to "Sir" [Mott and other recipients], 31 August 1916, folder 1761, box 100, Mott Papers.

78. Arthur S. Link, *Woodrow Wilson and the Progressive Era* (New York, 1954), 142–43.

79. Joseph Tumulty to Woodrow Wilson, c. 25 August 1916, with Rev. Father E. J. Flannery to Tumulty, 24 August 1916, in Arthur S. Link, ed., *The Papers of Woodrow Wilson*, vol. 38, *August 7–November 19, 1916* (Princeton, NJ, 1982), 83.

80. "Ethics for an International Policeman," 2 (quotes); *New York Times*, 12 September 1916, in Link, *The Papers of Woodrow Wilson*, 38:169.

81. Donald E. Davis and Eugene Trani, "The American YMCA and the Russian Revolution," *Slavic Review* 33 (September 1974), 469–91; "Elihu Root Accepts Mission to Russia," *New York Times*, 27 April 1917, p. 3; "Root Has Faith Russia Will Stand," *New York Times*, 5 August 1917, p. 1; "The Special Diplomatic Mission of the United States to the Provisional Government of Russia," *American Journal of International Law* 11 (October 1917), 757–62.

82. "Millions Raised for Y.M.C.A. War Relief Work," *New York Times*, 17 June 1917, SM7.

83. The work was partly funded from the War Emergency Fund. John Mott to George Creel, 8 February 1918, in Arthur S. Link, ed., *The Papers of Woodrow Wilson,* vol. 46, *January 1–March 12, 1918* (Princeton, NJ, 1984), 479.

84. "Address of John R. Mott, Member of the Special Mission of the United States of America to Russia at the Great Sobor of the Russian Orthodox Church, Moscow, June 19th, 1917," folder 2550, box 153, Mott Papers (quote). On Elihu Root's view of the mission, see *What We Are Fighting For: Speeches of the President on Flag Day, of Elihu Root to Russia, and Message to the Russian People from the American Rights League* (Hartford, CT, [1917]). For Mott, "Addresses of John R. Mott," in Elihu Root, *America's Message to the Russian People: Addresses by the Members of the Special Diplomatic Mission of the United States to Russia in the Year 1917* (Boston, 1918), 105–16.

85. John Mott to Cleveland H. Dodge, 24 July 1917, folder 1762, box 100, Mott Papers.

86. Arthur S. Link, *The Higher Realism of Woodrow Wilson and Other Essays* (Nashville, 1971), 3–20, 76–81.

87. Enclosure, Woodrow Wilson to John Mott, with George Creel to Wilson, 9 November 1917, in Arthur S. Link, ed., *The Papers of Woodrow Wilson,* vol. 44, *August 21–November 10, 1917* (Princeton, NJ, 1983), 551.

88. George Creel to Woodrow Wilson, 27 February 1918, with enclosure, Mott to Creel, 8 February 1918, in Link, *The Papers of Woodrow Wilson,* 46:479.

89. *New York Times*, 17 June 1917, SM7.

90. Harold Ickes to Henry Allen, 29 June 1920, p. 6, with E. C. Carter to William Sloane, vol. 8, Duplicate, folder 4, 1918–20, Armed Services: World War I, box 83, Y.USA.4-1, KFYMCAA.

91. "Report of Conference of Workers held at Peronne on 23/24 July, 1919," China: Chinese Laborers in France (2) Conference of Workers, Report 1919, 7, 3, 9 (quote), box 204, Y-21-5, KFYMCAA; on Ewing, see Charles Ewing and Bessie Ewing, *Death Throes of a Dynasty: Letters and Diaries of Charles and Bessie Ewing, Missionaries to China,* ed. E. G. Ruoff (Kent, OH, 1990).

92. Rev. E. W. Burt, quoted in "Report of Conference of Workers held at Peronne on 23/24 July, 1919," pp. 7, 31.

93. E. C. Carter to William Sloane (chairman, National War Work Council, YMCA), 18 October 1920, vol. 1, 1918–20, folder 1, Armed Services: World War I, box 77, Y.USA.4-1, KFYMCAA.

94. Charles R. Joy, "Analysis and Criticism of the Report of Major O. T. Kenan, Base Inspector, Base Section no. 4," Armed Services: World War I, box 83, Y.USA.4-1, KFYMCAA.

95. Ickes to Allen, 29 June 1920.

96. Calvin Coolidge, introduction to James L. Barton, *The Story of Near East Relief* (New York, 1930), viii, ix (quote).

97. Barton, *Near East Relief*, 10.

98. Ibid., xiii.

99. Ibid.; Herbert Hoover, *The Memoirs of Herbert Hoover: Years of Adventure, 1874–1920* (New York, 1961), 394 (quotes); Murray N. Rothbard,

"Hoover's 1919 Food Diplomacy in Retrospect," in L. Gelfand, ed., *Herbert Hoover: The Great War and Its Aftermath, 1914–1923* (Iowa City, 1979), 89–110; William C. Mullendore, *History of the United States Food Administration, 1917–1919* (Stanford, CA, 1941); Curti, *American Philanthropy*, 259–300.

100. Grabill, *Protestant Diplomacy and the Near East.*

101. Davis and Trani, "The American YMCA and the Russian Revolution," 470.

102. Ibid., 469 ("peak"); John Mott to Woodrow Wilson, 24 July 1918, folder 1763, box 100, Mott Papers (second quote); David S. Foglesong, *America's Secret War against Bolshevism: U.S. Intervention in the Russian Civil War, 1917–1920* (Chapel Hill, 1995), 158–63.

103. Davis and Trani, "The American YMCA and the Russian Revolution," 470, 484.

CHAPTER 10. TO MAKE A DRY WORLD:
THE NEW WORLD ORDER OF PROHIBITION

1. Charles Clayton Morrison, editor of the *Christian Century*, proclaimed the Versailles Treaty "not redemptive and … not Christian." Quoted in James L. Lancaster, "The Protestant Churches and the Fight for Ratification of the Versailles Treaty," *Public Opinion Quarterly* 31 (Winter 1967–68), 612.

2. *Union Signal*, 19 September 1918, p. 1.

3. Howard Russell to Richmond Hobson, 17 January 1919, box 3, Richmond Pearson Hobson Papers, LC (hereafter Hobson Papers).

4. Quoted in Robert A. Hohner, *Prohibition and Politics: The Life of Bishop James Cannon Jr.* (Columbia, SC, 1999), 127–28.

5. *Union Signal*, 19 September 1918, p. 1.

6. Susan Brook, "The World League Against Alcoholism: The Attempt to Export an American Experience" (M.A. thesis, University of Western Ontario, 1972), 39; "Convention Relating to the Liquor Traffic in Africa and Protocol," *American Journal of International Law*, Supplement: Official Documents 15 (October 1921), 322–28.

7. Brook, "World League Against Alcoholism," 45.

8. David M. Fahey, "Jones, Leifchild Stratten, Baron Rhayader (1862–1939)," *Oxford Dictionary of National Biography*, http://www.oxforddnb.com/view/article/39155 (accessed 9 May 2008).

9. Randall Jimerson, Francis X. Blouin, and Charles A. Isetts, eds., *Guide to the Microfilm Edition of Temperance and Prohibition Papers* (Ann Arbor, 1977), 205–7; Brook, "World League Against Alcoholism," 39–40, 60, 65; Robert Hercod, "Alcoholism as an International Problem," *British Journal of Inebriety* 23 (January 1926), 107–26; *New York Times*, 7 June 1919, p. 3. On Vandervelde's temperance interests, see Janet Polasky, *The Democratic Socialism of Emile Vandervelde: Between Reform and Revolution* (New York, 1995), 5, 165, 169, 171.

10. *SEAP*, 6:2911; Jimerson, Blouin, and Isetts, *Guide to the Microfilm Edition*, 206.

11. *Union Signal,* 19 September 1918, p. 1, quoting from Lillian Stevens's proclamation of 10 September 1911.

12. Richmond Hobson to Anna Gordon, 2 September 1915, box 3, Hobson Papers (quote); "Drink and Preparedness: An Interview with Richmond Hobson," *Christian Herald,* 3 May 1916, p. 556. See also Andrew Sinclair, *Prohibition: The Era of Excess* (Boston, 1962), 53.

13. Patricia Prestwich, *Drink and the Politics of Social Reform: Antialcoholism in France since 1870* (Palo Alto, CA, 1988), 128.

14. Arthur Newsholme, "Some International Aspects of Alcoholism with Special Reference to Prohibition in America," *British Journal of Inebriety* 19 (January 1922), 99.

15. *SEAP,* 4:2026–27.

16. Keith Dunstan, *Wowsers* (1968; Sydney, 1974), 109–32; Walter Phillips, "'Six O'clock Swill': The Introduction of Early Closing of Hotel Bars in Australia," *Historical Studies,* no. 75 (October 1980), 250–66.

17. Ella Boole, "Americanization the Imperative Need of the Hour," *Union Signal,* 6 June 1918, p. 5.

18. *Union Signal,* 5 December 1925, p. 6.

19. Cf. Lawrence Spinelli, *Dry Diplomacy: The United States, Great Britain, and Prohibition* (Wilmington, DE, 1989), 155.

20. *Union Signal,* 5 December 1925, p. 6.

21. Ibid. (quote); Crafts et al., *Intoxicating Drinks,* 225–26; Tyrrell, *Woman's World,* chap. 7.

22. In one historian's view, the WLAA was "little more than an office in London with a single representative." Another dismissed the World League as characterized by "American domination" and not "genuinely international." K. Austin Kerr, *Organized for Prohibition: A New History of the Anti-Saloon League* (New Haven, 1985), 220, 281, 246 (first quote); Brook, "World League Against Alcoholism," 59, 61 (last two quotes).

23. *Union Signal,* 23 November 1922, p. 3 (quote); Hohner, *Prohibition and Politics,* 154.

24. Treasurer's Report for the Year Ended 31st May 1918, World's WCTU Files, Frances Willard Memorial Library, Evanston, IL.

25. Ernest H. Cherrington, *The Evolution of Prohibition in the United States* (Westerville, OH, 1920), 367.

26. Julia Deane to Chester Rowell, 12 December 1922, Chester Harvey Rowell Correspondence, Bancroft Library, University of California, Berkeley; Henry Beach Carre to Anti-Saloon League of America, Report, April 1918 to December 1919, folder 39, reel 19, World League Against Alcoholism Series, Temperance and Prohibition Papers, microfilm, MHC-OHS (hereafter WLAA Series).

27. *New York Times,* 27 November 1920, p. 24; "Anti-Saloon League Speakers in Great Britain Enthusiastically Received," clipping, 26 April 1919, folder 39, reel 19, WLAA Series; *SEAP,* 3:1215; Woolley died in Spain during his tour. *Union Signal,* 24–31 August 1922, 9.

28. See generally folder 40, reel 19, WLAA Series; "Fact and Fiction," *Alliance News and Temperance Reformer,* May 1920, 76–77; *The Times,* 17 April 1920, p. 15.

29. *New York Times,* 27 November 1920, p. 24; "Anti-Saloon League Speakers in Great Britain Enthusiastically Received" (quote).

30. David Ostlund, "On the Dry Campaign in Sweden," press release, 27 September 1922, folder 71, reel 26, WLAA Series; *Hartford Courier,* 12 July 1922, ibid.; *Union Signal,* 7 December 1922, p. 3, 24–31 August 1922, p. 4.

31. Jack S. Blocker Jr., *Retreat from Reform: The Prohibition Movement in the United States, 1890–1913* (Westport, CT, 1976), 51, 71–72; Harry Gene Levine, "The Committee of Fifty and the Origins of Alcohol Control," *Journal of Drug Issues* 13 (Winter 1983), 95–116; Tyrrell, *Woman's World,* 257–63.

32. See, for example, William E. Johnson, *The Gothenburg System of Liquor Selling* (Chicago, 1903).

33. Henry Beach Carre to Executive Committee, Anti-Saloon League of America, 12 July 1919, folder 71, reel 26, WLAA Series.

34. *Union Signal,* 23 March 1916, p. 3, 16 April 1916, p. 3, 3 November 1916, p. 7.

35. "Noted American Drys Active in African Fight," *American Issue,* 24 June 1922 (quotes), and W. Chappell to Ernest Cherrington, 21 July 1922, folder 4, box 6, reel 26, WLAA Series; Richard L. Watson Jr., *Bishop Cannon's Own Story: Life as I Have Seen It* (Durham, NC, 1955), 224; Tyrrell, *Woman's World,* 86, 278.

36. *Union Signal,* 21 July 1921, p. 6.

37. Tarini Prasad Sinha, *"Pussyfoot" Johnson and His Campaign in Hindustan* (Madras, 1922).

38. William E. Johnson to Ernest H. Cherrington, 2 October 1920, folder 36, reel 22, WLAA Series.

39. Newspaper clipping, 6 August 1921, folder 36, reel 22, WLAA Series.

40. William E. Johnson to Ernest H. Cherrington, 2 October 1920, folder 36, reel 22, WLAA Series; "Johnson's Speaking Tour in India Subject of Great Interest in Empire," clipping, *American Issue,* 6 August 1921, in ibid.

41. Johnson to Cherrington, 2 October 1920; Sinha, *"Pussyfoot" Johnson.*

42. Sinha, *"Pussyfoot" Johnson,* 243–44; William E. Johnson to M. K. Gandhi, November 1921, cited in ibid., 205–6 (quote); *The Collected Works of Mahatma Gandhi* (Delhi, 1966), 21:508–9.

43. William E. Johnson, "India's Appeal to America," *American Issue,* 7 January 1922.

44. Sinha, *"Pussyfoot" Johnson,* 171–73, 193–95, 209–10.

45. Kenneth L. Roberts, *Why Europe Leaves Home* (1922; New York, 1977), 332. See, for heavy documentation of Johnson's British work, reel 19, WLAA Series.

46. *Union Signal,* 10–17 August 1921, p. 5.

47. W. J. Allison to Ernest H. Cherrington, 7 April 1920, folder 56, reel 25, WLAA Series.

48. *SEAP,* 6:2915.

49. *New York Times,* 27 August 1922, sec. 2, p. 5; "A Remarkable Interview: An Australian Who Was Convinced by Facts," *Grit,* 12 July 1923, p. 9; *Union Signal,* 10–17 August 1922, p. 5; *SEAP,* 6:2574.

50. *Union Signal,* 31 October 1925, p. 3.

51. Reported in ibid., 3 September 1925, p. 2.

52. "Guy Hayler: Veteran in the Cause," *White Ribbon Signal* (Sydney), 1 May 1935, p. 82, 12 June 1923, p. 4, 3 February 1928, p. 3; "World Prohibition Federation," *SEAP*, 6:2916 (quotes); David Fahey, "Temperance Internationalism: Guy Hayler and the World Prohibition Federation," *Social History of Alcohol and Drugs* 20 (Spring 2006), 247–75; "International Prohibition Confederation," *SEAP*, 3:1341–42.

53. Quoted in Fahey, "Temperance Internationalism," 261; Brook, "World League Against Alcoholism," 54.

54. "World-Wide Prohibition," *The Methodist* (Sydney, NSW), 8 March 1919.

55. "Alcoholism and the League of Nations," *White Ribbon Signal*, 12 July 1926, p. 2; Guy Hayler, "The New Europe and Prohibition," *Grit*, 27 December 1923, p. 10; on the World Prohibition Federation's international conferences, see *White Ribbon Signal*, 12 June 1923, p. 4; E. L. Hohenthal, "My Impressions of [the] Seventeenth International Anti-Alcohol Congress," *Grit*, 28 February 1924, p. 6; *Union Signal*, 21 October 1920, p. 6; Hercod, "Alcoholism as an International Problem," 107–26.

56. Fahey, "Temperance Internationalism," 264.

57. Prestwich, *Drink and the Politics of Social Reform*, 231.

58. Hercod, "Alcoholism as an International Problem," 107–26. On Légrain, see "Légrain, Paul-Maurice," *SEAP*, 4:1530; Patricia E. Prestwich, "Paul-Maurice Légrain (1860–1939)," *Addiction* 92 (October 1997), 1255–63.

59. *Union Signal*, 25 January 1923, p. 5, 7 December 1922, p. 10.

60. *Report of the Twenty-Third Convention of the Dominion Woman's Christian Temperance Union ...* ([Toronto], 1925), 62.

61. Erik Olssen, "Towards a New Society," in W. H. Oliver with B. R. Williams, eds., *The Oxford History of New Zealand* (Oxford, 1981), 263 (quote); *Union Signal*, 10–17 August 1922, p. 5.

62. "Swedish Women Give Big Dry Majority," newspaper clipping, 23 September 1922, folder 71, reel 26, WLAA Series; Ostlund, "On the Dry Campaign in Sweden."

63. Roberts, *Why Europe Leaves Home*, 353–54; *Glasgow Herald*, 4 November 1920; "Smoke Lifts off Scotia's Wet and Dry Battlefield," *Temperance Leader and League Journal*, 15 November 1920, folder 57, reel 25, WLAA Series; *Report of the Twenty-First Convention of the Dominion Woman's Christian Temperance Union ...* ([Toronto], 1920), 45; *Report of the Twenty-Second Convention of the Dominion Woman's Christian Temperance Union ...* ([Toronto], 1922), 75; and *Report of the Twenty-Third Convention*, 58.

64. *New York Times*, 2 December 1926, pp. 1, 3; *Report of the Twenty-Third Convention*, 58; "Ontario's Experiment: Shall We Follow Our Northern Neighbor's Example?" *Union Signal*, 18 April 1931, p. 6.

65. David Ostlund, "Iceland Losing Temporarily in Her Fight for Prohibition," circular, 28 April 1922; press release, 1 November 1933, both in folder 71, reel 26, WLAA Series; Greg Marquis, "'Brewers and Distillers Paradise': American Views of Canadian Alcohol Policies, 1919 to 1935," *Canadian Review of American Studies* 34, no. 2 (2004), 135–66.

66. Chester H. Rowell to Julia Deane, 22 December 1922, Chester Harvey Rowell Correspondence.

67. Célestin Cambiaire, *The Black Horse of the Apocalypse (Wine, Alcohol, and Civilization)* (Paris, 1932), 296–97; Ernest Cherrington, "Foreign Wet Influences in Our Politics," *Union Signal*, 1 September 1928, p. 9.

68. See, for example, James S. Roberts, "The Tavern and Politics in the German Labor Movement, c. 1870–1914," in Susanna Barrows and Robin Room, eds., *Drinking: Behavior and Belief in Modern History* (Berkeley, 1991), 98–111. On cafés, see Henry-Melchoir de Langle, *Le petit monde des cafés et débits parisiens au XIXe siècle* (Paris, 1990). For Britain, see Roberts, *Why Europe Leaves Home*, 278–82.

69. "How London Has Viewed Mr. 'Pussyfoot' Johnson," *New York Times*, 23 November 1919, p. 7.

70. Alexander Björkman and others to William Johnson, 6 January 1920, repr. in *American Issue*, 14 February 1920; Frederick A. McKenzie, *"Pussyfoot" Johnson: A Man among Men* (New York, 1920); Roberts, *Why Europe Leaves Home*, 303.

71. Roberts, *Why Europe Leaves Home*, 302.

72. Henry Beach Carre to Anti-Saloon League of America, Report, April 1918 to December 1919, folder 39, reel 19, WLAA Series.

73. Sinha, *"Pussyfoot" Johnson*, 73, 80.

74. *New York Times*, 30 December 1919, p. 2.

75. Frederick A. McKenzie, *The American Invaders* (1902; New York, 1976).

76. For Canada, see the *Canadian White Ribbon Tidings*, 1914–22; for Australia, *Grit* from 1907 to 1911, compared to 1926–30, shows this shift.

77. Cf. Clark, *Deliver Us from Evil*, 136, 139.

78. Ostlund, "Iceland Losing Temporarily"; press release, 1 November 1933, folder 71, reel 26, WLAA Series; *White Ribbon Signal*, 12 June 1929, p. 6; *SEAP*, 5:2031; *Union Signal*, 15 May 1926, p. 3.

79. Per Frånberg, "The Social and Political Significance of Two Swedish Restrictive Systems" (paper delivered at the International Conference on the Social History of Alcohol, Berkeley, CA, January 1984), 1; Ootlund, "On the Dry Campaign in Sweden"; *Time*, 27 August 1928; Svante Nycander, "Ivan Bratt: The Man Who Saved Sweden from Prohibition," *Addiction* 93 (January 1998), 17–25.

80. Sara Rowell Wright, "Canada's Struggles, Defeats, and Triumphs," *Union Signal*, 8 September 1928, p. 4; Clark, *Deliver Us from Evil*, 138; "Larger Liquor Flow from Canada Seen," *New York Times*, 12 November 1923, p. 19; *New York Times*, 2 December 1926, 1, p. 3; *Union Signal*, 30 June 1928, p. 4, and 29 September 1928, p. 3.

81. *Union Signal*, 15 February 1922, p. 4 (quote); K. Austin Kerr, "The Failure of Prohibition in New Zealand in 1925: A Research Note," *Social History of Alcohol Review*, no. 19 (Spring 1989), 14–16.

82. Ostlund, "On the Dry Campaign in Sweden," 3.

83. Roberts, *Why Europe Leaves Home*, 345–47; W. J. Allison to Ernest H. Cherrington, 7 April 1920, folder 56, reel 25, WLAA Series.

84. *Chicago Tribune*, quoted in *New York Times*, 27 September 1920, p. 15;

The Pioneer: The Official Organ of the Wesleyan Methodist Temperance and Social Welfare Department, no. 1 (June 1920), 92.

85. Quoted in Alison M. Parker, *Purifying America: Women, Cultural Reform, and Pro-Censorship Activism, 1873–1933* (Champaign, IL, 1997), 152.

86. Roger Openshaw, "'The Glare of Broadway': Some New Zealand Reactions to the Perceived Americanisation of Youth," *Australasian Journal of American Studies* 10 (July 1991), 50–51; *Union Signal*, 24 October 1925, p. 9 (quote); "Unclean Pictures," *Grit*, 2 July 1931, p. 7.

87. World League Against Alcoholism, *Proceedings of the International Congress, the World League Against Alcoholism, Winona Lake, Indiana, August 17–23, 1927* (Westerville, OH, 1927).

88. "Turkish Feminist a Delegate Here," *New York Times*, 16 August 1927, p. 28; "Report Dry Gains Abroad," *New York Times*, 21 August 1927, p. 6.

89. Wayne B. Wheeler, *How to Enforce National Prohibition* (n.p., 1927).

90. *New York Times*, 19 August 1927, p. 8. Methodist bishop Dr. F. H. Otto Melle of the German Federation against Alcoholism argued against Johnson, stating that local option, not prohibition, was the best strategy in Europe: "Expects World to Go Dry; Pussyfoot Johnson, at Winona Lake," *New York Times*, 24 August 1927, p. 11.

91. Quoted in Hohner, *Prohibition and Politics*, 158.

92. Kerr, *Organized for Prohibition*, 220 (quotes); "Wheeler, Wayne Bidwell," *SEAP*, 6:2833.

93. Hohner, *Prohibition and Politics*, 160–61.

94. "Sees World Turning to Prohibition," *New York Times*, 1 January 1930, p. 3.

CONCLUSION. THE JUDGMENTS OF HEAVEN:
CHANGE AND CONTINUITY IN MORAL REFORM

1. Braisted, *In This Generation*, 154.

2. Ibid. (first quote); Parker, *The Kingdom of Character*, 147, 168; Beahm, "Factors," 250 (second quote); Nathan D. Showalter, *The End of a Crusade: The Student Volunteer Movement for Foreign Missions and the Great War* (Lanham, MD, 1998).

3. Hogg, *Ecumenical Foundations*, 244–52; *Report of the International Missionary Council, Jerusalem, March 24–April 8, 1928*, 8 vols. (New York and London, 1928); for the women's missionary movement, see Hill, *The World Their Household*, 167.

4. Primer, *Protestants and American Business Methods*, 98–100.

5. Jeffrey A. Charles, *Service Clubs in American Society: Rotary, Kiwanis, and Lions* (Urbana, IL, 1993), 10, 124–40. On the British Soroptimists and other women's clubs, see James Hinton, *Women, Social Leadership, and the Second World War: Continuities of Class* (Oxford, 2002), 43–44.

6. Victoria de Grazia, *Irresistible Empire: America's Advance through Twentieth-Century Europe* (Cambridge, MA, 2005), 36–49; Brendan Goff, "The Heart-

land Abroad: The Rotary Club's Mission of Civic Internationalism, 1910–1950"
(Ph.D. diss., University of Michigan, 2008), chap. 1.

7. De Grazia, *Irresistable Empire*, 66.

8. Ironically, the Rockefeller-sponsored alternative had to adapt in the longer
run, too. Mary Brown Bullock, *An American Transplant: The Rockefeller Foundation and Peking Union Medical College* (Berkeley, 1982), 23, 134, 159.

9. *New York Times*, 19 September 1921, p. 14 (first quote); John S. Baick,
"Cracks in the Foundation: Frederick T. Gates, the Rockefeller Foundation, and
the China Medical Board," *Journal of the Gilded Age and Progressive Era* 3 (January 2004), 59–89, at 59.

10. *New York Times*, 19 September 1921, p. 14.

11. Warwick Anderson, *Colonial Pathologies: American Tropical Medicine,
Race, and Hygiene in the Philippines* (Durham, NC, 2006), chaps. 7, 8.

12. John Burnham, "New Perspectives on the Prohibition 'Experiment' of
the 1920's," *Journal of Social History* 2 (1968), 25–38; Jack S. Blocker Jr., "Did
Prohibition Really Work? Alcohol Prohibition as a Public Health Innovation,"
American Journal of Public Health 96 (February 2006), 233–43; Catherine Gilbert Murdock, *Domesticating Drink: Women, Men, and Alcohol in America,
1870–1940* (Baltimore, 1998), 118.

13. Beahm, "Factors," 234; Parker, *Kingdom of Character*, 168, 186; Braisted,
In This Generation, 154; Latourette, "Missionaries Abroad," 25 (quote); "Missionaries 'Add Prestige to Nation,'" *Boston Daily Globe*, 18 June 1922, 6.

14. Jun Xing, *Baptized in the Fire of Revolution*, 20.

15. Lian Xi, *Conversion of Missionaries*, 52.

16. Dana Robert, *American Women in Mission: A Social History of Their
Thought and Practice* (Macon, GA, 1997), 199.

17. Ruth Tucker, *From Jerusalem to Irian Jaya: A Biographical History of
Christian Missions*, rev. ed. (Grand Rapids, MI, 2004), 335–63.

18. Earl C. Kaylor Jr., "Lucy Whitehead McGill Waterbury Peabody," *NAW*,
2:37.

19. K. Austin Kerr, ed., *The Politics of Moral Behavior: Prohibition and Drug
Abuse* (Reading, MA, 1973), 97–102.

20. "Pasadena to Be Home of Movement," clipping from *Pasadena Star News*,
5 May 1922, folder 6, box 39, Hobson Papers.

21. Paper delivered at the Fifteenth International Congress against Alcoholism, held in Washington, DC, 21–26 September 1920, folder 5, box 41, Hobson
Papers.

22. Harvey Rosenfeld, *Richmond Pearson Hobson: Naval Hero of Magnolia
Grove* (Las Cruces, NM, 2001), 209.

23. Susan L. Speaker, "'The Struggle of Mankind against Its Deadliest Foe':
Themes of Counter-Subversion in Anti-Narcotic Campaigns, 1920–1940," *Jour-
nal of Social History* 34 (Spring 2001), 591–610, esp. 595; Michael Woodiwiss,
"Reform, Racism and Rackets: Drug and Alcohol Prohibition in the United
States," in Ross Coomber, ed., *The Control of Drugs and Drug Users: Reason or
Reaction* (Reading, Eng., 1998), 13–31 (quote at 21); Eric Schaefer, *Bold! Dar-
ing! Shocking! True! A History of Exploitation Films, 1919–1959* (Durham, NC,
1999), 221–22.

24. Richmond Hobson to Elizabeth Wright, 9 August 1929 [?], folder 8, box 71, Hobson Papers.

25. Rosenfeld, *Hobson*, 213.

26. Convention for Limiting the Manufacture and Regulating the Distribution of Narcotic Drugs, signed at Geneva on 13 July 1931; summary of the report, "Second Quinquennial Conference Held in Geneva, June 15–17, 1931," p. 2, folder 7, box 71, Hobson Papers; "Introduction to the Report on the Second Quinquennial World Conference on Narcotic Education Held in Geneva, Switzerland, June 15–17, 1931, by the Secretary-General," ibid.; "News from the Field," *Journal of Educational Sociology* 5 (October 1931), 133–35.

27. Rosenfeld, *Hobson*, 216.

28. Douglas Clark Kinder and William O. Walker III, "Stable Force in a Storm: Harry J. Anslinger and United States Narcotic Foreign Policy, 1930–1962," *Journal of American History* 72 (March 1986), 908–27.

29. Herbert Hoover, "Message to the Fifth Annual Conference of the International Narcotic Education Association and the World Narcotic Defense Association, New York City," in John T. Woolley and Gerhard Peters, *The American Presidency Project*, http://www.presidency.ucsb.edu/ws/?pid=23451 (accessed 16 June 2007); Frank Ninkovich, "The Rockefeller Foundation, China, and Cultural Change," *Journal of American History* 70 (March 1984), 799.

30. *Union Signal*, 28 November 1925, p. 5.

31. Ibid., 21 November 1925, p. 3, 31 October 1925, p. 3; George W. Henry in *New York Times,* 27 November 1920, p. 24.

32. Quoted in *Union Signal,* 31 October 1925, p. 3.

33. F.J.B., "The Car and Social Life," *Sydney Morning Herald*, 31 October 1927; *White Ribbon Signal* (Sydney), 12 November 1927, p. 2; "Motors and Sobriety: Why America Must Remain Dry," *White Ribbon Signal,* 12 March 1925, p. 6.

34. *Grit*, 2 March 1933, pp. 9, 10; "Edison Talks about Prohibition," *Grit*, 27 November 1930, pp. 9–10; "What Thomas A. Edison Thought of Prohibition," *White Ribbon Signal*, 1 January 1932, p. 1.

35. De Grazia, *Irresistible Empire*, chap. 1; see also Frank Costigliola, *Awkward Dominion: American Political, Economic, and Cultural Relations with Europe, 1919–1933* (Ithaca, NY, 1984).

36. "Pussyfootism," *The Forum,* 13 September 1922, p. 15; *New York Times*, 16 August 1927, p. 28.

37. The alcohol issue in this respect presaged American embroilment in international anti-drug diplomacy, for which see William O. Walker III, *Drug Control in the Americas,* rev. ed. (Albuquerque, 1989).

38. Lawrence Spinelli, *Dry Diplomacy: The United States, Great Britain, and Prohibition* (Wilmington, DE, 1989), 158.

39. Hercod, "Alcoholism as an International Problem," 118.

40. Benjamin Rhodes, "The Image of Britain in the United States, 1919–1929: A Contentious Relative and Rival," in B. J. McKercher, ed., *Anglo-American Relations in the 1920s: The Struggle for Supremacy* (Basingstoke, Eng., 1991), 200.

41. Joan Hoff Wilson, *American Business & Foreign Policy, 1920–1933* (Lexington, KY, 1971), x.

42. There is no adequate general synthesis of American Christian missionary impacts on a global scale. For a brief but dated account, see Latourette, "Missionaries Abroad." See also the studies listed in the introduction in notes 18–20. For a specific and highly pertinent example, see Clymer, *American Protestant Missionaries in the Philippines*. For the temperance missionaries' impact, see Tyrrell, *Woman's World*, chaps 4, 5, pp. 62–113.

43. Leitch and Leitch, *Seven Years in Ceylon*, 24.

44. For this theme, see Tyrrell, *Transnational Nation*, 7; Tyrrell, "American Exceptionalism and Uneven Global Integration: Pushes Away from the Global Society," in Bruce Mazlish, Nayan Chanda, and Kenneth Weisbrode, eds., *The Paradox of a Global USA* (Stanford, CA, 2007), 64–80.

45. Mary Leitch to Dear Friend, 2 September 1925, folder 36:13, Leitch (2), biographical file, box 43, WBMHL.

46. Mary Leitch to Rev. William Strong, 29 August 1925, biographical file, box 43, WBMHL.

47. Mary Leitch to Enoch Bell, 1 January 1927, biographical file, box 43, WBMHL.

48. Cornelius H. Patton to Enoch F. Bell, 15 February 1927, biographical file, box 43, WBMHL.

49. Mary Leitch to Dr. Alden Clark, 26 November 1935, biographical file, box 43, WBMHL.

50. John Bicknell to Mary Leitch, 8 December 1936, biographical file, box 43, WBMHL. Bicknell was president of Jaffna College (1916–36). http://www.tamil canadian.com/page.php?cat=52&id=2319 (accessed 1 August 2007).

51. Mary Leitch to Cosmo Gordon Brown, 17 May 1937, biographical file, box 43, WBMHL.

52. Crafts, *Primer*, 9.

53. Wilbur Crafts, "Studies of Internationalism Imperative," in addendum, [c. 1920–21], p. 8, with Crafts Notebooks.

54. Ibid.

55. James M. Goode, *Capital Losses: A Cultural History of Washington's Destroyed Buildings* (Washington, DC, 1979), 17–18.

56. *Twentieth Century Quarterly* 10, no. 3 (21 March 1911), 13.

57. *Twentieth Century Quarterly* 11, no. 11 (June 1914), 22.

58. Diary, box 1, Crafts Notebooks, 263, 270.

59. "Two More Squares for Library Annex Planned in House," *Washington Post*, 17 January 1928; Edward T. Folliard, "U.S. to Spend $25,000,000 in Building Here," *Washington Post*, 29 December 1929.

60. Quoted in Eugene C. Bianchi, "The Ecumenical Thought of Bishop Charles Henry Brent," *Church History* 33 (December 1964), 448.

61. Ibid.; *Report of the Preliminary Meeting at Geneva, Switzerland* (Geneva, 1920), 90–91.

62. Bianchi, "Ecumenical Thought," 448; Charles Henry Brent, *Understanding: Being an Interpretation of the Universal Christian Conference on Life and Work, held in Stockholm, August 15–30, 1925* (New York, 1925).

63. "Bishop Brent Opens Faith Conference," *New York Times*, 4 August 1927, p. 20; Bianchi, "Ecumenical Thought," 448; Paul A. Crow Jr., "The Concept

of Unity in Diversity in Faith and Order Conversations from the Lausanne to the Oberlin Conferences," *Church History* 33 (March 1964), 9. For conference papers, proceedings, decisions, and membership, see H. N. Bate, ed., *Faith and Order: Proceedings of the World Conference, Lausanne, August 3–21, 1927* (London, 1927), quote at 7.

64. *New York Times*, 28 November 1927, p. 24.

65. Alexander C. Zabriskie, *Bishop Brent: Crusader for Christian Unity* (Philadelphia, 1948); Arthur Stanwood Pier, *American Apostles to the Philippines* (Boston, 1950).

66. Charles Evans Hughes to Stephen G. Porter, 10 May 1923, in folder Communications with the Department of State, 1923, box 41, Brent Papers.

67. "An Appeal to My Colleagues," in folder Communications with the Department of State, 1923, box 41, Brent Papers; "Speech of the Right Reverend Charles H. Brent, Before the Second International Opium Conference at Geneva, Switzerland, November 19, 1924, ibid.; "Dr. Brent Condemns Opium Conference," *New York Times*, 8 December 1924, p. 21 (quote); "Opium Trade Spreads with Powers at Odds; Why the American Delegates Withdrew from International Conference," *New York Times*, 15 February 1925, p. XX10.

68. R. I. Jardine, "The Student and the Future: International Student Service and the Pacific," *Pacific Affairs* 4 (February 1931), 113.

69. John R. Mott, *The Continuation Committee Conferences in Asia, 1912–13* (New York, 1913); Harlan Beach, *Findings of the Continuation Committee Conferences, held in Asia, 1912–13* (New York, 1915).

70. Hogg, *Ecumenical Foundations*, 144–56.

71. Hopkins states that it was probably apocryphal that Mott signed up for "the world" as one of the first Student Volunteers. Mott left the space blank; though he was interested in India, he did not go (*Mott*, 706). However, an undated document in the SVM records does list his preferred destination as "the World." See "First One Hundred Student Volunteers," folder 5234, box 449, Archives of the Student Volunteer Movement for Foreign Missions, RG 42, YDSL.

72. http://nobelprize.org/nobel_prizes/peace/laureates/1946/mott-bio.html (accessed 5 February 2008).

73. http://nobelprize.org/nobel_prizes/peace/laureates/1946/mott-acceptance .html (accessed 5 February 2008).

74. William Appleman Williams, "The Legend of Isolationism in the 1920s," *Science and Society* 18 (Winter 1954), 1–20.

75. Akira Iriye, *Global Community: The Role of International Organizations in the Making of the Contemporary World* (Berkeley, 2002), 20–21, 23, 25.

76. William B. McAllister, "Conflicts of Interest in the International Drug Control System," in William O. Walker III, ed., *Drug Control Policy: Essays in Historical and Comparative Perspective* (University Park, PA, 1992), 145–46.

77. Carl Parini, *Heir to Empire: United States Economic Diplomacy, 1916–1923* (Pittsburgh, 1965), 8–9.

78. Davis and Trani, "The American YMCA and the Russian Revolution"; Ethan T. Colton, "With the Y.M.C.A. in Revolutionary Russia," *Russian Review* 14 (April 1955), 128–39.

79. De Grazia, *Irresistible Empire*, 62–67.

80. Charles H. Brent, "The Moral Side of the Opium Question," *The Christian Work: A Religious Weekly Review*, 22 March 1924, p. 367, folder Brent: Personal 1924, box 41, Brent Papers.

81. "Bishop Brent Dies at 66 in Lausanne," *New York Times*, 28 March 1929, p. 27.

82. "Mark Lawrence's Address at Mere Anglicanism—Charles Henry Brent: Excavating an Anglican Treasure," http://www.kendallharmon.net/t19/index .php/t19/print_w_comments/9762/ (accessed 9 February 2008). Lawrence's statement closely follows Zabriskie, *Bishop Brent*, 197.

INDEX

Note: Italicized page numbers refer to illustrations.